JAVASCRIPT® 24-HOUR TRAINER

D1303559

JavaScript® 24-Hour Trainer

Jeremy McPeak

Wiley Publishing, Inc.

JavaScript® 24-Hour Trainer

Published by
Wiley Publishing, Inc.
10475 Crosspoint Boulevard
Indianapolis, IN 46256
www.wiley.com

Copyright © 2011 Wiley Publishing, Inc.

Published simultaneously in Canada

ISBN: 978-0-470-64783-7

Manufactured in the United States of America

10 9 8 7 6 5 4 3 2 1

For general information on our other products and services please contact our Customer Care Department within the United States at (877) 762-2974, outside the United States at (317) 572-3993 or fax (317) 572-4002.

Wiley also publishes its books in a variety of electronic formats. Some content that appears in print may not be available in electronic books.

Library of Congress Control Number: 2010937810

This book is dedicated to my wife, Starla, and my sons, Hayden and Evan. Thank you for your love, support, and (especially) patience during the writing of this book. This book is also dedicated to my grandparents, Virginia and Don. Thank you for your love and support.

CREDITS

ACQUISITIONS EDITOR
Scott Myers

PROJECT EDITORS
Ed Connor
Deadline Driven Publishing

TECHNICAL EDITOR
John Peloquin

SENIOR PRODUCTION EDITOR
Debra Banninger

COPY EDITOR
Sadie Kleinman

EDITORIAL DIRECTOR
Robyn B. Siesky

EDITORIAL MANAGER
Mary Beth Wakefield

FREELANCER EDITORIAL MANAGER
Rosemarie Graham

MARKETING MANAGER
Ashley Zurcher

PRODUCTION MANAGER
Tim Tate

VICE PRESIDENT AND EXECUTIVE GROUP PUBLISHER
Richard Swadley

VICE PRESIDENT AND EXECUTIVE PUBLISHER
Barry Pruett

ASSOCIATE PUBLISHER
Jim Minatel

PROJECT COORDINATOR, COVER
Lynsey Stanford

COMPOSITOR
Craig Johnson,
Happenstance Type-O-Rama

PROOFREADER
Nancy Carrasco

INDEXER
Robert Swanson

COVER IMAGE
© seraficus / iStockPhoto

COVER DESIGNER
Michael Trent

ABOUT THE AUTHOR

JEREMY MCPEAK is a self-taught programmer who began his career by tinkering with websites in 1998. He is the coauthor of *Professional Ajax, Second Edition* (Wiley, 2007) and *Beginning JavaScript, Fourth Edition* (Wiley, 2009). He also contributes to Nettuts+ (`http://net.tutsplus.com`), providing articles and video tutorials for ASP.NET. He is currently employed by an oil and gas company building in-house conventional and web applications. Jeremy can be contacted via the p2p forums or through his website at `http://www.wdonline.com`.

ABOUT THE TECHNICAL EDITOR

JOHN PELOQUIN is a front-end engineer with experience ranging across JavaScript applications of all sizes. John earned his bachelor of arts degree in mathematics from the University of California at Berkeley and is currently a lead developer for a startup in the healthcare industry. When he is not coding or collecting errata, John is often found engaged in mathematics, philosophy, or juggling.

ACKNOWLEDGMENTS

FIRST AND FOREMOST, I want to thank God for the blessings he has bestowed upon me. Also, a huge thank-you goes to my wife for putting up with my late nights and sleep-deprived (grouchy) attitude.

Writing and producing a book requires a lot of people, and I know I cannot name everyone who has had a hand in this project. But a very big thank-you goes to Scott Meyers for making this book happen, and to Ed Conner for putting up with me while getting this book into its final, printed form. Thank you, John Peloquin, for providing your input and ensuring the text I wrote is accurate and meaningful. Thanks, Ginny Munroe, for stepping in for Ed in the latter stages of the project, and to Rosemarie Graham for organizing everything.

Lastly, thank you Nicholas C. Zakas, author of *Professional JavaScript, Second Edition* (Wiley, 2009) and coauthor of *Professional Ajax, Second Edition* (Wiley, 2007), for getting me into this business.

CONTENTS

PREFACE

JAVASCRIPT IS THE MOST POPULAR programming language in the world. It is used on all major Internet sites, and even those not so important. Whether you make a purchase from an online retailer, manage your funds using your bank's website, visit a news site to get caught up on current events, or simply read a blog written by one of the millions of bloggers worldwide, you have experienced JavaScript in some way.

Despite this popularity, there has always been some form of confusion regarding JavaScript. Some claim, because of its name, that it's a light version of Java, a programming language originally developed by Sun and now owned by Oracle. This is not the case at all. While JavaScript's syntax is similar to Java's, JavaScript is its own language used primarily to program the web pages you visit daily using a web browser. Its purpose is to provide interactivity for the user — making the web page or web application feel like a conventional application running on your computer.

JavaScript is a simple, yet complex, object-oriented language. While getting started with JavaScript takes little time, it can take years to master the language. And even then, masters of the language still find themselves learning something new about it.

This book aims to teach you JavaScript, to put you on the right path so that you can use the language to add interactivity to your web pages and applications. Don't worry if you don't know how to program. This book teaches you JavaScript from the very beginning — showing you the concepts behind the basics of all programming languages. You'll find that JavaScript can be a gateway to the world of programming. It was for your author.

WHOM THIS BOOK IS FOR

This book is for beginners at two levels: those who have never used JavaScript before, and those who have, but did not learn the language outside of a library such as jQuery.

To get the most out of this book you'll need an understanding of HTML and CSS, and how to use these two technologies to create web pages. JavaScript lives inside the web browser, and it's used to interact with a web page loaded into the browser. So being able to write HTML and style it with CSS is an important skill to have before you learn JavaScript.

WHAT THIS BOOK COVERS

JavaScript 24-Hour Trainer teaches you how to use JavaScript in your web pages from the absolute beginning: adding JavaScript to your page. From there the book moves on to introduce you to the fundamentals of JavaScript (and every programming language for that matter), such as syntax, variables, functions, decisions, and loops. From there you'll be introduced to object-oriented programming by looking at some of JavaScript's built-in objects, and you'll learn to write your own objects to represent complex data.

Building on that base, you'll learn how to use JavaScript to program the browser by creating and manipulating new windows and scripting frames. Then you'll learn how to interact with the HTML elements in a page by adding them, removing them, and modifying their styles. You'll learn how to react to a user's action by using events, and the different ways to do this for different browsers. You'll continue a study of the browser and page by learning how to animate elements, script HTML forms, and leverage Ajax to send and receive data from the server.

You'll then turn your studies toward errors, debugging, and best practices. You'll learn how to identify and avoid common mistakes, as well as how to handle errors that are caused by stimuli outside your control. For those tough-to-find errors, you'll learn how to debug your code with Firebug. After that you'll learn some conventions that professional JavaScript developers follow, as well as techniques for writing efficient and maintainable JavaScript.

HOW THIS BOOK IS STRUCTURED

This book consists of short lessons, each focusing on a particular aspect of the JavaScript language. It is not meant as an exhaustive resource or as an in-depth look at technical aspects of the language. The goal is to teach you what you need to know in order to start using JavaScript in your web pages and applications.

This book consists of 43 lessons. Most are reasonably short — much shorter than chapters in most other books. A couple of them are longer, but that is only because the content of that particular lesson warrants the bigger size.

The lessons are broken into three distinct sections:

➤ **Part I: Introduction to JavaScript:** This section teaches you the fundamentals of the JavaScript language. You can also apply the concepts in this section to just about any other programming language.

➤ **Part II: Programming the Browser:** The primary use of JavaScript is to manipulate the browser and the web page loaded into it. You'll learn how to use the language to do that.

➤ **Part III: Handling Errors, Debugging, and Best Practices:** Errors happen, and some can be avoided. You'll learn how to spot errors, deal with errors you can't control, and locate hard-to-find bugs with debugging and Firebug. You also learn techniques employed by professional developers that you can use to make your code more efficient and maintainable.

Most lessons contain a tutorial called "Try It," and each tutorial applies the concepts of the lesson in an example. You can also watch the DVD to see your author complete the tutorial, as well as offer commentary on the subject matter.

After you've finished reading the book and watching the DVD, you can visit Wrox's p2p forums, where your author offers support.

INSTRUCTIONAL VIDEOS ON DVD

Not everyone can learn straight from a book; kudos to those of you who can. For the rest of us (including your author), a visual and audible aid is often required. This is exactly why a DVD accompanies this book. Most of the book's lessons have a corresponding video tutorial, complete with commentary. So if seeing something done and hearing it explained help you understand a subject better than just reading about it, this book-and-DVD combination is just the thing for you.

CONVENTIONS

To help you get the most from the text and keep track of what's happening, this book uses a number of conventions.

> *Boxes like this one hold important, not-to-be forgotten information that is directly relevant to the surrounding text.*

> *Notes, tips, hints, tricks, and asides to the current discussion are offset and placed in italics like this.*

> *References like this one point you to the DVD to watch the instructional video that accompanies a given lesson.*

As for styles in the text:

➤ New terms and important words are *italicized* when introduced.

➤ Code appearing in text looks like this: `document.body`.

➤ URLs look like the following when inside text: `www.wrox.com`.

➤ Code blocks are presented in the following way:

```
A monofont type on its own line(s)
denotes code examples.
```

SUPPORTING PACKAGES AND CODE

As you work through the lessons in this book, you can choose to type the code and create all the files manually or you can use the supporting code files that accompany the book. All the code and other support files used in this book are available for download at www.wrox.com. On the site, simply locate the book's title (either by using the Search box or by using one of the title lists), and then click the Download Code link on the book's detail page to obtain all the source code for the book.

 Because many books have similar titles, you may find it easiest to search by ISBN; this book's ISBN is 978-0-470-64783-7.

Once you download the code, just decompress it with your favorite compression tool. Alternatively, you can go to the main Wrox code download page at www.wrox.com/dynamic/books/download.aspx to see the code available for this book and all other Wrox books.

ERRATA

Every effort is made to ensure that there are no errors in the text or in the code. However, no one is perfect, and mistakes do occur. If you find an error in this book or any Wrox book for that matter, such as a spelling mistake or faulty piece of code, your feedback is appreciated. By sending in errata, you can save a reader hours of frustration, and at the same time, you can help your author and Wrox provide even higher-quality information.

To find the errata page for this book, go to www.wrox.com and locate the title using the Search box or one of the title lists. Then, on the Book Search Results page, click the Errata link. On this page, you can view all errata that have been submitted for this book and posted by Wrox editors.

 A complete book list, including links to errata, is also available at www.wrox.com/misc-pages/booklist.shtml.

If you don't spot "your" error on the Errata page, click the Errata Form link and complete the form to send us the error you have found. We'll check the information and, if appropriate, post a message to the book's errata page and fix the problem in subsequent editions of the book.

P2P.WROX.COM

For author and peer discussion, join the P2P forums at p2p.wrox.com. The forums are a web-based system you can use to post messages relating to Wrox books and related technologies and interact with other readers and technology users. The forums offer a subscription feature to e-mail you topics of interest of your choosing when new posts are made to the forums. Wrox authors and editors, other industry experts, and your fellow readers are present on these forums.

At http://p2p.wrox.com you will find a number of different forums that will help you not only as you read this book, but also as you develop your own applications. To join the forums just follow these steps:

1. Go to p2p.wrox.com and click the Register link.

2. Read the terms of use and click Agree.

3. Complete the required information for joining as well as any optional information you wish to provide and click Submit.

4. You will receive an e-mail with information describing how to verify your account and complete the joining process.

 You can read messages in the forums without joining P2P, but in order to post your own messages you must join.

Once you join you can post new messages and respond to messages other users post. You can read messages at any time on the Web. If you would like to have new messages from a particular forum e-mailed to you, click the Subscribe to This Forum icon by the forum name in the forum listing.

For more information about how to use the Wrox P2P, be sure to read the P2P FAQs for answers to questions about how the forum software works as well as many common questions specific to P2P and Wrox books. To read the FAQs, click the FAQ link on any P2P page.

PART I
Introduction to JavaScript

Adding JavaScript to a Web Page

When JavaScript was first introduced to web pages, Netscape needed to find some mechanism that allowed JavaScript to be added to a web page without causing adverse effects in other browsers. After much debate, it was finally settled on to incorporate the `<script/>` element, which was later added to the HTML specification.

THE <SCRIPT/> ELEMENT

The primary means of adding JavaScript to a web page is by using the `<script/>` element. This element, introduced by Netscape, became part of the HTML 3.2 specification as a placeholder for a transition to HTML 4.01, in which the element was fleshed out and given the following attributes:

➤ `src`: Optional. Specifies an external script file to be executed.

➤ `type`: Required. Specifies the language used in the `<script/>` element's contents, and a value of `"text/javascript"` is typically used. Even though this attribute is required by the HTML specification, all browsers assume the language is JavaScript if this attribute is omitted.

➤ `language`: Deprecated. This attribute specifies the language used in the `<script/>` element's contents. This attribute is no longer used, as `type` has replaced it.

➤ `defer`: Optional. A Boolean (`true` or `false`) value that tells the browser whether to wait to execute any code within the `<script/>` element until after the browser loads the entire HTML document.

➤ `charset`: Optional. The character encoding of the external code file specified by the `src` attribute. This attribute is rarely used.

There are two ways to use <script/> elements: either by embedding JavaScript code directly into the page, in which case it is referred to as *inline code*, or by using the src attribute to refer to that external file.

To add inline code to a web page, place the code between the opening and closing tags, as the following code shows:

```
<script type="text/javascript">
function inlineScript() {
    var message = "Hello, World!";
    alert(message);
}

inlineScript();
</script>
```

Don't worry about the code just yet — you'll learn what this code does in due time. Even though browsers automatically assume that code within a <script/> element is JavaScript, it is considered good practice to include the type attribute. The browser stops loading the rest of the page when it encounters a <script/> element; it loads the code and interprets it before processing the rest of the HTML page.

It's important to note that inline code blocks, as shown in the previous code sample, should be included in a CDATA block in XHTML documents. Failing to do so does not currently result in an error in the browser. In fact, all major browsers still load the JavaScript and execute it normally. However, there is no guarantee that future browsers will behave as today's browsers do. So, if you use XHTML, future-proof your inline script by encapsulating it in a CDATA section, like this:

```
<script type="text/javascript">
<![CDATA[
function inlineScript() {
    var message = "Hello, World!";
    alert(message);
}

inlineScript();
]]>
</script>
```

Adding an external JavaScript file to the page incorporates the src attribute. It's possible to cut the JavaScript code from the previous example, without the <script> tags, and paste it into another file. Then, by using the src attribute, the page can reference the external JavaScript file like this:

```
<script type="text/javascript" src="sample.js"></script>
```

This <script/> element references an external JavaScript file called sample.js. Using the .js extension is a convention nearly all JavaScript developers use. It does not matter how the file is named — the browser will download it and interpret the file's contents as JavaScript code.

Just as with inline code, the browser halts processing of the HTML page when it encounters the <script> tag, but it also has to download the file before it begins interpreting it. After the browser loads the JavaScript from the external file, it resumes processing the HTML page.

Choosing whether to use inline or external scripts is ultimately up to you. However, the majority of developers use external JavaScript files for the following reasons:

➤ External scripts are much easier to maintain than inline scripts, especially if you use the same code in several pages. Imagine having to edit multiple HTML pages to make identical changes to blocks of inline code. That would certainly be a time-consuming task. With an external file, you simply make changes to one file.

➤ External scripts are cached by the browser, just as images and style sheets are. The browser downloads the script file once and uses it for subsequent page requests as long as the script file hasn't changed. This grants a certain performance gain in that the browser doesn't have to download the same code over and over again, whereas it does if the code is embedded in the HTML page.

How and where <script/> elements are placed in the page do matter — they are loaded and interpreted in the order in which they're placed in the page.

Tag Placement

The <script/> element is one of the few elements that can go almost anywhere in an HTML page: it can go within the <head/> element or the <body/> element. The more traditional place is within the <head/> element, along with the <style/> and <link/> elements. The following HTML demonstrates this:

```
<html>
<head>
    <title>Sample Page</title>
    <script type="text/javascript" src="sample.js"></script>
</head>
<body>

</body>
</html>
```

While this keeps resources for the HTML page in one place within the document, remember that the browser halts all processing of the HTML document once it encounters a <script/> element, in order to download and load the script that it references. So placing <script/> elements at the top of the document has the side effect of delaying the browser from loading the page's content. To users, this is a performance issue, as they see a blank web page while the browser downloads and loads the JavaScript.

Because of this, it's becoming a best practice to place all <script> tags just before the closing <body> tag, like this:

```
<html>
<head>
    <title>Sample Page</title>
</head>
<body>

    <script type="text/javascript" src="sample.js"></script>
</body>
</html>
```

This way, the browser loads and renders the entire page before loading JavaScript code. Even though the net download time is the same regardless of the <script> tags' placement, the user sees their requested web page sooner and perceives a faster web page.

TRY IT

In this lesson, you add an external JavaScript file to a web page.

Lesson Requirements

For this lesson, you need a text editor; any plain text editor will do. For Microsoft Windows users, Notepad is available by default on your system or you can download Microsoft's free Visual Web Developer Express (www.microsoft.com/express/web/) or Web Matrix (www.asp.net/webmatrix/). Mac OS X users can use TextMate, which comes as part of OS X, or download a trial for Coda (www.panic.com/coda/). Linux users can use the built-in VIM.

You also need a modern web browser. Choose any of the following:

- ➤ Internet Explorer 8+
- ➤ Google Chrome
- ➤ Firefox 3.5+
- ➤ Apple Safari 4+
- ➤ Opera 10+

Create a folder somewhere in your file system called JS24Hour, and create a subfolder called Lesson01. Store the files you create in this lesson in the Lesson01 folder you created.

Step-by-Step

Add an external JavaScript file to a web page by following these steps:

1. Open your text editor and type the following JavaScript code:

```
function inlineScript() {
    var message = "Hello, World!";
    alert(message);
}

inlineScript();
```

2. Save the file as lesson01_sample01.js.

3. Open another instance of your text editor and type the following HTML:

```
<html>
<head>
    <title>Sample Page</title>
</head>
```

```
<body>

    <script type="text/javascript" src="lesson01_sample01.js"></script>
</body>
</html>
```

4. Save this file as `lesson01_sample01.html`, and make sure you save it in the same location as `lesson01_sample.js`.

5. Open the HTML file in your web browser by double-clicking the file. You should see an alert box saying "Hello, World!" when the browser loads the page.

 Please select Lesson 1 on the DVD to view the video that accompanies this lesson. You can also download the sample code for all lessons from the book's website at `www.wrox.com`.

Variables and JavaScript Syntax

In the midst of teaching you how and where you add script to your pages, the previous lesson introduced the following simple script:

```
function inlineScript() {
    var message = "Hello, World!";
    alert(message);
}

inlineScript();
```

To fully understand what this code does, it's important to know the basics of the JavaScript language. The core of any language is its syntax — a set of rules that dictate how certain pieces of the language fit together. Think of a spoken language and how difficult it would be to communicate with others if that language did not have a set of rules that defined how words are arranged into complete and understandable sentences. The same is applicable to programming languages. In the case of JavaScript, the browser wouldn't know what to do with your code if it weren't for the rules set forth by the language specifications. Syntax defines how very small pieces of code fit together in order to perform some kind of work.

This lesson focuses on the syntax of one line of code in the listing at the top of the page — the variable declaration:

```
var message = "Hello, World!";
```

In this lesson, you learn about variables and the syntax required to make them.

VARIABLES

Developers write programs to make working with data easier. Large amounts of data are typically stored outside the program, via the file system or a database, but many times that data is brought into the application and stored in the computer's memory. Because of this, all programming languages need some way to access the data stored in memory in order to perform work on it.

Variables are parts of a programming language that grant programmers the ability to store and retrieve data stored in memory. You can think of a variable as a box — the box is empty when you create the variable, and the box is full when you assign that variable to hold data.

Some languages are very strict as to what type of data you can put in a particular box. These types of languages are called *strongly-typed* languages. For example, some languages have boxes for numbers and numbers only — trying to put pieces of text in a box for numbers results in an error.

JavaScript is not one of these strongly-typed languages. Instead, it is a *loosely-typed* language — it sees a variable as a box that can hold any type of data at any given time. That box may grow or shrink to accommodate the data you put into it, but it does not discriminate between what types of data can fit in the box. This means that a variable can contain a text value at one time, and a number value at another.

Defining a variable in JavaScript requires the use of a variable declaration *statement*. A statement is a small piece of code that performs some kind of action. Any given program is made up of one or more statements in a specific sequence. The following code shows a variable declaration statement:

```
var myVariable;
```

Most JavaScript statements end with a semicolon, as shown in this code. But it is also valid to omit them, as shown in the following code:

```
var myVariable
```

However, omitting the semicolon is considered a bad programming practice and is strongly discouraged. This code is considered bad code.

Variable declarations begin with the `var` *keyword*, a word reserved by the language for a specific use. The `var` keyword is used specifically for declaring variables. Following the `var` keyword is the variable's *identifier*, or name. Identifiers are made up of one or more characters, and they must follow these rules:

➤ An identifier's first character must be a letter, an underscore, or a dollar sign. Many JavaScript libraries make extensive use of the dollar sign. So, it is suggested that you avoid using it.

➤ All other characters can be letters, whole decimal numbers (0–9), underscores, or dollar signs.

➤ An identifier cannot be the same as a keyword or reserved word (more on these later).

 An identifier should briefly describe what the variable contains.

It is important to note the casing of each letter in the variable's identifier. JavaScript is a *case-sensitive* language: It distinguishes between uppercase and lowercase letters. The previous identifier, myVariable, is not the same as myvariable, Myvariable, mYVariable, or any such variation. It's important to always be aware of an identifier's case, as failing to do so is a very common cause of errors.

The myVariable identifier uses what's called *camel-case*. This means that the first letter of the identifier is lowercase, and each word in the identifier starts with an uppercase letter. Camel-casing isn't a requirement of JavaScript, but most of JavaScript's built-in identifiers use camel-case. As a programmer, it's a good idea to follow the conventions of the language you're using. In the case of JavaScript, that means following the camel-casing guidelines when naming your own identifiers.

The variable declaration statement in the previous code doesn't contain any data. It has been declared, but it has not been *initialized*, or assigned a value. To assign data to a variable, use the equals sign (=), also known as the assignment *operator*, to assign a value to the variable. An operator is a symbol or keyword that takes one or more operands as input and performs an action on those operands.

```
var myVariable;
myVariable = "some text";
```

This code declares and initializes myVariable in two separate statements. The first statement is a declaration statement (declaring the variable with the var keyword), and the second statement is an initialization statement (giving the variable an initial value). Notice there is no var keyword used in the initialization line. The var keyword is used only for declaring variables. Once a variable is declared, it is no longer necessary to use var for that variable.

The operands in an assignment operation, as shown in the initialization statement in the previous example, are on both sides of the assignment operator (the equals sign). The operand on the right is an expression or value that is assigned to the operand on the left (the variable).

Using two statements, as in the previous example, is sometimes necessary, as the data for a variable may not exist at the time the variable is declared. However, a variable can be declared and initialized in one statement. The following code shows this:

```
var myVariable = "some text";
```

Using one statement is preferred, as it is easier to read and results in a smaller file size.

A variable's value can be overwritten with another value at any time. Using the myVariable from the previous example, the following code overwrites the "some text" value with that of a number:

```
myVariable = 100;
```

The variable now contains the number 100. There is no limit to the number of times a variable can be overwritten.

A variable can also be assigned the value contained in another variable. The following line creates a new variable called myVariable2, and it is initialized with the value contained within myVariable:

```
var myVariable2 = myVariable;
```

So now the myVariable2 variable contains a value of 100. Even though these two variables contain the same value, and it may look as if they are linked, they are, in fact, independent from one another. In other words, modifying the value contained in `myVariable` has no effect on the data in `myVariable2`. This variable independence comes from the fact that numbers are a primitive data type in JavaScript.

Primitive Data Types in JavaScript

A *data type* is a type of value represented in a programming language, such as numbers, text, and `true`/`false` values (among other things). *Primitive data types* are the basic types of data provided by a programming language. They are the building blocks for more complex data types.

JavaScript has five primitive data types. They are:

- ➤ Number
- ➤ String (text)
- ➤ Boolean
- ➤ Undefined
- ➤ Null

JavaScript's primitive data types hold only one value at a time and are *immutable*. This means that once a primitive value is created, it cannot be changed. Instead, the variable's original value must be destroyed and replaced with a new value. A primitive variable directly contains the value it is assigned. Assigning a variable the value of a primitive data type copies the value of the second variable, and that copy is assigned to the first variable.

Consider the following code, which recreates the `myVariable` and `myVariable2` variables:

```
var myVariable = 5,
    myVariable2 = myVariable; // copies the number and assigns copy

myVariable = 6;                 // destroys old number value and assigns new
                                // number value in 2nd variable still intact
```

Before I discuss this code, you undoubtedly noticed some new syntax at the end of lines two, three, and four. These are *comments*. Comments are human-readable annotations in code. They are ignored by JavaScript and are meant to provide information to anyone reading the code. The types of comments presented in the previous code are single-line comments. They begin with two forward slashes (`//`), and anything after the slashes is considered a comment. Again, comments are completely ignored by JavaScript, but they give the reader insight about particular lines of code.

Something else you might have noticed is a comma separating the initialization of the `myVariable` and `myVariable2` variables, along with the omission of the `var` keyword in the second line. The first two lines of this code initialize two variables in a single statement. These multiple variable initialization statements begin with the `var` keyword, and each subsequent variable initialization is separated with a comma. You can initialize as many variables as you want within a single statement. Just start the statement with `var`, separate each initialization with a comma, and end the statement with a semicolon.

It does not matter if you initialize variables in one or multiple statements. It's a personal preference. For the sake of clarity, this book opts to use multiple statements to initialize variables.

The first line of code initializes the myVariable variable as containing a value of 5. This value is of the Number data type. The second line of code initializes the myVariable2 variable by copying the value contained within myVariable and assigning that copy to myVariable2. The third line of code reassigns a new value of 6 to myVariable — destroying its original value of 5. But myVariable2 still contains a value of 5, since it was assigned a copy of myVariable's original value. Thus, both variables are separate and independent of each other.

Every time a variable containing a value of a primitive data type is used in code, a copy of that value is made and used in its place. The only way to modify a variable's value is to assign the variable a new value.

Numbers

JavaScript is different from most other languages in that it does not distinguish between different types of numbers, such as integer and decimal numbers. Instead, all numbers are represented by the Number type, which consists solely of *floating-point numbers*, rational numbers with a very large value range.

In most JavaScript applications, numbers are used as numeric *literals*. This means that numbers appear directly in the code. The examples up to this point have used whole number, or integer, literals, like the following code:

```
var myNumber = 5;
```

But you can also use a numeric literal to assign a number with decimals, like this:

```
myNumber = 3.14;
```

Numbers are primarily used to perform mathematical calculations with arithmetic operators.

Using Arithmetic Operators

JavaScript has several operators to perform arithmetic calculations. The following table lists them:

Arithmetic Operators

OPERATOR	NAME	DESCRIPTION
+	Addition	Adds the operands together
−	Subtraction	Subtracts the right operand from the left operand
*	Multiplication	Multiplies the operands together
/	Division	Divides the left operand by the right operand
%	Modulus	Divides the left operand by the right operand and returns the remainder of the operation

Consider the following line of code:

```
var myNumber = 2 + 2;
```

This code creates a variable called `myNumber`. Its value is the result of a mathematic operation adding 2 and 2 together; thus, the value assigned to the `myNumber` variable is 4.

Mathematical operations are not limited to using numeric literals; variables containing a numeric value can be used in any mathematical expression. The following code uses the `myNumber` variable created earlier in another mathematical calculation:

```
myNumber = myNumber - 4;
```

Remember that assignment operations always go from right to left. So the expression on the right side of the equals sign (`myNumber - 4`) is evaluated, and the resulting value is assigned to the variable on the left side of the equals sign. Since `myNumber`'s value is 4, this code is essentially the same as the following:

```
myNumber = 4 - 4;
```

Arithmetic operations are not limited to one operation per statement; a statement can contain multiple operations, like the following code:

```
myNumber = 1 + 2 * 3 - 4 / 2;
```

Executing this statement results in the `myNumber` variable's containing a value of 5. JavaScript's arithmetic operators have a precedence order similar to the "My Dear Aunt Sally" order in mathematics. Multiplication and division operations have a higher precedence than addition and subtraction, so they execute first. The previous code could be rewritten to the following code after the multiplication and division operations have been performed:

```
myNumber = 1 + 6 - 2;
```

Also as in mathematics, you can use parentheses to give a higher precedence to certain operations. The following code adds some parentheses to the previous code sample:

```
myNumber = (1 + 2) * 3 - 4 / 2;
```

By placing parentheses around the `1 + 2` operation, you give it a higher precedence than multiplication or division, so it is executed first, followed by the multiplication and division operations, and finally by the subtraction operation. Because the `1 + 2` operation is executed first, the result value has changed from 5 to 7.

Operator precedence determines the outcome of mathematical operations. So it's important to keep operator precedence in mind when performing them.

The final operator, the *modulus* (or remainder) operator, is represented by a percent sign (`%`). It performs a division operation on the two operands and returns the remainder of the quotient. The following code demonstrates this:

```
var remainder = 3 % 2; // returns 1
var remainder2 = 2 % 2; // returns 0
```

The modulus operator is very handy when you're testing whether a numeric value is even or odd. If the result of a modulus operation by 2 is 0, the number is even. If it is any other number, the number it's odd. Look at the following code:

```
var isEven = 4 % 2; // 0 - so even
var isOdd = 1 % 2; // 1 - so odd
```

When a Number Is Not a Number

There are times when a numeric operation fails, such as one that divides by zero or breaks some other mathematical rule. Instead of registering an error and halting code execution (as many other languages do), JavaScript uses a special numeric value called NaN, meaning Not a Number, to indicate that a mathematical operation failed. The following code results in a value of NaN, since it is illegal to divide by zero:

```
var nan = 1 / 0;
```

Any operation involving a NaN value always results in NaN. This has the side effect of possibly ruining mathematical operations that contain multiple steps.

Strings

Strings are text values — sequences of zero or more characters. Strings are delimited by double-quote (") or single-quote characters ('). The following code shows two valid strings:

```
var str1 = "Hello, World";
var str2 = 'Hello, World (again)';
```

A string beginning with a double quote must end with a double quote; likewise, a string beginning with a single quote must end with a single quote. For example, the following code is not correct and results in an error because the beginning and ending quotes don't match:

```
var str3 = 'Hello, World (yes again!)"; // invalid string literal
```

It is, however, perfectly fine for a string delimited with double quotes to contain single quotes, like this:

```
var str4 = "Hello, Jeremy's World";
```

Similarly, strings delimited with single quotes can contain double quotes:

```
var str5 = 'Jeremy said, "Hello, World!"';
```

Unlike other languages, JavaScript does not discriminate between the type of quotes used to delimit strings. Using single quotes does not change how JavaScript treats the string compared to using double quotes. They're all the same, so which type of quote you use to delimit strings is completely up to you. The examples in this book primarily use double quotes.

A string delimited with single quotes cannot use a single quote inside the string. The following code is incorrect and will generate an error:

```
var str6 = 'Hello, Jeremy's World'; // error
```

This is incorrect because JavaScript thinks that the string ends after the `y` in `'Hello, Jeremy'`. It treats the second single quote as the end of the string and doesn't know what to do with the text `s World';`. The same is true for double-quote characters in a string delimited with double quotes, like this:

```
var str7 = "Jeremy said, "Hello, World!""; // error
```

JavaScript thinks the string in this statement is `"Jeremy said, "`, and it again doesn't know what to do with the remainder of the statement: `Hello, World!"";`.

In addition to quotation marks, JavaScript has many other special characters that cannot be typed within a string. They can, however, be represented with *escape sequences*. Think of an escape sequence as an HTML entity: It is a set of characters that represents a particular keystroke when rendered.

For example, HTML entities start with an ampersand (`&`) and end with a semicolon. The `&quot;` HTML entity looks funky in the HTML markup, but it renders as a double quotation mark in the browser. Similarly, the `\"` escape sequence in JavaScript looks funky in the code, but it is interpreted as a double quotation mark when it occurs in a JavaScript string.

As an example, the following code revisits the `str7` variable declaration and assigns it a string value containing escape sequences:

```
var str7 = "Jeremy said, \"Hello, World!\""; // valid string
```

Escape sequences in JavaScript begin with a backslash, and are followed by one or more characters to denote the special character the escape sequence represents. The following table lists the more commonly used escape sequences:

Escape Sequences

ESCAPE SEQUENCE	DESCRIPTION
\n	New line
\t	Tab
\'	Single quote (used when the string is delimited with single quotes)
\"	Double quote (used when the string is delimited with double quotes)
\\	Backslash

Escape sequences are used when you want to store such a character in a literal string.

Modifying Strings

Like the `Number` data type, strings are immutable. A string value cannot change once it has been created. Modifying a string value involves destroying the original string value and replacing it with a different value.

Say a variable called `str1` contains a string value of `"This is a string."`. The following code demonstrates this:

```
var str1 = "This is a string.";
```

The string value assigned to `str1` cannot technically be altered; however, a *concatenation*, or joining, operation can use the original value contained within `str1` and join it with another string value to create a new string value.

Concatenating two or more strings requires the use of the concatenation operator: the plus sign (+). The following code concatenates the original string value in `str1` with another string value to modify the data contained within `str1`:

```
str1 = str1 + " Hello, World!";
```

The value now contained within `str1` is `"This is a string. Hello, World!"`.

Focus on the code that appears to the right of the assignment operator (the equals sign). This expression is a concatenation operation. The first operand retrieves a copy of `str1`'s value (remember that values are not used directly; they are copied). The second operand is a string literal, and the concatenation operation joins the two values into one value — a value that is then assigned to the `str1` variable.

Note the space before `Hello` in the string literal. If the space had been left out, the concatenated string would be `"This is a string.Hello World!"`. JavaScript will not format strings automatically for you; you must do that yourself.

The same principle can be applied to multiple variables. Look at this code:

```
var firstString = "This is a string.";
var greetingString = "Hello,";
var name = "Jeremy";
var finalString = firstString + " " + greetingString + " " + name + "!";
```

This code initializes four strings. The first three are simple strings, and the fourth concatenates the first three into a greeting. Notice that this time, the first three string values do not contain spaces to help with formatting. Instead, the concatenation operation in the fourth line of code inserts spaces as needed. So the value assigned to `finalString` is this: `"This is a string. Hello, Jeremy!"`.

Converting Numbers to Strings

String concatenation may be confusing at first, especially since the + operator sign is typically used for mathematical operations. This operator pulls double duty as an addition operator and a string concatenation operator in many languages. In JavaScript, the confusion comes from the use of the + operator with values of differing types. Look at the following code as an example:

```
var possiblyConfusing = "This is the number " + 1;
```

This code declares and initializes a variable called `possiblyConfusing`. The expression on the right side of the equals sign consists of a string value, a + operator, and a number. JavaScript is smart enough to know that the string `"This is the number "` cannot be used in a mathematical operation.

Therefore, JavaScript converts the number 1 to a string and concatenates the two operands together. The value contained within the variable is "This is the number 1".

When a string is involved in an operation consisting of the + sign, as in the previous line of code, all non-string values to the right of the string are converted to string values. The operand to the left of the operator maintains its original value, but the end result is a string value

Keep that in mind as you look at the following code and determine the result of the operation:

```
var probablyConfusing = 1 + 2 + "45";
```

In this code, the expression to the right of the = operator consists of three operands. The first two are number values, and the third is a string. Since the two numbers are to the left of the string, they are treated as numbers, and the + operator performs an addition operation. So this code can be simplified to this:

```
var probablyConfusing = 3 + "45";
```

Now JavaScript sees a number value and a string value and treats the + operator as a concatenation operator. The final value that is assigned to the probablyConfusing variable is "345". Even though the string looks like a number, it is still a string. Any operation involving the + operator and a string results in a concatenation operation.

A string can be converted to a number using any other arithmetic operator. Look at the following example:

```
var probablyConfusing = "1" + 2 - 3;
```

In this code, the string "1" is concatenated with the numeric value 2. So this code can be simplified like this:

```
var probablyConfusing = "12" - 3;
```

The subtraction operation, however, is not a valid string operator. So JavaScript converts the string to a numeric value and performs the operation. The result of this code is 9, since "12" is converted to 12.

Converting Strings to Numbers

There are more ways to convert a string to a number, however. JavaScript provides two functions to convert strings to numbers: the parseInt() and parseFloat() functions. You'll learn much more about functions later, but for now all you need to know is that functions perform work on data.

Calling a function is as simple as using the function's identifier followed by a pair of parentheses, like this:

```
parseInt();
```

This executes the parseInt() function. However, it returns a value of NaN because it does not have any data to work with. Some functions, like parseInt(), accept data in the form of *arguments*, a set of special variables used by the function. For example, the parseInt() function accepts a string value to convert to a number, like this:

```
var num = parseInt("45");
```

This code converts the string `"45"` to the number 45 and stores it in the num variable. The `parseInt()` function returns an integer (a whole number) value. If a string containing a decimal number is passed to the `parseInt()` function, it drops the decimal and the numbers after it and returns the whole number. It does not round up. The following code demonstrates this:

```
num = parseInt("1.8392"); // returns 1
```

In this code, a string containing a decimal number is passed to the function. The result is the whole number: 1.

It is sometimes desirable to keep the numbers after the decimal. In cases such as these, use the `parseFloat()` function. An example is shown here:

```
var floatingNum = parseFloat("1.8392"); // returns 1.8392
```

In this code, the same string is passed to the `parseFloat()` function, and the result is the exact number passed to the function.

The `parseInt()` and `parseFloat()` functions parse the strings passed to them. They work by starting at the beginning of the string and look at each character in the string. The function determines if the character is a valid number. If it is, the function uses that numeric value to start building the number to return and looks at the next character. If the character isn't a number, JavaScript assumes the number has ended and stops parsing the string. This means that these two functions can parse strings that also contain alphabetical characters. The following code shows this:

```
var num = parseInt("1234abcd"); // returns 1234
var decNum = parseFloat("1.234abcd"); // returns 1.234
var num2 = parseInt("1234abcd5678"); // returns 1234
```

This code demonstrates how `parseInt()` and `parseFloat()` parse strings that contain alphabetical characters. In all three lines, the parsing functions begin parsing the strings with the first character, and they stop parsing when they encounter a non-numeric character. The third line demonstrates this better, since the string passed to `parseInt()` contains several numeric characters separated by a group of alphabetical characters.

The `parseInt()` function accepts an optional second argument called a *radix*. The radix determines what numeral system the string passed in the first argument is converted to. For example, we humans use a base 10 numeral system, but computers use a base 2 (binary) system. The binary number 100 is actually the base 10 number 4. When calling `parseInt()`, it's important to specify the radix; otherwise, JavaScript may interpret the string as a number of a different numeral system. So, if you want to convert a string to a number that we humans use, specify the radix of 10, like this:

```
var parsedNumber = parseInt("1043", 10); // 1043
```

Boolean

All computer systems use a binary system at their most basic level. The CPU and other processors are made up of transistors that are either turned on or turned off. The hard drive stores data by magnetically positively or negatively charging a tiny piece of the platter.

A *bit* is the simplest unit in a computer system. It can have only one of two states: It can either be turned on (1) or it can be turned off (0). In programming, the `Boolean` data type is typically the most basic data type, as it exactly represents the state of a bit. `Boolean` values are either `true` or `false` (on or off, respectively).

JavaScript has two `Boolean` literals: `true` and `false`. These values are different from the numeric equivalents of 1 and 0 even though they can be used to mean the same thing. You assign `Boolean` values like this:

```
var trueVar = true;
var falseVar = false;
```

Keep JavaScript's case-sensitivity in mind here. The `true` and `false` literal values are not the same as `True` and `False`, respectively.

Truthy and Falsy Values

JavaScript is somewhat unique in that `true` and `false` are not the only `Boolean` values in the language. In fact, all data types have values that are equivalent to `true` and `false`. JavaScript developers call these values *truthy* and *falsy*.

The `Number` data type's falsy values are the number zero (0) and `NaN`, , and all other numbers are considered truthy. The following code offers some examples of truthy and falsy number values:

```
var truthyVar = -56;
var truthyVar2 = 0.453;
var falseyVar = 0;
var falseyVar2 = 1 / 0;
```

The `String` data type follows along the same lines as numbers. An empty string (`""`) is a falsy value, whereas anything other than an empty string is a truthy value. The following lines of code show some examples:

```
truthyVar = " ";
truthyVar2 = "This is a string.";
falseyVar = "";
```

JavaScript has two more primitive data types, and they both serve as falsy values.

Undefined and Null

The `Undefined` and `Null` data types are special in JavaScript, primarily because they can have only one value each. The `Undefined` type's special value is called `undefined`, and `Null`'s special value is `null`. Many beginning JavaScript developers think these two values are synonymous. On the contrary, these values serve two different purposes.

When a variable is declared, but not initialized, its value is said to be undefined. Recall from earlier in this chapter when you were first introduced to variables. The following code was used as an example:

```
var myVariable;
myVariable = "some text";
```

The first line declares the `myVariable` variable by using the `var` keyword followed by the variable's name. No value is assigned to it. Therefore, its value is `undefined` until another value is assigned to it.

The `Null` data type comes into play when you are dealing with objects. Later lessons will delve into objects, but for now, think of an object as a thing that contains multiple types of data. An empty object is said to be `null`. The value of `null` is best used to assign a value to a variable that will later hold an object. The following line of code assigns `null` to a variable:

```
var obj = null;
```

Don't worry about the `Null` data type right now. Later lessons will revisit `null` in the context of discussing objects, where it'll make much more sense.

Determining a Variable's Data Type

Before you work with data stored in variables, it's important to know what kind of data is actually stored within the variable. This isn't necessarily a problem in strongly-typed languages, as you generally know what type of data you're working with. Because of JavaScript's loosely-typed nature, however, it needs some way to identify a variable's data type. The `typeof` operator is used for this specific purpose.

The `typeof` operator is a *unary* operator, meaning it operates on only one operand. This is in contrast to the arithmetic and concatenation operators, which are binary operators (they perform operations on two operands). The `typeof` operator returns a string value containing the type of data stored in a variable. The following list displays the possible values:

➤ `"number"`: For number values

➤ `"string"`: For string values

➤ `"boolean"`: For Boolean values (pure Boolean values — not truthy or falsy values)

➤ `"undefined"`: For uninitialized variables

➤ `"object"`: For `null`

These are fairly self-explanatory, except for `null`. Remember that `null` refers to an empty object. Therefore, its data type is considered to be an object.

Look at the following code for an example:

```
var myVariable = 3.14;
var variableType = typeof myVariable; // "number"
```

The first line of code creates the `myVariable` variable and initializes it with a number value of 3.14. The second line uses the `typeof` operator against the `myVariable` operand to get the variable's data type. In this case, the `typeof` operator returns `"number"`.

KEYWORDS AND RESERVED WORDS

Every programming language has a list of words that have specific uses. These are called keywords, and you've been introduced to several in this lesson. Keywords cannot be used as identifiers. The complete list of JavaScript's keywords is as follows:

break	else	new	var
case	finally	return	void
catch	for	switch	while
continue	function	this	with
default	if	throw	
delete	in	try	
do	instanceof	typeof	

JavaScript also has a set of words that are *reserved* words. These are words that are not currently used in the language, but are reserved for future use. Following is the complete list of reserved words:

abstract	enum	int	short
boolean	export	interface	static
byte	extends	long	super
char	final	native	synchronized
class	float	package	throws
const	goto	private	transient
debugger	implements	protected	volatile
double	import	public	

TRY IT

In this lesson, you learn about variables, primitive data types, and some of JavaScript's syntax.

Lesson Requirements

For this lesson, you need a text editor; any plain text editor will do. For Microsoft Windows users, Notepad is available by default on your system or you can download Microsoft's free Visual Web Developer Express (www.microsoft.com/express/web/) or Web Matrix (www.asp.net/webmatrix/). Mac OS X users can use TextMate, which comes as part of OS X, or they can download a trial for Coda (www.panic.com/coda/). Linux users can use the built-in VIM.

You also need a modern web browser. Choose any of the following:

➤ Internet Explorer 8+

➤ Google Chrome

➤ Firefox 3.5+

➤ Apple Safari 4+

➤ Opera 10+

Create a subfolder called `Lesson02` in the `JS24Hour` folder you created in Lesson 1. Store the files you create in this lesson in the `Lesson02` folder.

Step-by-Step

Create and initialize three variables. The first variable should contain a numeric value. The second variable's initialization should use the value of the first variable in an addition operation. The third variable should contain a string followed by the numeric value in the second variable. Use the `alert()` function to display the string value in the third variable.

1. Open your text editor, type the following code, and save the file as `lesson02_sample01.js`.

```
var myVariable = 3;
var myVariable2 = myVariable + 2;
var myVariable3 = "The value is: " + myVariable2;
alert(myVariable3); // alert the value
```

2. Open another instance of your text editor, type the following HTML, and save it as `lesson02_sample01.htm`:

```
<html>
<head>
    <title>Sample Page</title>
</head>
<body>
    <script type="text/javascript" src="lesson02_sample01.js"></script>
</body>
</html>
```

3. Open the HTML file in your browser. You will see an alert box displaying a value of `"The value is: 5"`.

 Please select Lesson 2 on the DVD to view the video that accompanies this lesson. You can also download the sample code for all lessons from the book's website at www.wrox.com.

3

Functions

Variables are certainly an important part of any programming language; developers could not create efficient and meaningful applications without them. However, a language without any means of organizing code can lead to inefficient applications. In fact, some early programming languages, such as those used for punch cards (and languages based on them like RPG II), lacked organizational constructs, which resulted in many lines of repeated code.

Consider an application that performs the same series of operations on multiple variables. The following shows an example of such an application:

```
var valueOne = 100;
valueOne = valueOne + 150;
valueOne = valueOne / 2;
valueOne = "The value is: " + valueOne; // results in "The value is: 125"

var valueTwo = 50;
valueTwo = valueTwo + 150;
valueTwo = valueTwo / 2;
valueTwo = "The value is: " + valueTwo; // results in "The value is: 100"

var valueThree = 2;
valueThree = valueThree + 150;
valueThree = valueThree / 2;
valueThree = "The value is: " + valueThree; // results in "The value is: 76"
```

This is code duplication. The same operations are duplicated three times for three variables. Imagine having to repeat these same operations over and over again for as many variables as your program needs. Also imagine needing to change the addition operation (+ 150) to a subtraction operation (- 150). Not only would you have to make three changes with this code, but you'd also need to make the same change to any other variable that used the same pattern of statements. It's time-consuming and makes updates more prone to error.

Believe it or not, many older programming languages require this type of programming — typing statement after statement as many times as needed to perform the same set of operations for as many variables as needed. Not only is it time-consuming to create, but it's a nightmare to maintain when updates are required. This is the primary reason most programming languages today have functions.

Functions are arguably the most important part of any programming language. They encapsulate one or more statements to perform a certain task, and you can *call*, or execute, them whenever you want. But in JavaScript functions are exceptionally important because they have *first-class* status. In programming, *first-class* means that functions can be created on-the-fly, they can be stored in variables, and they can be passed as arguments to other functions. In other words, functions are a type of value in JavaScript, and this is a powerful feature that makes JavaScript one of the best languages to program with.

You've already been introduced to a few functions. The `parseInt()` and `parseFloat()` functions convert string values to numeric values. You've also seen a function called `alert()`, which displays information in an alert box in the browser. You know how to call functions and pass arguments to them, so now it's time to learn how to write your own functions.

FUNCTION DECLARATIONS

Functions are declared in *function declaration* statements by means of the `function` keyword. Unlike the statements seen in Lesson 2 and at the beginning of this lesson, function declaration statements do not end with a semicolon. The following code shows the syntax of a function declaration statement:

```
function functionName(parameter1, parameter2, etc) {
    // statements here
}
```

Function declaration statements begin with the `function` keyword, followed by a space and the function's identifier. The identifier should be unique throughout the entire HTML page, but at the same time it should be meaningful. For example, there's no guesswork as to what a function called `sum()` does; anyone reading the code can instantly recognize that the function adds two or more numbers together. Contrast that with a function named `function4392()`. Not even the person who wrote a function with that name would be able to remember what the function does. Readability is very important in writing code — especially when you're revisiting the code to make updates.

Function identifiers follow the same rules for identifiers outlined in Lesson 2:

➤ The first character must be a letter, underscore, or dollar sign.

➤ All other characters can be letters, numbers, underscores, or dollar signs.

➤ An identifier cannot be the same as a keyword or reserved word.

After the identifier is a list of *parameters* separated by commas that are encapsulated within a pair of parentheses. Parameters are special variables that a function may need in order to properly do its work.

You may hear and read the terms parameter *and* argument *used interchangeably, but there is a distinction between them. The term* parameter *is more appropriately used to refer to an identifier between the parentheses in a function declaration. For example: "The function has three parameters." The term* argument *is more appropriately used to refer to a value passed to a function: "Pass the value 3 as an argument to the function."*

Parameters are optional. Functions do not have to have them, but on the other hand, a function can accept multiple arguments. Regardless of the amount of parameters a function has, the opening and closing parentheses are required in the declaration. The following example shows the difference between a zero-parameter function and a function accepting two parameters:

```
function noArgumentFunction() {

}

function twoArgumentFunction(paraOne, anotherValue) {
    var newValue = paraOne + anotherValue;
}
```

The first function does not define any parameters due to the lack of any identifiers inside the parentheses. The second function, however, lists two parameters, and you can see how they are used within the function's body — just like variables.

After the parameter list is an opening curly brace. This marks the beginning of the function's body, and a closing curly brace marks the end. When called, the function executes the statements within its body. Any statements outside the function's body are not executed by the function.

The function's body, or any amount of code occurring within a pair of curly braces, is sometimes referred to as a block of code.

Let's apply this information by modifying the code at the beginning of this lesson, and write a function to make the code easier to type and maintain. This function is called augmentValue(), and it accepts only one argument, called originalValue:

```
function augmentValue(originalValue) {
    var augmentedValue = originalValue;
    augmentedValue = augmentedValue + 150;
    augmentedValue = augmentedValue / 2;
    augmentedValue = "The value is: " + augmentedValue;

    return augmentedValue;
}
```

Compare the statements inside the function to the statements at the beginning of this lesson. The original value is stored within a variable and modified by the addition of 150, then divided in half, and finally converted into a string. With the exception of the last statement (the return statement), all statements in this function perform the same exact operations as the code listed at the beginning of this lesson. The only difference is the names of the variables.

The last line of the function uses the return keyword to exit the function and return the value stored within augmentedValue to the code that called the function. To use this function, simply call it by using its name, and pass a number value as an argument to the function (as with the parseInt() and parseFloat() functions in Lesson 2). The following code does just that:

```
var valueOne = augmentValue(100); // results in "The value is: 125"
var valueTwo = augmentValue(50);  // results in "The value is: 100"
var valueThree = augmentValue(2); // results in "The value is: 76"
```

When the function executes, the parameter originalValue contains the value passed to the function as an argument. So in the first line of this code, originalValue contains the value 100. When augmentValue() is called on the second line, originalValue contains 50, and in the final call to augmentValue(), originalValue is 2. The various operations are performed on each value, and the result is returned to the valueOne, valueTwo, and valueThree variables, respectively.

So isn't that easier? If you simply organize repetitive code into a function, the entire code is much easier to type, and maintenance becomes much simpler. Again, imagine that instead of adding 150 to the original value, you need to subtract 150 from it. In the old code you would have to make at least three changes and hope you don't forget to change the code anywhere else it's used. If you use a function, however, making that change is simple and easy because you have to make only one change to the function, and that one change is effective every time the function is called.

The use of functions is an example of code reuse as opposed to the code duplication seen at the beginning of this lesson. Instead of duplicating the same operations over and over again, you simply reuse one piece of code (the function) to get the same results. It makes application development and maintenance much easier.

It is not a requirement for functions to return a value; a function should return a value only if it needs to do so. In the case of augmentValue(), the function was written to replace code that resulted in a string value's being stored in a variable.

It's also important to note that functions immediately exit when they reach a return statement. Any statements following a return statement never execute. The following example rewrites the augmentValue() function to demonstrate this:

```
function augmentValue(originalValue) {
    var augmentedValue = originalValue;

    return augmentedValue;

    augmentedValue = augmentedValue + 150;
    augmentedValue = augmentedValue / 2;
    augmentedValue = "The value is: " + augmentedValue;
}
```

The bolded lines never execute in this version of `augmentValue()` because the function exits before those statements can execute. So, in effect, this function doesn't augment the original value at all; it simply returns the same value that is passed to the function.

There are a few circumstances where code might execute after a `return` statement, but do not worry about that right now.

You can also use the `return` statement without specifying a value to return. Developers use this technique to exit a function early if it does not need to return a value.

FUNCTIONS AS VALUES

Using the function declaration statement isn't the only way to create a function; you can create an *anonymous function*. Anonymous functions, as the name suggests, don't have a name, and they are quite useful despite that fact.

Anonymous functions look very much like the function statements of the previous section. The only difference is the lack of an identifier, as the following example shows:

```
function(parmOne, parmTwo) {
    // statements here
}
```

On its own, this is actually invalid code because the interpreter expects a named function declaration, but what makes functions powerful in JavaScript is that they themselves are a type of value. This means that a function can be assigned to a variable, and doing so gives the function the name of the variable. Assigning a function to a variable is called using a *function expression* statement. Such a statement is a cross between the variable initialization statement and the function declaration statement. The following code rewrites the `augmentValue()` function using a function expression:

```
var augmentValue = function(originalValue) {
    var augmentedValue = originalValue;
    augmentedValue = augmentedValue + 150;
    augmentedValue = augmentedValue / 2;
    augmentedValue = "The value is: " + augmentedValue;

    return augmentedValue;
};
```

This code creates an anonymous function, complete with a parameter and its statements, and assigns it to the `augmentValue` variable. Notice the semicolon after the function's closing curly brace. Even though this statement involves the creation of a function, it is still an assignment operation, and as such should end with a semicolon.

You execute this function exactly like any other function, as follows:

```
var valueOne = augmentValue(100);
```

Other than how the function is created and named, there is virtually no difference between declared functions and functions assigned to variables. You execute them the same way, they execute the body of code the same way, and they exit the same way.

PASSING FUNCTIONS TO OTHER FUNCTIONS

Because functions are values in JavaScript, you can use them as you would any other value in the sense that they can be assigned to variables, passed to other functions, and returned by functions. You've seen one way of assigning a function to a variable by using a function expression statement, but it's also possible to assign a function declared with a function declaration statement to a variable. Look at this code:

```
function sum(paramOne, paramTwo) {
    return paramOne + paramTwo;
}

var sumCopy = sum;
```

This code creates a new function called sum(). It accepts two arguments and returns their sum. The last line of this code creates a variable called sumCopy, and it is assigned the sum() function. Pay careful attention to this assignment, and notice the identifier sum is used without the trailing set of parentheses. When you omit the parentheses after the name of a function, you use the function as an actual value.

So what this code does is create the sum() function, and then assign the actual sum() function to the sumCopy variable; sumCopy is now a function allowing you to use it exactly as you would sum(), like this:

```
var sumOne = sum(1, 2); // 3
var sumTwo = sumCopy(1, 2); // 3
```

The variable name sumCopy used in this example is actually misleading because it's not really a copy of sum() — it is sum() with a different identifier. Great, so you have a function with two different names! But why? Well, take a look at the following code:

```
function sum(paramOne, paramTwo) {
    return paramOne + paramTwo;
}

function multiply(paramOne, paramTwo) {
    return paramOne * paramTwo;
}

function calculate(paramOne, paramTwo, calculator) {
    return calculator(paramOne, paramTwo);
}

var sumResult = calculate(1, 2, sum); // 3
var multiplyResult = calculate(1, 2, multiply); // 2
```

This code creates three functions: `sum()`, `multiply()`, and `calculate()`. The first two functions are self-explanatory, but the third, `calculate()`, isn't so obvious. It accepts three arguments: two numeric values and a function value (`calculator`). In the body of `calculate()`, the function assigned to `calculator` is called and the two numeric values are passed to the function contained within `calculator`.

When the `calculate()` function is called in the final two lines of code, the `sum()` and `multiply()` functions are passed as the third argument. By passing `sum()` in the next-to-last line, the `calculate()` function calls `sum()`, passing it the numeric values of 1 and 2, and returns the result of `sum()` to the `sumResult` variable. In the last line `multiply()` is passed to `calculate()`. So `calculate()` calls `multiply()` and returns the result of calling `multiply(1, 2)`.

Now look at another example:

```
var subtractionResult = calculate(1, 2, function(paramOne, paramTwo) {
    return paramOne - paramTwo;
}); // results in -1
```

This code uses the same philosophy as the code using `sum()` and `multiply()`, but an anonymous function is passed as the third argument to `calculate()`. This anonymous function subtracts the two values, resulting in a value of -1. So, you don't have to declare or name a function before you pass it as an argument to another function — it's usually sufficient to simply pass an anonymous function.

Code such as this is highly modular and flexible. Anytime you want to perform a mathematical operation on two numeric values, you can write a function to do it and pass it to the `calculate()` function to do the work for you. Granted, this particular example isn't all that useful, as you can directly call the `sum()` and `multiply()` functions without needing to call `calculate()`. But this technique of passing a function to another function is invaluable starting in Lesson 16, when you learn about events.

RETURNING FUNCTIONS

You can also return a function from a function as you would any other value. For example:

```
function someFunction() {
    return function() {
        alert("Hello!");
    };
}

var foo = someFunction(); // foo is now a function
foo(); // alerts the string "Hello!"
```

This code creates a function called `someFunction()`, and it returns an anonymous function to whatever called `someFunction()`. You can see this in the last two lines of this code. A variable called `foo` is assigned the return value of `someFunction()`, essentially making `foo` a function. Then, the `foo()` function is executed, alerting the text `Hello!` As in the previous section, the ability to return a function may not seem overly helpful. As you progress through the book, and especially in Lessons 20 and 23, you'll see many uses for returning a function from another function.

TRY IT

In this lesson, you learn about functions, how to write them, and how they are treated as values in JavaScript.

Lesson Requirements

For this lesson, you need a text editor; any plain text editor will do. For Microsoft Windows users, Notepad is available by default on your system or you can download Microsoft's free Visual Web Developer Express (www.microsoft.com/express/web/) or Web Matrix (www.asp.net/webmatrix/). Mac OS X users can use TextMate, which comes as part of OS X, or download a trial for Coda (www.panic.com/coda/). Linux users can use the built-in VIM.

You also need a modern web browser. Choose any of the following:

- ➤ Internet Explorer 8+
- ➤ Google Chrome
- ➤ Firefox 3.5+
- ➤ Apple Safari 4+
- ➤ Opera 10+

Create a subfolder called Lesson03 in the JS24Hour folder you created in Lesson 1. Store the files you create in this lesson in the Lesson03 folder.

Step-by-Step

Write a function with two parameters: a first and last name. Have the function concatenate a greeting message using the two arguments, and return the greeting to the caller.

1. Open your text editor and type the following code. Save the file as lesson03_example01.js.

```
function getGreeting(firstName, lastName) {
    var greeting = "Hello, " + firstName + " " + lastName + "!";

    return greeting;
}
```

This code creates a function called getGreeting(). It accepts a first name and a last name as arguments, and it uses those values to create a greeting message that is stored in the greeting variable. Then the value contained within greeting is returned to the caller.

2. Now call this function and alert the message by adding the following bolded code:

```
function getGreeting(firstName, lastName) {
    var greeting = "Hello, " + firstName + " " + lastName + "!";

    return greeting;
```

```
    }

    var message = getGreeting("John", "Doe");

    alert(message);
```

3. Resave the file.

4. Open another instance of your text editor and type the following HTML:

```
<html>
<head>
    <title>Lesson 3: Example 01</title>
</head>
<body>
    <script type="text/javascript" src="lesson03_example01.js"></script>
</body>
</html>
```

Save it as `lesson03_example01.htm`.

5. Open the HTML file in your browser. You will see an alert box displaying the message `Hello, John Doe!`

 Please select Lesson 3 on the DVD to view the video that accompanies this lesson. You can also download the sample code for all lessons from the book's website at `www.wrox.com`.

Making Decisions

Programming is much more than variables, functions, and calculations. If programming were as simple as those three things, computers wouldn't be anything more than giant calculators, and chances are good you wouldn't be reading this book.

What sets computers apart from other electronic calculation devices is their capability to simulate intelligence. Granted, it's the programmer who tells the computer how to behave and how and when to make decisions, but it's the computer that decides what action to take based on a set of criteria.

Making decisions is an important part of programming. At the core of decision making are *conditions*, and the program makes a decision based on whether or not a particular condition is met. There are a few control structures that use conditions to determine how code executes, but first let's look at how to write conditional statements.

CONDITIONAL STATEMENTS

In JavaScript, a conditional statement consists of an operation comparing two or more values to result in a Boolean value together with statements that may run, depending on the result. Recall from Lesson 2 that Boolean values consist of either `true` or `false`. A condition is said to have been met if the conditional statement results in `true`; otherwise, a value of `false` defines the condition as unmet. In order to get a `true` or `false` value, you typically use JavaScript's *comparison operators*.

Comparison Operators

Lesson 2 introduced several operators: the assignment operator to give a variable a value, the string concatenation operator to join two or more strings together, the `typeof` operator to determine a variable's data type, and mathematical operators to perform arithmetic operations. Similarly, JavaScript provides many operators to test conditions. These operators are binary operators, meaning they have a left side (the left operand) and a right side (the right operand). A comparison operator looks at both operands, compares them, and returns a `true` or `false` value after performing its test.

Let's introduce you to the less-than comparison operator. Like its mathematical counterpart's, its symbol is a less-than sign (<). This operator determines if the left operand is less than the right operand. The following code demonstrates the use of this operator:

```
5 < 6;
```

This reads as "Is 5 less than 6?" which of course is `true`. However, reversing the operands so that 6 is on the left and 5 is on the right (6 < 5) results in `false`.

JavaScript has many comparison operators, as the following table shows:

Comparison Operators

OPERATOR	NAME	DESCRIPTION
==	Equality	Tests if both operands are equal
===	Identity	Tests if both operands are equal and of the same type
!=	Inequality	Tests if both operands are not equal
!==	NonIdentity	Tests if both operands are not identical
<	Less Than	Tests if the left operand is less than the right operand
>	Greater Than	Tests if the left operand is greater than the right operand
<=	Less Than or Equal To	Tests if the left operand is less than or equal to the right operand
>=	Greater Than or Equal To	Tests if the left operand is greater than or equal to the right operand

Most of these operators are self-explanatory; the less-than, greater-than, less-than-or-equal-to, and greater-than-or-equal-to operators work the same way as their mathematical counterparts (with numbers, that is). However, the difference between the equality and identity operators, and between the inequality and nonidentity operators, isn't immediately obvious.

JavaScript's equality operator is lenient when comparing both operands; it *coerces* or converts the operands to the same type and then compares the converted values. Consider the following code:

```
"6" == 6; // true
"6" != 6; // false
```

The first line checks if a string value of `"6"` is equal to a numeric value of 6. Even though they look different, JavaScript says they are equal. The second line performs an inequality check: It determines if the string `"6"` is *not* the same as the number 6. Once again, looks can be deceiving. Even though the code compares a string with a number, JavaScript returns `false` because it converts both values and then compares them.

This is considered wrong in many programming circles, but thankfully this is where the identity and nonidentity operators come into play. These operators do not convert the operands to the same type. Instead, these operators leave the operands alone, and compare both operands' types and values. The following code performs the previous comparison, but instead uses the identical and not-identical operators:

```
"6" === 6; // false
"6" !== 6; // true
```

This is a more desirable result, and the use of the identity and nonidentity operators is therefore the recommended practice.

Operator Precedence

Like arithmetic operators, comparison operators have an order of precedence. The equality/inequality and identity/nonidentity operators have the lowest precedence, and the other comparison operators have the same higher level of precedence. This means that the less-than, greater-than, less-than-or-equal-to, and greater-than-or-equal-to operators perform their tests before the equality and identity operators perform theirs. Look at the following code for an example:

```
5 < 6 === true; // true
```

In this condition the less-than comparison is performed first since it has a higher precedence than the identical operator. The result of the less-than comparison is the Boolean value of `true`, which is then compared with the Boolean literal `true`. This condition can essentially be simplified as `true === true`. So the overall result of the condition is `true`.

Let's see another example:

```
false !== 6 >= 6; // true
```

Remember that the greater-than comparison has precedence over the identity comparison, so the `6 >= 6` comparison is made first. The number 6 is greater than or equal to 6, and the result of the comparison is `true`. With that conclusion, the overall condition can be simplified to `false !== true`, which of course is `true`, because `false` does not exactly equal `true`

Now look at a condition example involving some arithmetic operators:

```
3 * 4 > 11 + 2; // false
```

Comparison operators have a lower precedence than arithmetic operators. This means the arithmetic operations are performed before the comparison operation. After the arithmetic is performed, the condition is simplified to `12 > 13`, which is `false`.

The previous examples have been relatively simple, and knowing the operator precedence rules certainly helps in deciphering each conditional statement and its outcome. However, using parentheses can make the conditional statements much clearer, as well as ensure that you don't get unexpected results. Look at the following lines:

```
(5 < 6) === true; // true
false !== (6 >= 6); // true
(3 * 4) > (11 + 2); // false
```

These three lines are rewrites of the three previous examples of conditional statements in this section. Adding parentheses ensures that precedence is clear, and that's important when you (or someone else) are maintaining code. As a general rule, use parentheses.

Finally, a note of caution about comparison operators: Using more than one comparison operator in a condition can cause unexpected results. Consider the following condition as an example and determine its outcome:

```
5 > 4 > 3;
```

If you said `false`, you are correct. At a glance, it looks like the condition tests whether 4 is less than 5 and greater than 3. In normal mathematical notation, that is correct, but that's not the case in JavaScript.

Let's break this down. First, the comparison operators in this condition are all > operators and have the same precedence. Therefore, this condition is evaluated from left to right. The first comparison checks if 5 is greater than 4. Remember that comparisons result in a `true` or `false` value. So the result of the 5 > 4 comparison is `true`, and the overall condition can be simplified to `true` > 3. This second comparison is obviously `false`, as `true` is not greater than 3, and that makes the final result of the conditional statement `false`.

But what if you want to perform a check such as: "Is 4 less than 5 and greater than 3?" This type of check has to be split into two conditions, such as 5 > 4 and 4 > 3. These two conditions are then combined into a single expression with a different set of operators called *logical operators*.

Logical Operators

Logical operators combine multiple conditions into one expression. JavaScript has three logical operators, and the following table lists them and their symbols:

Logical Operators

OPERATOR	NAME
&&	Logical AND
||	Logical OR
!	Logical NOT

It's important to note that the AND and OR operators use two ampersands (&) and pipes (|), respectively. Using just one gives you strange results, as a single & and a single | are JavaScript's *bitwise operators* — operators that work on individual bits.

Like comparison and arithmetic operators, the logical AND and OR operators operate on a left operand and a right operand. The primary difference between logical and comparison operators is that the logical operators operate on Boolean values, so both the left and the right values must evaluate to either `true` or `false`. Typically, one or both operands is a conditional statement. The logical NOT operator is a unary operator, but it too operates on a Boolean value.

The logical AND and OR operators have the lowest precedence. All other operations (mathematical and conditional) are performed before the logical AND and OR operators perform their jobs. The logical NOT operator, on the other hand, has a higher precedence than all other mathematical and conditional operators. Let's look at these operators in more detail, starting with logical AND.

Logical AND

The logical AND operator (`&&`) behaves very much like the English word *and*. For example, "Is 4 less than 5 *and* greater than 3?" There are two conditions in this statement. The left condition is "Is 4 less than 5?" and the right condition is "Is 4 greater than 3?" If both conditions result in `true`, then the entire statement must be `true`. But if one or both conditions results in `false`, then the entire statement cannot be `true`, and thus is `false`. Let's translate this into a conditional expression. The following conditional expression is the code equivalent of "Is 4 less than 5 and greater than 3?"

```
5 > 4 && 4 > 3;
```

With the logical AND operator, both the left and the right operand must evaluate to `true` in order for the entire expression to result in `true`. This code results in `true` because 5 is greater than 4, and 4 is greater than 3. But look at this next expression and determine its final outcome:

```
5 > 4 && 3 < 2;
```

If you said `false`, you are correct. The left operand, the `5 > 4` condition, results in `true`. The right operand, the `3 < 2` condition, results in `false`. Therefore, the result of the entire expression is `false`, because both operands are not `true`.

The following table is a truth table that outlines all possible outcomes of the logical AND operator:

Logical AND Truth Table

LEFT OPERAND	RIGHT OPERAND	RESULT
true	true	true
true	false	false
false	true	false
false	false	false

JavaScript doesn't want to do any more work than is absolutely necessary; it exhibits a behavior called *short-circuiting*. This means that the right operand is evaluated only if the left operand does not determine the outcome of the logical operation.

Looking at the truth table, you can see that the logical AND operation returns `true` if, and only if, both operands are `true`. If the left operand is `true`, JavaScript has to evaluate the right operand in order to determine whether the logical operation returns `true` or `false`. If the left operand is `false`, JavaScript automatically knows that the logical AND operation cannot return `true`, so it ceases the evaluation of the expression and returns `false`.

Logical OR

Like the logical AND operator, the logical OR operator (||) behaves somewhat like its English counterpart, the word *or*. In English, the word "or" is often implicitly exclusive. For example, the question "Do you want a cookie or a cupcake?" implies you can pick only one of those choices. Logical OR, however, is implicitly inclusive. Consider the following question: "Is 4 less than 5 or less than 3?" This phrase has two conditions. The one on the left is "Is 4 less than 5?" and the condition on the right is "Is 4 less than 3?" Like this question, a logical OR operation looks at both conditional operands and returns `true` if one or more of them is `true`. The following expression is the JavaScript equivalent of this "or" question:

```
5 > 4 || 4 < 3;
```

The first operand, `5 > 4`, evaluates to `true`, but the second operand, `4 < 3`, does not. Even so, this expression returns `true` because at least one of the operands is `true`.

Remember that a logical AND operation returns `true` only if both operands are `true`; all other outcomes are `false`. With the logical OR operation, the outcome is `true` unless both operands are `false`.

To make it a bit clearer, here is the truth table for the logical OR operator:

Logical OR Truth Table

LEFT OPERAND	RIGHT OPERAND	RESULT
true	true	true
true	false	true
false	true	true
false	false	false

Like the logical AND operator, the logical OR operator can short-circuit. If the left operand evaluates to `true`, JavaScript doesn't bother to evaluate the right operand and returns `true`. If the left operand evaluates to `false`, however, JavaScript will check the right operand to determine the OR operation's outcome.

Logical NOT

The logical NOT operator (`!`) is a little different from AND and OR. One difference, as mentioned earlier, is that it operates on only one operand — the one to the right of the operator. Another difference is that it reverses the Boolean value returned by that operand. This is a useful behavior, as you'll see when covering the `if` statement. Keeping those two things in mind, look at the following example of the logical NOT operator:

```
!(4 < 3);
```

If you were to read this expression in your native language, it would read "4 is not less than 3." By reading it that way, you of course know the expression is true. However, it's important to know how to determine the outcome of the statement without translating it into spoken language.

First evaluate the `4 < 3` condition. Its result is `false`, so the simplified version of this expression is `!false`. The logical NOT operator has the behavior of reversing whatever Boolean value its operand contains. In this case, it reverses `false` to `true`.

Following is the NOT operator's truth table:

Logical NOT Truth Table

RIGHT OPERAND	RESULT
true	false
false	true

Assigning the Results of Conditions

Up to this point, the examples of conditional statements have shown isolated expressions for the sake of simplicity. The results of conditional statements are Boolean values, so it's quite possible to store a condition's result in a variable. The following line of code shows this:

```
var conditionalOutcome = (4 < 3) || (3 > 2); // true
```

It's quite simple, really: just declare a variable, use the assignment operator, and put the conditional expression to the right of the equals sign.

EXECUTING CODE BASED ON CONDITIONS

You've been introduced to the core of decisions with conditional statements and expressions. Now it's time to use those concepts and apply them to actually making decisions within your code.

Aside from loops covered in Lesson 5, JavaScript has two constructs to make decisions. The first is the `if` statement and the second is the `switch` statement. You use these statements to execute code based on the outcome of a condition.

The if Statement

You'll find yourself using the `if` statement in almost every program you write; it works very much as it does in spoken language. For example, "If it is cold outside, Sally will put on her coat." This sentence says that Sally will put on her coat (an action) *if* it's cold outside (a condition). Translating this to JavaScript could look something like this:

```
if (weatherType === "cold") {
    putCoatOn();
}
```

This code assumes a variable of type string called `weatherType`. It shows the syntax of the `if` statement. Notice the lack of semicolons, except for the statement within the code block. An `if` statement is made up of the `if` keyword followed by a condition surrounded by parentheses. In the case of this code, the condition is a string comparison comparing the value of `weatherType` to the value "cold". If this condition results in `true`, the code within the code block executes. If it's `false`, the code block is skipped and JavaScript begins executing the next line of code after the code block.

What if you want to do the reverse: to check if it isn't cold outside and perform an action based on that outcome? There are a few different actions you could take. For one, you could use the `!==` operator to see if the `weatherType` variable is not `"cold"`; or you could use the logical NOT operator, like this:

```
if (!(weatherType === "cold")) {
    // do something for warm weather
}
```

This is where the logical NOT can be useful. This code uses it to reverse the result of the comparison operator. If the comparison's result is `false`, the logical NOT operator changes it to `true` and executes the warm-weather code. If the comparison's result is `true` (meaning cold weather), then the NOT alters the value to `false`, thus skipping the warm-weather code.

To execute code for cold or warm weather, you could write these two `if` statements sequentially, like this:

```
if (weatherType === "cold") {
    putCoatOn();
}

if (!(weatherType === "cold")) {
    // do something for warm weather
}
```

But JavaScript provides a cleaner way: the `else` statement. Like the `if` statement, the `else` statement translates very well into spoken language: "If it's cold outside, Sally will put on her coat, or *else* she'll wear clothes for warm weather." The following code demonstrates the use of the `else` statement:

```
if (weatherType === "cold") {
    putCoatOn();
} else {
    // do something for warm weather
}
```

As you can see here, the `else` statement is added after the closing curly brace of the `if` code block, and it too has its own block of code. The `else` statement cannot be used on its own; it must be used in conjunction with an `if` statement.

The example, so far, of how Sally prepares for the weather is all well and good if warm and cold are the only weather conditions to plan for, but it's quite evident that other weather patterns exist in this world. It could be raining or windy. The point is, a simple if ... else statement block isn't enough for this example; it needs to take several other weather patterns into consideration.

JavaScript is accommodating by allowing you to use an if statement immediately after an else The else if statement is used in conjunction with the if statement, but before the final else statement. It is used like an else statement while providing the ability to test another condition. So, in other words, it looks exactly like an if statement, except that it features the word else before if. The following example includes more weather possibilities for Sally:

```
if (weatherType === "cold") {
    putCoatOn();
} else if (weatherType === "rainy") {
    getUmbrella();
} else if (weatherType === "windy") {
    putOnJacket();
} else {
    // do something for warm weather
}
```

This code includes new checks for rainy and windy weather, and you can easily add more else if statements to check for other weather conditions. With if ... else if ... else you can turn a dumb calculator-type application into a thinking program, able to handle different types of situations. It's very useful for checking for various conditions.

In this example, each condition checked the value of one variable, the weatherType variable. In this case there's a more efficient means to achieve the same results: the switch statement.

The switch Statement

The switch statement is a switch of sorts. You supply it with a value or an expression, and it switches to the code that matches the supplied value or expression. There are four important parts of the switch statement:

➤   The test expression

➤   One or more case statements to check for possible values of the supplied test expression

➤   The break statements

➤   The default statement

The last example in the previous section, the if ... else if ... else example, can be rewritten with a switch statement, as follows:

```
switch (weatherType) {
    case "cold":
        putCoatOn();
        break;
    case "rainy":
        getUmbrella();
        break;
```

```
        case "windy":
            putOnJacket();
            break;
        default:
            // do something for warm weather
            break;
    }
```

The `switch` statement's test expression follows the `switch` keyword and is contained within parentheses. This code uses the `weatherType` variable as the test expression, but you can use any valid expression inside the parentheses.

Next are the `case` statements. The `case` statements do the condition checking by using the value in the `case` statement and checking if it is equal to the `switch` statement's test expression. For example, the first `case` statement in this example can be translated as `if (weatherType == "cold")`. Case statements end with a colon (`:`) and each `case` statement is paired with a `break` statement. The code in between the `case` statement and the `break` statement is executed if the test expression matches the `case` statement's condition.

The `break` keyword is used to break out of the `switch` statement when a case is matched and the code within the case is executed. It is possible to omit the `break` statement: Doing so causes code execution to drop to the next case statement. If this happens, the case's conditional value is ignored, and JavaScript executes all code until it reaches either a `break` statement or the end of the `switch` code block. The following example demonstrates this:

```
switch (true) {
    case true:
        alert("Hello");
    case false:
        alert("World");
}
```

Running this code results in an alert window displaying the text `"Hello"`, because the first `case` statement matches the text expression (both values are `true`). After the user clicks OK to exit the alert window, code execution drops to the next `case` statement. JavaScript doesn't perform a check to see if `false` is equal to the test expression, but instead simply executes the code `alert("World")`. This results in another alert window displaying the text `"World"`.

As a general rule of thumb, use the `break` keyword at the end of each `case` statement's block of code to break out of the `switch` statement. Otherwise you might experience some unexpected results.

The final piece of the `switch` statement is the special `case` statement called `default`. The `default` case does not use the `case` keyword, and is the code that executes when no matching case could be found. It is optional, as the previous example shows. If it is omitted, however, keep in mind that no code will execute if no matching case is found. It's generally a good idea to include a `default` case unless you are absolutely certain that you do not need it.

The case expressions in this section use literal values to determine the code that executes when a match is found.

The Ternary Operator

Sometimes you want to assign a value to a variable based on a condition. The common thought is to use an `if ... else` statement like this:

```
var someVariable = null;

if (4 < 5) {
    someVariable = "4 is less than 5.";
} else {
    someVariable = "4 isn't less than 5.";
}
```

There is nothing technically wrong with this code. You initialize a variable called `someVariable` with a value of `null`, and then you assign a string value to `someVariable` dependent upon the outcome of the `if` statement's condition. It does, however, require six lines of code to essentially assign a value to `someVariable`. Thankfully, there is a shorter way of performing this same exact process, and it uses the ternary operator to do it. The ternary operator's syntax looks like this:

```
(<condition>) ? <return value if true> : <return value if false>;
```

To convert the previous `if ... else` block to use the ternary operator, the code would look like the following:

```
var someVariable = (4 < 5) ? "4 is less than 5." : "4 isn't less than 5.";
```

The ternary operator is handy in situations like this where you want to assign or return a value based on a condition. It is, however, limited to only returning a single value; you cannot execute multiple statements in a ternary operation like you can with `if ... else`.

TRY IT

In this lesson, you learn about conditional statements and how to use them to make decisions with the `if` and `switch` statements, as well as the ternary operator.

Lesson Requirements

For this lesson, you need a text editor; any plain text editor will do. For Microsoft Windows users, Notepad is available by default on your system or you can download Microsoft's free Visual Web Developer Express (www.microsoft.com/express/web/) or Web Matrix (www.asp.net/webmatrix/). Mac OS X users can use TextMate, which comes as part of OS X, or download a trial for Coda (www.panic.com/coda/). Linux users can use the built-in VIM.

You also need a modern web browser. Choose any of the following:

➤   Internet Explorer 8+

➤   Google Chrome

➤   Firefox 3.5+

➤ Apple Safari 4+

➤ Opera 10+

Create a subfolder called `Lesson04` in the `JS24Hour` folder you created in Lesson 1. Store the files you create in this lesson in the `Lesson04` folder.

Step-by-Step

Control code execution by using a condition to determine whether a number is less than three and greater than zero.

1. Open your text editor, type the following code, and save the file as `lesson04_sample01.js`.

```
var valueToTest = 2;

if ((3 > valueToTest) && (valueToTest > 0)) {
    alert("The value is less than 3 and greater than 0");
} else {
    alert("The value does not meet the needed criteria");
}
```

2. Open another instance of your text editor, type the following HTML, and save it as `lesson04_sample01.htm`:

```
<html>
<head>
    <title>Playing with if...else</title>
</head>
<body>
    <script type="text/javascript" src="lesson04_sample01.js"></script>
</body>
</html>
```

3. Open the HTML file in your browser. You will see an alert window displaying the text `"The value is less than 3 and greater than 0"`.

4. Change the value of the `valueToTest` variable to any number greater than three, save the JavaScript file, and reload the page to see a different message.

In this next exercise, your script will be more dynamic and require user input via the `prompt()` function. You have not seen this function yet, but it is very simple.

1. Open your text editor, type the following code, and save the file as `lesson04_sample02.js`.

```
var weatherType = prompt("What is it like outside?", "");

switch (weatherType) {
    case "sunny":
        alert("It's sunny outside! Go out and play!");
        break;
    case "rainy":
        alert("It's rainy outside! Stay inside!");
        break;
```

```
        case "cloudy":
            alert("It's cloudy outside. Stay in or go out.");
            break;
        case "windy":
            alert("It's windy outside! Carry a jacket!");
            break;
        case "cold":
            alert("It's cold outside! Don't forget your coat!");
            break;
        default:
            alert("I don't know that type of weather");
            break;

    }
```

2. Open another instance of your text editor, type the following HTML, and save it as `lesson04_sample02.htm`:

```
<html>
<head>
    <title>Weather Program</title>
</head>
<body>
    <script type="text/javascript" src="lesson04_sample02.js"></script>
</body>
</html>
```

3. Open the HTML file in your browser. A window will prompt you to answer a question. Answer the question and see how your program responds.

To get the sample database files, you can download Lesson 4 from the book's website at www.wrox.com.

 Please select Lesson 4 on the DVD to view the video that accompanies this lesson.

5

Loops

In Lesson 3, you learned how functions can greatly clean up your code by encapsulating repetitive operations and calculations to use throughout the application's code. There are times, however, when a function isn't the right tool for handling repetitive code.

For example, you want a particular line of code repeated 10 times — no more and no less. You can, of course, write that same line of code 10 times, but in doing so you condemn yourself to a maintenance nightmare in which you may have to make 10 changes to 10 lines of code. Functions don't solve the problem either. Although the code might be a little less complex, you still have to type (or copy and paste) 10 identical lines of code.

For this reason, programming languages have a concept called *looping*. In programming, looping means to repeat one or more lines of code while a particular condition is `true`. This functionality is useful, and you'll see loops used throughout the book. But for now, let's take a look at some loops.

LOOP BASICS

There are several different types of loops, but they all perform the same primary function of repeating code. They also share some similar features. For example, all loops repeat a code block based on the results of a condition. As long as the condition evaluates to `true`, the loop *iterates*, or repeats its code, and it immediately ends when the condition evaluates to `false`.

Loops can be grouped into two categories: *pre-test* and *post-test*. A pre-test loop tests its condition at the beginning of every iteration of the loop — even the first iteration. It's entirely possible for a pre-test loop to not execute its block of code at all. If the condition fails on the first iteration, the loop doesn't execute any code.

A post-test loop tests its condition at the end of each iteration. This means that a post-test loop's code block is executed at least once. After the code block executes, JavaScript evaluates the loop's conditional logic and determines whether the loop continues or exits.

Loops, while useful, can sometimes cause trouble when you're developing an application. Remember that loops repeat their code over and over again until their provided condition returns `false`. It is very easy to miss a flaw in the condition's logic and cause the loop to never end. This type of error is referred to as an *infinite loop*, and it is very common when applications are being developed. Always double-check the loop condition's logic; it can save you a lot of *debugging* time, or time spent locating and fixing errors.

It is also possible to break out of a loop early by using the `break` statement introduced with the `switch` statement in Lesson 4, and you can skip iterations by using a `continue` statement.

Let's now look at the different types of loops starting with the `for` loop.

THE FOR LOOP

The `for` loop's primary function is to repeat code a specified number of times. The `for` keyword denotes a `for` loop, which is followed by the loop's logic contained within parentheses. This logic consists of the following three things:

➤ An initialization of the loop counter

➤ A condition to determine how many times the loop iterates

➤ An increment statement to determine how the counter increments

The following is an example of the `for` loop's syntax:

```
for (var loopCounter = 0; loopCounter < 10; loopCounter++) {
    alert("This is loop iteration: " + loopCounter);
}
```

Focus on the logic inside the parentheses. The initialization, condition, and increment statement are separated by semicolons. The loop counter (the `loopCounter` variable, but it can be any variable) is initialized with a value of `0`. Computer scientists begin counting at `0` instead of `1` mainly because of the binary system that all computers are based upon. This is counter to what we humans have done for centuries; so it does take a while to get used to.

 Counters do not have to start at `0`; they can start at any integer value.

After the counter initialization is the condition. As long as the condition results in `true`, the loop iterates and repeats the code within the code block. If `false`, the loop immediately exits. The `for` loop is a pre-test loop; therefore, it can execute zero or more times. In this example the loop iterates as long as `loopCount` is less than `10`. The loop ends once `loopCount` equals `10` or more.

Following the condition is the increment portion of the loop's logic. The code here increments the loop counter by one at the end of each iteration of the loop. In this example you see a new operator, the increment operator (++). The increment operator is a unary operator that adds one to the value contained in the variable. The code `loopCounter++` is equivalent to `loopCounter = loopCounter + 1`.

The increment operator is a special unary operator in that it can either precede or follow the variable to be incremented: `++loopCounter` and `loopCounter++` are both valid statements. Where the increment operator is placed determines how the value is incremented. If it is placed before the variable (`++loopCounter`), the value contained within `loopCounter` is incremented by one, and the new value is returned to the caller. Consider the following code as an example:

```
var x = 1;
var y = ++x; // returns 2
```

Here a variable called x is initialized with a value of 1. In the second line the increment operator precedes the x variable. The value in x is incremented, and the new value of x is assigned to the y variable. So y contains a value of 2. Contrast that example with what happens when the ++ operator follows the variable, as shown here:

```
var x = 1;
var y = x++; // returns 1, but x is now 2
```

As in the previous example, this code initializes the x variable with a value of 1. In the second line, the current value of x (which is 1) is assigned to y, and then x is incremented by one to 2. So y contains 1, while x contains 2.

It's important to understand the difference between `++loopCounter` and `loopCounter++`, as unexpected results may occur if the increment operator is placed incorrectly.

 There is also a decrement operator: `--`. Instead of increasing by one, it decreases by one. It too can be placed before or after the variable, and other than decreasing by one, it behaves the same as the increment operator.

It's important to note that an increment or decrement operator does not have to be used in the increment portion of the `for` loop. You can increment the loop counter however you want to — with addition, subtraction, multiplication, or division. Look at the following code as an example:

```
for (var loopCounter = 0; loopCounter < 10; loopCounter = loopCounter * 2) {
    // code to repeat here
}
```

Here `loopCounter` is increased by being multiplied by 2 every time the loop iterates. But there's a flaw in the logic of this particular implementation. The `loopCounter` variable is initialized as 0. When `loopCounter` is incremented, 0 is multiplied by 2, resulting in 0. So `loopCounter` always has a value of 0, which is less than 10, and that means the loop runs forever.

The `for` loop is especially useful when you know exactly how many times to execute the same block of code, but sometimes you just need a loop that iterates as long as a condition is `true`. Enter the `while` loop.

THE WHILE LOOP

The `while` loop is simpler than the `for` loop. It does not require counters to function properly; all it needs is a condition. It is possible, however, to replicate the `for` loop's functionality with the `while` loop.

The `while` loop is a pre-test loop, so JavaScript tests the condition before the loop iterates. The loop's syntax looks like this:

```
while (condition) {
    // statements
}
```

It begins with the `while` keyword followed by conditional logic in parentheses and then the block of code that the loop repeats. Using the `while` loop can be as simple as the following example:

```
var counter = 0;

while (counter < 5) {
    alert(counter);
    counter++;
}
```

This code initializes the `counter` variable with a value of `0`. To determine if the loop should execute code, the value of `counter` (currently `0`) is compared to the number `5`. If the comparison results in `true`, then the code within the loop's code block executes. An alert window displays the value of `counter`, and `counter` is incremented via the `++` operator. As long as `counter` is less than 5, the loop executes. Otherwise the loop exits and JavaScript begins executing the next line of code after the loop.

THE DO-WHILE LOOP

The `do-while` loop is a post-test loop: its condition is tested at the end of each iteration. Other than that, the `do-while` loop is similar to the `while` loop. This type of loop is useful when you know you want the loop to iterate at least once.

The syntax of the `do-while` loop looks like this:

```
do {
    // statements
} while (condition);
```

With this loop, the code within the do block executes at least once, and then the condition is evaluated to determine if the loop iterates or exits. Notice the semicolon at the end of the while statement. This is the only time a semicolon is used to terminate a loop statement.

Look at this example of an implementation of the do-while loop:

```
var counter = 0;

do {
    alert(counter++);
} while (counter < 5);
```

This code results in the same outcome as the example for the while loop. First the counter variable is initialized with a value of 0. Then the code within the do code block is executed; it uses an alert window to display the value of counter and increments the variable in the same statement. Then the condition tests if the loop should continue or exit.

TRY IT

In this lesson you learn about looping with the for, while, and do-while loops. You will write an HTML page and a JavaScript file for each loop.

Lesson Requirements

For this lesson, you need a text editor; any plain text editor will do. For Microsoft Windows users, Notepad is available by default on your system or you can download Microsoft's free Visual Web Developer Express (www.microsoft.com/express/web/) or Web Matrix (www.asp.net/webmatrix/). Mac OS X users can use TextMate, which comes as part of OS X, or they can download a trial for Coda (www.panic.com/coda/). Linux users can use the built-in VIM.

You also need a modern web browser. Choose any of the following:

➤ Internet Explorer 8+

➤ Google Chrome

➤ Firefox 3.5+

➤ Apple Safari 4+

➤ Opera 10+

Create a subfolder called Lesson05 in the JS24Hour folder you created in Lesson 1. Store the files you create in this lesson in the Lesson05 folder.

Step-by-Step

Use a `for` loop and keep a running total of the even numbers from 0 to 20. In other words, add each even number together to get a total. Use the `continue` statement to achieve this. Use `alert()` to display the grand total when the loop exits.

1. Open your text editor and type the following code. Use the name `i` for the counter variable, and the name `total` for the variable that keeps track of the total.

```
var total = 0;

for (var i = 0; i < 20; i++) {

}

alert(total);
```

2. Add the bold line in the following code to the file. This line calculates `total`:

```
var total = 0;

for (var i = 0; i < 20; i++) {
    total = total + i;
}

alert(total);
```

3. This code adds the counter to `total` in each iteration of the loop. You want only the even numbers, so use the `continue` statement to skip an iteration when `i` is odd. Add the following bold lines of code:

```
var total = 0;

for (var i = 0; i < 20; i++) {
    if (i % 2) {
        continue;
    }

    total = total + i;
}

alert(total);
```

This code uses the modulus operator to determine whether `i` is even or odd. Remember, modulus operations return 0 if `i` is even. Because 0 is a false value, the `continue` statement is not executed. If `i` is odd, however, the modulus operation returns a nonzero number — a truth value. So, when that's the case, the `continue` statement executes and causes the loop to skip the current iteration.

4. Save the file as `lesson05_sample01.js`.

5. Open another instance of your text editor, type the following HTML, and save it as `lesson05_sample01.htm`.

```
<html>
<head>
    <title>Playing with for loops</title>
</head>
<body>
    <script type="text/javascript" src="lesson05_sample01.js"></script>
</body>
</html>
```

6. Open the HTML file in your browser. An alert window will display the value `190`.

Write a simple application using the `while` loop. The application should prompt the user to enter his or her name. The loop will use an alert window to display a greeting to the user, as well as a counter value, and it will continue to loop until the user types `exit`. The counter variable's name is `i`, and the variable to hold the user's name is `userName`.

1. Open your text editor and type the following code:

```
var i = 0;
var userName = prompt("Please enter your name. Type exit to exit", "");

while (userName !== "exit") {

}
```

2. Add the following bold lines to the file. The first line uses an alert window to display the message to the user. This line concatenates several string literals with the value the user typed, as well as incrementing the `i` variable by one. The increment operator is used before the variable to display a number to the user starting with `1`. The second line prompts the user to enter his or her name again.

```
var i = 0;
var userName = prompt("Please enter your name. Type exit to exit", "");

while (userName !== "exit") {
    alert("Hello, " + userName + ". You've run this " + ++i + " times.");

    userName = prompt("Please enter your name. Type exit to exit", "");
}
```

3. Save the file as `lesson05_sample02.js`.

4. Open another instance of your text editor, type the following HTML, and save it as `lesson05_sample02.htm`.

```
<html>
<head>
    <title>Playing with while loops</title>
</head>
```

```
<body>
    <script type="text/javascript" src="lesson05_sample02.js"></script>
</body>
</html>
```

5. Open the HTML file in your browser and enter a few names. Then, type `exit` to exit the loop.

Rewrite the `while` loop example using the `do-while` loop.

1. Open your text editor and type the following code. Save the file as `lesson05_sample03.js`.

```
var i = 0;

do {
    var userName = prompt("Please enter your name. Type exit to exit", "");
    alert("Hello, " + userName + ". You've run this " + ++i + " times.");
} while (userName !== "exit");
```

2. Open another instance of your text editor, type the following HTML, and save it as `lesson05_sample03.htm`.

```
<html>
<head>
    <title>Playing with do-while loops</title>
</head>
<body>
    <script type="text/javascript" src="lesson05_sample03.js"></script>
</body>
</html>
```

3. Open the HTML file in your browser and enter a few names. Then type `exit` to exit the loop. Notice that the alert window displays a greeting for `exit`. You can fix this behavior by using an `if` statement to determine if `exit` was typed. Add the bold lines from the following listing, save the JavaScript file, and reload the web page.

```
var i = 0;

do {
    var userName = prompt("Please enter your name. Type exit to exit", "");
    if (userName !== "exit") {
        alert("Hello, " + userName + ". You've run this " + ++i + " times.");
    }
} while (userName !== "exit");
```

 Please select Lesson 5 on the DVD to view the video that accompanies this lesson. You can also download the sample code for all lessons from the book's website at www.wrox.com.

Scope

In the Try It section of Lesson 5, you used a variable called i to count a for loop's iterations. Most programmers use the i identifier for that exact reason; it's used everywhere and all the time to count loop iterations. So if multiple developers were working on different pieces of the same application, wouldn't all these uses of i conflict with each other?

Thanks to scope, the answer is no. *Scope* is an important concept in programming, particularly in JavaScript. It's important to understand scope because it determines what variables a function can see and access.

GLOBAL SCOPE

Variables and functions defined outside of a function are created in the global scope. JavaScript's global scope is the topmost level of scope. It persists throughout the entire web page, and any variables and functions created in the global scope are accessible anywhere in the page.

Consider the following code:

```
var globalVar = "This is a global variable.";

function globalFunction() {
    globalVar = "This changes the value of globalVar";
}

globalFunction();
```

In this example, a variable called globalVar is created outside of any function; thus, it is a global variable and can be accessed anywhere in the page. Because the globalVar variable is a global variable, the globalFunction() function, which is also defined in the global scope, can access the variable and modify it. Since globalVar is global, its new value can be seen and accessed anywhere in the page; modifying a global variable's value makes the new value visible and usable everywhere.

Global variables and functions persist throughout the page, and they remain relevant to the page until the user navigates to a different one. Contrast that with *functional* scope, in which scope is limited only to the function.

FUNCTIONAL SCOPE

Think of scope as shown in Figure 6-1.

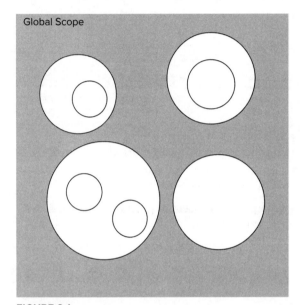

Global Scope

FIGURE 6-1

The shaded area outside the circles is the global scope. All variables and functions defined in this area have access to the other variables and functions in the same space. The circles represent functions: Some are globally defined while others are defined inside other functions. The boundary line of each circle is a barrier preventing access to the variables and functions defined within the circle from items outside the circle. However, a circle is contained within either another circle or the global space, and the items defined within a circle have complete access to the items defined outside the circle.

This figure shows the primary characteristic of scope in JavaScript. Items in a particular circle of scope have access to the items inside their containing circle, as well as items outside the circle. They cannot, however, penetrate the boundary into another circle — even one contained within itself.

The variables and functions defined within a function are said to have functional, or *local*, scope — they are local to their containing functions. They have access to global variables and functions, as well as to other variables and functions defined within the same function, but they cannot be accessed from outside the function in which they are defined. This can be shown in the following example:

```
var globalVar = "This is a global variable.";

function globalFunction() {
```

```
        var localVar = "This is a local variable";
        globalVar = localVar;
    }

    globalFunction();

    alert(localVar); // error; execution stops
    alert(globalVar); // "This is a local variable";
```

This example uses the global variable and function from the previous section, but adds a variable initialization within the function. This new variable is called `localVar`, a local variable to the `globalFunction()` function.

The second-to-last line of this example uses an alert window to display the value contained within `localVar`. The only problem here is that `localVar` cannot be accessed outside of the `globalFunction()` function because it is a local variable of that function — it is only accessible to code within the function. What this line actually does is try to find a global variable called `localVar`. Since it doesn't exist, an error occurs and code execution stops. Neither alert window displays.

When the function exits, all its local variables are destroyed. But notice that within the function, the `globalVar` variable was changed to contain the value contained within `localVar`. While the local variable `localVar` was destroyed, its value was copied to `globalVar` before the function exited.

The same behavior is seen with function parameters. The function sees them as local variables, and while all code within the context of the function can access those parameters, code outside the function cannot. Look at the following example:

```
    var globalVar;

    function globalFunction(paramOne) {
        globalVar = paramOne;
    }

    globalFunction("This is a parameter");

    alert(paramOne); // error; execution stops
    alert(globalVar); // "This is a parameter"
```

This code recreates the `globalFunction()` function by modifying it to accept a parameter. After the function declaration is the statement to execute `globalFunction()` by passing a string value to the function. The next-to-last line attempts to access a variable called `paramOne`, but such a variable does not exist within the global scope. So once again, an error occurs and code execution stops before an alert window pops up.

Let's make things a little more interesting. Look at the following code:

```
    var globalVar = "This is a global variable";

    function globalFunction(paramOne) {
        var localVar = "This is a local variable";

        function innerFunction() {
```

```
            var innerVar = "This is an inner function's variable";
            alert(globalVar);
            alert(paramOne);
            alert(localVar);
        }

        innerFunction();
        alert(innerVar); // error; execution stops
    }

    globalFunction("This is a parameter");

    // code execution never gets here, but if it did...
    innerFunction(); // error
```

This code yet again recreates the `globalFunction()` function. It accepts a parameter as in the previous example, but the body has drastically changed. A function called `innerFunction()` is declared inside `globalFunction()`'s body. This function is created within the scope of `globalFunction()`, so it has access to all other variables and functions within `globalFunction()`, as well as those within the global scope. In other words, it can directly access the `paramOne` and `localVar` variables of the outer `globalFunction()` function and the `globalVar` variable in the global context.

The `innerFunction()` function has its own local scope. While it can access the items in the outer function and global scopes, the outer scopes cannot access the `innerVar` variable defined within `innerFunction()`. Also, the `innerFunction()` function cannot be accessed outside of `globalFunction()`.

NO BLOCK-LEVEL SCOPES

The idea of scope can be confusing, especially when you're dealing with functions within a function within a function. Many other languages include a level of scope for every block of code — that is, a list of statements inside a pair of curly braces (`{}`). This means that `if` statements, loops, and `switch` statements have their own level of scope in other languages. This is not the case with JavaScript. Consider the following code:

```
if (true) {
    var hundred = 100;
}

alert(hundred);
```

In other languages the `hundred` variable would be destroyed after the `if` statement was executed, and so the last line would result in an error. JavaScript, on the other hand, adds the declared variable to the scope in which it was created (the global scope in this case, making it usable anywhere in the application).

The `function` code block is one of the few code blocks with its own scope. Most other code blocks, such as `if ... else`, loops, and switches, share the same scope as their container.

VARIABLE DECLARATIONS

Throughout this book, variable declarations and initializations have started with the var keyword. It is, in fact, possible to create a variable without using the var keyword, but doing so has the side effect of creating a global variable. Look at the following example:

```
function someFunction() {
    someVariable = "This creates a global variable";
}
someFunction();
alert(someVariable);
```

This code creates a function called someFunction(). Its only statement assigns a string value to a variable called someVariable. When this statement executes, the JavaScript engine looks for the someVariable variable to assign it a new value. The engine can't find it, and so creates it in the global scope. When the last line of this code executes, it displays the text "This creates a global variable".

Even though this may seem beneficial, omitting the var keyword can lead to unexpected errors. It is strongly recommended that you always use a var keyword to declare variables.

This behavior is caused, in part, by how JavaScript looks up identifiers.

IDENTIFIER LOOKUP

When you access a variable or a function in your code, the JavaScript engine begins to look up the item's identifier, starting in the current level of scope. If it cannot find a match in scope, it begins to look in the next level of scope — traveling up to every level of scope until it either finds a match or doesn't find one in the global scope. For example, consider the following code:

```
var globalVar = "Hello, Global Scope!";

function someFunction() {
    alert(globalVar);
}
```

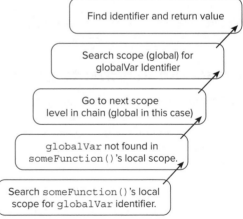

FIGURE 6-2

This code creates a global variable called globalVar and the someFunction() function to alert globalVar's value. When someFunction() executes, the JavaScript engine goes through a process to find the globalVar identifier starting at the bottom of Figure 6-2.

Because identifiers are looked up in this way, it's possible to override a variable or function defined in a higher level of scope with one in the local scope. Look at this example:

```
var aNumber = 100;

function overrideVar() {
```

```
        var aNumber = 101;
        alert(aNumber); // 101
}

overrideVar();
alert(aNumber); // 100
```

This code creates a global variable called aNumber; it has a value of 100. Next the code creates a function called overrideVar(). Inside this function, another variable called aNumber is initialized with a value of 101. The second line of the function uses the aNumber variable by passing it to the alert() function. JavaScript performs a lookup for the aNumber identifier, finds one in the current scope, and immediately stops searching for the identifier. Therefore the local aNumber variable is used in the call to alert(), so the alert window displays 101.

The local aNumber variable does not modify the global variable of the same name in any way, but any line of code inside overrideVar() uses the local aNumber variable instead of the global variable. The JavaScript engine simply finds the identifier in the local scope, and uses it because the engine found that variable's identifier first.

Outside the function, the global aNumber variable is intact. The aNumber variable inside the overrideVar() function is limited to the scope of that function, so the final line of code in this example calls the alert() function, passes the global aNumber variable, and displays the value 100 in the alert window.

TRY IT

In this lesson, you learn about JavaScript's scope and how it can affect your application. You will write a function to determine the area of triangles and rectangles.

Lesson Requirements

For this lesson, you need a text editor; any plain text editor will do. For Microsoft Windows users, Notepad is available by default on your system or you can download Microsoft's free Visual Web Developer Express (www.microsoft.com/express/web/) or Web Matrix (www.asp.net/webmatrix/). Mac OS X users can use TextMate, which comes as part of OS X, or they can download a trial for Coda (www.panic.com/coda/). Linux users can use the built-in VIM.

You also need a modern web browser. Choose any of the following:

➤ Internet Explorer 8+

➤ Google Chrome

➤ Firefox 3.5+

➤ Apple Safari 4+

➤ Opera 10+

Create a subfolder called Lesson06 in the JS24Hour folder you created in Lesson 1. Store the files you create in this lesson in the Lesson06 folder.

Step-by-Step

1. Open your text editor and type the following code:

```
function shapeArea(base, height, shape) {
    var area = 0;

    function triangle() {
        area = (base * .5) * height;
    }

    function rectangle() {
        area = base * height;
    }

    switch (shape) {
        case "triangle":
            triangle();
            break;

        case "rectangle":
            rectangle();
            break;

        case "square":
            rectangle();
            break;
    }

    return area;
}
```

This code creates a function called `shapeArea()`. It accepts three arguments: a number representing the shape's base, a number representing the shape's height, and a string containing the type of shape of which to compute the area. Inside the function, a local variable named `area` is initialized with the value of `0`.

Next are two inner functions: `triangle()` and `rectangle()`. They access the values passed to the `base` and `height` parameters of `shapeArea()`. Because of local scope, they have access to those values.

Then a `switch` statement switches through three possible values for the `shape` parameter: `triangle`, `rectangle`, and `square`. The appropriate inner function is called based on `shape`'s value. Finally, `area` is returned to the caller.

2. Save this file as `lesson06_sample01.js`.

3. Open another instance of your text editor, type the following HTML, and save it as `lesson06_sample1.htm`.

```
<html>
<head>
```

```
        <title>Lesson 6: Example 1</title>
        <script type="text/javascript" src="lesson06_sample01.js"></script>
        <script type="text/javascript">
            var area = shapeArea(2, 2, "square");
            alert(area);
        </script>
    </head>
    <body>

    </body>
</html>
```

4. Open the HTML file in your browser. An alert window will display the value 4.

To get the sample code files, you can download Lesson 6 from the book's website at www.wrox.com.

 Please select Lesson 6 on the DVD to view the video that accompanies this lesson.

7

Objects and Built-In Types

You live in an object-based world. Stop and think about the objects you come in contact with pretty much every second of every day. Whether you're driving to work or school, sitting at a table eating dinner, sleeping in a bed, or even walking in a field — you're interacting with objects. You don't even think about most of the objects you come in contact with every day. Interaction with objects is natural to you.

Before the 1990s, programmers primarily used procedural programming languages. These languages were based on the steps a program takes to reach the desired goal — very much like the examples thus far in this book. It wasn't until the 1990s that mainstream developers began to shift their thinking to involve objects.

Objects are a very important part of JavaScript: In fact, just about everything in JavaScript is an object. An understanding of what objects are and how to use them is required in order to use the language to its full potential. First let's talk a little more about what objects are and why they're useful.

WHAT ARE OBJECTS?

It's easiest to understand objects in a programming context by comparing them with real-world examples. Consider an automobile as an example. Automobiles come in a variety of colors, and are made by manufacturers that build them into different models. Some have vinyl interiors, while others have leather. Most automobiles come with an automatic transmission, and a small number of them have manual transmissions. The majority of automobiles have four wheels, and others have more than four. There are a variety of *properties*, or pieces of data, that help describe each individual automobile on the planet.

Automobiles are also defined by a set of actions they can perform. They propel themselves forward or backward by supplying fuel to an engine. They can change directions by moving their wheels to the right or left. They even have a communication device (the horn) that can honk to get the attention of another driver. These are *methods*, or actions, a driver can use to control an automobile.

In programming, objects are things that can have properties, or special variables, that contain data about them. They also have methods, which are similar to functions, which perform some type of action — usually on the data stored in properties. Just as the properties and methods of an automobile object define an automobile, the properties and methods of an object in programming define that object. Object-oriented programming is a type of programming intended to mimic the real world by using objects to organize and work with data — complex data, as opposed to the simple primitive data discussed in Lesson 2.

JavaScript has many object data types. Before looking into them, however, first look at how to use objects.

USING JAVASCRIPT OBJECTS

An object must be created before it can be used, and the most common way to create an object is by calling a *constructor*. A constructor is a special function that creates an *instance* of a particular data type.

Think back to Lesson 2, and recall the primitive data types in JavaScript: Number, String, and Boolean. While these primitive data types are not objects themselves, they do have what are called *wrapper* objects — objects that encapsulate the primitive types so that they can be represented as objects. Because of this, it's possible to create values of these types by using the appropriate constructors. A constructor has the same name as the data type it represents. For example, the String data type's constructor is String().

When calling a constructor, you use an operator called new. This tells JavaScript that you want to create a new object of the specified data type. After typing the new operator, you then call the data type's constructor function and pass it any necessary parameters. The following code shows an example of using a constructor to create a String object:

```
var message = new String("Hello, World!");
```

This is a variable-initialization statement that creates a String object containing the data "Hello, World!" and assigns it to the message variable.

Even though you can create a String value, or a value of any of the other primitive types, by calling its constructor, it is recommended that you use literal notation to create such values. You can still access the properties and methods of those data types.

Once an object is created, it is then possible to use the properties and methods (collectively known as *members*) of that data type. Accessing a data type's members involves the use of the dot (.) operator. Use this operator between the object's identifier and the member's identifier, like this:

```
var numberOfCharacters = message.length; // 13
```

This statement uses the String data type's `length` property, which returns the amount of characters and whitespace in the string. The property is accessed by means of the object's identifier (`message` in this code), followed by the dot operator, and then the property's identifier (`length`).

Properties are very much like variables attached to an object. Some properties are read-only — meaning they can return data, but they cannot be assigned a new value. The String data type's `length` property is a read-only property. Because of this, the following line is incorrect:

```
message.length = 10; // wrong; length is read-only
```

Accessing methods follows the same principle: use the object's identifier, followed by a dot, and then the method's identifier. The following code calls one of the String data type's methods:

```
var lowerCaseMessage = message.toLowerCase(); // "hello, world!"
```

Just as properties are like variables, methods are like functions. The primary difference between a method and a function is that methods perform some kind of work on or for the object. The `toLowerCase()` method is an example of this. It performs work using the String object's value by copying and converting all alphabetical characters to lowercase and returning the new value to the caller, the `lowerCaseMessage` variable in this code.

Now that you have an idea of how to use objects, let's start looking at JavaScript's built-in data types.

BUILT-IN DATA TYPES

JavaScript has many built-in data types. This lesson introduces you to the following types:

➤ Array

➤ Date

➤ Number

➤ String

Future lessons will introduce you to the Object and Function data types.

Array

Expanding on the automobile example at the beginning of this lesson, an automobile has a set of gears that determine how the vehicle moves. Putting an automobile into reverse moves it backward, whereas another gear moves the vehicle forward. Storing all possible gear values in an object's property could be problematic, as properties and variables typically contain only one piece of data at a time. The following code provides an example:

```
var gear = 1;
```

There are times, such as in the gear situation, when it's desirable to store multiple values in one variable or property. This is where *arrays* are helpful. The simplest definition of an array is an ordered collection of values.

Arrays are created in one of two ways. The first way uses the Array data type's constructor, like this:

```
var myArray = new Array(); // create a new array
```

The `Array()` constructor can accept a set of parameters containing the data to store in an array. The following line of code creates an array and adds possible values for an automobile's gears:

```
var gears = new Array(1, 2, 3);
```

This array is said to have three *elements*, or items. There is a much shorter and preferred method of creating arrays, however. By using *array literal notation*, you can create the same arrays with fewer keystrokes:

```
var myArray = [];
var gears = [ 1, 2, 3 ];
```

Array literal notation involves the use of square brackets, as shown in this code. The use of square brackets is a result of how you access each individual element in the array: *index notation*. You first use the array's identifier, followed by an opening square bracket, followed by the element's *index*, and then the closing square bracket.

Elements in an array are stored in a numerical sequence starting with zero. Remember from Lesson 5 when examples showed loops starting at zero? This is why. The first element in an array has an index of 0. The second element has an index of 1, the third element has an index of 2, and so on. You use an element's index number to access it in the array. The code to retrieve the third element in the gears array looks like this:

```
gears[2]; // 3
```

The code to retrieve the first element in the gears array looks like this:

```
gears[0]; // 1
```

It's OK if this is confusing to you, as it usually is for beginning developers. As humans, we typically start counting with the number one. Computers don't — they start counting at zero. JavaScript, as well as many other languages, follows the computer's pattern and starts counting at zero too. This means that counting to 10 actually involves 11 numbers: 0, 1, 2, 3, 4, 5, 6, 7, 8, 9, and 10. This is an important concept to understand, as this counting method is used throughout the language.

Each element in an array is very much like a variable; you can get data as shown in the previous examples or you can modify existing elements by assigning them new data. The following code changes the first element in the array:

```
gears[0] = 2; // changed from 1 to 2
gears[0] = 1; // changed back to 1
```

It's exactly like using normal variables, except you use index notation to access an element in the array.

The gears array has three elements, and this information is retrieved by means of the Array type's length property. It behaves much like the String type's length property, except that instead of counting characters, it counts the number of elements in the array. The following code shows an example of the length property:

```
var length = gears.length; // 3
```

The length property is especially useful when you're using a loop to iterate over an array. Instead of programming a specific end point for the loop, the length property can ensure that the loop iterates over each element and ends after the last element. The following code shows this:

```
for (var i = 0; i < gears.length; i++) {
    alert(gears[i]);
}
```

This code is the basis for looping through an array. The initialization portion of the for loop initializes a variable called i with a value of 0. The loop's condition tells the loop to repeat itself as long as i is less than the length of the gears array. It will iterate three times, and the value of i for each iteration is: 0, 1, 2. On the fourth iteration, the condition determines if i, which contains a value of 3, is less than the length of the gears array, which also is 3. Because 3 is not less than 3, the loop exits.

The length property always returns the number of elements in the array. This means that adding a new element to the gears array will cause gears.length to return 4. One way to add a new element to an array is to use index notation. The following line adds a new element to represent the gear of reverse:

```
gears[3] = -1;
```

This code adds a new element in an index position of 3, which is the fourth position in the array. While hard-coding the index position works in some cases, such as this example, there are times when you will not know how many elements are in an array. In times like these you can use the length property to add the new element at the next index position. For more flexible code, the previous line of code could be rewritten like this:

```
gears[gears.length] = -1;
```

In this example, the length property returns a value of 3, which is also the index number needed to add a new element at the end of the array. There is an easier way to achieve the same results, however, and it requires the use of one of the Array type's methods: the push() method, shown here:

```
gears.push(-1);
```

The push() method accepts one argument: the value to add to the array. Now that a new element has been added to the array, the length property returns 4 since there are now four elements in the array: 1, 2, 3, and -1.

As well as the `push()` method, the Array data type exposes a few other useful methods, as shown in the following table:

Useful Array Methods

METHOD	DESCRIPTION
`concat(array1, array2, ...)`	Joins two or more arrays into a single array.
`join(separator)`	Converts the array into a string. Each element is separated by the specified separator.
`pop()`	Removes the last element of the array and returns it to the caller.
`push(element)`	Adds a new element to the end of the array. Returns the new length.
`reverse()`	Reverses the order of the elements in the array.
`sort()`	Sorts the elements in the array.

The next few sections show you how to use some of these methods.

Joining Arrays

If you want to join multiple arrays together, you can use the `concat()` method. It does not alter the original arrays; instead, it creates a new array, populates it with the elements of all the specified arrays, and returns it to the caller. Let's depart from the automobile example and look at a family, as shown in this example:

```
var parents = ["John", "Jane" ];
var kids = [ "Jason", "Joe", "Jordan" ];
var pets = [ "Jackson", "Jimmy" ];
var family = parents.concat(kids, pets);
```

The first three lines of this code create three arrays, all representing portions of a family — the names of the parents, children, and pets. The final line of this code calls the `concat()` method on the `parents` array and passes the `kids` and `pets` arrays to the method. The newly created array, `family`, contains all the elements of the other arrays. This means `family` contains the names: John, Jane, Jason, Joe, Jordan, Jackson, and Jimmy.

The order in which the `concat()` method is called determines the order of the elements in the new array. In this example `concat()` is called on the `parents` array, so the elements in this array are the first elements in `family`. The `kids` array is the first argument passed to the method, so its elements can be found after `John` and `Jane` in `family`. The `pets` array is the last argument passed to `concat()`, so its elements appear at the end of `family`. Changing how `concat()` is called changes the order in which the provided arrays are joined together. For example, if the final line is var family = pets.concat(parents, kids), the elements of family would be in this order: Jackson, Jimmy, John, Jane, Jason, Joe, and Jordan.

Converting Arrays to Strings

Sometimes it's beneficial to convert an array to a string. In fact, it's more efficient to do this than to concatenate several strings together. Use the join() method to join the individual elements into a single string. It accepts one argument, specifying a separator to place between the element values. The following example uses the original family array from the previous section:

```
var familyString = family.join(", ");
```

This code passes a comma followed by a whitespace character to the join() method called on the family array. This results in familyString, containing the value "John, Jane, Jason, Joe, Jordan, Jackson, Jimmy". The separator passed to the method separates the element's values in the string.

As mentioned earlier, it's more efficient to use the join() method to concatenate array elements than it is to use the + operator to concatenate strings. For this reason you will see developers use something like the following code to generate strings:

```
var stringParts = [
    "John's family is: ",
    family.join(", ")
];

var familyString = stringParts.join("");
```

This code first creates an array called stringParts. Its first element is a string value, and its second element is the result of converting the family array. The final result of this code is the string "John's family is: John, Jane, Jason, Joe, Jordan, Jackon, Jimmy".

Like the concat() method, the join() method does not alter the original array.

Sorting Elements

Arrays are typically used for organizing similar pieces of data. Therefore, it might be desirable to sort that data in alphabetical order if the elements are string values or in numerical order if the data consists of numbers.

The sort() method makes sorting easy: It sorts the elements of the array in alphabetical order. The following example uses the family array yet again:

```
family.sort();
```

Unlike the other methods before it, the sort() method alters the original array The elements contained within family are now in the following order: Jackson, Jane, Jason, Jimmy, Joe, John, and Jordan.

The sort() method is case-sensitive: Words starting with an uppercase letter come before words starting with a lowercase letter. So Jackson comes before jackson as the result of a sort in JavaScript.

The sort() method sorts the elements in ascending order: There is not a method or a parameter to sort in descending order. However, there is a method, called reverse(), that can reverse the order of an ascending-ordered array.

Reversing Elements

The reverse() method alters the array by reversing the order of the array's elements. To get an idea of how this works, let's look at the kids array from an earlier section:

```
var kids = [ "Jason", "Joe", "Jordan" ];
kids.reverse();
```

The original kids array can be represented as in the following table:

INDEX	ELEMENT VALUE
0	Jason
1	Joe
2	Jordan

This table shows each element in the array and its index position. Calling the reverse() method reorders the elements in the array in reverse order, and the elements receive new index positions. The following table shows the array after calling reverse():

INDEX	ELEMENT VALUE
0	Jordan
1	Joe
2	Jason

By combining the use of sort() and reverse() methods, you can essentially sort an array in descending order, as in the following code:

```
family.sort().reverse();
```

Remember that many of the Array object methods return an array; sort() is one such method. Because of this, it's possible to chain method calls to perform multiple processes in a single statement. The call to sort() returns the sorted version of the family array, but instead of the result's being assigned to a variable, the return value is used to call the reverse() method. This is just one technique experienced developers use to write more efficient code.

Date

Every computer system needs to maintain date and time functionality. Many of today's operating systems rely on date and time to provide essential information and services. Similarly, every programming language needs some way to get the current date and time so that programmers can write meaningful and usable applications.

JavaScript uses the Date data type to handle this functionality. It provides access to information such as the current date and time, as well as any other date and time, so calculations can be performed. JavaScript's Date object uses the UNIX timestamp; in fact, it stores date information in this format. The UNIX timestamp is the number of milliseconds since the UNIX Epoch, January 1, 1970 at 12:00 a.m. GMT. For example, the UNIX timestamp for January 1, 2010 at 12:00 a.m. GMT is 1264982400000. The date and time contained within a Date object are based on your computer's date and time.

There are four ways to create a Date object. The first is the simplest, and it returns the current date and time. Simply call the constructor without passing any arguments to it, like this:

```
var date = new Date(); // current date and time
```

The second way to create a Date object is to pass a year, month, day, hours, minutes, seconds, and milliseconds to the Date constructor:

```
var date = new Date(2010, 0, 1, 0, 0, 0, 0); // January 1, 2010 12:00AM
var date2 = new Date(2010, 0, 1); // January 1, 2010 12:00AM
```

Most parameters are optional; omitting them causes 0 to be passed in their place. An important note to make here is that the month argument is passed as a zero-based number. So January is 0, February is 1, March is 2, and so on. If you are specifying hours, they must be passed in 24-hour format: 0 is midnight, 13 is 1:00 p.m., and 23 is 11:00 p.m.

You can also create Date objects by passing a string value, like this:

```
var date = new Date("January 1, 2010");
var date2 = new Date("Jan 1 2010");
var date3 = new Date("1 January 2010");
```

There are a variety of string variations you can pass to the constructor. If in doubt, try it out. Browsers, however, behave differently in creating a Date object this way. For example, Firefox does not support "01-01-2010" as a valid date format. So make sure to test Date object creation in multiple browsers when passing a string to the constructor.

The final way to create a Date object is to pass it a UNIX timestamp. This is perhaps the least-used method of Date object creation. The following line creates a Date object by passing a UNIX timestamp:

```
var copy = new Date(date.getTime()); // January 1, 2010 12:00AM
```

The Date object's `getTime()` method returns the UNIX timestamp of the Date object it was called on. So, this code makes a copy of the `date` Date object from the previous example by calling its `getTime()` method, passing it to the Date constructor, and assigning the new Date object to the `copy` variable.

JavaScript stores dates and times in UNIX timestamps. This isn't useful, so the Date data type exposes some methods that allow you to get more meaningful information from a Date object. The following table lists the more useful methods involving dates.

Date-Related Methods

METHOD	DESCRIPTION
`getFullYear()`	Returns the four-digit year.
`getMonth()`	Returns a zero-based number representing the month. January is 0, February is 1, and December is 11.
`getDate()`	Returns a number representing the day of the month.
`getDay()`	Returns a zero-based number representing the day of the week. Sunday is 0, Monday is 1, and Saturday is 6.
`toDateString()`	Converts the date portion of the object to a string and returns it in the format of `Fri Jan 1 2010`.
`setDate(dayOfMonth)`	Sets the day of the month according to the argument passed as `dayOfMonth`.
`setMonth(monthNumber)`	Sets the month according to the argument passed as `monthNumber`. Valid values are 0 through 11.
`setFullYear(yearNumber)`	Sets the year according to the four-digit year passed as `yearNumber`.

Unfortunately, the Date object does not return the name of the month or the day of the week; developers have to provide that functionality in their code. With arrays, however, it's a simple exercise. Look at this code:

```
var daysOfWeek = [ "Sunday", "Monday", "Tuesday", "Wednesday", "Thursday",
    "Friday", "Saturday" ];

var date = new Date(); // get current date

alert("Today is " + daysOfWeek[date.getDay()]);
```

The result of running this code depends on the day on which it is executed. If it were run on January 1, 2010, the alert window would display the text, "`Today is Friday`." Because array indexes are zero-based, as is the `getDay()` method of the Date object, you can use the value returned by `getDay()`

as the index for the correct day of the week. The same principle can be applied to months, which you'll see in the Try It section later.

Just as JavaScript's Date data type has methods for working with dates, it also exposes methods to work with the time portion of a Date object. The following table lists these time-based methods:

Time Related Methods

METHOD	DESCRIPTION
getHours()	Returns the hour in 24-hour format. Possible values are 0 through 23.
getMinutes()	Returns the minutes. Possible values are 0 through 59.
getSeconds()	Returns the seconds. Possible values are 0 through 59.
getMilliseconds()	Returns the milliseconds. Values range from 0 to 999.
setHours(newHour)	Sets the hours according to the argument newHours. Valid values for argument are 0 through 23.
setMinutes(newMinutes)	Sets the minutes according to the argument newMinutes. Valid values for argument are 0 through 59.
setSeconds(newSeconds)	Sets the seconds according to the argument newSeconds. Valid values for argument are 0 through 59.
setMilliseconds(newMS)	Sets the milliseconds according to the argument newMS. Valid values for argument are 0 through 999.

NUMBER

Lesson 2 thoroughly covered the Number data type. Number objects do not have any properties, but they do have some methods. The most useful, and perhaps the most used, Number method is the toFixed() method. This method formats the number to a fixed amount of decimal places, like this:

```
var num = 1.2345;
var fixedNum = num.toFixed(2); // 1.23
```

It accepts one argument specifying the amount of decimal places to include in the new number. It does not modify the original number; it copies it, formats the copy, and returns the copy to the caller.

The toFixed() method rounds the nearest decimal place up or down. The previous example looked at the decimal place after the hundredths and determined that it should be rounded down. The next example uses the toFixed() method to round up:

```
var num = 1.54321;
var fixedNum = num.toFixed(0); // 2
```

This code chops all decimal places off the number. The `toFixed()` number looks at the first decimal place to determine whether to round the number up or down. Since it is greater than or equal to five, `toFixed()` rounds the number up to 2.

The `toFixed()` method can chop off only zero to 20 decimal places.

String

The beginning of this lesson introduced you to two members of the String data type: the `length` property and the `toLowerCase()` method. The `length` property is String's only property, but unlike the Number type, the String type has a multitude of useful methods. They don't alter the original string in any way. Instead, they make a copy, perform their operation on the copy, and return the copy to their caller.

The following table lists several useful String methods that will be covered in this section:

Useful String Methods

METHOD	DESCRIPTION
charAt(index)	Gets the character at the specified index.
indexOf(searchString)	Returns the index position of the first found occurrence of the provided string. Returns –1 if no match was found.
lastIndexOf(searchString)	Returns the index position of the last found occurrence of the provided string. Returns –1 if no match was found.
replace(toReplace, replaceWith)	Searches for a substring in the string that matches the provided toReplace argument, and replaces the first match with the provided replaceWith.
split(separator)	Splits a string into an array using the provided separator.
substr(startIndex, numberOfChars)	Extracts the characters of the string starting at the startIndex position and selecting the amount of characters specified by numberOfChars. Omitting numberOfChars selects the remainder of the string.
substring(startIndex, endIndex)	Extracts the characters from the string starting at the position specified by startIndex and ending with the character before endIndex. Omitting endIndex results in the rest of the string's being selected.
toLowerCase()	Returns the string in all-lowercase characters.
toUpperCase()	Returns the string in all-uppercase characters.

Searching for Substrings

String objects have two useful methods to search for *substrings*, or smaller strings that occur within a larger string. They are the indexOf() and lastIndexOf() methods. These methods are useful when you want to determine if a particular string contains a keyword or phrase. Both methods accept a substring as an argument, and JavaScript will search for that substring within the String object the method is called on. These methods are case-sensitive: They do not report a match unless an exact match is found.

The difference between the two methods is how they search for the substring. Look at the following example:

```
var welcomeString = "Hello, Jeremy! Wonderful day, isn't it, Jeremy?";

alert(welcomeString.indexOf("Jeremy")); // 7
alert(welcomeString.lastIndexOf("Jeremy")); // 40
alert(welcomeString.indexOf("JavaScript")); // -1
```

The indexOf() method begins searching at the beginning of the string for the specified substring. It then starts searching the string and doesn't stop until it either finds a match or reaches the end of the string. When it finds a match, it immediately returns the index of the match. In this code, indexOf("Jeremy") returns 7 because the substring was found starting at the seventh character position.

The lastIndexOf() method begins searching at the end of the string as opposed to the beginning, and it doesn't stop until it either finds a match or reaches the beginning of the string. When it finds a match of the specified substring, it, too, immediately returns the index position of the match. In this example, lastIndexOf() finds a match that starts at an index position of 40.

If indexOf() or lastIndexOf() does not find a match, it returns a value of -1.

Extracting Substrings

There are times when extracting pieces of a string is beneficial, and JavaScript's String data type allows this with the substr() and substring() methods. Both of these methods provide the same end result, but they do so based on different parameter values.

The substr() method accepts two parameters. The first is required, and it's the index at which to start the extraction. The second parameter is optional. If specified, it determines how many characters after the starting index to extract, including the starting character. If the second parameter is omitted, the substr() method extracts all characters after the starting index. The following code uses the substr() method to extract a portion of a string:

```
var message = "JavaScript 24-Hour Trainer";
var subString = message.substr(11, 7); // 24-Hour
```

This code uses the substr() method to extract the 24-Hour portion of the string contained within the message variable. The 2 in 24-Hour is the twelfth character in the string — making the starting index 11 (again, remember that indexes start at 0) — and the phrase is 7 characters long. Passing these two values to the substr() method extracts the phrase 24-Hour and assigns it to the subString variable. The string contained within message is not altered.

The substring() method can provide the same results, but it does so with slightly different data. It still requires a starting index, and the substring() method behaves like substr() if the second parameter is omitted. But if it is specified, it is the index at which to stop the extraction. An important, and often forgotten, behavior of the substring() method is that the extraction includes the characters *up to* the ending index; it does not include the character *at* the ending index. The following code rewrites the previous example by using the substring() method:

```
var message = "JavaScript 24-Hour Trainer";
var substring = message.substring(11, 18); // 24-Hour
```

Use the method that makes the most sense to you. The substr() method is obviously the better choice if you know the exact length of the desired substring. The substring() method is the better choice when you don't know how long the desired substring is, and can be a powerful tool combined with the indexOf() and lastIndexOf() methods.

Converting to an Array

In many ways strings are closely related to arrays. In fact, many programming languages see a string as an array of characters. Unfortunately, JavaScript is not one of these languages. While String objects have a length property like array objects, you cannot use index notation to access individual characters as you can with elements in an array. Instead, String objects have a charAt() method. Pass an index to this method and you can retrieve, but not edit, an individual character at the specified index.

It is possible, however, to convert a string to an array by using the split() method: it splits a string into an array of substrings. The method knows where to split the string according to the argument passed to it. If you supply an empty string as an argument, this method creates an array in which each individual character is an element. The following code demonstrates this:

```
var message = "Hello, World!";
var messageArray = message.split(""); // converts to array
```

Once the string is in array form, you can access the individual characters using index notation. This method is also quite useful when you have a string containing a list of items delimited by a consistent delimiting character, such as a comma. Look at this code:

```
var fruitsString = "orange,apple,banana";
var fruitsArray = fruitsString.split(","); // creates array with 3 elements
```

This code creates an array by splitting the fruitsString string at each comma. The resulting array contains three elements: orange, apple, and banana.

Replacing Text

The replace() method accepts two arguments: the string to replace, and the string to replace it with. This method searches the string starting at the beginning and looks for the first occurrence of the specified substring. It does not replace all occurrences of the specified substring — only the first, as shown in the following code:

```
var message = "Today is Monday. Yesterday was Monday.";
var newMessage = message.replace("Monday", "Tuesday");
alert(newMessage); // Today is Tuesday. Yesterday was Monday.
```

This code first creates a string value that contains an error. It says that today is Monday and yesterday was Monday. To fix this error, the second line of code uses the `replace()` method to change `"Monday"` to `"Tuesday"` and returns the new string to the `newMessage` variable. When the alert window displays the new message, it reads, "Today is Tuesday. Yesterday was Monday."

As with all the other String methods discussed in this lesson, the original string (`message` in this case) is not altered.

TRY IT

In this lesson, you learn how to use objects and some of JavaScript's built-in object types. Here, you apply some of the knowledge and concepts you gained from previous sections .

Lesson Requirements

For this lesson, you need a text editor; any plain text editor will do. For Microsoft Windows users, Notepad is available by default on your system or you can download Microsoft's free Visual Web Developer Express (www.microsoft.com/express/web/) or Web Matrix (www.asp.net/webmatrix/). Mac OS X users can use TextMate, which comes as part of OS X, or they can download a trial for Coda (www.panic.com/coda/). Linux users can use the built-in VIM.

You also need a modern web browser. Choose any of the following:

➤ Internet Explorer 8+

➤ Google Chrome

➤ Firefox 3.5+

➤ Apple Safari 4+

➤ Opera 10+

Create a subfolder called `Lesson07` in the `JS24Hour` folder you created in Lesson 1. Store the files you create in this lesson in the `Lesson07` folder.

Step-by-Step

Write an application that prompts the user to enter his or her name. Display the name and today's date in an alert window. Use a function to get the name of the month, and use another function to abbreviate it to three characters.

1. Open your text editor and type the following function.

```
function getMonthName(index) {
    var months = [ "January", "February", "March", "April", "May", "June",
        "July", "August", "September", "October", "November", "December" ];

    return months[index];
}
```

This `getMonthName()` function creates an array containing the names of the month, and returns the element at the provided index.

2.   Now add the following bolded function:

```
function getMonthName(index) {
    var months = [ "January", "February", "March", "April", "May", "June",
        "July", "August", "September", "October", "November", "December" ];

    return months[index];
}

function abbrName(text) {
    return text.substr(0, 3);
}
```

This new function, `abbrName()`, uses the `substr()` method to select the first three characters of the provided text and returns it to the caller.

3.   Add the following bolded code:

```
function getMonthName(index) {
    var months = [ "January", "February", "March", "April", "May", "June",
        "July", "August", "September", "October", "November", "December" ];

    return months[index];
}

function abbrName(text) {
    return text.substr(0, 3);
}

var date = new Date();
var messageParts = [
    "Hello, ",
    prompt("Please enter your name", "Please enter your name"),
    ". Today is ",
    abbrName(getMonthName(date.getMonth())),
    " ",
    date.getDate(),
    ", ",
    date.getFullYear()
];
```

The first line of this code creates a Date object containing today's date. This Date object will be used to display date information to the user.

The second statement creates an array called `messageParts`. This array's purpose is to contain elements that will be concatenated into the message to display to the user. The first element is a simple string. The second element calls the `prompt()` function to prompt the user to enter his or her name. The fourth element gets the current month from the date object and passes it to the `getMonthName()` function. The return value of `getMonthName()` is then passed to the `abbrName()` function. So the fourth element in the array is a string containing the first three characters of the current month.

4. Alert the user to the message by adding the following bolded code:

```
function getMonthName(index) {
    var months = [ "January", "February", "March", "April", "May", "June",
        "July", "August", "September", "October", "November", "December" ];

    return months[index];
}

function abbrName(text) {
    return text.substr(0, 3);
}

var date = new Date();
var messageParts = [
    "Hello, ",
    prompt("Please enter your name", "Please enter your name"),
    ". Today is ",
    abbrName(getMonthName(date.getMonth())),
    " ",
    date.getDate(),
    ", ",
    date.getFullYear()
];

alert(messageParts.join(""));
```

This line calls the `join()` method, passing it an empty string to concatenate the elements without a noticeable separator.

5. Save the file as `lesson07_sample01.js`.

6. Open another instance of your text editor, type the following HTML, and save it as `lesson07_sample01.htm`.

```
<html>
<head>
    <title>Lesson 7: Objects</title>
</head>
<body>
    <script type="text/javascript" src="lesson07_sample01.js"></script>
</body>
</html>
```

7. Open the HTML file in your browser. An alert window will display the name provided to the prompt window in a message containing today's date.

 Please select Lesson 7 on the DVD to view the video that accompanies this lesson. You can also download the sample code for all lessons from the book's website at www.wrox.com.

8

Custom Objects

The built-in objects discussed in Lesson 7 go a long way in making applications easier to write and maintain, but they stop short of allowing developers to tailor objects to their personal needs and those of their applications. For example, what if it were your job to write an application that emulates a two-dimensional Cartesian coordinate plane? How would the Array, Date, Number, and String data types help you achieve that goal? It could be done, but it would take a lot of time and effort to write a proper application.

The fact is that JavaScript or any object-oriented programming language for that matter wouldn't be useful without the capability to create objects other than the built-in objects provided by the language. Being able to build your own objects and data types makes it possible to write flexible and maintainable applications.

At the heart of JavaScript's object-oriented design is the Object data type. It's the basis of all objects and reference types in JavaScript, and you'll look at how to use it in this lesson.

THE OBJECT DATA TYPE

There are two ways to create a basic object. The first is to use the Object data type's constructor, like this:

```
var coordinates = new Object();
```

This code calls the `Object()` constructor using the `new` keyword and assigns it to the `coordinates` variable. As with the Array data type, there is a much simpler (and preferred) way to create an object, by using *object literal notation*:

```
var coordinates = {};
```

Object literal notation uses curly braces as opposed to the square braces used to denote an array literal.

A plain object isn't usable. There's not much you can do with one, but JavaScript is a dynamic language. You can add properties to objects on-the-fly. All you need to do is assign a value to a property, like this:

```
var coordinates = {};
coordinates.x = 0;
coordinates.y = 0;
```

It's possible to take this code a step further and define the object and its properties in one statement. Doing so produces something like the following code:

```
var coordinates = {
    x : 0,
    y : 0
};
```

This statement starts like any other assignment statement. The `var` keyword denotes a variable declaration or initialization, followed by the variable's identifier (`coordinates` in this case), and then the assignment operator. Next is an opening curly brace denoting an object literal, but then things start looking different.

Inside the curly braces is a list of property definitions separated by commas. Property definitions inside an object literal consist of the property's name, a colon (`:`), and then the property's value. Each definition is separated from the next by a comma; otherwise JavaScript wouldn't know where one property definition ends and another begins. In this code two properties are defined for the `coordinates` object. They are `x` and `y`, and this code assigns them both a value of `0`.

After an object and its properties are defined, you can use them as you would any other object. Look at the following code:

```
var text = "X is " + coordinates.x + " and Y is " + coordinates.y;
alert(text);
```

The `x` and `y` properties of the `coordinates` object are concatenated with other string values. The final result is assigned to the `text` variable, and the second statement displays the contents of `text` to the user. This functionality would work well as a method, so let's add a method that performs this action to the `coordinates` object.

Method definitions follow the same principles as property definitions; the only difference is that the value to the right of the colon is a function. The following bolded code adds a method definition to the `coordinates` object:

```
var coordinates = {
    x : 0,
    y : 0,
    sayCoordinates : function() {
        var text = "X is " + this.x + " and Y is " + this.y;
        alert(text);
    }
};
```

First, notice that a comma was added to the end of `y`'s definition. Since it is no longer the last member in the definition list, it needs a comma to separate it from the definition of `sayCoordinates()`.

The code within the new method's body is very similar to the code in the previous example. But there's one change: A new keyword, called `this`, is used where the `coordinates` identifier was previously used. The `this` keyword is a special variable used inside a function; it points to the object on which the function is invoked as a method. The `sayCoordinates()` method is a member of `coordinates`. As such, it executes within the context of the `coordinates` object. Because of this, the `this` variable points to the `coordinates` object. The context in which `this` is used can easily be translated into spoken language. A statement like `this.x = 0;` translates to "Set the x property of this object to 0." When you see `this`, think "this object."

Outputting Objects

Custom objects have many uses in JavaScript development, but they're primarily used for data exchange. To continue the Cartesian plane example, a single point in 2D space must have two pieces of information: the x, or horizontal, information, and the y, or vertical, information. In order for the application to know where the current point is in 2D space, a function called `getCurrentPoint()` needs to return the x and y coordinates for the current point. JavaScript does not have a data type that represents coordinate data, but as you've seen in this lesson, a custom object can do it easily. The following code shows an example of what such a function might look like:

```
function getCurrentPoint() {
    // set initial values for current coordinates
    var currentX = 0;
    var currentY = 0;

    // code here to get the current x and y
    // and assign it to the variables

    return {
        x : currentX,
        y : currentY
    };
}
```

This function first initializes two local variables called `currentX` and `currentY` with a value of 0. Then, as stated by the comments, some code determines the x and y data and assigns the appropriate values to the `currentX` and `currentY` variables. Finally, the function returns an object, created with object literal notation, with two properties, x and y, that contain the values needed for the current point. Notice that this object has no identifier, and is not assigned to any local variable within the function. This code demonstrates how you can return any type of data without specifically creating and assigning it to a variable first.

To use this function, you might write code similar to this:

```
var point = getCurrentPoint();

alert(point.x);
alert(point.y);
```

The first line calls the `getCurrentPoint()` function and assigns the resulting value to the `point` variable, which is now an object. The next two lines of code show the `point` object in use by accessing the `x` and `y` properties.

Objects as Input

Just as returning an object to represent complex data is beneficial, so too is accepting objects as arguments in functions. Your fictional Cartesian plane application needs to draw a dot at a specific point on the graph, and a function called `drawPoint()` provides this ability for the application. The function might look like the following:

```
function drawPoint(x, y) {
    // do something with x
    // do something with y
}
```

Here, a traditional function accepts two arguments, and it performs some type of work with those arguments to draw a point on the screen. There's nothing wrong with this function, but it could fit better in an object-oriented environment by accepting an object containing coordinate data as an argument:

```
function drawPoint(point) {
    // do something with point.x
    // do something with point.y
}

var point = getCurrentPoint(); // get coordinates
drawPoint(point); // draw the dot on the screen
```

By means of a simple change, this function fits very well into an object-based environment. It's much easier to call since it now accepts one argument containing complex data.

CREATING CUSTOM DATA TYPES

Custom objects have their uses, but if you plan on using multiple objects that have the same properties and methods, a better solution is to write a custom data type that allows you to create objects using the `new` keyword and constructor functions.

The first step in creating a custom data type is to create the constructor function. Constructor functions closely resemble regular functions, except you define the data type's members inside the function. Constructor functions, by convention, begin with an uppercase letter. This is to help distinguish constructor functions from regular functions. The following code creates a data type called Point:

```
function Point(x, y) {
    this.x = x;
    this.y = y;
    this.getDistance = function(point) {
```

```
        var x2 = Math.pow(point.x - this.x, 2);
        var y2 = Math.pow(point.y - this.y, 2);

        return Math.sqrt(x2 + y2);
    };
}
```

This Point constructor accepts two arguments, x and y coordinates. It accepts individual pieces of data, as opposed to the single object shown at the end of the previous section. This is a personal choice: The philosophy behind it is that individual pieces of data are combined to construct a singular complex piece of data. It would be perfectly fine for the constructor function to accept a custom object containing x and y properties.

Inside the constructor function two properties, x and y, are assigned the values passed to the constructor function. Notice the use of the `this` variable. Remember that `this` refers to the current object, and the current object, in this case, is the object being created by the calling of the `Point()` constructor function with the `new` keyword. So the first two statements in the constructor create x and y properties by assigning their values. If `this` were omitted and `var` were used in its place, x and y would simply be variables.

After creating the x and y properties, the constructor function creates a method called `getDistance()`. This method accepts a Point object as an argument, and it uses the `Math` object to work out the Euclidean distance formula to determine the distance between the point represented by the current object and the Point object passed to the method.

To create a Point object, simply call the constructor by using the `new` keyword, and pass it some data, like this:

```
var point1 = new Point(0, 0);
var point2 = new Point(1, 1);
```

With more than one Point object created, you can determine the distance between the two points by calling the `getDistance()` method on one of the objects and passing the other as an argument, like this:

```
var distance = point1.getDistance(point2);
```

When calling a constructor you create, it is very, very important to remember to include the `new` keyword. Not doing so results in near-catastrophic circumstances. Custom constructor functions use the special `this` variable to create properties and methods for the object the constructor function is making. If the `new` keyword is omitted, the `this` variable points to the global object.

Because of this, the constructor function creates the properties and methods defined within it on the global object. Not only is the global object polluted with properties and methods it doesn't need, but a new object is not created. There is no warning or error given by JavaScript; it simply executes the code. The only clue you have is that your code will not work as expected. So always, always remember to use the `new` keyword when calling a constructor function.

TRY IT

In this lesson, you learn how to create your own objects and use them in your code.

Lesson Requirements

For this lesson, you need a text editor; any plain text editor will do. For Microsoft Windows users, Notepad is available by default on your system or you can download Microsoft's free Visual Web Developer Express (www.microsoft.com/express/web/) or Web Matrix (www.asp.net/webmatrix/). Mac OS X users can use TextMate, which comes as part of OS X, or they can download a trial for Coda (www.panic.com/coda/). Linux users can use the built-in VIM.

You also need a modern web browser. Choose any of the following:

➤   Internet Explorer 8+

➤   Google Chrome

➤   Firefox 3.5+

➤   Apple Safari 4+

➤   Opera 10+

Create a subfolder called Lesson08 in the JS24Hour folder you created in Lesson 1. Store the files you create in this lesson in the Lesson08 folder.

Step-by-Step

Write a Person data type that has two properties: firstName and lastName. It should also have a method called getFullName() to concatenate the two properties together and return the result of that concatenation, and a method to greet other Person objects.

1.   Open your text editor and type the following function:

```
function Person(firstName, lastName) {

}
```

This is the basis of the constructor function for your Person data type. The function has two parameters: firstName and lastName.

2.   Now add the following bolded code:

```
function Person(firstName, lastName) {
    this.firstName = firstName;
    this.lastName = lastName;
}
```

This code adds the firstName and lastName properties to the data type. Their values come from the values passed to the constructor.

3. Add the following bolded code:

```
function Person(firstName, lastName) {
    this.firstName = firstName;
    this.lastName = lastName;
    this.getFullName = function() {
        return this.firstName + " " + this.lastName;
    };
}
```

This code adds the `getFullName()` method. It concatenates the `firstName` and `lastName` properties and returns the result of that operation. The result of the concatenation is not stored in a variable; it is directly returned to the caller.

4. Now it's time to add the `greet()` method. It's bolded in the following code:

```
function Person(firstName, lastName) {
    this.firstName = firstName;
    this.lastName = lastName;
    this.getFullName = function() {
        return this.firstName + " " + this.lastName;
    };

    this.greet = function(person) {
        alert("Hello, " + person.getFullName());
    };
}
```

The `greet()` method accepts a Person object as an argument, and it calls the `getFullName()` method on that Person object to get the person's name and use it in a greeting message. The message is displayed in an alert window.

5. Once again, add the bolded code that follows. Feel free to pass your own name to one of the constructor calls.

```
function Person(firstName, lastName) {
    this.firstName = firstName;
    this.lastName = lastName;
    this.getFullName = function() {
        return this.firstName + " " + this.lastName;
    };

    this.greet = function(person) {
        alert("Hello, " + person.getFullName());
    };
}

var person1 = new Person("Jeremy", "McPeak");
var person2 = new Person("John", "Doe");

person1.greet(person2);
```

6. Save the file as `lesson08_sample01.js`.

7. Open another instance of your text editor, type the following HTML, and save it as
`lesson08_sample01.htm`:

```
<html>
<head>
    <title>Lesson 8: Custom Objects</title>
</head>
<body>
    <script type="text/javascript" src="lesson08_sample01.js"></script>
</body>
</html>
```

8. Open the HTML file in your browser. An alert window displays the result of calling
`person.getFullName()`: a string containing the values passed to the `Person()` constructor.

 *Please select Lesson 8 on the DVD to view the video that accompanies this
lesson. You can also download the sample code for all lessons from the book's
website at* www.wrox.com.

Prototypes and Inheritance (The Function Object)

The latter half of Lesson 8 taught you how to create your own data types by creating a constructor function in conjunction with the `this` variable to create properties and methods. We'll pick up with the Point data type; its code is repeated here for your convenience:

```
function Point(x, y) {
    this.x = x;
    this.y = y;
    this.getDistance = function(point) {
        var x = Math.pow(point.x - this.x, 2);
        var y = Math.pow(point.y - this.y, 2);

        return Math.sqrt(x + y);
    };
}
```

This implementation has a slight flaw. When calling the constructor with the `new` keyword, JavaScript creates a Point object, and in doing so it has to recreate everything within the constructor every time it's called. That is, the x and y properties, and a new Function object to serve as the `getDistance()` method. In JavaScript, functions are objects, too — complete with their own properties and methods.

In an object-oriented environment, creating a new object should also create its properties. Properties, and more importantly their values, are specific to each instance of a data type, and they should rarely be shared with all other instances of a particular data type. For example, a Point object's x and y properties contain values that are independent from another Point object's x and y properties. Changing one Point's x property should not affect another Point object's x property. So a Point's x and y properties should be created when the Point object is created.

A Point object's methods, however, are another matter. From a developer's standpoint, you want a Point object to behave like every other Point object in an application. A change made to a Point object's behavior should be reflected in all other Point objects; otherwise you could not depend on any object to behave how you need it to behave.

In JavaScript, an instance of the Function data type is created every time a function is defined or declared. That means that with every call to the `Point()` constructor, JavaScript creates a new function instance for the `getDistance()` method. JavaScript shouldn't have to create new behavior with every new object that is created; it should use an already existing behavior and share that behavior with all objects of the same type. This is achieved by means of the `prototype` property.

USING THE PROTOTYPE OBJECT

Every Function object has a `prototype` property. It is an object that contains properties and methods that are shared among all instances of a particular data type. That means that a change made to any property or method of a particular data type's `prototype` object is seen by all instances of that data type. The `prototype` object is very much a prototype for every object created with a constructor; the properties and methods defined on a data type's `prototype` become members of an object.

That being said, properties generally should be created only in the constructor, not the `prototype` object, because properties are typically pieces of data that are unique to each instance of a data type. On the other hand, the shared nature of the `prototype` object makes it an ideal place to create methods.

To access a Function object's `prototype` object, use the function's name, followed by a dot and the word `prototype`. The following code rewrites the Point data type to include the use of the prototype property:

```
function Point(x, y) {
    this.x = x;
    this.y = y;
}

Point.prototype.getDistance = function(point) {
    var x = Math.pow(point.x - this.x, 2);
    var y = Math.pow(point.y - this.y, 2);

    return Math.sqrt(x + y);
};
```

Here, the `getDistance()` method is moved out of the constructor and added to the `Point.prototype` object. This is advantageous for two reasons:

➤ Only one Function object is created and assigned to `getDistance`. Calling the `Point()` constructor now does not create a new Function object for `getDistance()`.

➤ The `getDistance()` method is shared among all Point objects. Changes made to the method are seen by all Point objects.

Even though this method is now created on the prototype, you still access the method from an object in the same way, as shown in this code:

```
var point1 = new Point(0, 0);
var point2 = new Point(1, 1);

point1.getDistance(point2);
```

This works because of the way JavaScript looks up identifiers on objects. When accessing this getDistance() method, JavaScript first performs a search for the getDistance identifier on the object itself — looking for an identifier with the same name. If JavaScript finds a match, it returns the match's value (remember: Functions can be values). However, if it does not find a match, JavaScript searches for the getDistance identifier in the data type's prototype object and returns either the value if a match is found or undefined if one could not be found.

Because of this behavior, it's possible to override methods defined in the prototype object. To do this, simply assign a value to the getDistance identifier, like this:

```
var point1 = new Point(0, 0);
var point2 = new Point(1, 1);

point1.getDistance = function(point) {
    alert("This method no longer works.");
};

point1.getDistance(point2); // message in alert window
```

Look at the bold portion of this code. Here, a new function object is created and assigned to the getDistance member on the object. You might think that this code alters the getDistance() method on the prototype, but it doesn't. The Point.prototype.getDistance() method can only be modified by directly accessing it through the prototype object (that is Point.prototype.getDistance = *new value*). This code actually creates a new getDistance() method on the point1 object itself, essentially overriding the getDistance() method defined on the prototype.

So now when the getDistance() method on point1 is accessed, JavaScript searches for the getDistance identifier, finds a match on the point1 object, and returns the newer function. The original getDistance() method on the prototype object is still intact, and the following code demonstrates this:

```
point2.getDistance(point1); // returns 2
```

Here, the code calls the point2.getDistance() method. The point2 object does not actually have a getDistance member, so JavaScript pulls the value from Point.prototype.getDistance — the function that performs the distance calculation.

Be wary of overriding methods in this manner. The whole idea behind using the prototype object is that members, usually methods, don't have to be created for each object. Besides, overriding a method like this can cause undesired results.

 It is worth reiterating that properties typically don't belong on the prototype. Properties generally should be created inside the constructor.

INHERITING MEMBERS FROM OTHER OBJECTS

All objects in JavaScript *inherit* from the Object data type. Inheritance is an object-oriented concept not too dissimilar from the idea or definition probably running through your head. It's not the type of inheritance by which one gets an heirloom from a family member, or a specific genetic trait, like eye or hair color. It's the type of inheritance by which a sedan has the properties and behaviors of an automobile.

In object-oriented programming, inheritance is all about reusing code. You have a *base data type* (called the base type, super type, or parent type), and you extend that data type by creating a new data type (called a sub-type or child type) that inherits properties and methods from the base type while also providing new functionality specific to the child-type.

Let's say you've been commissioned to write a portion of an application that keeps track of all employees within a given company. The portion you are in charge of is to write a data type that represents an individual employee. The application needs to know the person's name and title. You incorporated a modified version of your Person data type created in Lesson 8, and another developer on your team is already using it for the portion of the app he is responsible for. The modified Person type looks like this:

```
function Person(firstName, lastName) {
    this.firstName = firstName;
    this.lastName = lastName;
}

Person.prototype.getFullName = function() {
    return this.firstName + " " + this.lastName;
};
```

It's a simple data type. It has properties for the person's first and last name, as well as a method to concatenate the two into the person's full name. A lot of work is already done with this data type. Wouldn't it be great if you could use it without altering it (otherwise, your coworker's code may break), while still adding the functionality you need? Inheritance allows you to do so.

 There are a number of inheritance patterns in JavaScript, each with its pros and cons. This book teaches you just one pattern.

The first step is to create a new data type that will inherit from the Person data type. This new type is called Employee, and the constructor function has three parameters: the employee's first and last name, and his or her position.

```
function Employee(firstName, lastName, position) {
    this.position = position;
}
```

This constructor function creates a `position` property and assigns it the value passed to the argument of the same name, but nothing is done with the `firstName` and `lastName` parameters. As it stands right now, Employee objects have only one property. So Employee needs some way of gaining the firstName and lastName properties of the Person type. This is where the call() method of Function objects comes into play.

The call() method allows you to call a function as if it was a method of a specific object. In other words, it calls a method with a specified value for the this variable. The idea is probably easier to understand with some code. The following bolded code adds a new line to the Employee() constructor function:

```
function Employee(firstName, lastName, position) {
    Person.call(this, firstName, lastName);
    this.position = position;
}
```

So what happens here is that the value of this (the Employee object being created) is passed to the call() method, which gives the this variable in Person() the value of the Employee object being created. So, essentially, Person() executes as if it were Employee().

The other arguments passed to the call() method reflect the parameters of the Person() function: firstName and lastName. The result of this code is that firstName and lastName properties are added to Employee objects when they are created. So, Employee has now inherited Person's properties, but it still needs to inherit the getFullName() method.

If getFullName() were defined inside the constructor, inheritance would be complete and you'd be done. But the method is defined in Person's prototype, so you'll use something called *prototype chaining* to inherit Person's prototype. The process of prototype chaining is a simple one: Simply create a new instance of the base-type and assign it to the sub-type's prototype, as in this bolded code:

```
function Employee(firstName, lastName, position) {
    Person.call(this, firstName, lastName);
    this.position = position;
}

Employee.prototype = new Person();
```

Prototype chaining gets its name because it adds another prototype to the search list, much as one would add a new link to a chain. Now when you create an Employee object and call the getFullName() method, JavaScript first looks at the object for a match. It does not find a match, so it looks at Employee's prototype and doesn't find a match there either. So it looks at Person's prototype, since that is a new "link" in the "chain" of prototypes, finds a match, and executes it. Of course, the more prototypes you add to the chain, the more JavaScript has to search for items in prototypes. So it's a good idea to keep prototype chains relatively small.

You can now create an Employee object and use the firstName, lastName, and position properties, as well as call the getFullName() method. The following code demonstrates this:

```
var employee = new Employee("Jeremy", "McPeak", "Author");

alert(employee.firstName); // Jeremy
alert(employee.lastName); // McPeak
alert(employee.getFullName()); // Jeremy McPeak
```

There's still more to be done, however, so now it's time to...

TRY IT

In this lesson, you learn how to use prototypes to make your code more efficient by creating fewer objects. You also learn about the Function's `call()` method, and how to chain prototypes to make inheriting a data type's prototype possible. In this section you learn how to override a base-type's method in a sub-type.

Lesson Requirements

For this lesson, you need a text editor; any plain text editor will do. For Microsoft Windows users, Notepad is available by default on your system or you can download Microsoft's free Visual Web Developer Express (www.microsoft.com/express/web/) or Web Matrix (www.asp.net/webmatrix/). Mac OS X users can use TextMate, which comes as part of OS X, or download a trial for Coda (www.panic.com/coda/). Linux users can use the built-in VIM.

You also need a modern web browser. Choose any of the following:

➤ Internet Explorer 8+

➤ Google Chrome

➤ Firefox 3.5+

➤ Apple Safari 4+

➤ Opera 10+

Create a subfolder called `Lesson09` in the `JS24Hour` folder you created in Lesson 1. Store the files you create in this lesson in the `Lesson09` folder.

Step-by-Step

The `getFullName()` method needs to include the employee's position. Follow these steps to override Person's `getFullName()` method to provide that functionality.

1. Open your text editor and type the following function:

```
function Person(firstName, lastName) {
    this.firstName = firstName;
    this.lastName = lastName;
}

Person.prototype.getFullName = function() {
    return this.firstName + " " + this.lastName;
};

function Employee(firstName, lastName, position) {
    Person.call(this, firstName, lastName);
    this.position = position;
```

```
    }

    Employee.prototype = new Person();
```

This is the Employee data type from this lesson.

2. Now add a method called `getFullName()` to Employee's prototype object. It is bold in the following code:

```
// Person omitted for printing

function Employee(firstName, lastName, position) {
    Person.call(this, firstName, lastName);
    this.position = position;
}

Employee.prototype = new Person();
Employee.prototype.getFullName = function() {

};
```

3. The Person data type's `getFullName()` method has functionality that we want to use. To save time recoding that portion of the method, use the `call()` method to call Person's `getFullName()` method and assign the result to a variable. The new code is bold in the following:

```
// Person omitted for printing

function Employee(firstName, lastName, position) {
    Person.call(this, firstName, lastName);
    this.position = position;
}

Employee.prototype = new Person();
Employee.prototype.getFullName = function() {
    var fullName = Person.prototype.getFullName.call(this);
};
```

This code calls the `Person.prototype.getFullName()` method in the context of the current object (the Employee object). The `call()` method has to be used here because `getFullName()` for Employee objects now has a new value (the method you're creating right now).

4. Append the employee's position to the string in `fullName` and return it:

```
function Employee(firstName, lastName, position) {
    Person.call(this, firstName, lastName);
    this.position = position;
}

Employee.prototype = new Person();
Employee.prototype.getFullName = function() {
    var fullName = Person.prototype.getFullName.call(this);

    return fullName + ", " + this.position;
};
```

5. Once again, add the bold code:

```
function Employee(firstName, lastName, position) {
    Person.call(this, firstName, lastName);
    this.position = position;
}

Employee.prototype = new Person();
Employee.prototype.getFullName = function() {
    var fullName = Person.prototype.getFullName.call(this);

    return fullName + ", " + this.position;
};

var employee = new Employee("Jeremy", "McPeak", "Author");

alert(employee.getFullName());
```

6. Save the file as `lesson09_sample01.js`.

7. Open another instance of your text editor, type the following HTML, and save it as `lesson09_sample01.htm`.

```
<html>
<head>
    <title>Lesson 9: Prototypes and Inheritance</title>
</head>
<body>
    <script type="text/javascript" src="lesson09_sample01.js"></script>
</body>
</html>
```

8. Open the HTML file in your browser. An alert window displays the result of calling `employee.getFullName()`: a string containing the values passed to the `Employee()` constructor.

To get the sample code files you can download Lesson 9 from the book's website at www.wrox.com.

 Please select Lesson 9 on the DVD to view the video that accompanies this lesson.

PART II
Programming the Browser

10

The window Object

The JavaScript language is based upon a standard called ECMAScript, and you can find ECMAScript used in a variety of applications and technologies. Flash has its own ECMAScript version called ActionScript, which is similar to JavaScript.

ECMAScript is most widely used, however, in web browsers, and chances are pretty good that you purchased this book and DVD to learn how to use JavaScript this way. Your wait is over (kind of).

The web browser is a JavaScript developer's platform, and every platform has what's called an *Application Programming Interface*, or *API*. An API is a set of objects and data types that allow a developer to interact with a particular platform. The web browser has two main APIs: the Browser Object Model (BOM) and the Document Object Model (DOM).

The BOM is an API to program certain aspects of the browser. It enables you to determine what web browser a user is currently using, to open and resize windows, and to navigate to a different page or website. Its primary focus is the browser window.

The DOM is another API that allows you to manipulate the HTML page loaded into the browser. You can find, add, and remove elements within the HTML document, change their appearance, and completely relocate them to different parts of the screen. The DOM's focus is the HTML document.

This lesson introduces you to the main object in the BOM: the window object. This object represents the browser window that contains the HTML page, and it allows you to manipulate many aspects of the browser window. Its most important purpose is to serve as JavaScript's global scope.

THE GLOBAL SCOPE

You've seen many references to global scope throughout this book. Every JavaScript implementation has a global scope, and in the browser the global scope is the window object. It is the topmost object, and all other objects related to the browser window or HTML document are considered members of the window object.

Variables and Functions Are Properties and Methods

You have, in fact, used the `window` object in every lesson so far. The `alert()` and `prompt()` functions are actually methods of the `window` object. In JavaScript the `window` object is implied, so it's possible to access its properties and methods without explicitly specifying `window` before a variable or method. For example, as far as the browser is concerned, the following two lines of code are identical:

```
window.alert("Hello, Browser!");
alert("Hello, Browser!");
```

This concept can be taken a step further with variables and functions. When you create a variable or function in the global scope, you actually create a property or method of the `window` object. Look at this code:

```
var someVariable = "Some value"; // is same as window.someVariable = "Some value";

function showSomeVariable() {
    alert(window.someVariable); // explicitly use window
}

window.showSomeVariable(); // explicitly use window
```

Here a variable called `someVariable` is created and given a string value. Next a function called `showSomeVariable()` is declared; its body contains a call to the `alert()` method and passes the `window.someVariable` property to it. The final line of this code explicitly uses the `window` object to execute the `showSomeVariable()` method. The result of this code can be seen in Figure 10-1.

FIGURE 10-1

All global variables and functions are members of the `window` object; thus, you can access them by explicitly using the `window` object. However, it is conventional to omit the explicit use of `window` unless there is a reason to use it. You'd want to use it, for example, to deal with scope when a local variable within a function has the same name as a global variable. Consider the following code:

```
var someVariable = "Global value";

function showSomeVariable() {
    var someVariable = "Local value";

    alert(someVariable); // Local value
    alert(window.someVariable); // Global value
}
```

In this code a global variable called `someVariable` is initialized with a string value. Next the `showSomeVariable()` function is declared, and its first statement is the initialization of a variable called `someVariable` — the same name as the global variable. Inside the function, the `someVariable` identifier refers to the local variable. In order to access the global variable with the same name, you must prepend it with `window`; otherwise, JavaScript retrieves the local variable.

The general rule of thumb is to omit `window` unless you absolutely need to explicitly specify the global object.

The this Variable

In Lesson 8, you learned how to create custom data types by writing a constructor function and using the this variable inside it to create properties. The end of Lesson 8 instructed you to always use the new keyword when calling a constructor function. Now that you know that global functions are actually methods of the window object, you can begin to see what happens when you call a constructor function without the new keyword. First, here is some code that correctly calls a custom data type's constructor:

```
function Person(firstName, lastName) {
    this.firstName = firstName;
    this.lastName = lastName;
}

var person = new Person("Jeremy", "McPeak");
```

This code creates a Person data type and correctly calls the constructor for that data type. A new Person object is created and assigned to the person variable. There is nothing wrong with this code. Compare it to the following code, which omits the new keyword:

```
var person2 = Person("Jeremy", "McPeak");
```

Here a statement calls the Person() function without prefixing it with new. JavaScript sees the call as being like any other function call and executes it. Because Person("Jeremy", "McPeak") is the same as window.Person("Jeremy", "McPeak"), the this variable is bound to the window object; therefore, the code within the function creates two global variables, firstName and lastName, and assigns them a value of whatever was passed to the function. Also, since Person() does not return a value, the person2 variable contains a value of undefined. So not only has this code added unnecessary variables to the global scope, but code depending on person2 breaks because person2 is undefined instead of a Person object.

Again, it is very, very important to always use the new keyword when calling a constructor function.

SHOWING AND USING DIALOG BOXES

Dialog boxes have a vital role in just about every application. They provide all sorts of information to the user, such as general information and error messages, and they can allow the user to input data or make a decision. Web browsers are no exception, and the window object gives developers access to three dialog boxes: the alert dialog, the prompt dialog, and the confirm dialog. When the browser displays one of these, JavaScript execution is halted until the box is closed. You've seen two of these dialog boxes used throughout the previous lessons, but let's go over all of them to be thorough.

The Alert Dialog Box

The alert dialog box is used to display a message to the user. The window contains one OK button, which is used to close the dialog. Closing the alert box does not cause any special JavaScript to run; it's simply a box to display information. Figure 10-2 shows an alert box in the Chrome browser.

FIGURE 10-2

The code that generates the alert box in this figure is as follows:

```
alert("Hello, Alert box!");
```

Use the `alert()` method to show this type of dialog. Its only parameter is the data to display to the user. If you want to get a user's input with a dialog box, use the `prompt()` method.

The Prompt Dialog Box

The prompt dialog box's purpose is to prompt the user to input data. Figure 10-3 shows what a prompt dialog box looks like in Chrome.

The prompt box might look different in other browsers, but they all have the same basic components: a message to the user, a textbox, an OK button, and a Cancel button. The following code generates the prompt seen in Figure 10-3:

FIGURE 10-3

```
var name = prompt("Please enter your name.", "Default Text");
```

The `prompt()` method accepts two arguments. The first is the message to display to the user. The second is optional and determines the default text entered in the textbox.

Clicking OK causes the prompt method to return the text typed into the textbox to the caller. In the case of this code, the value of the `name` variable depends on what text is in the textbox when the user clicks OK. If the user clicks Cancel, the `prompt()` method returns `null`. Therefore, when relying on the `prompt()` method to get data from the user, make sure the data returned is not `null`, like this:

```
if (name != null) {
    // do something with data
}
```

The `prompt()` method is an obtrusive means of getting data from the user. From a user-interface perspective, form elements within a web page are a better means of acquiring text-based user input. Not only can form elements take on the look and feel of your web application, but you can acquire multiple pieces of data without having to display an ugly pop-up window for user input.

There is, however, a dialog box that gets input from the user that is ideal in some situations.

The Confirm Dialog Box

Sometimes you want the user to decide how your program should behave. You see this type of dialog box frequently in some operating systems. For example, a dialog box may ask you if you really do want to delete a file when you press the Delete key with a file selected. It waits for your input and deletes the file if you chose Yes. This is the idea behind the confirm dialog box. Its purpose is to provide the user with a yes-or-no option, and your application can process data according to the user's input.

You can show the confirm dialog box by calling the `confirm()` method. It accepts an argument containing a message to display to the user, and it returns a Boolean value based on the button the user presses. The following code uses the `confirm()` method in an `if` statement:

```
if (confirm("Is it sunny today?")) {
    alert("Let's go outside");
} else {
    alert("Let's stay inside");
}
```

Here a confirm dialog box is shown in Figure 10-4 to the user, asking if it's sunny outside. If the user clicks OK, the `confirm()` method returns `true` and an alert box displays the text "`Let's go outside`." If the user clicks Cancel, he or she sees a message that says, "`Let's stay inside`."

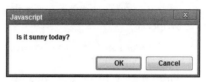

FIGURE 10-4

The confirm dialog box allows your application to be considerate of the user by asking the user's permission to execute code that performs an obtrusive action, such as navigating unexpectedly to another web page using the `location` object.

THE LOCATION OBJECT

The `window` object has a property called `location`; it's an object that contains information about the current URL loaded in the browser. The two main uses of the `location` object are to reload the current page and to navigate to a new page.

Reloading the Page

There are many ways to reload a web page in the browser. It's common to find the `<meta/>` element used to reload the page after a set amount of time, but JavaScript is typically a better solution, as you can control how the page refreshes itself to fit the needs of your application.

To reload the page you use the `reload()` method. It accepts an optional Boolean argument that determines if the browser performs a full refresh in the event that the webserver says the document hasn't been modified. If the webserver responds that a web page hasn't been modified since it was last requested by the browser, the browser normally loads the page from its cache. By passing a value of `true` to the `reload()` method, you can ensure that the document is always retrieved from the webserver; omitting the parameter lets the browser load the page from the cache. The following code demonstrates the use of the `reload()` method:

```
location.reload(true);
```

Here the `reload()` method is called on the `location` object. Remember that `window` is implied, so this code actually translates to `window.location.reload(true)`. A value of `true` is passed to this method, so it will always retrieve the page from the webserver.

Navigating to Another Page

Navigating away from the current page to another is probably the most common action for which the location object is used. There are two ways to do this: The first is to use the location object's href property, like this:

```
location.href = "http://www.google.com";
```

This code assigns a new URL to the href property, and the browser automatically navigates to the page (Google's search page in this case). You can, however, simplify this code by omitting the href property:

```
location = "http://www.google.com";
```

This code performs the same function as the previous example, and it's actually the preferred method of navigating to a different page.

TRY IT

In this lesson you learn about the window object and its global nature. You also learn about the dialog boxes it provides you with, as well as the ability to reload the page and navigate to another page.

Lesson Requirements

For this lesson, you need a text editor; any plain text editor will do. For Microsoft Windows users, Notepad is available by default on your system or you can download Microsoft's free Visual Web Developer Express (www.microsoft.com/express/web/) or Web Matrix (www.asp.net/webmatrix/). Mac OS X users can use TextMate, which comes as part of OS X, or they can download a trial for Coda (www.panic.com/coda/). Linux users can use the built-in VIM.

You also need a modern web browser. Choose any of the following:

➤ Internet Explorer 8+

➤ Google Chrome

➤ Firefox 3.5+

➤ Apple Safari 4+

➤ Opera 10+

Create a subfolder called Lesson10 in the JS24Hour folder you created in Lesson 1. Store the files you create in this lesson in the Lesson10 folder.

Step-by-Step

Write a simple application that either navigates to a different page or reloads the current page, based on the user's input.

1. Open your text editor and type the following code:

```
if (confirm("Do you want to go to Google?")) {
    location = "http://www.google.com";
}
```

This code shows a confirm dialog box asking the user if he or she wants to go to another web page. If the user clicks OK, the browser will go to Google's website.

2. Now add an `else` block to reload the page. It is bolded in the following code:

```
if (confirm("Do you want to go to Google?")) {
    location = "http://www.google.com";
} else {
    location.reload(true);
}
```

3. Save the file as `lesson10_sample01.js`.

4. Open another instance of your text editor, type the following HTML, and save it as `lesson10_sample01.htm`:

```
<html>
<head>
    <title>Lesson 9: The window Object</title>
</head>
<body>
    <script type="text/javascript" src="lesson10_sample01.js"></script>
</body>
</html>
```

5. Open the HTML file in your browser. A dialog box will ask whether or not you want to go to Google. Click OK to go there, or Cancel to reload the current page.

To get the sample code files you can download Lesson 10 from the book's website at www.wrox.com.

 Please select Lesson 10 on the DVD to view the video that accompanies this lesson.

11

Scripting Windows

Dialog boxes and the `location` object are far from all the `window` object has to offer developers. In fact, this object is often used to open and manipulate new windows.

OPENING NEW WINDOWS

Even though the advent of pop-up blockers greatly (and rightly) diminished the use of opening new windows through script, you can still find the practice legitimately used by many web-based applications. The key to this functionality is the `open()` method. It accepts four optional arguments, and returns the `window` object of the newly created window (dubbed the *child window* in this text).

The first parameter of the method is the URL of the web page you want to open in the child window; passing an empty string causes the child window to open a blank page. The second parameter, if specified, is the name you want to give to the new window. This name corresponds with the value given to the `target` attribute in hyperlinks. The following HTML is an example:

```html
<a href="http://www.microsoft.com" target="childWindow">Microsoft.com</a>
```

If you were to open a new window with JavaScript and give it the name `childWindow`, clicking this link would load `www.microsoft.com` in the newly opened window. Of course, omit the second parameter if you do not wish the window to be a target for links.

The third parameter is a list of options and properties that determine how the child window looks. These options and properties include, but are not limited to, width, height, and whether user interface elements are visible to the user. There's a lengthy list of options to choose from, and you'll see a shortened list in a few moments. For now, let's just stick with height and width with this simple example:

```javascript
var childWindow = open("http://www.google.com", "googleWindow",
    "height=400, width=400");
```

Here the `open()` method is called (the `window` object is implied before `open()`), and the child's `window` object is stored in the `childWindow` variable. The first argument passed to the method is the URL for Google's home page. Its name is `googleWindow`, so any hyperlink in the main document with the same `target` value opens its URL in this new window. Notice the third argument: It looks a little different from other arguments you've seen so far. The third argument is a string that contains one or more options separated by commas. In this example the `height` and `width` options are assigned values of `400`, and a comma separates the two options. Figure 11-1 shows the window this code opens in Chrome.

FIGURE 11-1

The third parameter is completely optional; you don't have to specify any options or settings for the new window. If you do, however, you can add any of the following options to control how the window looks or behaves.

New Window Options

OPTION	POSSIBLE VALUES	DESCRIPTION
height	integer	The height of the new window in pixels
left	integer	The horizontal position of the new window
location	yes, no	Shows the location bar (Doesn't work in Opera)
menubar	yes, no	Shows the menu bar (Doesn't work in Opera or Safari)

OPTION	POSSIBLE VALUES	DESCRIPTION
resizable	yes, no	Determines whether or not the user can resize the window
scrollbars	yes, no	Shows the horizontal and/or vertical scrollbars if the page is too large to fit in the window
status	yes, no	Shows the status bar (Doesn't work in Opera)
toolbar	yes, no	Shows the toolbar (Doesn't work in Opera)
top	integer	The vertical position of the new window
width	integer	The width of the new window in pixels

Keep in mind this list is not exhaustive, but these are the most commonly used options for a new window. Consider the following code to get an idea of how to apply some of these options:

```
var childWindow = open("http://www.google.com", "googleWindow",
    "height=400, width=400, resizable=no, menubar=no");
```

Here two more options are added to the `open()` method's third parameter. The new window is no longer resizable by the user, and it does not display the menu bar. Figure 11-2 shows the window generated from this code in Internet Explorer 8.

FIGURE 11-2

The fourth parameter is a Boolean value that determines whether the URL specified in the first argument creates a new entry or replaces the current entry in the browser's history list if the page is loaded into an already existing window. If `true`, the URL replaces the current document in the history list. If `false`, a new entry is created in the history.

MANIPULATING WINDOWS

Unfortunately, you can't change the properties listed in the previous table once a window is opened. You can, however, change the window's dimensions and position. Instead of using the `height`, `width`, `top`, and `left` properties in the previous table, you must use four special methods that perform these actions.

Before looking at these methods, especially the positional methods, you need to know how coordinates are translated on the screen. The computer screen is a coordinate system of pixels. The top left pixel on the screen is the origin, or 0, 0 (x, y). As you move down the y-axis of the screen, each pixel is a consecutive positive number. So the pixel directly below the origin has a vertical position of 1, the pixel below that has a vertical position of 2, and so on. As you move to the right on the x-axis, each pixel is a consecutive positive number. This means the pixel directly to the right of the origin has a horizontal position of 1, the one next to it has a horizontal position of 2, and so on. Figure 11-3 illustrates this coordinate plane.

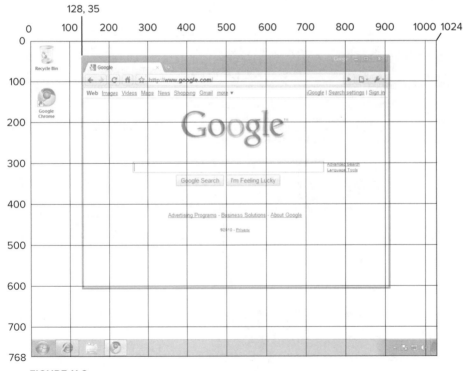

FIGURE 11-3

You use this coordinate system to position a window by specifying its horizontal and vertical position when using the `moveTo()` method. The following code opens a window and positions it on the screen at (100, 100). Figure 11-4 shows the results of the following code:

```
var childWindow = open("http://www.google.com", "", "height=300, width=300");

childWindow.moveTo(100, 100);
```

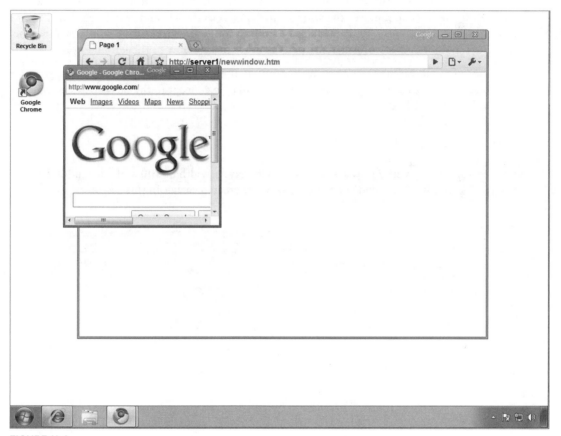

FIGURE 11-4

Here, the `moveTo()` method moves the window 100 pixels to the right and 100 pixels down from the origin. The first argument passed to `moveTo()` is the new horizontal (x) position, and the second is the new vertical (y) position. This method moves the window in relation to the entire screen. So this code moves the window 100 pixels from the left and top edges of the screen. If you wanted to move the window from its current position of (100, 100) by four pixels to the left and two pixels down, you could use this line of code:

```
childWindow.moveTo(100 - 4, 100 + 2);
```

You can, however, use another method called `moveBy()` to perform the same action. This method moves the window by the specified values in relation to the window's current position. So instead of performing arithmetic, as in the previous example, simply use the `moveBy()` method and supply the number of pixels to move the window by, like this:

```
childWindow.moveBy(-4, 2);
```

This line of code provides the same results as the previous example. Instead of moving the window to the coordinates (-4, 2), it moves the window four pixels to the left and two pixels down from its current position of (100, 100). Given a specific point on the screen, positive numbers move the window to the right and down; negative numbers move the window to the left and up.

Repositioning windows isn't the only way you can manipulate them after creating them; you can also change their height and width with methods similar in concept to the `moveTo()` and `moveBy()` methods. The first method is `resizeTo()`, and it allows you to specify the new width and height of the window, like this:

```
childWindow.resizeTo(100, 200);
```

Here the `resizeTo()` method resizes the window to have a width of 100 and a height of 200. Figure 11-5 shows what this code does to the window created earlier in this section.

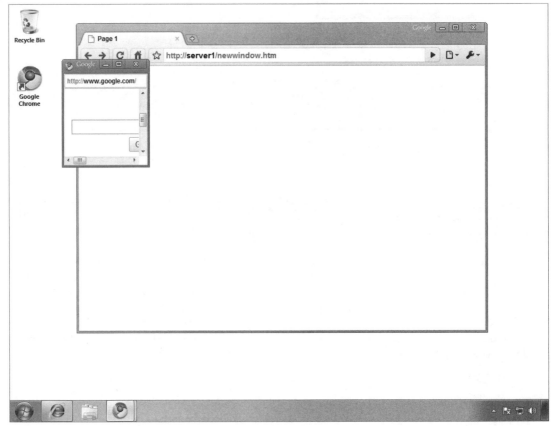

FIGURE 11-5

If you want to resize the window in relation to its current dimensions, simply use the `resizeBy()` method. The following code shrinks the window's width by 50 pixels and expands its height by 100:

```
childWindow.resizeBy(-50, 100);
```

Browsers allow you to manipulate the parent window by using these methods. It is strongly recommended that you do not do so. Our primary goal as web developers is to provide usable and friendly web applications to our users. Resizing and moving the main window breaks the friendliness of our applications. As a general rule of thumb, move and resize only the windows you open, and leave the windows the user opens alone.

Changing a window's size or position isn't the only way to interact with a window created with the `open()` method. Parent and child windows can communicate with each other using JavaScript.

CODING BETWEEN WINDOWS

Remember that the `open()` method returns the new window's `window` object, so you can access just about anything within the window by using the child's `window` object. For example, look at this code:

```
var childWindow = open("http://www.google.com");

childWindow.alert("Hello there!");
```

Here a new window is opened to `www.google.com`, and its `window` object is assigned to the `childWindow` variable. The next line uses this object and calls its `alert()` method, displaying an alert box in the child window. So by executing this code, the JavaScript code in the main window communicates with the `window` object of the child window. Using this methodology, you can tell the child window to navigate to a different page by using the `location` object, like this:

```
childWindow.location = "http://www.microsoft.com";
```

Here the child window navigates to Microsoft's website by assigning a new value to the `location` object.

Cross-window communication is not a one-way street — the child window also has the ability to communicate with the parent's `window` object by using the `opener` keyword. This keyword is used inside the child window to reference the parent window. The following code demonstrates the use of the `opener` property:

```
opener.alert("Hello from the child!");
```

In this code, an alert box displays a message in the parent window even though it is executed from the child window. You can also access the parent's `location` object — simply prefix it with `opener` as shown here:

```
opener.location = "http://www.google.com";
```

In this line of code, the child window tells the parent window to navigate to Google's home page. The fun doesn't end here, however. Not only can you access the `window` objects of both parent and child windows, but you can also access each window's JavaScript code. The following code is an HTML page. Let's refer to it as Page 1:

```
<html>
<head>
    <title>Page 1</title>
    <script type="text/javascript">
        function showMessage(message) {
            alert(message);
        }

        var childWindow = open("page2.htm");
    </script>
</head>
<body>

</body>
</html>
```

Focus on the `<script/>` element. It creates a function called `showMessage()` that accepts one argument called `message`. The value passed to this function is then passed to the `alert()` method. The last line of the `<script/>` element opens a new window, which we'll call Page 2. Its HTML follows:

```
<html>
<head>
    <title>Page 2</title>
    <script type="text/javascript">
        opener.showMessage("Hello from Page 2!");
    </script>
</head>
<body>

</body>
</html>
```

The script in this page has only one line; it uses the `opener` object to call the `showMessage()` method (remember that global variables and functions are actually properties and methods of the `window` object). So this is what happens when you load Page 1 into a browser:

1. Page 1 creates the `showMessage()` function and opens a new window.

2. Page 2 loads into the new window and calls the `showMessage()` function in the parent window, passing it a string value.

3. The `showMessage()` function executes, displaying "Hello from Page 2!" in an alert box in Page 1.

The ability for JavaScript code to communicate between windows is pretty cool, and it can be very helpful when you are writing applications that require multiple windows. There is, however, one issue with cross-window JavaScript communication: security.

SECURITY

JavaScript's success is in part the result of its security policies, and one such policy relevant to this discussion is the same-origin policy. This states that a JavaScript script in one window can access and interact with a web page (and its JavaScript) in another window if, and only if, the web pages in both windows are from the same origin. In other words, if the pages in both windows do not come from the same domain (among finer details), JavaScript in one window cannot communicate with the web page and its JavaScript in the other window.

Two web pages or JavaScript scripts are determined to be of the same origin if the following criteria are met:

➤ The protocols must match. HTTP is the primary protocol used on the Internet, and two pages or scripts must use the same protocol in order to be considered as coming from the same origin. This means `http://www.wrox.com` is not of the same origin as `https://www.wrox.com`. One URL uses the HTTP protocol, and the other uses HTTPS.

➤ The host names or domain names must match. A web page's domain name is unique. In order to be considered as coming from the same origin, two pages or scripts must come from the same domain. This includes subdomains. For example, `http://p2p.wrox.com` is not the same domain as `http://www.wrox.com`. Even though the primary domain, `wrox.com`, is the same, the subdomains are not. Therefore, these two URLs are not considered to be from the same origin.

➤ The ports must match. By default, HTTP traffic uses port 80. When you request a website, your browser uses port 80 to send the HTTP request to the server. So, the URL of `http://www.wrox.com` is the same as that of `http://www.wrox.com:80`. There are some webservers, however, that are configured to use a different port (a common one is 8080) to provide other web-based services. To be considered as having the same origin, the ports of both scripts or pages must match. This means `http://www.wrox.com` is not from the same origin as `http://www.wrox.com:8080`.

Two web pages or JavaScript scripts are considered to be from the same origin only when these three criteria are met. This means you cannot open a window to `http://www.google.com` and interact with its web page and JavaScript. You can change the window's size and position, and you can access the `location` object, but you cannot interact with any JavaScript. JavaScript's security will not allow it.

TRY IT

In this lesson, you learn about creating new windows and how to interact with them by changing their position and size, and you learn about interacting with the objects and JavaScript code (if security permits).

Lesson Requirements

For this lesson, you need a text editor; any plain text editor will do. For Microsoft Windows users, Notepad is available by default on your system or you can download Microsoft's free Visual Web Developer Express (`www.microsoft.com/express/web/`) or Web Matrix (`www.asp.net/webmatrix/`). Mac OS X users can use TextMate, which comes as part of OS X, or they can download a trial for Coda (`www.panic.com/coda/`). Linux users can use the built-in VIM.

You also need a modern web browser. Choose any of the following:

➤ Internet Explorer 8+

➤ Google Chrome

➤ Firefox 3.5+

➤ Apple Safari 4+

➤ Opera 10+

Create a subfolder called `Lesson11` in the `JS24Hour` folder you created in Lesson 1. Store the files you create in this lesson in the `Lesson11` folder.

Step-by-Step

Write a simple web page that opens a new window with a blank page and write text to it.

1. Open your text editor and type the following code:

```
<html>
<head>
    <title>Page 1</title>
    <script type="text/javascript">
        var childWindow = open("");

    </script>
</head>
<body>

</body>
</html>
```

The JavaScript in this page opens a blank page in a new window by not specifying a URL for the window to open.

2. Now add the bold code shown here:

```
<html>
<head>
    <title>Page 1</title>
    <script type="text/javascript">
        var childWindow = open("");

        childWindow.document.write("Hello, new Window!<br/>");
        childWindow.document.write("How are you today?");
    </script>
```

```
</head>
<body>

</body>
</html>
```

This new code uses the `document` object's `write()` method to write directly into the page in the new window. The first line writes some text and an HTML `<br/>` element. The second line writes more text, which, when rendered in the browser, is on a second line.

3. Save the file as `lesson11_sample01.htm`.

4. Open the HTML file in your browser. You'll see a new window open, and it will contain the text written into the document.

To get the sample code files you can download Lesson 11 from the book's website at `www.wrox.com`.

 Please select Lesson 11 on the DVD to view the video that accompanies this lesson.

12

Scripting Frames

The previous two lessons focused on the `window` object — a programmatic representation of the browser window. The browser window typically contains one web page, and thus only one `window` object. The `<frameset/>` element, however, allows web developers to divide a browser window into two or more smaller window panes.

Each of these panes is itself a browser window, and as such has a full-fledged `window` object. In fact, some browsers allow you to move and resize an individual frame with the moving and resizing methods you learned in Lesson 11 (it is highly recommended that you do not use these methods on a frame).

Arguably the most important aspect of dealing with frames as a JavaScript developer is accessing code and objects across frames. Over the course of this lesson you'll see many similarities between cross-frame scripting and cross-window scripting.

FRAMES AND THE WINDOW OBJECT

The easiest way to delve into frame scripting is with a demonstration. The first item you'll look at is the frameset page. Its HTML is as follows:

```
<html>
<head>
    <title>Frameset Page</title>
</head>
<frameset rows="50%,*">
    <frame name="frmTop" src="frame_top.htm" />
    <frame name="frmBottom" src="frame_bottom.htm" />
</frameset>
</html>
```

This is a simple frameset page: It divides the page into upper and lower regions. The frame on top, named `frmTop`, loads the `frame_top.htm` page into it, and the bottom frame, `frmBottom`, loads `frame_bottom.htm`. Make note of each frame's name, as they are key when you are accessing them through script.

The browser creates a hierarchy of three `window` objects when it loads this frameset page. The first `window` object belongs to the main window — the one that loaded the frameset page. This is referred to as the *parent* window.

The second and third `window` objects are *child objects* of the parent window. The first of these is created for the first frame in the frameset (`frmTop`), and the next is created for the `frmBottom` frame. Figure 12-1 is a visual representation of the relationship and hierarchy of these three `window` objects — a family tree, if you will.

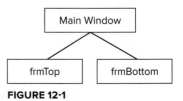

FIGURE 12-1

This illustration also doubles as a guide to communicating between frames. You can see that the parent window has a direct relationship to its children. So it is safe to assume that accessing the children from the parent in JavaScript is done directly. You access a child frame's `window` object much as you access an opened window's `window` object. In Lesson 11 you learned that the `open()` method returns the `window` object of the newly created window, and that you can assign that object to a variable, like this:

```
var newWindow = open("");
```

Retrieving a frame's `window` object is even simpler, as the browser automatically creates a variable using the name of the frame as the variable's identifier. So to call the `alert()` method of the top frame from the frameset page, you write code like this:

```
frmTop.alert("Hello, Top!");
```

The same principle is used for accessing the bottom frame. The following bolded code adds a `<script/>` element to the frameset page:

```
<html>
<head>
    <title>Frameset Page</title>
    <script type="text/javascript">
    function sayHello(message) {
        alert(message);
    }
    </script>
</head>
<frameset rows="50%,*">
    <frame name="frmTop" src="frame_top.htm" />
    <frame name="frmBottom" src="frame_bottom.htm" />
</frameset>
</html>
```

Inside the `<script/>` element is a simple function called `sayHello()`. It accepts one argument that is then displayed in an alert box. There is nothing in this main page that calls this function; instead, it is called from within the HTML pages loaded into each frame.

Think back to Lesson 11, and remember how child windows access their parent with the `opener` keyword. Accessing the main frameset `window` object from a page loaded into a frame is just as simple; the difference is that instead of using `opener`, you use the `parent` keyword.

The following is the source code for `frame_top.htm`. Focus on the bold line:

```
<html>
<head>
    <title>Top Frame</title>
    <script type="text/javascript">
    parent.sayHello("Hello from Top!");
    </script>
</head>
<body>

</body>
</html>
```

This single statement uses the `parent` keyword to access the parent's `window` object and calls `sayHello()`. When the browser loads this page into the top frame, it executes this line of code, which results in an alert box displaying the text "Hello from Top!"

The source code for `frame_bottom.htm` is similar:

```
<html>
<head>
    <title>Bottom Frame</title>
    <script type="text/javascript">
    parent.sayHello("Hello from Bottom!");
    </script>
</head>
<body>

</body>
</html>
```

The code in this page goes through the same process. The only difference is the message that the alert box displays when the browser loads this page and executes the JavaScript code.

As you can see from these examples, scripting between the parent window and child frames is very much like scripting between parent and child windows. The only difference is in how you refer to the child and parent `window` objects. But what if you want to script between two individual frames?

Using JavaScript to script between frames is slightly different from, but almost as straightforward as, using it to script between parent and child. Refer back to Figure 12-1 and take note of how, in the illustration, each `window` object is linked. Notice that there is no direct link between the two child frames; instead, the only thing linking them is the parent window. This is indicative of how you access the code and objects of one child frame from its sibling frame.

Let's say you want to access the top frame and call its `alert()` method from the bottom frame. To do this you must first reference the parent window with the `parent` keyword, and then use `frmTop`, the name of the top frame. The following code shows you what this might look like:

```
parent.frmTop.alert("Called from frame_bottom.htm");
```

Here the `parent` keyword is used to refer to the `window` object of the main page. Then the top frame's `window` object is accessed via the frame's name, `frmTop`, and the `alert()` method is called. This has the result of showing an alert box, but it isn't evident that the alert box belongs to the `frmTop` frame. Modify the JavaScript in `frame_bottom.htm` to write some text in the top frame. Following is a new version of `frame_bottom.htm`:

```
<html>
<head>
    <title>Bottom Frame</title>
    <script type="text/javascript">
    parent.frmTop.document.write("Hello from frame_bottom.htm");
    </script>
</head>
<body>

</body>
</html>
```

Here, the bold line of code is the only thing that changes from the previous line of code. It uses the parent object to access the frmTop object. From there this code uses frmTop's document object to write some text to the page. The result of this code can be seen in Figure 12-2.

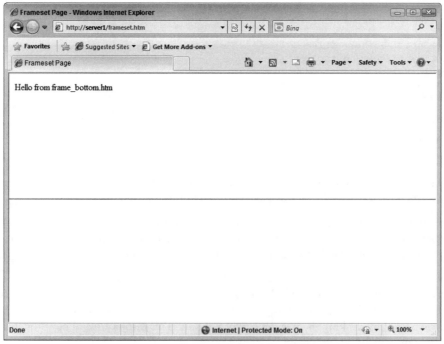

FIGURE 12-2

Despite the extra step of using the `parent` object, scripting between two frames is still a straightforward process. You simply navigate through the tree to get to the object you want.

There is also an object called `top`, and it gives you direct access to the topmost page's `window` object — the main frameset page. This is extremely helpful when a page has nested framesets, as shown in Figure 12-3.

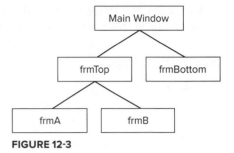

FIGURE 12-3

In this diagram `frmTop` is itself a frameset, dividing the frame into two frames, `frmA` and `frmB`; `frmTop` is now a parent of `frmA` and `frmB`. If code within `frmA` accesses an object in `frmBottom`, the code to get from `frmA` to `frmBottom` looks like this:

```
parent.parent.frmBottom
```

Here the first parent refers to `frmA`'s parent, which is `frmTop`. The next parent references `frmTop`'s parent, the main frameset page. From this object you can directly access `frmBottom`. The more nested framesets you add, the more tedious it becomes to script between frames. The `top` object helps you avoid having to climb the tree to the topmost page. Instead of typing `parent.parent` `.frmBottom`, you simply type this:

```
top.frmBottom
```

It's a shortcut to get to the top of the `window` object tree if you need it. You'll see this object used in the next section.

TRY IT

In this lesson, you learn how to script frames. You learn how the browser automatically creates a variable to allow access to a frame. You also learn about the `parent` and `top` objects that allow you to navigate the `window` object hierarchy created by framesets.

Lesson Requirements

For this lesson, you need a text editor; any plain text editor will do. For Microsoft Windows users, Notepad is available by default on your system or you can download Microsoft's free Visual Web Developer Express (`www.microsoft.com/express/web/`) or Web Matrix (`www.asp.net/webmatrix/`). Mac OS X users can use TextMate, which comes as part of OS X, or they can download a trial for Coda (`www.panic.com/coda/`). Linux users can use the built-in VIM.

You also need a modern web browser. Choose any of the following:

➤ Internet Explorer 8+

➤ Google Chrome

➤ Firefox 3.5+

➤ Apple Safari 4+

➤ Opera 10+

Create a subfolder called `Lesson12` in the `JS24Hour` folder you created in Lesson 1. Store the files you create in this lesson in the `Lesson12` folder.

Step-by-Step

Take another look at Figure 12-3. Use it as a blueprint and create five web pages to use in framesets. The JavaScript in `frmA` will write text into `frmBottom`, and the JavaScript in `frmB` will call a function in `frmTop` that will call a function in the main window to write text in `frmB`.

1. Open your text editor and type the following HTML:

```
<html>
<head>
    <title>Frameset Page</title>
    <script type="text/javascript">
    function writeInB(message) {
        frmTop.frmB.document.write(message);
    }
    </script>
</head>
<frameset rows="50%,*">
    <frame name="frmTop" src="frame_top.htm" />
    <frame name="frmBottom" src="frame_bottom.htm" />
</frameset>
</html>
```

Save it as `frameset_main.htm`. This is the main frameset page that is loaded into the browser, and it divides the screen into top and bottom frames. The JavaScript in this page defines a function called `writeInB()`. It'll access the `frmB` frame (a child in `frmTop`) and write a message in it using the `document.write()` method.

2. Open another instance of your text editor and type the following HTML:

```
<html>
<head>
    <title>Top Frame</title>
    <script type="text/javascript">
    function callParentFunction() {
        parent.writeInB("Calling from frmTop");
    }
    </script>
</head>
<frameset cols="50%,*">
    <frame name="frmA" src="frame_a.htm" />
    <frame name="frmB" src="frame_b.htm" />
</frameset>
</html>
```

Save it as `frame_top.htm`. This is another frameset page that loads in the top frame of `frameset_main.htm`. It divides the available screen into two columns. The JavaScript in this page defines a function called `callParentFunction()`. It calls the `writeInB()` function defined in `frameset_main.htm`.

3.   Open another instance of your text editor and type the following HTML:

```html
<html>
<head>
    <title>Bottom Frame</title>
</head>
<body>
    <h1>Bottom Frame</h1>
</body>
</html>
```

Save this file as `frame_bottom.htm`. This page loads in the bottom frame in `frameset_main.htm`. This page does not contain any JavaScript.

4.   Now you need to write the HTML for the pages loaded into the `frame_top.htm` frameset. So once again, open another instance of your text editor, and type the following HTML:

```html
<html>
<head>
    <title>Frame A</title>
    <script type="text/javascript">
    top.frmBottom.document.write("Hello from frmA!");
    </script>
</head>
<body>
    <h1>Frame A</h1>
</body>
</html>
```

Save this as `frame_a.htm`. The JavaScript in this page does not define a function, but it does use the `top` object to refer to the `frameset_main.htm`'s `window` object. Then it accesses the `frmBottom` object and writes a message to that frame.

5.   The final HTML file you need to write is `frame_b.htm`. Once again, open a new instance of your text editor and type the following HTML:

```html
<html>
<head>
    <title>Frame B</title>
    <script type="text/javascript">
    parent.callParentFunction();
    </script>
</head>
<body>
    <h1>Frame B</h1>
</body>
</html>
```

Save it as `frame_b.htm`. The JavaScript code in this file uses the parent object to access the `window` object of `frame_top.htm`, and it calls the `callParentFunction()` function defined in that page.

6. Open the `frameset_main.htm` file in your browser. You should see something similar to Figure 12-4.

```
Frameset Page - Windows Internet Explorer Platform Preview 1.9.7766.6000          [- □ x]
Page  Debug  Report Issue  Help

Frame A                                  Calling from frmTop

                                         Frame B




────────────────────────────────────────────────────────────────────────

Hello from frmA!






Done [Document Mode: IE 5]
```

FIGURE 12-4

To get the sample code files, you can download Lesson 12 from the book's website at www.wrox.com.

 Please select Lesson 12 on the DVD to view the video that accompanies this lesson.

13

The Document Object Model

In conventional applications, the operating system provides user interface elements and behaviors that enable developers to provide a rich experience for the user. Developing such applications is convenient, as the entire application is typically written in one language. The developer needs to know only one language to write code to interface with a data store (such as a database), code to process that data, code to display that data to the user, and code to interact with the user.

Web developers don't have it that easy. The data store interaction and processing are written in one language (like PHP, Python, or C#), and the user interface is typically a combination of HTML, CSS, and JavaScript. HTML is used for basic output/input for the user, which is a rather static and boring experience. CSS can spice up the application a little, but it isn't designed to do much more than determine how the browser renders the elements. So, to create a rich interactive experience, developers must turn to JavaScript.

But JavaScript is only part of the equation. There has to be an interface that enables a JavaScript developer to interact with a web page while it's loaded in the browser; such an interface exists, and it's called the Document Object Model (DOM).

WHAT IS THE DOM?

The DOM is a browser-independent Application Programming Interface (API) — a set of objects, properties, and methods that defines how HTML documents are structured, accessed, and manipulated with JavaScript. It's a standard put forth by the W3C (a standards body) that, when implemented in a browser, provides a means to literally change everything in the HTML page while it is loaded in the browser. There are multiple levels, or versions, of the DOM with each new version building on the last. The latest version is DOM Level 3.

To achieve this level of programmability, every HTML element in the document is represented by an object, and these objects are organized in a tree-like hierarchal structure. This structure is very similar in concept to the file system on a computer. Figure 13-1 shows a screenshot of Windows Explorer in Windows 7.

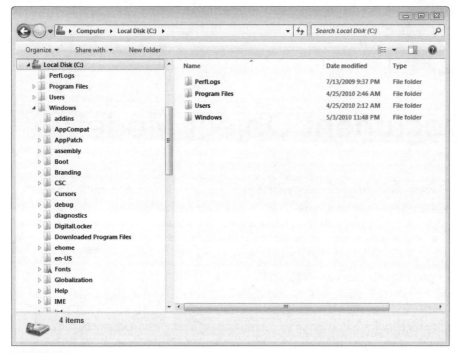

FIGURE 13-1

At the very top of the tree is c:\, or the root directory. Inside the root are a list of child directories; these are branches that can contain either more branches (directories) or leaves (files). To find a particular file, you start at the root and navigate through the appropriate directories until you find it. The DOM is very similar because HTML documents are structured in a very treelike way. Look at the following HTML:

```
<html>
<head>
    <title>Sample Page</title>
</head>
<body>
    <p>This is some text.</p>
    <p>This is more text.</p>
    <p>Here is text with a <span>span element</span>.</p>
</body>
</html>
```

If you were to diagram this HTML document as a tree, it would look like Figure 13-2.

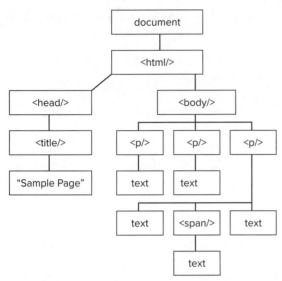

FIGURE 13-2

You start at the top of the tree with what is called the root element, the document. In the DOM, each point in the tree is called a *node*. There are several types of nodes, and the more notable ones are:

➤ Document node type represents the entire document.

➤ Element node type represents an element.

➤ Attr node type represents an attribute.

➤ Text node type represents text within an element.

The Document node is sometimes referred to as the *root node*. The root node contains other nodes, such as the doctype declaration (if specified) and the *document element*, the <html/> element, which is also sometimes referred to as the *root element*.

The document element contains HTML elements that are represented as *child nodes*. In the case of this example, the document element node has two child nodes: <head/> and <body/>, and to these nodes the <html/> element node is a *parent node*. These two child nodes are also related to each other as *sibling nodes*; all child nodes that share the same parent node are siblings.

The <head/> and <body/> nodes also contain their own children. The <head/> element node contains a <title/> node; this contains a text node containing the text Sample Page. This text node is the end of that particular branch.

The <body/> node contains three child nodes — three <p/> elements. The first two <p/> nodes only contain text, but the third has three children:

➤ The text node of Here is text with a

➤ The <span/> element node

➤ The text node of .

As you add elements and text to the web page, a corresponding node is added to the DOM representing that page.

 HTML attributes are nodes, too, but they are represented differently in the tree. For the sake of simplicity, attributes have been omitted from this particular discussion.

To get any use out of the DOM, it's important to know how to get around in the DOM tree.

NAVIGATING THE DOM

Using the parent, child, and sibling relationships, you can traverse the entire DOM tree using the `Node` data type's properties and methods. The `Node` data type is not part of the JavaScript language. Instead, it is provided by the browser to represent nodes in the DOM. It is the most basic of DOM types (most other DOM data types inherit from `Node`), but it provides the necessary tools to get from one node to another. The following table lists some of the more useful members:

Useful *Node* Members

MEMBER	DESCRIPTION
childNodes	A `NodeList` (special array) that contains all children of the specified node. The list is empty if the node has no children.
firstChild	The first child node of the specified node. Returns `null` if no such node exists.
lastChild	The last child node of the specified node. Returns `null` if no such node exists.
nextSibling	The node immediately following the specified node. Returns `null` if no such node exists.
previousSibling	The node immediately preceding this node. Returns `null` if no such node exists.
ownerDocument	The document that the specified node belongs to.
parentNode	The parent node of the specified node. Returns `null` if no such node exists.
nodeName	The name of the node. If the node is an element, this returns the tag name. If the node is text, it returns `"#text"`.
nodeValue	The value of the node. If it is a text node, the actual text is returned; if an element, `null`.
hasChildNodes()	Returns a Boolean value specifying whether the node has any children.

Using some of these members, you can get from the top of the tree (the document) to the `<span/>` element in the example HTML from the previous section, like this:

```
document.firstChild.firstChild.nextSibling.lastChild.childNodes[1];
```

Let's break this down object by object. This line starts off at the top of the tree with `document`, and its first child is the `<html/>` element. So `document.firstChild` returns `<html/>`. The `firstChild` property is used on the `<html/>` node, getting the `<head/>` element because it's the first child node of `<html/>`. Then `nextSibling` is used, returning the `<body/>` element node. The `<body/>` node's `lastChild` property returns the third `<p/>` element, and since this `<p/>` element has three children, you get the `<span/>` element by specifying the second child in the `childNodes` collection.

This certainly seems like a lot of work, doesn't it? Maintenance would be a nightmare because even slight changes to the HTML markup would require you to rewrite this code. Thankfully, the `document` object provides you with some methods to make selecting particular element nodes much easier.

SELECTING ELEMENT NODES

The first method is `getElementsByTagName()`. It accepts a string argument containing the name of the elements you want to retrieve, and it returns a `NodeList` of all the elements in the page that have the specified tag name. Using the example HTML provided earlier in this lesson, the following example selects all the `<p/>` elements:

```
var paragraphs = document.getElementsByTagName("p");
```

Here the `getElementsByTagName()` method returns a `NodeList` of three elements. A `NodeList` is a special array. It has a `length` property, and you access each element in the list with a numeric index. The primary difference, however, is that a `NodeList` is *live*: any change to the elements within the document is reflected. It is easy to demonstrate this by modifying the example HTML. The following code adds a few elements to the page:

```
<html>
<head>
    <title>Sample Page</title>
</head>
<body>
    <p>This is some text.</p>
    <p>This is more text.</p>
    <p>Here is text with a <span>span element</span>.</p>
    <script type="text/javascript">
        var paragraphs = document.getElementsByTagName("p");

        alert(paragraphs.length); // 3
    </script>
    <p>Another paragraph.</p>
    <script type="text/javascript">
        alert(paragraphs.length); // 4
    </script>
</body>
</html>
```

The bold portion of this code adds a script element to call getElementsByTagName(), selecting all <p/> elements currently in the document and assigning the resulting NodeList to the paragraphs variable. Keep in mind that at this point in the document, only three <p/> elements are found in the document, so the alert() call in the first <script/> element alerts the value of 3.

After the first <script/> element is another <p/> element, bringing the total number to four. Then another <script/> element adds another line of JavaScript, alerting the length of paragraphs again; it alerts 4.

So by using the getElementsByTagName() method, you can get to the <span/> element much more easily by selecting all <span/> elements and getting the first element in the NodeList, as shown in the following code:

```
var theSpan = document.getElementsByTagName("span")[0];
```

That's much easier, isn't it? But you can make it easier still by making a slight modification to the HTML markup and using the getElementById() method. This method's purpose is simple: to select only one element that has an id attribute with a specific value. This functionality and simplicity make the getElementById() method the most frequently used method in JavaScript development.

The following code modifies the original HTML from the beginning of this lesson by adding an id attribute to the <span/> element.

```
<html>
<head>
    <title>Sample Page</title>
</head>
<body>
    <p>This is some text.</p>
    <p>This is more text.</p>
    <p>Here is text with a <span id="foo">span element</span>.</p>
</body>
</html>
```

After this simple change, the <span/> element can be instantly found in the document with the following code:

```
var theSpan = document.getElementById("foo");
```

The getElementById() method is, by far, the easiest way to select single elements in a document. It's also much more maintainable than other methods, as long as the id attribute doesn't change.

If an element with a specified id value cannot be found in the document, getElementById() returns null. Because of this, where you use the getElementById() method is crucial: It can be reliably used only after the browser has loaded the desired HTML element into the DOM. Remember in Lesson 1 when I advised you to place <script/> elements at the bottom of the body? This is another reason — so that all elements can be loaded into the DOM before any script attempts to access them.

TRY IT

In this lesson, you learned about the DOM and how to navigate and find nodes in the tree.

Lesson Requirements

For this lesson, you need a text editor; any plain text editor will do. For Microsoft Windows users, Notepad is available by default on your system or you can download Microsoft's free Visual Web Developer Express (www.microsoft.com/express/web/) or Web Matrix (www.asp.net/webmatrix/). Mac OS X users can use TextMate, which comes as part of OS X, or they can download a trial for Coda (www.panic.com/coda/). Linux users can use the built-in VIM.

You also need a modern web browser. Choose any of the following:

➤ Internet Explorer 8+

➤ Google Chrome

➤ Firefox 3.5+

➤ Apple Safari 4+

➤ Opera 10+

Create a subfolder called Lesson13 in the JS24Hour folder you created in Lesson 1. Store the files you create in this lesson in the Lesson13 folder.

Step-by-Step

You will write a web page using the HTML provided in this lesson that selects a particular element and changes the text it contains using the nodeValue property.

1. Open your text editor and type the following code:

```
<html>
<head>
    <title>Sample Page</title>
</head>
<body>
    <p>This is some text.</p>
    <p>This is more text.</p>
    <p>Here is text with a <span id="foo">span element</span>.</p>
</body>
</html>
```

This is the same HTML provided earlier in the lesson. Save this file as lesson13_example01.htm.

2. Now add the following bold code:

```
<html>
<head>
    <title>Sample Page</title>
</head>
```

```
<body>
    <p>This is some text.</p>
    <p>This is more text.</p>
    <p>Here is text with a <span id="foo">span element</span>.</p>
    <script type="text/javascript">
        var theSpan = document.getElementById("foo");

        theSpan.childNodes[0].nodeValue = "span element containing new text";
    </script>
</body>
</html>
```

This new code retrieves the `<span/>` element with an `id` of `foo`. It then uses the `childNodes` `NodeList` to select the text node contained within the element (`firstChild` could be used in place of `childNodes[0]`), and assigns a new value to the text node.

3. Resave the document and load it into your browser.

To get the sample code files, you can download Lesson 13 from the book's website at www.wrox.com.

 Please select Lesson 13 on the DVD to view the video that accompanies this lesson.

14

Adding HTML with JavaScript

The Document Object Model (DOM) is about much more than finding particular elements in the page. Remember that JavaScript's purpose in web development is to provide a higher level of interactivity with the user, and there will be times when you want to add elements dynamically to the web page according to the user's input.

The DOM allows you to create new HTML elements and add them to the page on-the-fly. You can do this in one of two ways: with creation methods provided by the DOM standard, and with the innerHTML property. The results of these two methods look identical on the surface, but which one you should choose depends on the final result you want to achieve.

DOM CREATION METHODS

The document object is an instance of the DOM data type called Document. Its members provide many useful methods allowing you to create other DOM objects like elements and text nodes. Here you'll look at how to create these types of objects, starting with HTML elements.

Before you begin, however, the following code shows the HTML document this lesson works with:

```
<html>
<head>
    <title>Sample Page</title>
</head>
<body>
    <script type="text/javascript">

    </script>
</body>
</html>
```

It is a simple web page with a sole <script/> element in the body. The script covered in this lesson will go inside the <script/> element.

Creating Elements

The `Document` data type specifies a method called `createElement()`. It accepts one argument, a string containing the tag name of the element you want to create. It creates an element outside of the currently loaded document and returns an element object. You use it like this:

```
var el = document.createElement("div");
```

Here you create a `<div/>` element by calling the `createElement()` method and passing it the tag name of div. You do not include any angle brackets — simply the tag name of the element. The resulting element object is saved in the `el` variable.

This new object is an instance of the `HTMLElement` data type (another data type included with the DOM), and, more specifically, of an `HTMLDivElement`. You can see this by calling `alert(el)` in any browser except Internet Explorer 8 and previous versions. Figure 14-1 shows the result of `alert(el)` in Internet Explorer 9.

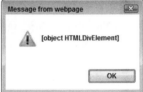

The fact that this element is an `HTMLDivElement` isn't necessarily important for the sake of this discussion. But it is important to understand that every HTML element in the HTML specification has a corresponding data type in the DOM specification. This means there are many new data types included with the DOM. For the sake of simplicity, however, you will be introduced to them only when they're relevant.

FIGURE 14-1

In the DOM, all HTML element objects are instances of the `HTMLElement` and `Element` data types, and because of this all element objects have a certain set of properties and methods you can use to add attributes to the element. The following table lists some of these members:

Useful HTMLElement and Element Members

MEMBER NAME	DESCRIPTION
id	Gets or sets the value of the id attribute for the element
className	Gets or sets the value of the class attribute
setAttribute(name, value)	Sets an attribute on the element with the specified value
getAttribute(name)	Gets the value of the specified attribute; returns null if the attribute does not exist
removeAttribute(name)	Removes the specified attribute from the element

So, by using a few of these members, you can add more content to an element. The bold lines in the following code do just that:

```
var el = document.createElement("div");

el.id = "myDiv";
el.setAttribute("align", "center");
```

In this code, the new `<div/>` element is given an `id` of `myDiv`, and an `align` property is added to the element with the `setAttribute()` method. If you were to write the HTML that this code generates, it would look like this:

```
<div id="myDiv" align="center"></div>
```

Keep in mind, however, that this element is not yet loaded into the document. You have created the element by using the `createElement()` method of the document, but it currently exists outside the document. To load it into the document, you need to use the `appendChild()` method or other insertion methods.

Adding Elements to the Document

The `appendChild()` method is a member of the `Node` data type, the same data type that you looked at in the previous lesson. You see, each HTML element object is an instance of a variety of data types. Not only is an element an instance of `HTMLElement` and `Element`, but it is an instance of the `Node` data type as well. So if you wanted to add this `<div/>` element to the web page's `<body/>` element, you could do so by finding the `<body/>` element's object and using its `appendChild()` method. Finding `<body/>` in the DOM is very easy: It's a property of the `document` object. The bold line in the following code adds the `<div/>` element created earlier to the page:

```
var el = document.createElement("div");

el.id = "myDiv";
el.setAttribute("align", "center");

document.body.appendChild(el);
```

The page's structure looks like Figure 14-2 after this code executes.

The `appendChild()` method *appends* the provided child node to the calling node. So this code places the new element as the last child in the page's body.

Sometimes you will want to append a new node, but not in every case. The `insertBefore()` method exists for this reason. It too adds a new node as a child of an existing node, but it gives you the ability to decide where, in the list of children, to place it.

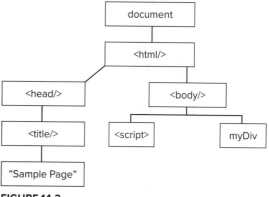

FIGURE 14-2

The `insertBefore()` method accepts two arguments. The first is the new node to insert, and the second is a reference node to place the new node in front of. The bold lines in the following code create a new `<div/>` element and insert it before `el` from the previous example:

```
var el = document.createElement("div");

el.id = "myDiv";
```

```
el.setAttribute("align", "center");

document.body.appendChild(el);

var el2 = document.createElement("div");

el2.id = "myDiv2";
el2.setAttribute("align", "center");

document.body.insertBefore(el2, el);
```

Figure 14-3 shows what the DOM structure looks like after this code is executed.

The elements don't contain any data at the moment, so seeing the results of this code requires tools that can give us an idea of what the DOM currently looks like. I'll save the introduction to those tools until later in the book; now let's add some text to these elements so you can physically see them in the browser.

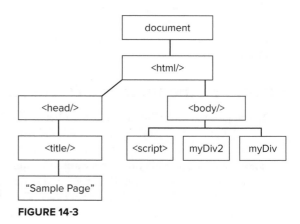

FIGURE 14-3

Creating and Adding Text Nodes

In the DOM, pieces of text are organized into individual nodes. So it's no surprise that the DOM method to create text actually creates a text node. The method to create a text node is aptly named createTextNode(). It accepts only one argument: the text that is contained within the node. Its usage looks like this:

```
var text = document.createTextNode("Hello, DOM methods!");
```

Here a text node containing the text Hello, DOM methods! is created and assigned to the text variable. Text nodes inherit from the Node data type as well, so they can be passed to the appendChild() method like this:

```
var el = document.createElement("div");
var text = document.createTextNode("Hello, DOM methods!");

el.id = "myDiv";
el.setAttribute("align", "center");

el.appendChild(text);
document.body.appendChild(el);
```

In this code, the bold lines create and append a text node to the el element from the previous examples.

One thing you might notice in this code is that the text node is appended to the <div/> element before the element is added to the body. Technically, it doesn't matter in what order you append nodes to elements and the document. But remember this: The DOM is a liability as far as performance is concerned. Every time you make a change to the document, the browser has to redraw the page. So, the goal is to limit the amount of times you change the document.

In the example provided here, the text node is added to the `<div/>` element while both nodes are outside the document itself. This is ideal, as adding the `<div/>` element to the document (complete with a child text node) requires only one write operation to the document.

Also, as the name of the method implies, `createTextNode()` creates text, not HTML. The `createTextNode()` method converts less-than and greater-than signs (< and >) to their HTML entity equivalents (`&lt;` and `&gt;`). To demonstrate this, let's return to our ongoing example and add a text node containing the < and > symbols with the following code:

```
var el = document.createElement("div");
var text = document.createTextNode("Hello, DOM methods!");

el.id = "myDiv";
el.setAttribute("align", "center");

el.appendChild(text);
document.body.appendChild(el);

var el2 = document.createElement("div");
var text2 = document.createTextNode("<b>Will this be bold?</b>");

el2.id = "myDiv2";
el2.setAttribute("align", "center");

el2.appendChild(text2);
document.body.insertBefore(el2, el);
```

The new lines of code are in bold. The first new line creates a text node containing HTML markup, which will be converted to HTML entities. The second new line adds that node to the `<div/>` element in `el2`. You can see the results of this code in Figure 14-4.

FIGURE 14-4

Using DOM methods to create elements is verbose and time-consuming. The payoff, however, is that you have references to the objects you create — you don't have to search the DOM for them. Making modifications to the `<div/>` element contained within the `el` variable is as easy as using that variable. So, DOM creation methods are ideal if you plan on modifying those same objects later on, but there is a faster and easier way to add HTML to a page if all you want to do is display it and forget it.

USING THE INNERHTML PROPERTY

The `innerHTML` property is a property all HTML elements have, and it provides a simple and effective means of adding HTML to the page. It is an invention of Microsoft that debuted in Internet Explorer 4 in 1997. It became so popular that developers clamored for other browser makers to include the property. Today, all major browsers support `innerHTML`.

The `innerHTML` property gets or sets the HTML contained within a given element. You can assign it a string containing HTML, and that HTML will be displayed in the browser. The following code shows an example:

```
var el = document.getElementById("someElement");
el.innerHTML = "<b>This is my new HTML!</b>";
```

Here the HTML contained within the `el` element is changed to some bolded text. In the case of this code, any preexisting HTML is removed from `el` and replaced with the HTML assigned to the `innerHTML` property. It is possible to keep any preexisting HTML by doing something like what you see in the following code:

```
el.innerHTML = el.innerHTML + "<b>This is my new HTML!</b>";
```

Here the existing HTML is preserved and some new HTML is appended.

The `innerHTML` property is really that simple, but it is surrounded by controversy. Type "innerHTML" into Google, and you'll find many articles for and against its use. Despite the ongoing debate, it is an incredibly useful tool. When it is used to update only the contents of an element, its speed and simplicity cannot be beat.

TRY IT

In this lesson, you learn how to add content to the page using JavaScript, the DOM creation methods, and the `innerHTML` property.

Lesson Requirements

For this lesson, you need a text editor; any plain text editor will do. For Microsoft Windows users, Notepad is available by default on your system or you can download Microsoft's free Visual Web Developer Express (www.microsoft.com/express/web/) or Web Matrix (www.asp.net/webmatrix/). Mac OS X users can use TextMate, which comes as part of OS X, or they can download a trial for Coda (www.panic.com/coda/). Linux users can use the built-in VIM.

You also need a modern web browser. Choose any of the following:

➤ Internet Explorer 8+

➤ Google Chrome

➤ Firefox 3.5+

➤ Apple Safari 4+

➤ Opera 10+

Create a subfolder called Lesson14 in the JS24Hour folder you created in Lesson 1. Store the files you create in this lesson in the Lesson14 folder.

Step-by-Step

You will write a web page and its content, a shopping list, using the DOM creation methods and innerHTML.

1. Open your text editor and type the following code:

```
<html>
<head>
    <title>Lesson 14 Example 1</title>
</head>
<body>
    <script type="text/javascript">

    </script>
</body>
</html>
```

Save this file as lesson14_example01.htm.

2. Now add the following bold code:

```
<html>
<head>
    <title>Lesson 14 Example 1</title>
</head>
<body>
    <script type="text/javascript">
        var shoppingList = [
            "Eggs",
            "Milk",
            "Juice",
            "Diapers",
            "Bread"
        ];

        for (var i = 0; i < shoppingList.length; i++) {

        }
    </script>
</body>
</html>
```

This adds an array called `shoppingList`. Each element contains an item to purchase at the store. After the array definition is a `for` loop to iterate over each item in the shopping list.

3. Add the following bold code:

```
<html>
<head>
    <title>Lesson 14 Example 1</title>
</head>
<body>
    <script type="text/javascript">
        var shoppingList = [
            "Eggs",
            "Milk",
            "Juice",
            "Diapers",
            "Bread"
        ];

        var ul = document.createElement("ul");

        for (var i = 0; i < shoppingList.length; i++) {
            ul.innerHTML = ul.innerHTML + "<li>" + shoppingList[i] + "</li>";
        }

        document.body.appendChild(ul);
    </script>
</body>
</html>
```

This new code creates an unordered list element (`<ul/>`) outside of the `for` loop. Its list item elements (`<li/>`) are generated with `innerHTML` inside the loop, so that the existing HTML is preserved with each iteration of the loop. When the loop exists, the `<ul/>` element is appended to the `<body/>` element. The browser renders the HTML as seen in Figure 14-5.

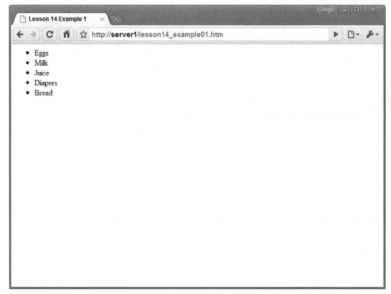

FIGURE 14-5

To get the sample code files, you can download Lesson 14 from the book's website at www.wrox.com.

 Please select Lesson 14 on the DVD to view the video that accompanies this lesson.

15

Modifying Element Style

Human beings are visual creatures. We can identify visual cues, no matter how subtle, and decipher their meaning. For example, the Windows operating system differentiates between active and inactive windows with visual cues––changing the color, the opacity, and other visual elements of the window. In Windows 7, inactive windows display themselves with more of a faded, transparent look than the color-rich, drop-shadow-encased active window. It's a subtle but effective means of telling users which window is currently active.

The ability to change how a particular user interface element looks is an extremely important feature of an application programming interface (API), and the DOM, combined with the styling power of CSS, gives you this ability.

In this lesson, you learn how you can leverage the power of the DOM and CSS to change the appearance elements in a web page. You can modify an element's style in two ways:

➤ Change individual CSS properties using the `style` property.

➤ Change the value of the element's `class` attribute.

USING THE STYLE PROPERTY

The `style` property is an object that maps to an element's `style` attribute. It provides access to individual CSS properties, allowing you to change all CSS properties that the browser supports. You access the `style` property like this:

```
document.getElementById("someElement").style.color = "red";
```

Here, an element with an `id` of `someElement` is retrieved, and its `color` property is set to `red`. Assuming this element is a `<div/>` element, this code essentially translates to the following HTML:

```
<div id="someElement" style="color: red"></div>
```

The relationship between the HTML `style` attribute and the JavaScript `style` property is usually overlooked by those new to JavaScript and the DOM. The `style` property is usually, and incorrectly, thought of as the doorway to all style information that affects an element — the belief being that an element's style, whether defined in an external style sheet or by means of the inline `style` attribute, can be retrieved with the `style` object. For example, assume the following style sheet:

```
<style type="text/css">
#someElement { color: red; }
</style>
```

It is not uncommon to see code that attempts to retrieve this information using the `style` object, like this:

```
var someEl = document.getElementById("someElement");

alert(someEl.style.color); // empty string
```

When this code is executed in a browser, an alert box displays an empty string (i.e., nothing) — it looks Figure 15-1.

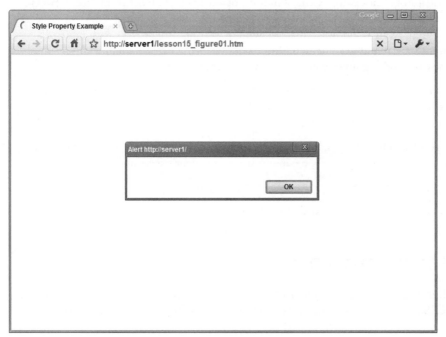

FIGURE 15-1

This happens because the `style` object has no link to any style rules that affect the HTML element — only the CSS properties defined in the `style` attribute. The previous code looks at the `style` attribute, searches for the `color` property, finds none, and returns an empty string. But you can get this information once it is set by using either the `style` property or the `style` attribute, like this:

```
<div id="someElement" style="color: red;">Hello</div>
...
```

```
var someEl = document.getElementById("someElement");
alert(someEl.style.color); // red
someEl.style.color = "blue";
alert(someEl.style.color); // blue
```

Always remember that the `style` object links, and only links, to the HTML element's `style` attribute. Just remember that while the HTML attribute contains a string of CSS, the DOM `style` property is an object.

By comparing the actual CSS property — `color` in this case — with the JavaScript equivalent, you can see they are the same. Many CSS property names, accessed in JavaScript via the `style` property, are exactly the same as the CSS properties used in a style sheet. There are some, however, that are different and have to be changed in order to work in JavaScript.

For example, the CSS property to change an element's background color is `background-color`. This particular CSS property cannot be used in JavaScript as is because the hyphen (-) cannot be used in an identifier. So in order that an element's background color can be changed with JavaScript and the `style` object, the hyphen in `background-color` is dropped, and the first letter of `color` is capitalized, like this:

```
document.getElementById("someElement").style.backgroundColor = "blue";
```

Many CSS properties use hyphens, and converting them to their JavaScript equivalents follows the same pattern: Drop the hyphen and camel-case the letter after the hyphen. The JavaScript equivalent of `border-left-color`, for example, is `borderLeftColor`.

There are a few exceptions to the camel-casing rule. Consider the CSS float property, for example. The word "float" is a reserved word in JavaScript, and as such, the code `element.style.float` will not change the float of the specified element. Instead, you must use the `cssFloat` and `styleFloat` (for IE8 and below) properties.

By using the `style` object, and the properties it allows you to modify, you can essentially replicate a style rule for a single HTML element, like this:

```
var someEl = document.getElementById("someElement");

someEl.style.color = "red";
someEl.style.backgroundColor = "gray";
someEl.style.border = "1px solid black";
```

Here, an element with an `id` of `someElement` is retrieved from `document`, its text color is changed to red, it is given a background color of gray, and a one-pixel black border is placed around it. Making many changes to an element's style in this manner, however, brings up a couple of issues you should be mindful of:

➤ Each change to an element's style is an individual call to DOM properties — which, as you learned in the previous lesson, you want to limit as much as possible for performance reasons.

➤ The philosophy behind CSS is to separate style from markup and behavior. This separation makes maintenance and modifications much easier because all the style information is grouped into style sheets — eliminating the need to search through HTML and JavaScript for style information.

For these reasons, editing an element's style one property at a time is considered the incorrect approach. There are situations in which you may want to, but for the most part the better solution is to manipulate an element's CSS class using the `className` property.

USING THE CLASSNAME PROPERTY

HTML elements have a class attribute that allows you to assign one or more CSS classes. This attribute is accessed through the DOM via the `className` property, and you use it like this:

```
someEl.className = "a-CSS-class";
```

Using the `className` property addresses the two previous issues rather nicely:

➤ Modifying an element's CSS class, which can contain multiple CSS properties, changes an element's style with only one call to the DOM.

➤ CSS data is kept separate from JavaScript; the only link between the CSS style sheet and the JavaScript code is the CSS class name. This makes maintenance much easier.

Another advantage to using the `className` property is that it requires less JavaScript code. The last example in the previous section used three lines of code to change an element's color, background color, and border. But place that style information in a CSS class, like this:

```
.a-CSS-class {
    color: red;
    background-color: gray;
    border: 1px solid black;
}
```

It takes only one line of JavaScript code:

```
someEl.className = "a-CSS-class";
```

You can also assign multiple CSS classes to the `className` property, just as you would with the `class` attribute. The following code demonstrates this:

```
someEl.className = "a-CSS-class b-CSS-class";
```

Just make sure to put a space between the class names.

TRY IT

In this lesson you learn how to manipulate an element's style by using the `style` and `className` properties.

Lesson Requirements

For this lesson, you need a text editor; any plain text editor will do. For Microsoft Windows users, Notepad is available by default on your system or you can download Microsoft's free Visual Web

Developer Express (www.microsoft.com/express/web/) or Web Matrix (www.asp.net/webmatrix/). Mac OS X users can use TextMate, which comes as part of OS X, or they can download a trial for Coda (www.panic.com/coda/). Linux users can use the built-in VIM.

You also need a modern web browser. Choose any of the following:

- ➤ Internet Explorer 8+
- ➤ Google Chrome
- ➤ Firefox 3.5+
- ➤ Apple Safari 4+
- ➤ Opera 10+

Create a subfolder called Lesson15 in the JS24Hour folder you created in Lesson 1. Store the files you create in this lesson in the Lesson15 folder.

Step-by-Step

You will write a web page and dynamically change an element's style.

1. Open your text editor and type the following code:

```
<html>
<head>
    <title>Lesson 15: Example 1</title>
    <style type="text/css">
    .message-style1 {
        color: navy;
        font-weight: bold;
        background-color: gray;
    }
    </style>
</head>
<body>
    <div id="divMessage">
        Here is a message.
    </div>
    <input type="button" value="Toggle Style" />
    <script type="text/javascript">

    </script>
</body>
</html>
```

2. Now add the following bold code:

```
<html>
<head>
    <title>Lesson 15: Example 1</title>
    <style type="text/css">
    .message-style1 {
        color: navy;
```

```
            font-weight: bold;
            background-color: gray;
        }
    </style>
</head>
<body>
    <div id="divMessage">
        Here is a message.
    </div>
    <input type="button" value="Toggle Style" />
    <script type="text/javascript">
    function toggleStyle() {
        var divMessage = document.getElementById("divMessage");

        if (divMessage.className === "message-style1") {
            divMessage.className = "";
        } else {
            divMessage.className = "message-style1";
        }
    }
    </script>
</body>
</html>
```

The new code adds a function called `toggleStyle()`. It retrieves the `<div/>` element with an `id` of `divMessage`, and it sets the element's `className` property according to its current value. If the element has a `className` of `message-style1`, then `className` is set to an empty string — effectively removing any styles applied to the element. If the element's `className` does not equal `message-style1`, then `className` is assigned that value.

3. Now modify the following bold line:

```
<html>
<head>
    <title>Lesson 15: Example 1</title>
    <style type="text/css">
    .message-style1 {
        color: navy;
        font-weight: bold;
        background-color: gray;
    }
    </style>
</head>
<body>
    <div id="divMessage">
        Here is a message.
    </div>
    <input type="button" value="Toggle Style" onclick="toggleStyle()" />
    <script type="text/javascript">
    function toggleStyle() {
        var divMessage = document.getElementById("divMessage");

        if (divMessage.className === "message-style1") {
            divMessage.className = "";
```

```
            } else {
                divMessage.className = "message-style1";
            }
        }
        </script>
    </body>
    </html>
```

An event handler is added to the `<input/>` element to execute the `toggleStyle()` function when the button is clicked. Don't worry about events right now; you'll begin learning about them in the next lesson. For now, simply know that `toggleStyle()` executes when you click the button.

4. Save this HTML file as `lesson15_example01.htm`. Open it in your browser, and click the button several times. You will see the `<div/>` element's style change with every click.

To get the sample code files you can download Lesson 15 from the book's website at `www.wrox.com`.

 Please select Lesson 15 on the DVD to view the video that accompanies this lesson.

16

Introduction to Events

A web application is usually divided into two distinct parts. The first is usually referred to as the *back end* or *server side*. It is powered by PHP, ASP.NET, Ruby, or any other server-side technology to validate, process, and format data. While there's always some level of complexity involved with an application, the server-side portion of a web application is typically more straight-forward than the client portion — the second part — because it has to do something only when data is sent or requested by the user.

The client portion, or *front end*, is the interface used by the user to input and view information, as well as to interact with the application as a whole. The client portion is made up of HTML, CSS, and JavaScript. HTML and CSS are sufficient for providing a user interface for a web application, but JavaScript is what can make an interface dynamic and responsive.

The user interface of a web application is usually in a reactive state — it waits for the user to perform a particular action before it knows to do something. Look at Google's search page as an example. When you first visit the page, you see something similar to Figure 16-1.

You see nothing but a search form, but the moment you move your mouse pointer or type in the search field, the page reacts to your actions. Moving your mouse causes the tool bar at the top to fade into view, and typing text into the search field causes Google's autocomplete feature to activate, as shown in Figure 16-2.

These subtle features on Google's search page are a prime example of how JavaScript can enrich the user's experience. But how does JavaScript know when to execute certain code based on a user's actions?

The answer is *events*. An event is something that happens, usually outside the developer's control, and that is handled by code. For example, pressing a key while the cursor is in the search field on Google's search page causes an event called `keypress` to *fire*, or take place. The developers of Google's search page lack control over when you press a key, but they can write what is called an *event handler* to handle the `keypress` event. This event handler executes JavaScript code every time you press a key while typing in the search field. By reacting to your users' actions, you can enrich their experiences while they use your app — just as the developers of Google's search page enhance your experience.

FIGURE 16-1

FIGURE 16-2

Unfortunately, events are one area in client-side development in which there are very noticeable differences in the various browsers. On one hand you have the browsers that support and implement the standard DOM event model; these are Internet Explorer 9, Firefox, Chrome, Safari, and Opera. On the other hand are Internet Explorer 8 and below, which use their own proprietary event model. Thankfully, there are similarities between the two event models; their differences, and how to cope with them, will be discussed in later lessons.

Now, though, you'll be introduced to the many different kinds of events you can "listen" for in order to execute code when they happen. You'll apply this information in future lessons.

 The events covered in this introduction are part of the W3C DOM event standard, and most pertain to events attached to HTML elements.

MOUSE EVENTS

The mouse is arguably the most important input device when it comes to the Web. Unless inputting information into a form, the average user doesn't use the keyboard all that much, and certainly doesn't use it to interact with a web page. No, pointing devices reign on the Web, and so the events associated with the mouse are the most commonly handled.

The mouse can generate a variety of events, but they all fall into two categories: movement-based and button-based.

Movement-Based Events

On a web page, a user generates an event every time he or she moves the mouse. In some cases, moving the mouse pointer one pixel in either direction can generate three events (or more, depending on the browser). These events are:

➤ `mousemove`: This event occurs when the mouse pointer is moved while it's over an element.

➤ `mouseover`: This event occurs when the mouse pointer moves over an element.

➤ `mouseout`: This event occurs when the mouse pointer moves away from an element.

Button-Based Events

Movement is just part of the equation when it comes to mouse-based events; it's also very useful to know when the user clicks the mouse button. Usually, clicking a button on the mouse generates three events, and they occur in the following order:

➤ `mousedown`: This event occurs when a mouse button is pressed over an element.

➤ `mouseup`: This event occurs when a mouse button is released over an element.

➤ `click`: This event occurs when the mouse button is clicked over an element. A `click` event happens when both a `mousedown` and a `mouseup` occur over the same location.

There is a fourth button event:

➤ dblclick: This event occurs when the mouse button is clicked twice, in quick succession, over the same position. If a click event is handled on the same element, the click event is handled before dblclick.

KEYBOARD EVENTS

The second-most-important input device, for web applications, is the keyboard. It is what users use to supply data to web applications. There are three keyboard events, and they are similar in concept to the three primary events of the mouse button. Pressing a key generates the following three events in the provided order:

➤ keydown: This event occurs when a key is pressed down.

➤ keyup: This event occurs when a key is released.

➤ keypress: This event occurs when a key is pressed and released.

There is usually some confusion about keyboard events, as they may seem redundant. But there are subtle differences in the ways they are used, and it's important to know the difference between a character and a key. A key is a physical button on the keyboard, and a character is a value that results from a key's being pressed.

The keypress event is traditionally used to detect the character being typed. In fact, the keypress event fires only if an alphanumeric or symbol (such as a period or tilde) key was pressed and released. For example, you can handle the keypress event on a textbox and filter out alphabetical characters so that only numbers and symbols appear in the textbox.

The keypress event does not fire for keys such as Backspace, Shift, or Enter, but the keyup and keydown events do. These two events fire when any key is pressed and released. You can actually detect when the user presses the Backspace key and prevent the deletion of characters — not that you should do that, of course.

BASIC EVENTS

Not all events occur from a user's actions. Some occur when something happens from within the HTML document. The user didn't do anything, but something took place within the window or document, and you may want to execute some code when one of these events occurs.

For example, there are some events that fire in relation to the window. They are:

➤ load: This element occurs when the window is finished loading the document and all other resources, such as JavaScript, style sheets, and images.

➤ unload: This element occurs when the document is unloaded from the window. For example, it fires on the current page when you navigate to another page.

➤ abort: This element occurs when the loading of the page is aborted, usually because the user has pressed the cancel button.

➤ resize: This event occurs when the window is resized.

➤ error: This event occurs when a JavaScript error takes place.

The beautiful thing about events is that the object related to an event, like the window object, doesn't care if you, or anyone for that matter, write code to handle the event. All the object knows is that it needs to execute an event handler when the associated event occurs, and if one exists, it executes it.

TRY IT

There isn't anything to try for this lesson. Events are an integral part of client-side development, and it's important to understand the concepts involved. This lesson is primarily meant to be a primer on events. In the next lesson, you learn one of the many ways you can handle events — by using HTML attributes.

 There is no video to accompany this lesson.

17

Assigning Event Handlers with HTML Attributes

The previous lesson introduced you to many events that you can handle in your JavaScript code. That leads to the question "How do you handle events in JavaScript?"

The answer isn't as straightforward as most would like. There are many ways you can "wire up" JavaScript code to handle an event, and over the course of this lesson, and those following, you'll learn the many ways you can set up functions to handle events.

You'll start this journey by learning how to use HTML attributes to handle events. Admittedly, HTML attribute event handlers aren't used as often as they used to be, but they are very useful when you need to handle an event quickly.

WIRING UP EVENT HANDLERS

Let's start with an example element. Following is a normal `<div/>` element:

```
<div id="myDiv">Hello, Events!</div>
```

This element has an `id` of `myDiv`, and it contains a small bit of text. It's an ordinary element now, but you can add some specialness to it by handling the `click` event. To handle this event, add an attribute called `onclick` to the opening tag, like this:

```
<div id="myDiv" onclick="">Hello, Events!</div>
```

The name of an attribute used to handle events is the word `on` followed by the name of the event. In this example the event handler `onclick` handles the `click` event. If you wanted to handle the `mouseover` event, the attribute's name would be `onmouseover`.

Also keep in mind that even though `<div/>` elements don't interact with mouse clicks by default, you can add that functionality by handling the `click` event. In fact, you can add custom functionality to just about any HTML element by handling events.

Let's now add some code to execute when this element is clicked. HTML attributes allow you to assign any JavaScript code as the attribute's value. So changing this element's text color is as simple as using the `this` variable, followed by the `style` object, and then the `color` CSS property, like this:

```
<div id="myDiv" onclick="this.style.color = 'red'">Hello, Events!</div>
```

When you're using HTML attributes to handle events, the `this` variable refers to the element that originated the event. Here `this` refers to the `<div/>` element; when the `<div/>` element is clicked, its text color changes to red.

Note the use of single quotes around `red`. Single quotes are used here because the `onclick` attribute uses double quotes to contain its value. If you were to use double quotes around `red`, it would look like this:

```
<div id="myDiv" onclick="this.style.color = "red"">Hello, Events!</div>
```

And this would result in the browser's thinking the value of the `onclick` attribute is `"this.style .color = "`, which obviously doesn't result in the intended outcome. Always keep quotation marks in mind, especially when dealing with HTML attribute event handlers.

Attributes also have the rather unusual trait of allowing more than one JavaScript statement in the attributes' value. To demonstrate this, the following code adds another statement that calls the `alert()` method:

```
<div id="myDiv" onclick="this.style.color = 'red'; alert('You clicked me!')">
    Hello, Events!
</div>
```

You can use as many statements as you want; simply use a semicolon at the end of each statement so that the JavaScript engine knows when a statement ends and a new one begins. But if you want to execute multiple statements in an event handler, it's best to group those statements into a function. Doing so is advantageous for the following reasons:

➤ Performing repeated tasks is much easier since all you have to call is a single function, as opposed to repeating the same statements over and over. In other words, code reuse.

➤ Maintaining the code is easier. Organizing the code in function form makes mistakes easier to spot and fix. Maintenance is much easier when you're using the same code in multiple elements' `onclick` event handlers; making changes to a function is much simpler than making changes to multiple attributes.

With this in mind, let's rewrite the previous example by using a function. Let's also add another HTML element that handles the `click` event and calls the same function, like this:

```
<script type="text/javascript">
function changeToRed(that) {
    that.style.color = "red";
    alert("You clicked me!");
```

```
    }
    </script>

    <div id="myDiv" onclick="changeToRed(this)">Hello, Events!</div>
    <p id="myPara" onclick="changeToRed(this)">Hello, Events 2!</p>
```

Look at the JavaScript function first. It's called `changeToRed()`, and it accepts an object called `that`. This parameter name is traditionally used to contain the `this` object (this and that... get it?), which is its use here. The first line uses the `that` variable to change the element's text color to red, and then an alert box displays a generic message to the user.

Now look at the HTML. The `<div/>` element was changed to call the `changeToRed()` function and passes `this` as an argument. Another element, a `<p/>` element, was added, and its `onclick` event handler was set to call `changeToRed()` as well, passing it a reference to that element by using the `this` variable. Even though `<p/>` is a different element from `<div/>`, the results will be the same: The `<p/>` element's text color will change to red, and an alert box displays a message to the user.

So, by taking the original statements and placing them within a function, you've essentially made the code usable by virtually any element in the page, and also made it easier to maintain.

CANCELLING DEFAULT BEHAVIOR

The `<div/>` and `<p/>` elements don't have any default behavior when a user clicks them. So the examples up to this point work as expected. But what if you want to provide the same functionality for an `<a/>` element — an element that does do something by default when it's clicked (such as navigate to a different page)?

When a user clicks a link in a web page, the browser looks at the `<a/>` element and determines if an `onclick` event handler is defined for that element. If one is found, the browser executes the JavaScript code first, and then it navigates to the page defined in the `href` attribute. Let's apply this process to a link that handles the `click` event by calling `changeToRed()`, like the following code:

```
    <a href="http://www.wrox.com" onclick="changeToRed(this)">Click me!</a>
```

In the case of this element, the browser goes through the following steps:

1. The browser finds the `onclick` attribute and executes `changeToRed()`.

2. The `<a/>` element's text color changes to red.

3. An alert box pops up and the browser stays on the page until the user clicks the OK button.

4. The browser navigates to another page once the OK button is clicked.

What if you want to disable the link's default behavior of navigating to a different page? There are some good reasons to do so; when you get into later lessons, such as Ajax, you'll see why you may want to disable a link's default behavior to enhance the user's experience on your web page.

But for now, just imagine you want the user to see your totally awesome ability to change the link's text color to red. After all, if it weren't for the alert box, anyone clicking the previous link would have no idea the text color had changed to red, because the browser navigates to a different page before the user has a chance to see the change. To disable the default behavior of an `<a/>` element, or any element for that matter, just ensure that the event handler returns `false`. This can be done in two ways.

First, simply tack the statement `return false` after the call to `changeToRed()`, like this:

```
<a href="http://www.wrox.com"
    onclick="changeToRed(this); return false">Click me!</a>
```

But in doing this you've made your code more difficult to manage and maintain — especially if you plan on doing the same thing with other `<a/>` elements. The better solution is to move the `return false` statement into `changeToRed()`, like this:

```
function changeToRed(that) {
    that.style.color = "red";
    alert("You clicked me!");
    return false;
}
```

Then you can simply use the `return` keyword in the event handler to return the value returned by `changeToRed()`, as shown in the following code:

```
<a href="http://www.wrox.com" onclick="return changeToRed(this)">Click me!</a>
```

Even though `changeToRed()` returns `false`, it returns only to the calling code — the `onclick` event handler. The event handler must return `false` in order to disable the link's default behavior. So that's why the `onclick` event handler is set to return `changeToRed()` — because the function returns `false`. Now when a user clicks this link, the browser goes through the following process:

1. The browser finds the `onclick` event handler and executes the `return` statement, which executes the `changeToRed()` function.

2. The `<a/>` element's text color changes to red.

3. An alert box pops up.

4. After the user clicks the OK button, `changeToRed()` returns `false` to the `onclick` event handler.

5. The event handler returns `false` (because `changeToRed()` returns `false`) to the browser.

6. The browser stays on the same page, cancelling the link's default behavior of navigating to the page specified in the `href` attribute.

Now that you know the theory behind HTML attribute event handlers, try applying them to an actual application.

TRY IT

In this lesson, you learn how to use HTML attributes to handle events.

Lesson Requirements

For this lesson, you will need a text editor; any plain text editor will do. For Microsoft Windows users, Notepad is available by default on your system or you can download Microsoft's free Visual Web Developer Express (www.microsoft.com/express/web/) or Web Matrix (www.asp.net/webmatrix/). Mac OS X users can use TextMate, which comes as part of OS X, or download a trial for Coda (www.panic.com/coda/). Linux users can use the built-in VIM.

You also need a modern web browser. Choose any of the following:

➤ Internet Explorer 8+

➤ Google Chrome

➤ Firefox 3.5+

➤ Apple Safari 4+

➤ Opera 10+

Create a subfolder called Lesson17 in the JS24Hour folder you created in Lesson 1. Store the files you create in this lesson in the Lesson17 folder.

Step-by-Step

You will write a web-based calculator using HTML attribute event handlers.

1. Open your text editor and type the following HTML:

```html
<html>
<head>
    <title>Lesson 17: Example 01</title>
    <style type="text/css">
    td {
        border: 1px solid gray;
        width: 50px;
    }

    #results {
        height: 20px;
    }
    </style>
</head>
<body>
    <table border="0" cellpadding="2" cellspacing="2">
        <tr>
            <td colspan="4" id="results"></td>
        </tr>
        <tr>
            <td><a href="#">1</a></td>
            <td><a href="#">2</a></td>
            <td><a href="#">3</a></td>
            <td><a href="#">+</a></td>
        </tr>
```

```
        <tr>
            <td><a href="#">4</a></td>
            <td><a href="#">5</a></td>
            <td><a href="#">6</a></td>
            <td><a href="#">-</a></td>
        </tr>
        <tr>
            <td><a href="#">7</a></td>
            <td><a href="#">8</a></td>
            <td><a href="#">9</a></td>
            <td><a href="#">x</a></td>
        </tr>
        <tr>
            <td><a href="#">Clear</a></td>
            <td><a href="#">0</a></td>
            <td><a href="#">=</a></td>
            <td><a href="#">/</a></td>
        </tr>
    </table>
    <script type="text/javascript">
    </script>
</body>
</html>
```

This is the markup used for this application, and a table makes up the bulk of the HTML. The first row has a `<td/>` element with an `id` of `results`. This is the display of the calculator. The subsequent rows consist of four cells on each row, and each cell contains a link. The `href` attribute of these links is set to #, which prohibits the browser from navigating away from the page. However, this is a little unnecessary, as your JavaScript code will cancel the links' default behavior.

2. Now add the JavaScript function that you see bold in the following code:

```
<html>
<head>
    <title>Lesson 17: Example 01</title>
    <style type="text/css">
    td {
        border: 1px solid gray;
        width: 50px;
    }

    #results {
        height: 20px;
    }
    </style>
</head>
<body>
    <table border="0" cellpadding="2" cellspacing="2">
        <tr>
            <td colspan="4" id="results"></td>
        </tr>
        <tr>
            <td><a href="#">1</a></td>
```

```
                <td><a href="#">2</a></td>
                <td><a href="#">3</a></td>
                <td><a href="#">+</a></td>
            </tr>
            <tr>
                <td><a href="#">4</a></td>
                <td><a href="#">5</a></td>
                <td><a href="#">6</a></td>
                <td><a href="#">-</a></td>
            </tr>
            <tr>
                <td><a href="#">7</a></td>
                <td><a href="#">8</a></td>
                <td><a href="#">9</a></td>
                <td><a href="#">x</a></td>
            </tr>
            <tr>
                <td><a href="#">Clear</a></td>
                <td><a href="#">0</a></td>
                <td><a href="#">=</a></td>
                <td><a href="#">/</a></td>
            </tr>
        </table>
        <script type="text/javascript">
        function addDigit(digit) {
            var resultField = document.getElementById("results");

            resultField.innerHTML += digit;

            return false;
        }
        </script>
    </body>
</html>
```

This new function, called addDigit(), accepts an argument called digit. It uses the value by appending it to the innerHTML of the <td/> element with an id of results. The function returns false.

3. Add the bold function in the following code:

```
<html>
<head>
    <title>Lesson 17: Example 01</title>
    <style type="text/css">
    td {
        border: 1px solid gray;
        width: 50px;
    }

    #results {
        height: 20px;
    }
    </style>
```

```
    </head>
    <body>
        <table border="0" cellpadding="2" cellspacing="2">
            <tr>
                <td colspan="4" id="results"></td>
            </tr>
            <tr>
                <td><a href="#">1</a></td>
                <td><a href="#">2</a></td>
                <td><a href="#">3</a></td>
                <td><a href="#">+</a></td>
            </tr>
            <tr>
                <td><a href="#">4</a></td>
                <td><a href="#">5</a></td>
                <td><a href="#">6</a></td>
                <td><a href="#">-</a></td>
            </tr>
            <tr>
                <td><a href="#">7</a></td>
                <td><a href="#">8</a></td>
                <td><a href="#">9</a></td>
                <td><a href="#">x</a></td>
            </tr>
            <tr>
                <td><a href="#">Clear</a></td>
                <td><a href="#">0</a></td>
                <td><a href="#">=</a></td>
                <td><a href="#">/</a></td>
            </tr>
        </table>
        <script type="text/javascript">
        function addDigit(digit) {
            var resultField = document.getElementById("results");

            resultField.innerHTML += digit;

            return false;
        }

        function calculate() {
            var resultField = document.getElementById("results");

            resultField.innerHTML = eval(resultField.innerHTML);

            return false;
        }
        </script>
    </body>
</html>
```

This function, called `calculate()`, retrieves the element with an `id` of `results` (the first
`<td/>` element), and uses the `eval()` method to execute the contents of the element's
`innerHTML`. The `eval()` method is new to you: It accepts a string value and executes that

string as JavaScript. Although it is useful, `eval()` is typically thought of as "evil" because it leads to sloppy code that can't be maintained and it makes JavaScript execution slower. There are, however, some legitimate uses for `eval()`, one of which is to execute mathematical computations. Its use here is benign, and used in this example for simplicity's sake.

4. Now add a function to clear the results. It is bold in the following code:

```html
<html>
<head>
    <title>Lesson 17: Example 01</title>
    <style type="text/css">
    td {
        border: 1px solid gray;
        width: 50px;
    }

    #results {
        height: 20px;
    }
    </style>
</head>
<body>
    <table border="0" cellpadding="2" cellspacing="2">
        <tr>
            <td colspan="4" id="results"></td>
        </tr>
        <tr>
            <td><a href="#">1</a></td>
            <td><a href="#">2</a></td>
            <td><a href="#">3</a></td>
            <td><a href="#">+</a></td>
        </tr>
        <tr>
            <td><a href="#">4</a></td>
            <td><a href="#">5</a></td>
            <td><a href="#">6</a></td>
            <td><a href="#">-</a></td>
        </tr>
        <tr>
            <td><a href="#">7</a></td>
            <td><a href="#">8</a></td>
            <td><a href="#">9</a></td>
            <td><a href="#">x</a></td>
        </tr>
        <tr>
            <td><a href="#">Clear</a></td>
            <td><a href="#">0</a></td>
            <td><a href="#">=</a></td>
            <td><a href="#">/</a></td>
        </tr>
    </table>
    <script type="text/javascript">
    function addDigit(digit) {
```

```
                        var resultField = document.getElementById("results");

                        resultField.innerHTML += digit;

                        return false;
                    }

                function calculate() {
                        var resultField = document.getElementById("results");

                        resultField.innerHTML = eval(resultField.innerHTML);

                        return false;
                    }

                function reset() {
                        var resultField = document.getElementById("results");

                        resultField.innerHTML = "";

                        return false;
                    }
                </script>
            </body>
            </html>
```

The reset() function resets the calculator's value, setting the innerHTML of the results field to an empty string.

5. Wire up the events for each <a/> element. Don't forget to use the return keyword before calling the appropriate function.

```
        <html>
        <head>
            <title>Lesson 17: Example 01</title>
            <style type="text/css">
            td {
                border: 1px solid gray;
                width: 50px;
            }

            #results {
                height: 20px;
            }
            </style>
        </head>
        <body>
            <table border="0" cellpadding="2" cellspacing="2">
                <tr>
                    <td colspan="4" id="results"></td>
                </tr>
    <tr>
                    <td><a href="#" onclick="return addDigit(1)">1</a></td>
                    <td><a href="#" onclick="return addDigit(2)">2</a></td>
```

```
                    <td><a href="#" onclick="return addDigit(3)">3</a></td>
                    <td><a href="#" onclick="return addDigit('+')">+</a></td>
                </tr>
                <tr>
                    <td><a href="#" onclick="return addDigit(4)">4</a></td>
                    <td><a href="#" onclick="return addDigit(5)">5</a></td>
                    <td><a href="#" onclick="return addDigit(6)">6</a></td>
                    <td><a href="#" onclick="return addDigit('-')">-</a></td>
                </tr>
                <tr>
                    <td><a href="#" onclick="return addDigit(7)">7</a></td>
                    <td><a href="#" onclick="return addDigit(8)">8</a></td>
                    <td><a href="#" onclick="return addDigit(9)">9</a></td>
                    <td><a href="#" onclick="return addDigit('*')">x</a></td>
                </tr>
                <tr>
                    <td><a href="#" onclick="return reset()">Clear</a></td>
                    <td><a href="#" onclick="return addDigit(0)">0</a></td>
                    <td><a href="#" onclick="return calculate()">=</a></td>
                    <td><a href="#" onclick="return addDigit('/')">/</a></td>
                </tr>
            </table>
            <script type="text/javascript">
            function addDigit(digit) {
                var resultField = document.getElementById("results");

                resultField.innerHTML += digit;

                return false;
            }

            function calculate() {
                var resultField = document.getElementById("results");

                resultField.innerHTML = eval(resultField.innerHTML);

                return false;
            }

            function reset() {
                var resultField = document.getElementById("results");

                resultField.innerHTML = "";

                return false;
            }
            </script>
        </body>
    </html>
```

Note that the links for clearing and totaling the calculator call the reset() and calculate() functions, respectively. All other links call the addDigit() function, and pass it a value representing their respective number or operation.

To work the calculator, click the appropriate links to perform arithmetic operations. Figure 17-1 shows an example of the calculator in action.

FIGURE 17-1

To get the sample code files, you can download Lesson 17 from the book's website at www.wrox.com.

 Please select Lesson 17 on the DVD to view the video that accompanies this lesson.

18

Using Early DOM Event Handlers

The HTML event handler attributes certainly work, and every browser continues to support them despite the fact that they were invented in very early versions of Netscape. However, as you may have surmised, handling events with HTML attributes can become a tedious endeavor mainly because you have to locate and add attributes to every element you want the user to interact with. Keep in mind that all those years ago, the majority of websites were primarily static, and the developers responsible for generating those websites had complete control over each page's HTML. It was also a time before the idea of separating markup (HTML) from style (CSS) and behavior (JavaScript) really gained traction.

The fourth generation of browsers, primarily Internet Explorer 4 and Netscape 4, introduced a new way of assigning event handlers by using what are now referred to as *DOM Level 0 event handlers*. Think of a "level" as a version; these event handlers are called DOM Level 0 event handlers because they existed before any W3C DOM standard. Yet all browsers support them. Even to this day, DOM Level 0 event handlers are widely used and are an integral part of many web applications.

Early DOM event handlers are so popular because they are supported by all browsers (something you'll appreciate in coming lessons), and you can use them in JavaScript code, effectively decoupling JavaScript from HTML.

ASSIGNING EVENT HANDLERS

DOM Level 0 event handlers are properties of DOM objects as well as the `window` object. So in order to assign an event handler, you must first retrieve an object from the DOM (or the `window`). The event handler property names closely resemble those of HTML attribute event handlers: they are lowercase and consist of `on` followed by the event's name.

For example, you handle the `window` object's `load` event by creating a function and assigning it to the `onload` property, like this:

```
function handleOnload() {
    alert("Loaded!");
}

onload = handleOnload;
```

Notice the lack of parentheses to `handleOnload` in the last line of this code. When assigning an event handler, it is important that you assign either a function or `null` (`null` tells the browser not to handle the event). Failing to assign one of these two values to an event handler property results in an error.

In the case of this code, executing `handleOnload()` when assigning it to the `onload` event handler does not actually assign the function — it assigns the *result* of the function's being executed. The result of a function is determined by a `return` statement within the function. Since `handleOnload()` does not contain a return statement, the result of the function's being executed is `undefined`. In the following line, `undefined` is assigned to `onload`:

```
onload = handleOnload(); // error; undefined assigned to onload
```

The value of `undefined` is not a function, nor is it `null`, so this code results in an error. It is possible, however, to write a function that returns another function. Let's modify `handleOnload()` to do just that with the following code:

```
function handleOnload() {
    return function() {
        alert("Loaded!");
    }
}
```

Since `handleOnload()` now returns a function, and that function is the desired function to handle the event, you can execute `handleOnload()` as you assign it to an event handler, as seen in the first line of this code:

```
onload = handleOnload(); // now it's ok; it returns a function
onload = handleOnload; // does not cause an error, but does not alert a message
```

The second line of this code is technically correct, but it does not result in the desired outcome of an alert window displaying the message "Loaded!" when the event fires. This is because the function `handleOnload()`, not the function `handleOnload()` returns, is assigned as the event handler. Always be mindful of how you assign your event handlers; assign the function you want to have execute when the event fires.

Despite the examples in this lesson, you will more than likely see event handlers assigned in slightly a different way — by having an anonymous function assigned to them, like this:

```
onload = function() {
    alert("Loaded!");
};
```

The advantage to this format is readability. The event handler and the function assigned to it are grouped together in the same statement — making it much easier to read and understand what the code does. In the grand scheme of things, it doesn't really matter how you assign a function to an event handler — as long as you do it correctly, of course.

Unlike the event handlers in Lesson 17, you cannot pass a value to DOM Level 0 event handlers. So you can't pass this as an argument as you did with the HTML attribute event handlers. You can, however, use this inside the event handler to refer to the element or object where the event occurred. For example:

```
var someElement = document.getElementById("divElement");

someElement.onclick = function() {
    this.style.color = "red";
};
```

This code gets an element with an id of divElement, and it assigns a function to handle the click event. When a user clicks the element, the color of the text it contains changes to red. Although you lose the ability to pass data to DOM Level 0 event handlers, you can still access the object where the event fired by using this inside the function.

 The browser actually passes an event object to DOM Level 0 event handlers. You learn about this object in Lessons 21 and 22.

TRY IT

In this lesson, you learn how to use early DOM event handlers.

Lesson Requirements

For this lesson, you need a text editor; any plain text editor will do. For Microsoft Windows users, Notepad is available by default on your system or you can download Microsoft's free Visual Web Developer Express (www.microsoft.com/express/web/) or Web Matrix (www.asp.net/webmatrix/). Mac OS X users can use TextMate, which comes as part of OS X, or download a trial for Coda (www.panic.com/coda/). Linux users can use the built-in VIM.

You also need a modern web browser. Choose any of the following:

- ➤ Internet Explorer 8+
- ➤ Google Chrome
- ➤ Firefox 3.5+
- ➤ Apple Safari 4+
- ➤ Opera 10+

Create a subfolder called `Lesson18` in the `JS24Hour` folder you created in Lesson 1. Store the files you create in this lesson in the `Lesson18` folder.

Step-by-Step

You will rewrite the calculator application from Lesson 17. Instead of using HTML attribute event handlers, you will use the DOM Level 0 event handlers to decouple the HTML from the JavaScript.

1. Open your text editor and type the following HTML:

```html
<html>
<head>
    <title>Lesson 18: Example 01</title>
    <style type="text/css">
    td {
        border: 1px solid gray;
        width: 50px;
    }

    #results {
        height: 20px;
    }
    </style>
</head>
<body>
    <table border="0" cellpadding="2" cellspacing="2">
        <tr>
            <td colspan="4" id="results"></td>
        </tr>
        <tr>
            <td><a href="#">1</a></td>
            <td><a href="#">2</a></td>
            <td><a href="#">3</a></td>
            <td><a href="#">+</a></td>
        </tr>
        <tr>
            <td><a href="#">4</a></td>
            <td><a href="#">5</a></td>
            <td><a href="#">6</a></td>
            <td><a href="#">-</a></td>
        </tr>
        <tr>
            <td><a href="#">7</a></td>
            <td><a href="#">8</a></td>
            <td><a href="#">9</a></td>
            <td><a href="#">*</a></td>
        </tr>
        <tr>
            <td><a href="#">Clear</a></td>
            <td><a href="#">0</a></td>
            <td><a href="#">=</a></td>
            <td><a href="#">/</a></td>
        </tr>
    </table>
```

```
        <script type="text/javascript">
        function addDigit(digit) {
            var resultField = document.getElementById("results");

            resultField.innerHTML += digit;

            return false;
        }

        function calculate() {
            var resultField = document.getElementById("results");

            resultField.innerHTML = eval(resultField.innerHTML);

            return false;
        }

        function reset() {
            var resultField = document.getElementById("results");

            resultField.innerHTML = "";

            return false;
        }
        </script>
    </body>
</html>
```

Save it as `lesson18_example01.htm`. This is almost the exact same page as in Lesson 17; the only differences are the content in the `<title/>` element, that none of the `<a/>` elements use the `onclick` attribute, and that the text of the multiplication link was changed to an asterisk (*) instead of x. The `addDigit()`, `calculate()`, and `reset()` functions remain untouched.

2. Now handle the `load` event as shown by the bold code:

```
<html>
<head>
    <title>Lesson 18: Example 01</title>
    <style type="text/css">
    td {
        border: 1px solid gray;
        width: 50px;
    }

    #results {
        height: 20px;
    }
    </style>
</head>
<body>
    <table border="0" cellpadding="2" cellspacing="2">
        <tr>
            <td colspan="4" id="results"></td>
```

```
        </tr>
        <tr>
            <td><a href="#">1</a></td>
            <td><a href="#">2</a></td>
            <td><a href="#">3</a></td>
            <td><a href="#">+</a></td>
        </tr>
        <tr>
            <td><a href="#">4</a></td>
            <td><a href="#">5</a></td>
            <td><a href="#">6</a></td>
            <td><a href="#">-</a></td>
        </tr>
        <tr>
            <td><a href="#">7</a></td>
            <td><a href="#">8</a></td>
            <td><a href="#">9</a></td>
            <td><a href="#">*</a></td>
        </tr>
        <tr>
            <td><a href="#">Clear</a></td>
            <td><a href="#">0</a></td>
            <td><a href="#">=</a></td>
            <td><a href="#">/</a></td>
        </tr>
    </table>
    <script type="text/javascript">
    function addDigit(digit) {
        var resultField = document.getElementById("results");

        resultField.innerHTML += digit;

        return false;
    }

    function calculate() {
        var resultField = document.getElementById("results");

        resultField.innerHTML = eval(resultField.innerHTML);

        return false;
    }

    function reset() {
        var resultField = document.getElementById("results");

        resultField.innerHTML = "";

        return false;
    }

    onload = function() {
        var links = document.getElementsByTagName("a");
        var length = links.length;
```

```
        };
        </script>
    </body>
</html>
```

This isn't entirely necessary since the code runs after the HTML is loaded into the browser. However, it does keep the global scope from being polluted with unnecessary variables — the links and length variables in this case.

3. Now loop through the elements in the links node list:

```
<html>
<head>
    <title>Lesson 18: Example 01</title>
    <style type="text/css">
    td {
        border: 1px solid gray;
        width: 50px;
    }

    #results {
        height: 20px;
    }
    </style>
</head>
<body>
    <table border="0" cellpadding="2" cellspacing="2">
        <tr>
            <td colspan="4" id="results"></td>
        </tr>
        <tr>
            <td><a href="#">1</a></td>
            <td><a href="#">2</a></td>
            <td><a href="#">3</a></td>
            <td><a href="#">+</a></td>
        </tr>
        <tr>
            <td><a href="#">4</a></td>
            <td><a href="#">5</a></td>
            <td><a href="#">6</a></td>
            <td><a href="#">-</a></td>
        </tr>
        <tr>
            <td><a href="#">7</a></td>
            <td><a href="#">8</a></td>
            <td><a href="#">9</a></td>
            <td><a href="#">*</a></td>
        </tr>
        <tr>
            <td><a href="#">Clear</a></td>
            <td><a href="#">0</a></td>
            <td><a href="#">=</a></td>
            <td><a href="#">/</a></td>
        </tr>
```

```
    </table>
    <script type="text/javascript">
    function addDigit(digit) {
        var resultField = document.getElementById("results");

        resultField.innerHTML += digit;

        return false;
    }

    function calculate() {
        var resultField = document.getElementById("results");

        resultField.innerHTML = eval(resultField.innerHTML);

        return false;
    }

    function reset() {
        var resultField = document.getElementById("results");

        resultField.innerHTML = "";

        return false;
    }

    onload = function() {
        var links = document.getElementsByTagName("a");
        var length = links.length;

        for (var i = 0; i < length; i++) {
            var link = links[i];
            var innerHTML = link.innerHTML;

        }
    };
    </script>
</body>
</html>
```

This is a normal `for` loop, looping through every `<a/>` element in the links node list. The first statement creates two variables, `link` and `innerHTML`. The `link` variable contains the `<a/>` object at the specified index, and the `innerHTML` variable contains the `<a/>` element's HTML.

4. Use a `switch` element to assign the appropriate functionality for each `<a/>` element object. Do so based on the element's `innerHTML`:

```
<html>
<head>
    <title>Lesson 18: Example 01</title>
    <style type="text/css">
    td {
        border: 1px solid gray;
```

```
        width: 50px;
    }

    #results {
        height: 20px;
    }
    </style>
</head>
<body>
    <table border="0" cellpadding="2" cellspacing="2">
        <tr>
            <td colspan="4" id="results"></td>
        </tr>
        <tr>
            <td><a href="#">1</a></td>
            <td><a href="#">2</a></td>
            <td><a href="#">3</a></td>
            <td><a href="#">+</a></td>
        </tr>
        <tr>
            <td><a href="#">4</a></td>
            <td><a href="#">5</a></td>
            <td><a href="#">6</a></td>
            <td><a href="#">-</a></td>
        </tr>
        <tr>
            <td><a href="#">7</a></td>
            <td><a href="#">8</a></td>
            <td><a href="#">9</a></td>
            <td><a href="#">*</a></td>
        </tr>
        <tr>
            <td><a href="#">Clear</a></td>
            <td><a href="#">0</a></td>
            <td><a href="#">=</a></td>
            <td><a href="#">/</a></td>
        </tr>
    </table>
    <script type="text/javascript">
    function addDigit(digit) {
        var resultField = document.getElementById("results");

        resultField.innerHTML += digit;

        return false;
    }

    function calculate() {
        var resultField = document.getElementById("results");

        resultField.innerHTML = eval(resultField.innerHTML);

        return false;
```

```
        }

        function reset() {
            var resultField = document.getElementById("results");

            resultField.innerHTML = "";

            return false;
        }

        onload = function() {
            var links = document.getElementsByTagName("a");
            var length = links.length;

            for (var i = 0; i < length; i++) {
                var link = links[i];
                var innerHTML = link.innerHTML;

                switch (innerHTML) {
                    case "Clear":
                        link.onclick = reset;
                        break;

                    case "=":
                        link.onclick = calculate;
                        break;
                }

            }
        };
        </script>
    </body>
</html>
```

If the link's innerHTML is "Clear", you know it is the link used to clear the contents of
the result field; assign its onclick property the reset() function. Similarly, if the link's
innerHTML is an equals sign (=), assign the calculate() function to the link's onclick
event handler.

5. Wire up the events for the other links:

```
<html>
<head>
    <title>Lesson 18: Example 01</title>
    <style type="text/css">
    td {
        border: 1px solid gray;
        width: 50px;
    }

    #results {
        height: 20px;
    }
    </style>
</head>
```

```
<body>
    <table border="0" cellpadding="2" cellspacing="2">
        <tr>
            <td colspan="4" id="results"></td>
        </tr>
        <tr>
            <td><a href="#">1</a></td>
            <td><a href="#">2</a></td>
            <td><a href="#">3</a></td>
            <td><a href="#">+</a></td>
        </tr>
        <tr>
            <td><a href="#">4</a></td>
            <td><a href="#">5</a></td>
            <td><a href="#">6</a></td>
            <td><a href="#">-</a></td>
        </tr>
        <tr>
            <td><a href="#">7</a></td>
            <td><a href="#">8</a></td>
            <td><a href="#">9</a></td>
            <td><a href="#">*</a></td>
        </tr>
        <tr>
            <td><a href="#">Clear</a></td>
            <td><a href="#">0</a></td>
            <td><a href="#">=</a></td>
            <td><a href="#">/</a></td>
        </tr>
    </table>
    <script type="text/javascript">
    function addDigit(digit) {
        var resultField = document.getElementById("results");

        resultField.innerHTML += digit;

        return false;
    }

    function calculate() {
        var resultField = document.getElementById("results");

        resultField.innerHTML = eval(resultField.innerHTML);

        return false;
    }

    function reset() {
        var resultField = document.getElementById("results");

        resultField.innerHTML = "";

        return false;
```

```
        }

        function getHandlerFunction(innerHTML) {
            return function() {
                addDigit(innerHTML);

                return false;
            };
        }

    onload = function() {
        var links = document.getElementsByTagName("a");
        var length = links.length;

        for (var i = 0; i < length; i++) {
            var link = links[i];
            var innerHTML = link.innerHTML;

            switch (innerHTML) {
                case "Clear":
                    link.onclick = reset;
                    break;

                case "=":
                    link.onclick = calculate;
                    break;

                default:
                    link.onclick = getHandlerFunction(innerHTML);
            }
        }
    };
    </script>
    </body>
    </html>
```

Because there are only two links that have special capabilities (`clear` and `calculate`), the rest of the links can fall under the `default` switch.

To handle the `click` event of these links, write a function called `getHandlerFunction()`, as shown in bold in the preceding code. It should accept one argument containing the element's `innerHTML`, and it should return a function to handle the link's `click` event.

6.   Load the page in your browser. It will behave exactly as Lesson 17's calculator does.

To get the sample code files, you can download Lesson 18 from the book's website at `www.wrox.com`.

 Please select Lesson 18 on the DVD to view the video that accompanies this lesson.

19

Using Standard DOM and IE Event Handlers

One problem with DOM Level 0 event handlers is that only one function can be assigned to an event handler; assigning another function to the same event handler property overwrites any previous function value assigned to that property. This isn't such a big problem if you own all the code within the web page, as you can write one function that calls as many functions as needed, like the following code:

```
onload = function() {
    doSomething();
    doSomethingElse();
    andDoSomethingElse();
};
```

But if you use code written by a third party, it might rely on the same event handler for initialization, like this:

```
// code from third party module or library
onload = function() {
    initializeLibrary();
};
```

If that is the case, the outcome will be one of the following: Either your function overwrites the third party's function or vice versa. Nice, eh? It is fortunate that there is a solution to this particular problem, enabling you to add as many event handlers to a specific event as you want. Unfortunately, the solution varies between browsers that support the standard DOM event model (Firefox, Chrome, Safari, Opera, and Internet Explorer 9) and those that support the Internet Explorer (IE) event model (versions 8 and below; version 9 supports both event models).

STANDARD EVENT HANDLERS

The standard event model, specified in DOM Level 2, centers around two methods that are members of virtually every element object in the DOM. They are addEventListener() and removeEventListener(). Their purpose is to register or remove event handlers (or listeners — as in, they *listen* for the event to fire) on a single object.

Let's look at addEventListener() first. Its usage is fairly straightforward. You first obtain an object to call the method on, such as window or an element object from the DOM. Then you call the addEventListener() method and pass it three arguments:

➤   The event to handle or listen for (click, mouseover, mouseout, load, etc.)

➤   The function to call when the event fires

➤   A Boolean value indicating whether to use *event capture* or *event bubbling*

Before we get any further, let's talk about event capture and bubbling.

Life as a client-side developer in the late 1990s was tough. OK, that's a lie. It was one of Dante's nine circles of Hell. The two browsers vying for dominance were Netscape 4 and Microsoft Internet Explorer 4. These browsers had different and incompatible DOMs, and thus different event models. Netscape 4's event model captured the event, whereas Internet Explorer used event bubbling.

When it came time for the W3C to work on a standard for an event model, it took both implementations and fused them together. So in the standard event model there are three phases to an event:

➤   Event capturing

➤   The event reaches the event target (the object in the DOM you specified a listener for).

➤   Event bubbling

That's great, but what does it all mean? Consider an HTML document with the structure shown in Figure 19-1, and imagine that an event listener is listening for the click event on the <span/> element.

FIGURE 19-1

When the user clicks that element the capture phase begins, and the click event is first received by the window — or, rather, the window captures the event and executes any click event listeners for the document. The event then moves down to the document that captures and executes any click event listeners for the document. The event continues down to the next element, the <div/> element, and captures and executes any click event listeners for that element. From there, the <p/> element captures the event (and executes any click listeners for that element). Then the event finally reaches the target, the <span/> element, and the listeners for the click event on the target execute. So, with event capturing, the event starts at the top of the document's tree (the document object), and gets passed down to each descendant, executing every click event listener for each descendant, until it reaches the target (Figure 19-2).

When the event finally reaches the event target, the bubbling phase begins — bubbling is the exact opposite of capture. The event starts at the target (the <span/> element in this case) and executes the click event listeners for the target. The event then bubbles up to each parent in the DOM tree, executing the click listeners at each parent until it reaches the window object (Figure 19-3).

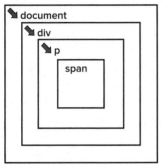

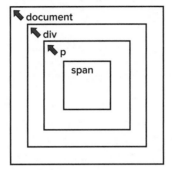

FIGURE 19-2   **FIGURE 19-3**

In standards-compliant browsers you have to choose whether you want to use event capture or event bubbling. Since the only version of Internet Explorer to support the standard event model is IE9, the decision is practically made for you: bubbling. That is, of course, if you want your code to work the same in all browsers. In other words, the third argument passed to addEventListener() is almost always false, meaning bubbling (passing true indicates capture).

Let's finally apply this with some code. The following is an example of addEventListener() in use:

```
var spanEl = document.getElementById("someElement");

function clickHandler1() {
    alert("You clicked me!");
}

function clickHandler2() {
    alert("You clicked me (I like repeating myself)!");
}

spanEl.addEventListener("click", clickHandler1, false);

spanEl.addEventListener("click", clickHandler2, false);
```

This code first retrieves an element from the document with getElementById(). Then, two functions are defined; both will handle the click event for the <span/> element. It then calls addEventListener() to add a listener for the click event on this element (notice the omission of on), and the listener is set to use event bubbling. Then another event listener is registered for the click event using the clickHandler2() function. When the user clicks this <span/> element an alert box will display the text "You clicked me!" Then, after the user clicks the box's OK button, another alert box will display the text "You clicked me (I like repeating myself)!" When you assign multiple functions to handle the same event on the same object, the functions are called in the order they are assigned.

If you want to remove a listener registered with `addEventListener()`, use the `removeEventListener()` method. It accepts the same three arguments passed to `addEventListener()`, and the values passed to `removeEventListener()` must exactly match the values that were passed to `addEventListener()` when you registered the listener. For example, the following code shows the incorrect and the correct ways to remove the second listener registered in the previous code:

```
// incorrect
spanEl.removeEventListener("click", clickHandler2, true);

// correct
spanEl.removeEventListener("click", clickHandler2, false);
```

In the first statement, the third argument passed to `removeEventListener()` is `true`; the statement attempts to remove a listener for the `click` event with the provided function, which is using event capture. While this statement does not result in an error, it is incorrect because the listener was registered to use event bubbling.

Now look at the second statement. It too attempts to remove a listener for the `click` event with the provided function, and the third argument is `false`. Since all three values match the values originally passed to `addEventListener()`, that specific listener is removed and the associated function will not execute when the event fires.

 In the standard event model, the `this` variable used inside a function handling an event refers to the object that fired the event.

IE EVENT HANDLERS

Around the time that the W3C was working on the DOM Level 2 event specification, Microsoft released version 5 of IE. The browser offered new ways to register and unregister event handlers: the `attachEvent()` and `detachEvent()` methods.

Using these two methods is similar to using the standard event model; you retrieve an object from the document, call the `attachEvent()` method to register an event handler (or `detachEvent()` to remove a handler) and pass it two arguments:

➤ The event, prepended with `on`, to handle

➤ The function to execute when the event fires

The proprietary IE event model doesn't support event capture — only bubbling. So there is no third parameter for these methods. The following code shows the IE equivalent of the registration code in the previous section:

```
var spanEl = document.getElementById("someElement");

spanEl.attachEvent("onclick", clickHandler1);

spanEl.attachEvent("onclick", clickHandler2);
```

Here the attachEvent() method is called twice, registering two onclick event handlers. Notice the use of on in onclick. Unlike with addEventListener() and removeEventListener(), you must use the name of the event handler as opposed to the name of the event. The result of this code is almost the same as earlier: Two alert boxes display two messages when the <span/> element is clicked. Except in this case, the handlers are executed in reverse order. Unlike addEventListener(), multiple functions assigned to handle the same event on the same object execute in the reverse order of how they were assigned.

Removing the second event handler is as simple as calling detachEvent() and passing the same values:

```
// remove the second listener
spanEl.detachEvent("onclick", clickHandler2);
```

In the proprietary IE event model, the this *variable used inside a function handling an event refers to the* window *object.*

TRY IT

In this lesson, you learn how to assign event handlers using standard and IE methods.

Lesson Requirements

For this lesson, you need a text editor; any plain text editor will do. For Microsoft Windows users, Notepad is available by default on your system or you can download Microsoft's free Visual Web Developer Express (www.microsoft.com/express/web/) or Web Matrix (www.asp.net/webmatrix/). Mac OS X users can use TextMate, which comes as part of OS X, or download a trial for Coda (www.panic.com/coda/). Linux users can use the built-in VIM.

You also need a modern web browser. Choose any of the following:

- ➤ Internet Explorer 8+
- ➤ Google Chrome
- ➤ Firefox 3.5+
- ➤ Apple Safari 4+
- ➤ Opera 10+

Create a subfolder called Lesson19 in the JS24Hour folder you created in Lesson 1. Store the files you create in this lesson in the Lesson19 folder.

Step-by-Step

You will rewrite the calculator application from Lesson 18 using standard and IE-specific event handlers.

1. Open your text editor and type the following HTML:

```
<html>
<head>
    <title>Lesson 19: Example 01</title>
    <style type="text/css">
    td {
        border: 1px solid gray;
        width: 50px;
    }

    #results {
        height: 20px;
    }
    </style>
</head>
<body>
    <table border="0" cellpadding="2" cellspacing="2">
        <tr>
            <td colspan="4" id="results"></td>
        </tr>
        <tr>
            <td><a href="#">1</a></td>
            <td><a href="#">2</a></td>
            <td><a href="#">3</a></td>
            <td><a href="#">+</a></td>
        </tr>
        <tr>
            <td><a href="#">4</a></td>
            <td><a href="#">5</a></td>
            <td><a href="#">6</a></td>
            <td><a href="#">-</a></td>
        </tr>
        <tr>
            <td><a href="#">7</a></td>
            <td><a href="#">8</a></td>
            <td><a href="#">9</a></td>
            <td><a href="#">*</a></td>
        </tr>
        <tr>
            <td><a href="#">Clear</a></td>
            <td><a href="#">0</a></td>
            <td><a href="#">=</a></td>
            <td><a href="#">/</a></td>
        </tr>
    </table>
    <script type="text/javascript">
    function addDigit(digit) {
```

```javascript
        var resultField = document.getElementById("results");

        resultField.innerHTML += digit;

        return false;
}

function calculate() {
        var resultField = document.getElementById("results");

        resultField.innerHTML = eval(resultField.innerHTML);

        return false;
}

function reset() {
        var resultField = document.getElementById("results");

        resultField.innerHTML = "";

        return false;
}

function getHandlerFunction(innerHTML) {
        return function() {
            addDigit(innerHTML);

            return false;
        };
}

onload = function() {
        var links = document.getElementsByTagName("a");
        var length = links.length;

        for (var i = 0; i < length; i++) {
            var link = links[i];
            var innerHTML = link.innerHTML;
            var func = null;

            switch (innerHTML) {
                case "Clear":
                    func = reset;
                    break;

                case "=":
                    func = calculate;
                    break;

                default:
                    func = getHandlerFunction(innerHTML);
            }

            link.addEventListener("click", func, false);
```

```
        }
    };
    </script>
</body>
</html>
```

Save it as `lesson19_example01.htm`. There are a few changes in this version, and the important ones are in bold. A new variable, called `func`, is declared and initialized as `null`. The purpose of this variable is to contain the function used in the call to `addEventListener()`, making the code a little easier to read while saving you from typing `link.addEventListener()` several times.

The `case` statements within the `switch` block remain the same, except that `func` is assigned the appropriate function in each case. Finally, a new line is added to the `for` loop, adding a `click` event listener to the `<a/>` element.

2. Now copy and paste that code into a new instance of your text editor. Make the changes specified in the following code (the changes are in bold):

```
<html>
<head>
    <title>Lesson 19: Example 02</title>
    <style type="text/css">
    td {
        border: 1px solid gray;
        width: 50px;
    }

    #results {
        height: 20px;
    }
    </style>
</head>
<body>
    <table border="0" cellpadding="2" cellspacing="2">
        <tr>
            <td colspan="4" id="results"></td>
        </tr>
        <tr>
            <td><a href="#">1</a></td>
            <td><a href="#">2</a></td>
            <td><a href="#">3</a></td>
            <td><a href="#">+</a></td>
        </tr>
        <tr>
            <td><a href="#">4</a></td>
            <td><a href="#">5</a></td>
            <td><a href="#">6</a></td>
            <td><a href="#">-</a></td>
        </tr>
        <tr>
            <td><a href="#">7</a></td>
            <td><a href="#">8</a></td>
```

```
        <td><a href="#">9</a></td>
        <td><a href="#">*</a></td>
    </tr>
    <tr>
        <td><a href="#">Clear</a></td>
        <td><a href="#">0</a></td>
        <td><a href="#">=</a></td>
        <td><a href="#">/</a></td>
    </tr>
</table>
<script type="text/javascript">
function addDigit(digit) {
    var resultField = document.getElementById("results");

    resultField.innerHTML += digit;

    return false;
}

function calculate() {
    var resultField = document.getElementById("results");

    resultField.innerHTML = eval(resultField.innerHTML);

    return false;
}

function reset() {
    var resultField = document.getElementById("results");

    resultField.innerHTML = "";

    return false;
}

function getHandlerFunction(innerHTML) {
    return function() {
        addDigit(innerHTML);

        return false;
    };
}

onload = function() {
    var links = document.getElementsByTagName("a");
    var length = links.length;

    for (var i = 0; i < length; i++) {
        var link = links[i];
        var innerHTML = link.innerHTML;
        var func = null;

        switch (innerHTML) {
            case "Clear":
```

```
                    func = reset;
                    break;

              case "=":
                    func = calculate;
                    break;

              default:
                    func = getHandlerFunction(innerHTML);
           }

           link.attachEvent("onclick", func);
        }
     };
     </script>
  </body>
</html>
```

Save this as `lesson19_example02.htm`. The changes make it work with IE —
`addEventListener()` becomes `attachEvent()`, on is added to `click`, and the third
parameter originally passed to `addEventListener()` is removed.

3.   Open each file in the appropriate browser to test it. You'll see that the application works
very much as it did in Lesson 17 and Lesson 18.

To get the sample code files, you can download Lesson 19 from the book's website at `www.wrox.com`.

 *Please select Lesson 19 on the DVD to view the video that accompanies this
lesson.*

20

Writing Cross-Browser Event Handlers

In ye olden days, the common approach to cross-browser scripting was similar to the solution at the end of Lesson 19: Create multiple pages for each browser type. The solution worked, but the amount of time involved grew according to how many different browsers you wanted to support. As years moved on, the accepted approach was simply to branch code (using an `if` statement to determine what method to use) when needed, like this:

```
// assume el variable is an element object
if (typeof addEventListener === "function") {
    el.addEventListener("click", function() {
        alert("You clicked me!");
    }, false);
} else if (typeof attachEvent !== "undefined") {
    el.attachEvent("onclick", function() {
        alert("You clicked me!");
    });
} else {
    el.onclick = function() {
        alert("You clicked me!");
    };
}
```

What you see here is a type of browser detection called *feature detection* — the detection of certain features, like `addEventListener()`. The idea is to determine whether the browser supports a particular feature and, if so, to use it. If the feature isn't supported, you fall back to a feature you know will work. In the preceding example the code checks for the `addEventListener()` method (which all standards-compliant browsers support) and uses it if it is found. If the browser does not support `addEventListener()`, then the code attempts to identify the browser as a version of IE and, if so, uses `attachEvent()`. If the browser does not support either `addEventListener()` or `attachEvent()`, then the code falls back to the DOM Level 0 `onclick` event handler.

The JavaScript engine in IE8 and below can do quirky things because of how different components in the browser are made. For example `typeof attachEvent` *actually returns "object" instead of "function." That is why the preceding code checks if* `attachEvent` *is not undefined. User-defined functions, however, are type "function."*

Most of the time, however, you write code for two types of browsers: standard compliant browsers and IE8 and below. So, the preceding code can be simplified to the following:

```
// assume el variable is an element object
if (typeof addEventListener === "function") {
    el.addEventListener("click", function() {
        alert("You clicked me!");
    }, false);
} else {
    el.attachEvent("onclick", function() {
        alert("You clicked me!");
    });
}
```

This code follows the same idea as before, except now `attachEvent()` is the fallback instead of the DOM Level 0 `onclick` event handler.

How you check for a feature is important. Nine times out of ten you want to check for standards compliance first because the standards will rarely change. For example, you can check for `attachEvent()` first, such as this:

```
// WRONG!
if (typeof attachEvent !== "undefined") {
    el.attachEvent("onclick", function() {
        alert("You clicked me!");
    });
} else {
    el.addEventListener("click", function() {
        alert("You clicked me!");
    }, false);
}
```

This does work, but consider the case of IE 9. It supports not only its own proprietary event model, but the standard event model as well. As a developer, you want to use the features put forth by the standards as much as possible, and you can ensure that this happens by checking for standard features before proprietary ones.

Now, in the old days, code branching such as this would be littered throughout a JavaScript file. Naturally, the next evolution was to refactor that code into its own function, like this:

```
function setEventHandler(obj, evt, fn) {
    if (typeof addEventListener === "function") {
        obj.addEventListener(evt, fn, false);
    } else {
        obj.attachEvent("on" + evt, fn);
```

```
    }
}

setEventHandler(el, "click", function() {
    alert("You clicked me!");
});
```

This code creates a function called `setEventHandler()`. It accepts three arguments: the object to assign an event handler to, the name of the event to handle (without the on prefix), and the function to handle the event. Inside the function, an `if` statement determines whether `addEventListener()` or `attachEvent()` should be used to assign an event handler to the provided object. Notice the call to `attachEvent()` inside the `else` block. Remember that the name of the event was passed to the function without the on prefix, so the prefix must be added in the call to `attachEvent()`.

The final statement of this code shows how the function is called by adding a `click` event handler on an element object. This way you call the `setEventHandler()` function whenever you need to wire up events for a particular object. But this approach, too, has its own drawbacks — one being suboptimal performance. Every call to `setEventHandler()` causes a slight performance hit for the following reasons:

➤ The JavaScript engine has to make a decision before it can execute `addEventListener()` or `attachEvent()`. This decision takes longer than simply executing one of the event handler methods.

➤ The engine has to look up the `addEventListener` identifier.

These problems bring us to modern JavaScript techniques, which you study in this lesson.

WRITING AN EVENT UTILITY OBJECT

Every aspect of JavaScript programming in the browser is object-oriented. Naturally, any tools and utilities you write should also incorporate object-oriented concepts that organize your code into one or more objects. In the case of events, you'll begin work on an object containing utility methods that work in all modern browsers.

Start by creating an object called `eventUtility`, shown in the following code:

```
var eventUtility = {};
```

This code uses object literal notation to create a singleton object. You do not need to create a new data type for this utility because it does not need any instance data; it's simply a utility in which all the necessary data is passed to its methods. Now add an `if` statement to branch your code, as shown before. Check if `addEventListener` is a feature supported by the browser:

```
var eventUtility = {};

if (typeof addEventListener === "function") {

} else {

}
```

Now the `eventUtility` object needs a method to add event handlers to an object. Call this method `addEvent`, and assign it a function that calls either `addEventListener()` or `attachEvent()`, such as the following code in bold:

```
var eventUtility = {};

if (typeof addEventListener === "function") {
    eventUtility.addEvent = function(obj, evt, fn) {
        obj.addEventListener(evt, fn, false);
    };
} else {
    eventUtility.addEvent = function(obj, evt, fn) {
        obj.attachEvent("on" + evt, fn);
    };
}
```

This new code creates an `addEvent()` method as a member of the `eventUtility` object. Actually, there are two definitions of `addEvent()`, but only one is actually assigned to `eventUtility.addEvent`. Notice the three parameters of `addEvent()` in both declarations; they are the same. This is very important because you want to be able to call `addEvent()` and have it work correctly regardless of what browser the user is using. The following code will add an event handler to an element to handle the `click` event, and it'll work in any modern browser (even IE6):

```
eventUtility.addEvent(el, "click", function() {
    alert("You clicked me!");
});
```

Let's take a look and see how this is more advantageous to the `setEventHandler()` function shown at the beginning of this lesson.

➤ Now the `if` statement, with its attendant performance problems (with the `addEventListener` lookup and the actual decision), is executed only once — when the browser loads the code. Unfortunately, this decision cannot be circumvented.

➤ The `addEvent()` method is immediately available to call because the browser executes the `if ... else` statement and assignment operations immediately after the browser loads the JavaScript code — much as it does with the `setEventHandler()` function.

➤ Calls to `addEvent()` execute only the code needed to assign an event handler to an object. There are no decisions or extraneous lookups for other identifiers. This is in contrast to `setEventHandler()`, which needs extra code in order to work.

Even though the `eventUtility` object makes working with events a little easier (and faster), the implementation doesn't quite match that of techniques used by modern-day JavaScript experts. So let's look at how this code can be transformed into modern-day JavaScript.

MODERNIZING YOUR EVENT UTILITY

An updated `eventUtility` object starts as before with an object literal:

```
var eventUtility = {};
```

Next, add a method called `addEvent()` to the object, like this:

```
var eventUtility = {
    addEvent : function() {

    }
};
```

Notice that this method does not specify any parameters. That is because this function declaration is actually going to execute and return another function to `addEvent`. Let's add some of that code now:

```
var eventUtility = {
    addEvent : function() {

    }()
};
```

The only thing this code adds is a set of parentheses at the end of the function statement. Remember that in order for a function to execute, the function's identifier must be followed by a set of parentheses, as in this call to `alert()`:

```
alert("Hello, JavaScript!");
```

You can apply the same concept to anonymous functions by simply adding a set of parentheses to the end of the function statement, like this:

```
function() {
    alert("Hello, JavaScript!");
}();
```

This code doesn't actually work because it has a syntax error, but you can make it work by surrounding the function and parentheses with another set of parentheses, like this:

```
(function() {
    alert("Hello, JavaScript!");
}());
```

So when the JavaScript engine loads this code, it executes the anonymous function that, in turn, executes the `alert()` method inside it. This type of function is sometimes referred to as a *self-executing function*.

Returning to your event utility object, you have an anonymous function that executes after the browser loads the JavaScript code, but it isn't returning anything worthwhile to `addEvent`. So let's change that with the following bold code:

```
var eventUtility = {
    addEvent : (function() {
```

```
            if (typeof addEventListener === "function") {
                return function(obj, evt, fn) {
                    obj.addEventListener(evt, fn, false);
                };
            }
        }())
    };
```

This new code first encapsulates the self-executing function in parentheses. It then adds an `if` block that looks somewhat similar to code in your original `eventUtility` code; it returns a function to `addEvent` as opposed to directly assigning the function to `eventUtility.addEvent` as in the previous version. Let's finish this new version by adding an `else` block for browsers that do not support `addEventListener`. The new code is in bold:

```
var eventUtility = {
    addEvent : (function() {
        if (typeof addEventListener === "function") {
            return function(obj, evt, fn) {
                obj.addEventListener(evt, fn, false);
            };
        } else {
            return function(obj, evt, fn) {
                obj.attachEvent("on" + evt, fn, false);
            };
        }
    }())
};
```

Once again, the contents of the `else` block are somewhat similar to those of the previous version. The main difference is that a function is returned to `addEvent` instead of being assigned directly; the end result, however, is the same. When the self-executing function does its thing, it returns one of two functions to `addEvent`; which function depends on what event model the browser supports.

This event utility, as shown in this lesson, does not offer a means to remove an event handler. However, the code in the Try It section, as well as the code download, does. The functionality operates according to the same principles discussed in this lesson.

TRY IT

In this lesson, you learn how to write your own event utility to handle cross-browser issues.

Lesson Requirements

For this lesson, you need a text editor; any plain text editor will do. For Microsoft Windows users, Notepad is available by default on your system or you can download Microsoft's free Visual Web

Developer Express (www.microsoft.com/express/web/) or Web Matrix (www.asp.net/webmatrix/). Mac OS X users can use TextMate, which comes as part of OS X, or download a trial for Coda (www.panic.com/coda/). Linux users can use the built-in VIM.

You also need a modern web browser. Choose any of the following:

- ➤ Internet Explorer 8+
- ➤ Google Chrome
- ➤ Firefox 3.5+
- ➤ Apple Safari 4+
- ➤ Opera 10+

Create a subfolder called Lesson20 in the JS24Hour folder you created in Lesson 1. Store the files you create in this lesson in the Lesson20 folder.

Step-by-Step

You will rewrite the calculator application from Lessons 17, 18, and 19 using the event utility object.

1. Open your text editor and type the following JavaScript:

```
var eventUtility = {
    addEvent : (function() {
        if (typeof addEventListener === "function") {
            return function(obj, evt, fn) {
                obj.addEventListener(evt, fn, false);
            };
        } else {
            return function(obj, evt, fn) {
                obj.attachEvent("on" + evt, fn);
            };
        }
    }()),
    removeEvent : (function() {
        if (typeof removeEventListener === "function") {
            return function(obj, evt, fn) {
                obj.removeEventListener(evt, fn, false);
            };
        } else {
            return function(obj, evt, fn) {
                obj.detachEvent("on" + evt, fn);
            };
        }
    }())
};
```

Save it as eventutility.js.

2. Now open another instance of your text editor and type the following HTML:

```html
<html>
<head>
    <title>Lesson 20: Example 02</title>
    <style type="text/css">
    td {
        border: 1px solid gray;
        width: 50px;
    }

    #results {
        height: 20px;
    }
    </style>
</head>
<body>
    <table border="0" cellpadding="2" cellspacing="2">
        <tr>
            <td colspan="4" id="results"></td>
        </tr>
        <tr>
            <td><a href="#">1</a></td>
            <td><a href="#">2</a></td>
            <td><a href="#">3</a></td>
            <td><a href="#">+</a></td>
        </tr>
        <tr>
            <td><a href="#">4</a></td>
            <td><a href="#">5</a></td>
            <td><a href="#">6</a></td>
            <td><a href="#">-</a></td>
        </tr>
        <tr>
            <td><a href="#">7</a></td>
            <td><a href="#">8</a></td>
            <td><a href="#">9</a></td>
            <td><a href="#">*</a></td>
        </tr>
        <tr>
            <td><a href="#">Clear</a></td>
            <td><a href="#">0</a></td>
            <td><a href="#">=</a></td>
            <td><a href="#">/</a></td>
        </tr>
    </table>
    <script type="text/javascript" src="eventutility.js"></script>
    <script type="text/javascript">
    function addDigit(digit) {
        var resultField = document.getElementById("results");

        resultField.innerHTML += digit;

        return false;
```

```
        }

        function calculate() {
            var resultField = document.getElementById("results");

            resultField.innerHTML = eval(resultField.innerHTML);

            return false;
        }

        function reset() {
            var resultField = document.getElementById("results");

            resultField.innerHTML = "";

            return false;
        }

        function getHandlerFunction(innerHTML) {
            return function() {
                addDigit(innerHTML);

                return false;
            };
        }

        onload = function() {
            var links = document.getElementsByTagName("a"),
                length = links.length;

            for (var i = 0; i < length; i++) {
                var link = links[i],
                    innerHTML = link.innerHTML,
                    func = null;

                switch (innerHTML) {
                    case "Clear":
                        func = reset;
                        break;

                    case "=":
                        func = calculate;
                        break;

                    default:
                        func = getHandlerFunction(innerHTML);
                }

                eventUtility.addEvent(link, "click", func);
            }
        };
    </script>
</body>
</html>
```

Save it as `lesson20_example01.htm`. Not much changed in this version. The `eventUtility` object contained within the external JavaScript file is referenced, and the utility is used to assign the `click` event handlers to the `<a/>` element objects. Open this file in multiple browsers and you'll find that it works in them all.

To get the sample code files, you can download Lesson 20 from the book's website at `www.wrox.com`.

 Please select Lesson 20 on the DVD to view the video that accompanies this lesson.

21

The Standard Event Object

Over the course of the past several lessons you've learned how you can handle events with HTML attributes, DOM object properties, and DOM object methods. But one vital piece of information has been withheld from you: how to access a special object that contains information about any event. Not surprisingly, the manner in which you access this object differs according to the user's browser: standards-supporting browsers use the standard Event object, and legacy versions of Internet Explorer (IE) use their own proprietary event object.

This lesson focuses on the standard Event object. You'll be introduced to IE's legacy event object in the next lesson.

ACCESSING THE EVENT OBJECT

When you have a moment, flip through the previous lessons regarding event handling. Pay attention to the functions assigned to handle events; notice that none of these functions accept any arguments. This is by design, as you, the developer, do not call event handlers; the browser does. So, it makes little sense to write a function that accepts arguments.

Or does it?

In actuality, the functions you wire to events should accept one argument, because, according to the standard event model, the browser passes an Event object to the function handling an event, like this:

```
eventUtility.addEvent(document, "click", function(event) {
    alert(event);
});
```

This code sets an event handler on the document object for the click event. When you click anywhere on the page, you see an alert box similar to that shown in Figure 21-1 (assuming a standards-compliant browser).

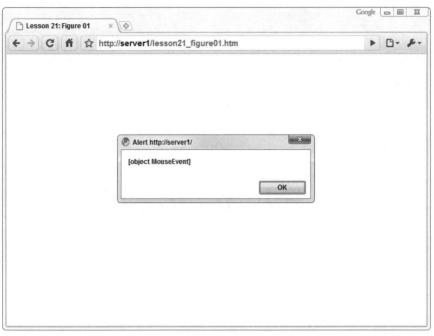

FIGURE 21-1

The MouseEvent mentioned in Figure 21-1 is a data type that inherits from Event, and it contains information related to the click event, such as which mouse button was clicked, the mouse pointer's coordinates, and a variety of other information. You'll look at MouseEvent objects in future lessons. For now, let's just focus on basic Event objects.

EVENT OBJECTS

Most of the time an Event object contains the majority of information you'll want about a particular event. It contains information regarding the type of event that occurred and the element that received the event.

Determining the Event That Occurred

To determine what event took place, you use the type property, like this:

```
eventUtility.addEvent(document, "click", function(event) {
    alert(event.type); // click
});
```

This property returns a string containing the name of the event (without a preceding on). This is extremely helpful when you use one function to handle a variety of events. For example, look at the following code:

```
function eventHandler(event) {
    if (event.type === "click") {
```

```
        alert("You clicked me!");
    } else if (event.type === "keypress") {
        alert("You pressed a key!");
    }
}

eventUtility.addEvent(document, "click", eventHandler);

eventUtility.addEvent(document, "keypress", eventHandler);
```

In this code a function called `eventHandler()` accepts an argument called `event` (event is the modern conventional identifier for the parameter of event handlers. Sometimes you may see just plain e used; that's old-school). Inside the function, an `if` statement determines whether or not the event that caused the function to execute was the `click` event. If so, an alert box displays the message "You clicked me!" There's also an `else...if` statement that checks if the event was the `keypress` event, and an alert box says, "You pressed a key!" if this event did indeed fire. The two final lines of this code set the `eventHandler()` function to handle the `click` and `keypress` events on the `document` object.

Using one function to handle a variety of events is actually quite common; the ability to discern what type of event occurred is an important ability that the `Event` object gives you.

Accessing the Event Target

Another piece of vital information `Event` objects provide you with is the `target` property. This property returns the DOM element object associated with the element that received the event. So if you wanted to you could manipulate the element that received the event, or use the element to locate a sibling or parent element using the DOM properties you learned about in Lesson 13. Let's look at an example that uses the following HTML:

```
<body>
    <div id="divElement"
        style="width: 100px; height: 100px; background-color: red; "></div>
</body>
```

This is a snippet of an HTML page showing the contents of the `<body/>` element. It has a `<div/>` element styled to look like a red square. You can set up an event handler to change the background color of this element when it is clicked, and you can do so in a variety of ways. One is to assign a `click` event handler for the `<div/>` element itself, like this:

```
eventUtility.addEvent(document.getElementById("divElement"), "click",
function(event) {
    var bgColor = event.target.style.backgroundColor;
    var color = "red";

    if (bgColor === color) {
        color = "green";
    }

    event.target.style.backgroundColor = color;
});
```

This event handler toggles the background color of this `<div/>` element between red and green. The first statement of the event handler creates two variables: one to contain the current background color of the element, called `bgColor`, and another to contain the text "red," called `color`.

The next statement determines the element's background color. If it is currently red, `color` is changed to `green`; otherwise, `color` stays as `red`. The final line changes the element's `backgroundColor` to the value contained within the `color` variable.

This code works, but what if you want to add another `<div/>` element to the document and provide the same functionality for it? Here's the HTML:

```
<body>
    <div id="divElement"
         style="width: 100px; height: 100px; background-color: red; "></div>
<br/><br/>
    <div id="divElement2"
         style="width: 100px; height: 100px; background-color: red; "></div>

</body>
```

Well, you could set up another `click` event handler for the new element, but a better solution is to use something called *event delegation*. Event delegation is a technique whereby you set a single event handler on a parent element. This way any event that occurs within that parent element, including its children, gets fired, and the event's target is whatever element (the parent or children) the event originated at.

This might be easier to understand with Figure 21-2.

Figure 21-2 shows an element that contains two child elements. Assume a `click` event handler is set on the parent element. You can click anywhere within the bounds of the parent element, and the click event is handled by your handler. This includes Child-A and Child-B. So when you click Child-B, it receives the click event, but because it is a child of the parent (and because the event bubbles up to the parent), the event handler executes and the event's target is Child-B.

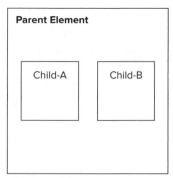

FIGURE 21-2

So, forget all about the event handler for the `divElement` `<div/>` element, and look at the following code, which uses event delegation:

```
eventUtility.addEvent(document, "click", function(event) {
    var eSrc = event.target;

    if (eSrc.tagName.toUpperCase() === "DIV") {
        var bgColor = eSrc.style.backgroundColor;
        var color = "red";

        if (bgColor === color) {
            color = "green";
        }

        eSrc.style.backgroundColor = color;
```

```
        }
    });
```

One thing about event delegation: It does involve a little bit more code. So let's look at it starting with the first line. A variable called `eSrc` is set to contain the event's target; it makes referring to the event target much easier (`eSrc` is your author's convention for naming this variable; it is short for "event source").

The next bit of code uses the `tagName` property to determine whether the element is a `<div/>` element (the `tagName` property usually returns the element's tag name in all-uppercase letters, but in some instances, like with XHTML documents, it doesn't. So, it's a good habit to use `toUpperCase()` to ensure uniformity. Remember that because the `click` event handler was set up on the `document` object, any mouse click anywhere in the page will cause the `click` event to fire and the event handler to execute. So you need to ensure that the event target is the element that you want to manipulate. In the case of this example, we want to manipulate any `<div/>` element in the page, so our simple check of the element's `tagName` property is sufficient. From there the code is largely the same as before. The code determines the element's background color and changes it.

When you need to handle one or more events on a variety of elements, use event delegation. It actually performs better and more efficiently than one or more event handlers set on a variety of elements.

The event's type and target are major pieces of information, and you'll use them quite often. Let's apply this knowledge with a simple example.

TRY IT

In this lesson you learn how to retrieve basic information regarding an event in the standard event model.

Lesson Requirements

For this lesson, you need a text editor; any plain text editor will do. For Microsoft Windows users, Notepad is available by default on your system or you can download Microsoft's free Visual Web Developer Express (www.microsoft.com/express/web/) or Web Matrix (www.asp.net/webmatrix/). Mac OS X users can use TextMate, which comes as part of OS X, or download a trial for Coda (www.panic.com/coda/). Linux users can use the built-in VIM.

You also need a modern web browser. Choose any of the following:

➤   Internet Explorer 8+

➤   Google Chrome

➤   Firefox 3.5+

➤   Apple Safari 4+

➤   Opera 10+

Create a subfolder called `Lesson21` in the `JS24Hour` folder you created in Lesson 1. Store the files you create in this lesson in the `Lesson21` folder.

Step-by-Step

You will write a simple toolbar with three buttons. They will have a normal state, a state when the mouse pointer moves over them, and a state when they're clicked. Use event delegation to handle the events for the buttons.

1. Open your text editor and type the following HTML:

```
<html>
<head>
    <title>Lesson 21: Example 01</title>
    <style type="text/css">
        #divContainer {
            background-color: silver;
            height: 50px;
            padding: 2px;
        }

        span {
            display: inline-block;
            width: 50px;
            height: 50px;
        }

        .button-normal {
            background-color: gray;
        }

        .button-over {
            background-color: navy;
        }

        .button-click {
            background-color: yellow;
        }
    </style>
</head>
<body>
    <div id="divContainer">
        <span class="button-normal">

        </span>
        <span class="button-normal">

        </span>
        <span class="button-normal">

        </span>
    </div>
    <script type="text/javascript" src="eventutility.js"></script>
```

```
    <script type="text/javascript">

    </script>
</body>
</html>
```

Save it as `lesson21_example01.htm`. There's nothing very exciting here. A `<div/>` element contains three `<span/>` elements, and they're styled to look like a rough, oversize toolbar. There are three CSS classes of note: `button-normal`, `button-over`, and `button-click`. These three classes are the three different states a button can be in.

2. Now add the bold JavaScript code:

```
<html>
<head>
    <title>Lesson 21: Example 01</title>
    <style type="text/css">
        #divContainer {
            background-color: silver;
            height: 50px;
            padding: 2px;
        }

        span {
            display: inline-block;
            width: 50px;
            height: 50px;
        }

        .button-normal {
            background-color: gray;
        }

        .button-over {
            background-color: navy;
        }

        .button-click {
            background-color: yellow;
        }
    </style>
</head>
<body>
    <div id="divContainer">
        <span class="button-normal">

        </span>
        <span class="button-normal">

        </span>
        <span class="button-normal">

        </span>
```

```
    </div>
    <script type="text/javascript" src="eventutility.js"></script>
    <script type="text/javascript">
    function mouseHandler(event) {
        var eSrc = event.target;
        var type = event.type;

        if (eSrc.tagName.toUpperCase() === "SPAN") {

        }
    }
    </script>
</body>
</html>
```

This code adds a function called `mouseHandler()`, and it accepts a single argument that the browser passes to the function. The first statement creates two variables, `eSrc` and `type`. These variables hold the event target and event type, respectively.

After the variable declarations, an `if` statement determines if the event target is a `<span/>` element. This check is sufficient since they're the only `<span/>` elements in the document. If there were other `<span/>` elements, you could use the `className` property to determine whether the target had one of the three CSS classes.

3. Now add more code; it's bold in the following:

```
<html>
<head>
    <title>Lesson 21: Example 01</title>
    <style type="text/css">
        #divContainer {
            background-color: silver;
            height: 50px;
            padding: 2px;
        }

        span {
            display: inline-block;
            width: 50px;
            height: 50px;
        }

        .button-normal {
            background-color: gray;
        }

        .button-over {
            background-color: navy;
        }

        .button-click {
            background-color: yellow;
        }
    </style>
```

```
    </head>
    <body>
        <div id="divContainer">
            <span class="button-normal">

            </span>
            <span class="button-normal">

            </span>
            <span class="button-normal">

            </span>
        </div>
        <script type="text/javascript" src="eventutility.js"></script>
        <script type="text/javascript">
        function mouseHandler(event) {
            var eSrc = event.target;
            var type = event.type;

            if (eSrc.tagName.toUpperCase() === "SPAN") {
                if (type === "mouseover") {
                    if (eSrc.className !== "button-click") {
                        eSrc.className = "button-over";
                    }
                } else if (type === "mouseout") {
                    if (eSrc.className !== "button-click") {
                        eSrc.className = "button-normal";
                    }
                } else if (type === "click") {
                    if (eSrc.className !== "button-click") {
                        eSrc.className = "button-click";
                    } else {
                        eSrc.className = "button-over";
                    }
                }
            }
        }
        </script>
    </body>
</html>
```

This code goes through an if ... else if ... else if chain checking for the different event types. If a mouseover event occurs, you want to change the element's className property to button-over — but only if its CSS class isn't button-click. You want clicked buttons to persist their state, as that mimics the behavior of pretty much every toolbar ever created. Next check for the mouseout event, and change the CSS class of the element to button-normal (again, only if the class isn't button-click). Finally comes the check for the click event, and you will toggle the CSS class between button-click and button-over. You use button-over here because, when you click a button in the toolbar, the mouse pointer is over the element.

4. Add the code that sets the `click`, `mouseover` and `mouseout` event handlers to the document object. It is bold in the following code:

```
<html>
<head>
    <title>Lesson 21: Example 01</title>
    <style type="text/css">
        #divContainer {
            background-color: silver;
            height: 50px;
            padding: 2px;
        }

        span {
            display: inline-block;
            width: 50px;
            height: 50px;
        }

        .button-normal {
            background-color: gray;
        }

        .button-over {
            background-color: navy;
        }

        .button-click {
            background-color: yellow;
        }
    </style>
</head>
<body>
    <div id="divContainer">
        <span class="button-normal">

        </span>
        <span class="button-normal">

        </span>
        <span class="button-normal">

        </span>
    </div>
    <script type="text/javascript" src="eventutility.js"></script>
    <script type="text/javascript">
    function mouseHandler(event) {
        var eSrc = event.target,
        var type = event.type;

        if (eSrc.tagName.toUpperCase() === "SPAN") {
            if (type === "mouseover") {
                if (eSrc.className !== "button-click") {
                    eSrc.className = "button-over";
```

```
                }
            } else if (type === "mouseout") {
                if (eSrc.className !== "button-click") {
                    eSrc.className = "button-normal";
                }
            } else if (type === "click") {
                if (eSrc.className !== "button-click") {
                    eSrc.className = "button-click";
                } else {
                    eSrc.className = "button-over";
                }
            }
        }
    }

    eventUtility.addEvent(document, "mouseover", mouseHandler);
    eventUtility.addEvent(document, "mouseout", mouseHandler);
    eventUtility.addEvent(document, "click", mouseHandler);
    </script>
  </body>
</html>
```

Save the file and load it into any browser (except IE8 and below). You'll see that as you move your mouse pointer over a button, the background color changes to navy. When you move your mouse pointer off a button, it will change back to gray . When you click a button, the element's background color will change to yellow. Clicking a button that is yellow will change it to navy.

To get the sample code files, you can download Lesson 21 from the book's website at www.wrox.com.

 Please select Lesson 21 on the DVD to view the video that accompanies this lesson.

22

Internet Explorer's Event Object

Internet Explorer's (IE) event model has its roots in early versions of the browser, and it has remained virtually the same for over 12 years. In fact, the organizations behind Chrome, Safari, and Opera saw fit to implement it in their browsers — only Firefox doesn't support it. Despite this rather broad support, IE's event model is still considered to be incorrect, and its use in any standards-supporting browser is discouraged.

The key to IE's event model is an object called `event`. This object is populated with event information every time an event is handled. In this lesson you will learn how to access the `event` object and glean event information from it.

ACCESSING THE EVENT OBJECT

The `event` object is a global object, so it is actually a property of `window`. You can therefore access it rather easily, as shown in the following code:

```
eventUtility.addEvent(document, "click", function() {
    alert(event);
});
```

Here an event handler is assigned to the `click` event for the `document` object. When you click anywhere in the document an alert box, shown in Figure 22-1, simply displays the text "[object]".

When an event handler is assigned with the `attachEvent()` method, which the `eventUtility.addEvent()` method uses, the `event` object is also passed as a parameter to the handling function, much as the standard `Event` object is in standards-supporting browsers. The following code shows this:

```
eventUtility.addEvent(document, "click", function(event) {
    alert(event);
});
```

There is no difference between the global event object and the event object passed to the handling function.

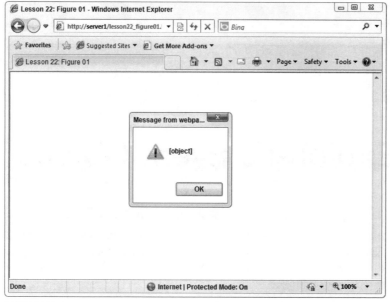

FIGURE 22-1

THE EVENT OBJECT

In Lesson 21 I mentioned that the standard event model uses multiple types of Event objects to represent different events (such as MouseEvent objects). In contrast, IE's event object is a multipurpose object that contains not only basic event information, but information regarding mouse- and keyboard-based events. Despite this difference, you can gather the same information from the event object that you can from the standard Event and MouseEvent objects, but you may have to use different property names to get at that information.

Determining the Event That Occurred

To determine what event took place, use the type property. You do this exactly as you saw in Lesson 21:

```
eventUtility.addEvent(document, "click", function(event) {
    alert(event.type); // click
});
```

It returns a string containing the name of the event without the preceding on, and you can use it exactly as you would the standard Event object. The following example is an exact duplicate of the code from Lesson 21:

```
function eventHandler(event) {
    if (event.type === "click") {
        alert("You clicked me!");
    } else if (event.type === "keypress") {
        alert("You pressed a key!");
    }
}

eventUtility.addEvent(document, "click", eventHandler);

eventUtility.addEvent(document, "keypress", eventHandler);
```

This code uses the type property to determine the event that occurred and display an appropriate message for that event. It is a simple property supported by all browsers. Unfortunately, discerning the target of the event, while simple, isn't the same as with the standard Event object.

Accessing the Event Target

The standard Event object provides the target property to access the HTML element that the event originated from. IE's version of target is called srcElement, and it can be used exactly as you would use target. Let's revisit the example from Lesson 21 with the following HTML:

```
<body>
    <div id="divElement"
        style="width: 100px; height: 100px; background-color: red; "></div>
</body>
```

Once again, this is a snippet of an HTML page. The <div/> element is styled to look like a red square, and you can set up an event handler to change the background color of this element when it is clicked, like this:

```
eventUtility.addEvent(document.getElementById("divElement"), "click",
    function(event) {
        var bgColor = event.srcElement.style.backgroundColor;
        var color = "red";

        if (bgColor === color) {
            color = "green";
        }

        event.srcElement.style.backgroundColor = color;
    });
```

Just as in Lesson 21, this event handler toggles the background color of this <div/> element between red and green. The first statement initializes two variables. The first, bgColor, contains the current background color of the element, and `color`, the second, contains the text `red`. The function then determines what color to change the element's background to, and then does so by changing the element's `backgroundColor`. This code achieves the same results as the code in Lesson 21, but uses the `srcElement` property instead of `target`.

Also, because of the bubbling nature of IE's event model, you can use event delegation to provide the same functionality to as many elements as you want. Here, once again, is the updated HTML from the previous lesson:

```
<body>
    <div id="divElement"
        style="width: 100px; height: 100px; background-color: red; "></div>
<br/><br/>
    <div id="divElement2"
        style="width: 100px; height: 100px; background-color: red; "></div>
</body>
```

The event handler to toggle the background color of both `<div/>` elements looks like this:

```
eventUtility.addEvent(document, "click", function(event) {
    var eSrc = event.srcElement;

    if (eSrc.tagName.toUpperCase() === "DIV") {
        var bgColor = eSrc.style.backgroundColor;
        var color = "red";

        if (bgColor === color) {
            color = "green";
        }

        eSrc.style.backgroundColor = color;
    }
});
```

This code was extremely easy to modify for IE. Only the first line of the function was changed from `event.target` to `event.srcElement`. The remainder of the function is untouched. So the `tagName` property allows you to determine whether or not the event source was a `<div/>` element. If it was, the element's background color is changed to either red or green.

TRY IT

In this lesson, you learn how to use IE's `event` object to retrieve basic information regarding an event.

Lesson Requirements

For this lesson, you need a text editor; any plain text editor will do. For Microsoft Windows users, Notepad is available by default on your system or you can download Microsoft's free Visual Web Developer Express (www.microsoft.com/express/web/) or Web Matrix (www.asp.net/webmatrix/).

Mac OS X users can use TextMate, which comes as part of OS X, or download a trial for Coda (www.panic.com/coda/). Linux users can use the built-in VIM.

You also need a modern web browser. Choose any of the following:

- ➤ Internet Explorer 8+
- ➤ Google Chrome
- ➤ Firefox 3.5+
- ➤ Apple Safari 4+
- ➤ Opera 10+

Create a subfolder called Lesson22 in the JS24Hour folder you created in Lesson 1. Store the files you create in this lesson in the Lesson22 folder.

Step-by-Step

You will rewrite the toolbar script from Lesson 21 for IE. Use event delegation to handle the events for the buttons.

1. Open your text editor and type the following HTML. It is the final HTML from lesson21_example01.htm:

```
<html>
<head>
    <title>Lesson 21: Example 01</title>
    <style type="text/css">
        #divContainer {
            background-color: silver;
            height: 50px;
            padding: 2px;
        }

        span {
            display: inline-block;
            width: 50px;
            height: 50px;
        }

        .button-normal {
            background-color: gray;
        }


        .button-over {
            background-color: navy;
        }

        .button-click {
            background-color: yellow;
        }
    </style>
</head>
```

```
<body>
    <div id="divContainer">
        <span class="button-normal">

        </span>
        <span class="button-normal">

        </span>
        <span class="button-normal">

        </span>
    </div>
    <script type="text/javascript" src="eventutility.js"></script>
    <script type="text/javascript">
    function mouseHandler(event) {
        var eSrc = event.target,
            type = event.type;

        if (eSrc.tagName.toUpperCase() === "SPAN") {
            if (type === "mouseover") {
                if (eSrc.className !== "button-click") {
                    eSrc.className = "button-over";
                }
            } else if (type === "mouseout") {
                if (eSrc.className !== "button-click") {
                    eSrc.className = "button-normal";
                }
            } else if (type === "click") {
                if (eSrc.className !== "button-click") {
                    eSrc.className = "button-click";
                } else {
                    eSrc.className = "button-over";
                }
            }
        }
    }

    eventUtility.addEvent(document, "mouseover", mouseHandler);
    eventUtility.addEvent(document, "mouseout", mouseHandler);
    eventUtility.addEvent(document, "click", mouseHandler);
    </script>
</body>
</html>
```

2. Save it as `lesson22_example01.htm`.

3. Modify the HTML and JavaScript using the following bold lines of code:

```
<html>
<head>
    <title>Lesson 22: Example 01</title>
    <style type="text/css">
        #divContainer {
            background-color: silver;
            height: 50px;
```

```
                padding: 2px;
            }

            span {
                display: inline-block;
                width: 50px;
                height: 50px;
            }

            .button-normal {
                background-color: gray;
            }


            .button-over {
                background-color: navy;
            }

            .button-click {
                background-color: yellow;
            }
        </style>
</head>
<body>
    <div id="divContainer">
        <span class="button-normal">

        </span>
        <span class="button-normal">

        </span>
        <span class="button-normal">

        </span>
    </div>
    <script type="text/javascript" src="eventutility.js"></script>
    <script type="text/javascript">
    function mouseHandler(event) {
        var eSrc = event.srcElement,
            type = event.type;

        if (eSrc.tagName.toUpperCase() === "SPAN") {
            if (type === "mouseover") {
                if (eSrc.className !== "button-click") {
                    eSrc.className = "button-over";
                }
            } else if (type === "mouseout") {
                if (eSrc.className !== "button-click") {
                    eSrc.className = "button-normal";
                }
            } else if (type === "click") {
                if (eSrc.className !== "button-click") {
                    eSrc.className = "button-click";
                } else {
```

```
                        eSrc.className = "button-over";
                }
            }
        }
    }

    eventUtility.addEvent(document, "mouseover", mouseHandler);
    eventUtility.addEvent(document, "mouseout", mouseHandler);
    eventUtility.addEvent(document, "click", mouseHandler);
    </script>
</body>
</html>
```

The change is minor: You change the `<title/>` element and the first statement of the `mouseHandler()` function (from `event.target` to `event.srcElement`).

4. Open this page in any browser supporting the IE event model (any version of IE since IE5, Chrome, Safari, or Opera), and see that it behaves exactly like the version supporting the standard event model.

To get the sample code files, you can download Lesson 22 from the book's website at www.wrox.com.

 Please select Lesson 22 on the DVD to view the video that accompanies this lesson.

23

Writing Cross-Browser Event Code

The challenge in dealing with two different event models is deciding how to meld them together to make working with them as painless as possible. It's a problem that all JavaScript developers face at one point or another, and their solutions are as varied as they are. The best solutions, however, are the simplest.

In this lesson you'll look at simple solutions to cross-browser event discrepancies, and at the end of the lesson you'll add functionality to the eventUtility object.

ACQUIRING THE EVENT TARGET

The previous two lessons detailed the differences between different types of basic event information. To acquire a reference to the element object that generated the event, standards-based browsers use the target property, and Internet Explorer (IE) 8 and below use the srcElement property. Despite the two very different names, both properties provide the exact same information: the element where the event was raised.

The simplest way to acquire this information is to write a function that accepts an event object as an argument and uses the appropriate property to get the event target. Such a function could look something like this:

```
function getTarget(event) {
    if (typeof event.target !== "undefined") {
        return event.target;
    } else {
        return event.srcElement;
    }
}
```

This function, called `getTarget()`, determines whether to use the `target` or `srcElement` property. It's a simple solution to a simple problem. Let's add a tiny bit of complexity to it so that it fits into the patterns used by the `eventUtility` object. Add the following bold code to the `eventUtility` object:

```
var eventUtility = {
    addEvent : (function() {
        // removed for printing
    }()),
    removeEvent : (function() {
        // removed for printing
    }()),
    getTarget : (function() {
        if (typeof addEventListener !== "undefined") {
            return function(event) {
                return event.target;
            }
        } else {
            return function(event) {
                return event.srcElement;
            }
        }
    }())
};
```

This `eventUtility.getTarget()` method looks very much like the `addEvent()` and `removeEvent()` methods. It determines whether to use standards-based code or IE's proprietary code by checking if the `addEventListener` identifier is not undefined. Notice a slight change to the feature detection code. Originally the `getTarget()` function checked for `event.target` to determine standards compliance, but the `eventUtility.getTarget()` method uses `addEventListener` for detection. This is because of how `getTarget()` and `eventUtility.getTarget()` are called.

The original `getTarget()` function was accepting an event object as an argument, so you could use that object to determine what properties it implements. The `eventUtility.getTarget()` method, however, isn't being called as the result of an event; it is immediately executing when it is loaded by the browser. Since `addEventListener()` and `event.target` are both pieces of the standard event model, it's pretty safe to test for `addEventListener()` and assume the browser also supports the `target` property.

So now you have a method that you can call to get the target of an event. Let's look at how you can add more functionality to `eventUtility`.

CANCELING DEFAULT BEHAVIOR REDUX

Remember from Lesson 17, the lesson dealing with HTML attribute event handlers, how the event handler could return `false` and cancel the default action associated with the event (if any)? Well, you may or may not have noticed from the many calculator examples that returning `false` doesn't work with `addEventListener()`. You can tell it doesn't work by opening one of those pages, clicking one of the links, and looking at the URL in the location bar. You'll see a pound sign (#) at the end of the URL, as shown in Figure 23-1.

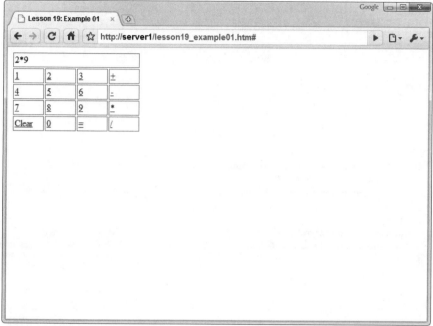

FIGURE 23-1

This isn't such a bad thing because seeing `return false` in an event handler doesn't make it very clear what that statement does. But at the same time, the ability to cancel an event's default behavior is very useful. Fortunately there is another way to cancel an event, but once again you'll have to deal with two different implementations.

The standard `Event` object (as supported by Chrome, Firefox, Safari, Opera, and IE9) has a method called `preventDefault()`. It doesn't accept any arguments; you simply call the method and the browser cancels the default behavior of the event. So instead of returning `false`, you simply add the following line of code to the function handling the event:

```
// call preventDefault() on event object to cancel event
event.preventDefault();
```

Canceling an event in IE8 and below requires a different approach. IE's `event` object has a property called `returnValue`, and you assign it a value of `false` in order to cancel the event. The following code demonstrates this:

```
// set returnValue as false to cancel event
event.returnValue = false;
```

So you have two completely different ways to perform the same action in a variety of browsers. As with the `getTarget()` method you added to `eventUtility`, a method is the simplest and most effective means of performing event cancellation across browsers. Let's skip writing a separate function and add the method to the `eventUtility` object. The following code adds a new method called `preventDefault()`. It is in bold text:

```
var eventUtility = {
    addEvent : (function() {
        // removed for printing
    }()),
    removeEvent : (function() {
        // removed for printing
    }()),
    getTarget : (function() {
        // removed for printing
    }()),
    preventDefault : (function() {
        if (typeof addEventListener !== "undefined") {
            return function(event) {
                event.preventDefault();
            }
        } else {
            return function(event) {
                event.returnValue = false;
            }
        }
    }())
};
```

The self-executing function returns one of two functions according to whether or not `addEventListener` is defined. Once again, it's assumed that if the browser supports `addEventListener()` it supports the standard `Event` object's `preventDefault()` method, as opposed to IE's `returnValue` property.

Now that you've added these two new pieces to the `eventUtility` object, let's revisit the calculator and toolbar examples.

TRY IT

In this lesson, you learn how to handle cross-browser discrepancies by writing a unified application programming interface (API) that performs work in all browsers.

Lesson Requirements

For this lesson, you will need a text editor; any plain text editor will do. For Microsoft Windows users, Notepad is available by default on your system or you can download Microsoft's free Visual Web Developer Express (www.microsoft.com/express/web/) or Web Matrix (www.asp.net/webmatrix/). Mac OS X users can use TextMate, which comes as part of OS X, or download a trial for Coda (www.panic.com/coda/). Linux users can use the built-in VIM.

You also need a modern web browser. Choose any of the following:

➤ Internet Explorer 8+

➤ Google Chrome

➤ Firefox 3.5+

➤ Apple Safari 4+

➤ Opera 10+

Create a subfolder called Lesson23 in the JS24Hour folder you created in Lesson 1. Store the files you create in this lesson in the Lesson23 folder.

Step-by-Step

You will rewrite the toolbar script from Lesson 21 for IE. Use event delegation to handle the events for the buttons.

1. Open eventutility.js in your text editor and add the getTarget() and preventDefault() methods to the object. They are bold in the following code:

```
var eventUtility = {
    addEvent : (function() {
        if (typeof addEventListener !== "undefined") {
            return function(obj, evt, fn) {
                obj.addEventListener(evt, fn, false);
            };
        } else {
            return function(obj, evt, fn) {
                obj.attachEvent("on" + evt, fn);
            };
        }
    }()),
    removeEvent : (function() {
        if (typeof removeEventListener !== "undefined") {
            return function(obj, evt, fn) {
                obj.removeEventListener(evt, fn, false);
            };
        } else {
            return function(obj, evt, fn) {
                obj.detachEvent("on" + evt, fn);
            };
        }
    }()),
    getTarget : (function() {
        if (typeof addEventListener !== "undefined") {
            return function(event) {
                return event.target;
            }
        } else {
            return function(event) {
                return event.srcElement;
            }
        }
    }()),
    preventDefault : (function() {
        if (typeof addEventListener !== "undefined") {
            return function(event) {
```

```
                event.preventDefault();
            }
        } else {
            return function(event) {
                event.returnValue = false;
            }
        }
    }())
};
```

2. You will now write a modified version of the calculator. This new version will contain several improvements: for example, it will use the new functionality of the event utility, event delegation, and an API to control the calculator (as opposed to functions). Open another instance of your text editor and type the following code:

```
<html>
<head>
    <title>Lesson 23: Example 01</title>
    <style type="text/css">
    td {
        border: 1px solid gray;
        width: 50px;
    }

    #results {
        height: 20px;
    }
    </style>
</head>
<body>
    <table border="0" cellpadding="2" cellspacing="2">
        <tr>
            <td colspan="4" id="results"></td>
        </tr>
        <tr>
            <td><a href="#">1</a></td>
            <td><a href="#">2</a></td>
            <td><a href="#">3</a></td>
            <td><a href="#">+</a></td>
        </tr>
        <tr>
            <td><a href="#">4</a></td>
            <td><a href="#">5</a></td>
            <td><a href="#">6</a></td>
            <td><a href="#">-</a></td>
        </tr>
        <tr>
            <td><a href="#">7</a></td>
            <td><a href="#">8</a></td>
            <td><a href="#">9</a></td>
            <td><a href="#">*</a></td>
        </tr>
        <tr>
```

```
                <td><a href="#">Clear</a></td>
                <td><a href="#">0</a></td>
                <td><a href="#">=</a></td>
                <td><a href="#">/</a></td>
            </tr>
        </table>
        <script type="text/javascript" src="eventutility.js"></script>
        <script type="text/javascript">
        var calculator = {
            resultField : document.getElementById("results"),
            reset : function() {
                this.resultField.innerHTML = "";
            },

            calculate : function() {
                this.resultField.innerHTML = eval(this.resultField.innerHTML);
            },

            addDigit : function(digit) {
                this.resultField.innerHTML += digit;
            }
        };
        </script>
    </body>
</html>
```

As you can see from this code, the `reset()`, `calculate()`, `addDigit()`, and `getHandlerFunction()` functions are gone. Instead there is a `calculator` object, defined with object literal notation, and it contains a `resultField` property (the HTML element), a `reset()` method, a `calculate()` method, and an `addDigit()` method. This new `calculator` object is an improvement over the previous list of functions. Not only is the calculator's functionality organized into a single entity (the `calculator` object), but the HTML element object representing the result field is cached in the `resultField` property. The various methods can use this property instead of having to perform a DOM search every time they're called.

3. Now add the event delegation code, shown in bold here:

```
<html>
<head>
    <title>Lesson 23: Example 01</title>
    <style type="text/css">
    td {
        border: 1px solid gray;
        width: 50px;
    }

    #results {
        height: 20px;
    }
    </style>
</head>
<body>
```

```
<table border="0" cellpadding="2" cellspacing="2">
    <tr>
        <td colspan="4" id="results"></td>
    </tr>
    <tr>
        <td><a href="#">1</a></td>
        <td><a href="#">2</a></td>
        <td><a href="#">3</a></td>
        <td><a href="#">+</a></td>
    </tr>
    <tr>
        <td><a href="#">4</a></td>
        <td><a href="#">5</a></td>
        <td><a href="#">6</a></td>
        <td><a href="#">-</a></td>
    </tr>
    <tr>
        <td><a href="#">7</a></td>
        <td><a href="#">8</a></td>
        <td><a href="#">9</a></td>
        <td><a href="#">*</a></td>
    </tr>
    <tr>
        <td><a href="#">Clear</a></td>
        <td><a href="#">0</a></td>
        <td><a href="#">=</a></td>
        <td><a href="#">/</a></td>
    </tr>
</table>
<script type="text/javascript" src="eventutility.js"></script>
<script type="text/javascript">
var calculator = {
    resultField : document.getElementById("results"),
    reset : function() {
        this.resultField.innerHTML = "";
    },

    calculate : function() {
        this.resultField.innerHTML = eval(this.resultField.innerHTML);
    },

    addDigit : function(digit) {
        this.resultField.innerHTML += digit;
    }
};

eventUtility.addEvent(document, "click", function(event) {
    var target = eventUtility.getTarget(event);

    if (target.tagName.toUpperCase() === "A") {
        var innerHTML = target.innerHTML;

        switch (innerHTML) {
            case "Clear":
                calculator.reset();
```

```
                        break;

                case "=":
                    calculator.calculate();
                    break;

                default:
                    calculator.addDigit(innerHTML);
            }

            eventUtility.preventDefault(event);
        }
    });
    </script>
</body>
</html>
```

The only event you need to handle is the `click` event, and you need to handle it at the document level. The first line of the event handler gets the event target by using the new `getTarget()` method. Next, the code determines if the target is an `<a/>` element, and then the switch block determines what `calculator` method to execute. The final statement within the `if` block cancels the default event's behavior, and you'll see evidence of its working by running it in any browser and seeing no pound sign in the URL.

4. Now you will modify the toolbar script to use the new `getTarget()` method. Open `lesson22_example01.htm` and save it as `lesson23_example02.htm`. Change the bold line in the following code:

```
<html>
<head>
    <title>Lesson 23: Example 02</title>
    <style type="text/css">
        #divContainer {
            background-color: silver;
            height: 50px;
            padding: 2px;
        }

        span {
            display: inline-block;
            width: 50px;
            height: 50px;
        }

        .button-normal {
            background-color: gray;
        }

        .button-over {
            background-color: navy;
        }

        .button-click {
            background-color: yellow;
```

```
            }
        </style>
    </head>
    <body>
        <div id="divContainer">
            <span class="button-normal">

            </span>
            <span class="button-normal">

            </span>
            <span class="button-normal">

            </span>
        </div>
        <script type="text/javascript" src="eventutility.js"></script>
        <script type="text/javascript">
        function mouseHandler(event) {
            var eSrc = eventUtility.getTarget(event),
                type = event.type;

            if (eSrc.tagName.toUpperCase() === "SPAN") {
                if (type === "mouseover") {
                    if (eSrc.className !== "button-click") {
                        eSrc.className = "button-over";
                    }
                } else if (type === "mouseout") {
                    if (eSrc.className !== "button-click") {
                        eSrc.className = "button-normal";
                    }
                } else if (type === "click") {
                    if (eSrc.className !== "button-click") {
                        eSrc.className = "button-click";
                    } else {
                        eSrc.className = "button-over";
                    }
                }
            }
        }

        eventUtility.addEvent(document, "mouseover", mouseHandler);
        eventUtility.addEvent(document, "mouseout", mouseHandler);
        eventUtility.addEvent(document, "click", mouseHandler);
        </script>
    </body>
</html>
```

It's a simple change, but the page now works in every modern browser. Go ahead and open it and you'll find it works just fine.

To get the sample code files, you can download Lesson 23 from the book's website at www.wrox.com.

 Please select Lesson 23 on the DVD to view the video that accompanies this lesson.

24

Dragging and Dropping

JavaScript can add rich interactivity to any web page, interactivity that once was available only with conventional applications. For example, take a look at your computer's desktop. Chances are you have one icon that you can click and drag to anywhere you want. That's a level of interactivity that users want, and it would be impossible to supply that interactivity on a web page without JavaScript or plugins like Flash, Silverlight, and so on.

In this lesson, you learn how to:

➤ Get the mouse pointer's location.

➤ Move an element on the page.

➤ Use events to facilitate drag-and-drop.

You then apply this information by writing a drag-and-drop script.

GETTING THE MOUSE POINTER'S LOCATION

For drag-and-drop, the most important piece of information you need is the mouse pointer's coordinates. But you actually need this information represented in two different ways. First you need to know the mouse pointer's coordinates in relation to the page; without them you don't know where to drag the item to.

You also need to know the mouse pointer's position in relation to the HTML element you want to drag. This is important because you want to maintain the mouse pointer's position on the element while you drag it to a new location. Without this information, clicking and dragging an element would result in the element's top left corner snapping to the mouse pointer, as shown in Figure 24-1.

Let's start by getting the mouse pointer's location in relation to the page.

Before

After

FIGURE 24-1

Client Coordinates

To get this information, look once again to the event object in both the standards and Internet Explorer (IE) event models. Thankfully, both event models are in lockstep when it comes to this type of information. You won't have to expand the functionality of the eventUtility object at all, as the properties have the same names and uses.

There are actually two sets of coordinates relating to the mouse pointer that you can retrieve from an event object. The first set is the pointer's location in relation to the entire screen. You get this information by using the screenX and screenY properties, like this:

```
eventUtility.addEvent(document, "click", function(event) {
    alert("X Coordinate is: " + event.screenX); // pointer's
horizontal position
    alert("Y Coordinate is: " + event.screenY); // pointer's vertical
 position
});
```

This information can be useful, but it isn't suited well for drag-and-drop. The screen is a fixed size, so regardless of where your mouse moves on the screen, you're limited to only the dimensions of the screen when using screenX and screenY. Most of all, the screenX and screenY coordinates are in relation to the entire screen, which isn't information you want. A better solution is to use a set of coordinates that are in relation to the *client area*, the part of the window that displays the document (also called the *viewport*). Figure 24-2 outlines this area.

Viewport

FIGURE 24-2

You can get this information by using the `clientX` and `clientY` properties, like this:

```
eventUtility.addEvent(document, "click", function(event) {
    alert("X Coordinate is: " + event.clientX); // pointer's horizontal
position
    alert("Y Coordinate is: " + event.clientY); // pointer's vertical
position
});
```

Like the screen coordinate system, the client coordinate system is a fixed size (the size of the viewport). For example, clicking the top-left corner of the viewport always results in a `clientX` value of 0 — regardless of whether the page is horizontally scrolled. The `clientX` and `clientY` coordinates are in relation to the viewport, not the document, but you can obtain two more pieces of information to combine with the client coordinates to accurately get the pointer's position: the `document.body.scrollTop` and `document.body.scrollLeft` properties.

The `scrollTop` and `scrollLeft` are properties of all element objects, and they get the vertical or horizontal position of the scrollbar for the element. When used on the `body` object, these properties return the amount of pixels the scrollbars have been scrolled. When the scrollbar is at the top (or to the left for horizontal scrollbars), the position is 0.

To get the mouse pointer's accurate position in the document, you combine the client coordinates with the body's scroll positions, like this:

```
var x = event.clientX + document.body.scrollLeft;
var y = event.clientY + document.body.scrollTop;
```

Element Coordinates

Every element has a set of properties that allow you to get position and size information for that element. They aren't part of any W3C standard, but every major browser has implemented them since they were first introduced in IE4. They are:

➤ `offsetLeft`: Gets the left position of an element relative to its nearest positioned ancestor.

➤ `offsetTop`: Gets the top position of an element relative to its nearest positioned ancestor.

➤ `offsetWidth`: Gets the width of an element relative to its nearest positioned ancestor. The value returned by this property also includes the element's padding, margin, and border width.

➤ `offsetHeight`: Gets the height of an element relative to its nearest positioned ancestor. The value returned by this property also includes the element's padding, margin, and border width.

These four properties are extremely helpful when you need to know the position and dimensions of an element as it is rendered by the browser. For the purposes of drag-and-drop the only properties you'll need to look at are `offsetLeft` and `offsetTop`.

To find the mouse pointer's coordinates in relation to an element, you use the element's `offsetLeft` and `offsetTop` properties and then subtract the event object's `clientX` and `clientY` properties, like this:

```
eventUtility.addEvent(document, "click", function(event) {
    var eSrc = eventUtility.getTarget(event);
    var x = event.clientX + document.body.scrollLeft;
    var y = event.clientY + document.body.scrollTop;

    var relativeX = eSrc.offsetLeft - x;
    var relativeY = eSrc.offsetTop - y;
});
```

In this code, the `eventUtility` object gets the event target by using the `getTarget()` method and assigning the returned value to `eSrc`. Then two variables, `relativeX` and `relativeY`, are created and assigned their respective values by the offset coordinates' being calculated with the mouse pointer's coordinates. Again, these relative coordinates are important because it is necessary for accurately emulating the behavior users are accustomed to seeing in their operating systems.

With these two sets of coordinates, you are well on your way to having all the pieces to writing a drag-and-drop script. There's just one more piece to the puzzle: events.

EVENTS USED IN DRAG-AND-DROP

Drag-and-drop is a series of operations governed completely and totally by the mouse. The user clicks an item and moves the mouse while keeping the mouse button pressed. When the mouse button is released, the item is "dropped" at the mouse pointer's location. To make drag-and-drop work on a web page you have to handle at least three mouse-related events:

➤ `mousedown`: Fires when the mouse button is pressed while the mouse pointer is over an object.

➤ `mouseup`: Fires when the mouse button is released while the mouse pointer is over an object.

➤ `mousemove`: Fires when the mouse pointer is moved over an object.

The `mousedown` event initiates the drag process, the `mousemove` event is used to move the element in sync with the mouse pointer (dragging), and the `mouseup` event ends the drag process and drops the element at the pointer's location.

So let's put all this knowledge to work and try it out.

TRY IT

In this lesson, you learn about the event object's `clientX` and `clientY` properties and an element's `offsetLeft` and `offsetTop` properties. In this section you learn how to use them in creating a drag-and-drop script.

Lesson Requirements

For this lesson, you need a text editor; any plain text editor will do. For Microsoft Windows users, Notepad is available by default on your system or you can download Microsoft's free Visual Web Developer Express (www.microsoft.com/express/web/) or Web Matrix (www.asp.net/webmatrix/). Mac OS X users can use TextMate, which comes as part of OS X, or download a trial for Coda (www.panic.com/coda/). Linux users can use the built-in VIM.

You also need a modern web browser. Choose any of the following:

➤ Internet Explorer 8+

➤ Google Chrome

➤ Firefox 3.5+

➤ Apple Safari 4+

➤ Opera 10+

Create a subfolder called `Lesson24` in the `JS24Hour` folder you created in Lesson 1. Store the files you create in this lesson in the `Lesson24` folder.

Step-by-Step

1. Start by typing the following HTML:

```
<html>
<head>
    <title>Lesson 24: Example 01</title>
    <style type="text/css">
    .draggable {
        position: absolute;
        cursor: move;
    }

    .box {
        width: 100px;
        height: 100px;
    }

    .navy {
        background-color: navy;
    }

    .green {
        background-color: Green;
    }
    </style>
</head>
<body>
<div class="navy box draggable"></div>
```

```
<div class="green box draggable"></div>

<script type="text/javascript" src="eventutility.js"></script>
<script type="text/javascript">

</script>
</body>
</html>
```

This is the basis of your web page. It has a style sheet containing four CSS classes: draggable, box, navy, and green.

The draggable class sets the element's position to absolute, making it possible for an element with this class to be moved anywhere in the page. It also changes the mouse pointer to the move symbol. This is a visual cue for the user so that she knows the element is movable. This class is used to make an element draggable. The JavaScript you write will determine whether the element uses this class, and the user will be able to drag it to anywhere on the page.

The box class is purely for presentation. When applied to an element, it renders the element as a square with 100-pixel sides.

The navy and green classes, too, are purely for presentation. They change the element's background color to navy and green, respectively.

In the <body/> of the page are two <div/> elements. The first uses the navy, box, and draggable classes to render the element as a navy box with an absolute position. The second uses the green, box, and draggable classes.

2. Now you want to add some JavaScript. The first little bit is the mouseHandler() function, which you use to handle a variety of events. The new code is in bold:

```
<html>
<head>
    <title>Lesson 24: Example 01</title>
    <style type="text/css">
    .draggable {
        position: absolute;
        cursor: move;
    }

    .box {
        width: 100px;
        height: 100px;
    }

    .navy {
        background-color: navy;
    }

    .green {
        background-color: Green;
    }
```

```
        </style>
    </head>
    <body>
    <div class="navy box draggable"></div>
    <div class="green box draggable"></div>

    <script type="text/javascript" src="eventutility.js"></script>
    <script type="text/javascript">
    function mouseHandler(event) {
    var eSrc = eventUtility.getTarget(event);
        var type = event.type;
        var x = event.clientX + document.body.scrollLeft;
        var y = event.clientY + document.body.scrollTop;

        switch (type) {
            case "mousedown":
                if (eSrc.className.indexOf("draggable") > -1) {


                }
                break;
            case "mouseup":

                break;
            case "mousemove":

                break;
        }
    }

    eventUtility.addEvent(document, "mousedown", mouseHandler);
    eventUtility.addEvent(document, "mouseup", mouseHandler);
    eventUtility.addEvent(document, "mousemove", mouseHandler);
    </script>
    </body>
    </html>
```

With this code, some of the pieces start coming together. Event handlers for the mousedown, mouseup, and mousemove events are set up for the document object, and the mouseHandler() function handles all three events.

The first statement in the function creates four variables. The first is eSrc, the event target. Next is type, the event type. Next are the x and y variables to contain the mouse pointer's coordinates.

Because this function handles multiple events, you need to determine what event took place. A switch statement uses the event type, and a case block is written for each of the three events.

When the user causes a mousedown event to fire, you use the indexOf() string method to determine if the target has a CSS class of draggable. You want to drag only those elements with this CSS class, so all the code to initiate the drag-and-drop sequence will be placed inside the `if` code block.

3. To facilitate the drag-and-drop process, create an object outside the `mouseHandler()` function called `dragObj`. Its responsibility is to initialize the element for dragging, as well as to contain information regarding the state of the dragging process. Add the following code:

```html
<html>
<head>
    <title>Lesson 24: Example 01</title>
    <style type="text/css">
    .draggable {
        position: absolute;
        cursor: move;
    }

    .box {
        width: 100px;
        height: 100px;
    }

    .navy {
        background-color: navy;
    }

    .green {
        background-color: Green;
    }
    </style>
</head>
<body>
<div class="navy box draggable"></div>
<div class="green box draggable"></div>

<script type="text/javascript" src="eventutility.js"></script>
<script type="text/javascript">
var dragObj = {
    setDragObj : function(el, mouseX, mouseY) {
        this.el = el;
        this.relativeLeft = el.offsetLeft - mouseX;
        this.relativeTop = el.offsetTop - mouseY;
    },
    dragTo : function(x, y) {
        this.el.style.left = x + this.relativeLeft + "px";
        this.el.style.top = y + this.relativeTop + "px";
    },
    dragging : false,
    el : null,
    relativeTop : 0,
    relativeLeft : 0
};
```

```
function mouseHandler(event) {
    var eSrc = eventUtility.getTarget(event);
    var type = event.type;
    var x = event.clientX + document.body.scrollLeft;
    var y = event.clientY + document.body.scrollTop;

    switch (type) {
        case "mousedown":
            if (eSrc.className.indexOf("draggable") > -1) {

            }
            break;
        case "mouseup":

            break;
        case "mousemove":

            break;
    }
}

eventUtility.addEvent(document, "mousedown", mouseHandler);
eventUtility.addEvent(document, "mouseup", mouseHandler);
eventUtility.addEvent(document, "mousemove", mouseHandler);
</script>
</body>
</html>
```

This `dragObj` object has four properties:

➤   `dragging`: A Boolean value to set whether or not an element is being dragged

➤   `el`: The element to drag

➤   `relativeTop`: The vertical position of the mouse cursor relative to the element

➤   `relativeLeft`: The horizontal position of the mouse cursor relative to the element

The `dragObj` object also has two methods:

➤   `setDragObj()`: Accepts the element to drag and the mouse pointer's *x* and *y* coordinates as arguments. This method initiates all the data needed to drag an element. It sets the `el` property to the element that will be dragged, and it sets the `relativeLeft` and `relativeTop` properties by taking the element's offset coordinates and subtracting the mouse pointer's coordinates.

➤   `dragTo()`: Accepts a set of coordinates as arguments, and uses the element's `style` object to set its `left` and `top` properties to the sum of the supplied coordinates and the relative coordinates. The string `px` is appended to each value. It's always a good idea to add the unit when setting an element's size and position. A standards-compliant browser will not resize or position the element without the unit.

4. Now use `dragObj` to facilitate the drag-and-drop sequence. Add the following bold code:

```
<html>
<head>
    <title>Lesson 24: Example 01</title>
    <style type="text/css">
    .draggable {
        position: absolute;
        cursor: move;
    }

    .box {
        width: 100px;
        height: 100px;
    }

    .navy {
        background-color: navy;
    }

    .green {
        background-color: Green;
    }
    </style>
</head>
<body>
<div class="navy box draggable"></div>
<div class="green box draggable"></div>

<script type="text/javascript" src="eventutility.js"></script>
<script type="text/javascript">
var dragObj = {
    setDragObj : function(el, mouseX, mouseY) {
        this.el = el;
        this.relativeLeft = el.offsetLeft - mouseX;
        this.relativeTop = el.offsetTop - mouseY;
    },
    dragTo : function(x, y) {
        this.el.style.left = x + this.relativeLeft + "px";
        this.el.style.top = y + this.relativeTop + "px";
    },
    dragging : false,
    el : null,
    relativeTop : 0,
    relativeLeft : 0
};

function mouseHandler(event) {
    var eSrc = eventUtility.getTarget(event);
    var type = event.type;
```

```
            var x = event.clientX + document.body.scrollLeft;
            var y = event.clientY + document.body.scrollTop;

            switch (type) {
                case "mousedown":
                    if (eSrc.className.indexOf("draggable") > -1) {
                        dragObj.dragging = true;
                        dragObj.setDragObj(eSrc, x, y);
                    }
                    break;
                case "mouseup":
                    dragObj.dragging = false;
                    break;
                case "mousemove":
                    if (dragObj.dragging) {
                        dragObj.dragTo(x, y);
                    }
                    break;
            }
        }

        eventUtility.addEvent(document, "mousedown", mouseHandler);
        eventUtility.addEvent(document, "mouseup", mouseHandler);
        eventUtility.addEvent(document, "mousemove", mouseHandler);
        </script>
        </body>
        </html>
```

The first new lines of code go inside the if block in the mousedown case. You set the dragging property of dragObj to true, and you call the setDragObj() method to get the element ready to drag.

Next you add one line of code under the mouseup case; you set the dragging property to false.

Then, in the mousemove case, you determine if dragObj.dragging is true. If the user is holding down the mouse button while it's over an element with the CSS class of draggable, then dragObj.dragging will be true. If it is true, you want to call the dragTo() method to move the element to the current mouse pointer's coordinates.

When the user releases the mouse button, dragObj.dragging will be false, and the element will stop moving when the mousemove event fires.

5. Save this file as lesson24_example01.htm, and open it in any browser. Drag the green box to another location on the page, and then do the same for the navy box.

One thing you may notice is that the navy box is always behind the green box. In traditional drag-and-drop implementations, whatever item is currently being dragged should be the topmost item on the screen. For example, drag your text editor window and your browser windows over each other, and you'll see that the window you're currently dragging is over the other window, as shown in Figure 24-3.

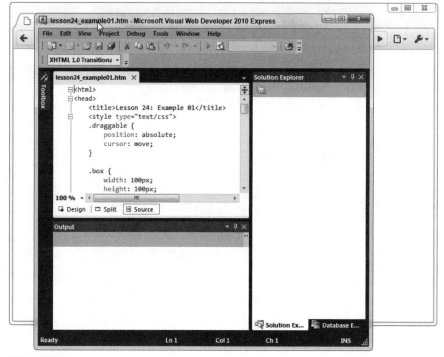

FIGURE 24-3

You can add the same functionality to your drag-and-drop script by modifying an element's
`z-index` CSS property.

6. In order to make this work as easily as possible, add a `zIndex` property to `dragObj` and give
it an initial value of `1`, as shown in the following bold code:

```
<html>
<head>
    <title>Lesson 24: Example 01</title>
    <style type="text/css">
    .draggable {
        position: absolute;
        cursor: move;
    }

    .box {
        width: 100px;
        height: 100px;
    }

    .navy {
        background-color: navy;
    }

    .green {
```

```
            background-color: Green;
        }
    </style>
</head>
<body>
<div class="navy box draggable"></div>
<div class="green box draggable"></div>

<script type="text/javascript" src="eventutility.js"></script>
<script type="text/javascript">
var dragObj = {
    setDragObj : function(el, mouseX, mouseY) {
        this.el = el;
        this.relativeLeft = el.offsetLeft - mouseX;
        this.relativeTop = el.offsetTop - mouseY;
        this.el.style.zIndex = this.zIndex++;
    },
    dragTo : function(x, y) {
        this.el.style.left = x + this.relativeLeft + "px";
        this.el.style.top = y + this.relativeTop + "px";
    },
    dragging : false,
    el : null,
    relativeTop : 0,
    relativeLeft : 0,
    zIndex : 1
};

function mouseHandler(event) {
    var eSrc = eventUtility.getTarget(event);
    var type = event.type;
    var x = event.clientX + document.body.scrollLeft;
    var y = event.clientY + document.body.scrollTop;

    switch (type) {
        case "mousedown":
            if (eSrc.className.indexOf("draggable") > -1) {
                dragObj.dragging = true;
                dragObj.setDragObj(eSrc, x, y);
            }
            break;
        case "mouseup":
            dragObj.dragging = false;
            break;
        case "mousemove":
            if (dragObj.dragging) {
                dragObj.dragTo(x, y);
            }
            break;
    }
}

eventUtility.addEvent(document, "mousedown", mouseHandler);
eventUtility.addEvent(document, "mouseup", mouseHandler);
```

```
        eventUtility.addEvent(document, "mousemove", mouseHandler);
    </script>
</body>
</html>
```

This new code also adds a line to `setDragObj()`, setting the `style.zIndex` property to an incremented value of the `dragObj.zIndex` property.

7. Resave the file and refresh your browser. Now drag the two boxes around on the page. You'll see that whichever box you drag becomes the topmost box — as with the drag-and-drop feature of your operating system.

To get the sample code files, you can download Lesson 24 from the book's website at www.wrox.com.

 Please select Lesson 24 on the DVD to view the video that accompanies this lesson.

25

Timers and Animating Elements

Users have come to expect a certain level of polish in the applications they use — particularly their operating systems. Every new version adds more visual goodness that, while not entirely necessary, enhances the user's experience. Features like menus that fade in and out, and windows that scale while maximizing and minimizing, are perfect examples of how unobtrusive animations can add visual flair while still maintaining the original functionality of showing or hiding a menu or resizing a window.

In Lesson 24 you allowed a user to click an element and drag it to wherever he wishes; you essentially wrote an animation script. The animation was limited and dependent upon the user's action, but the element moved to a different set of coordinates in sync with the mouse pointer — a movement animation.

Animations such as the fading in and out in menus aren't so dependent on user interaction. Sure, the user has to initiate an event to cause the animation to run, but a menu fades in over a certain period — not in relation to where the user moves the mouse pointer.

This type of animation is akin to motion pictures or cartoons — a character's fluid movement is broken into a number of frames that are shown in rapid sequence. Each frame is shown for a certain time (usually one thirtieth of a second) to mimic movement on the screen.

On a web page, you modify an element (the character) bit-by-bit (or frame by frame) over a certain period using timers. In this lesson you'll learn about two methods that are used for timing. Then you'll use the timers to create an animation.

SETTING A DELAY — THE SETTIMEOUT() METHOD

The first method is the `setTimeout()` method. It is a member of the `window` object, so it is global. It's essentially a delay: Its purpose is to execute a function once after a certain amount of time has elapsed. It accepts two arguments: a function to execute and the amount of time in milliseconds to wait before executing the code. Its syntax looks like the following:

```
function doSomething() {
    alert("Hello, timeout!");
}

var timer = setTimeout(doSomething, 1000);
```

The setTimeout() method returns a numeric value, which is the timer's unique ID number. While it's not necessary to use this ID number, it does come in handy, as you'll see in a few moments.

In this code the setTimeout() method is called by passing the doSomething() function as the first argument, and a number value of 1000 as the second argument. Remember, the second parameter is the amount of time in milliseconds. The number 1000 actually represents one second.

After the setTimeout() method executes, the JavaScript engine waits one second and then executes doSomething(). The engine, however, does not delay any statements that may appear after the setTimeout() call — it delays only the execution of doSomething(). For example, look at the following code:

```
function doSomething() {
    alert("Hello, timeout!");
}

var timer = setTimeout(doSomething, 1000);
alert("After setTimeout() call");
```

This code adds a statement to the end of the previous example. When this code executes, the setTimeout() call queues the doSomething() function to be called in one second, and then an alert box displays the text "After setTimeout() call." Then, and only after a second has passed since the call to setTimeout(), doSomething() executes. So the engine does not delay all code; it delays only the code specified as the first argument to setTimeout().

Even though setTimeout() is a one-shot timer, you can use a form of *recursion* (a function's calling itself) to call setTimeout() every time doSomething() executes. Look at the following code, which removes the alert() call from the previous example and adds a new line (bolded) to doSomething():

```
function doSomething() {
    alert("Hello, timeout!");
    timer = setTimeout(doSomething, 1000);
}

var timer = setTimeout(doSomething, 1000);
```

It's a simple modification, but it drastically changes how the code behaves. It creates an infinite loop. The call to setTimeout() outside the function initiates the loop by setting a one-second timeout before executing doSomething(). Then, when the second expires, doSomething() executes, which sets another one-second timeout to call doSomething() again. Every time doSomething() executes, a new one-second timeout is set to call doSomething().

Notice how the timer variable is reused. Since doSomething() executes when a timeout expires, the timeout ID stored in timer becomes useless. So instead of a new variable being created, timer is reused to store the new timeout's ID. This is advantageous because, as you may have guessed, a loop such as the preceding one could potentially be troublesome. A never-ending loop, especially one that pops up an alert window every second, can be very annoying.

Thankfully, when setTimeout() was added to Netscape 2 a companion method called clearTimeout() was included as well. As its name implies it cancels a timeout set with setTimeout(), and it accepts a timeout ID as an argument. Look at the following code to see it in action:

```
function doSomething() {
    alert("Hello, timeout!");
    timer = setTimeout(doSomething, 1000);
}

var timer = setTimeout(doSomething, 1000);
clearTimeout(timer);
```

Calling clearTimeout() and passing it timer cancels the timeout set in the statement before it can expire. Remember that setTimeout() doesn't stall the execution of the rest of the code. As a result, the timeout is cleared and doSomething() never executes.

 Calling clearTimeout() *on an expired timer ID has no effect and doesn't throw an error.*

Many years ago setTimeout() was often used to execute a function a certain number of times at particular time intervals, as the following code demonstrates:

```
function doSomething() {
    if (counter < 5) {
        alert("Hello, timeout!");
        counter++;
        timer = setTimeout(doSomething, 1000);
    }
}

var counter = 0;
var timer = setTimeout(doSomething, 1000);
```

This code adds a counter variable, and as long as the value of counter is less than 5, setTimeout() delays the execution of doSomething() again. If counter is greater than 5, the timeout isn't issued again and the loop exits.

This method of repeating a function with a time delay is still used today, but setTimeout() is usually more appropriately used to defer execution of a function. If you want to repeat a function call at regular time intervals, look to the setInterval() method.

SETTING AN INTERVAL — THE SETINTERVAL() METHOD

The setInterval() method, as implied in the previous section, executes a function at regular intervals of time. The following code executes the doSomething() function at regular intervals of one second:

```
function doSomething() {
    alert("Hello, timeout!");
}

var timer = setInterval(doSomething, 1000);
```

doSomething() will execute every second until either it is canceled in code or a different page is loaded in the browser. Like setTimeout(), the setInterval() method returns a unique timer ID that can be passed to the clearInterval() companion method. The following code re-creates the timeout with a timer code from the previous section, using setInterval() and clearInterval():

```
function doSomething() {
    if (counter < 5) {
        alert("Hello, timeout!");
        counter++;
    } else {
        clearTimeout(timer);
    }
}

var counter = 0;
var timer = setInterval(doSomething, 1000);
```

There's no need to call setInterval() more than once; its job is to repeat the provided function for as long as it's allowed to. So the code determines if counter is less than 5 and, if it isn't, calls clearTimeout() to clear the timer.

 setInterval() *waits until the specified amount of time has passed before executing the provided function for the first time.*

The setInterval() and clearInterval() methods are widely used to perform animations, and you'll use them now to create an animation script that resizes a box.

TRY IT

In this lesson, you learn about timers and what they're used for. In this section you use one of them, setInterval(), to animate an element.

Lesson Requirements

For this lesson, you need a text editor; any plain text editor will do. For Microsoft Windows users, Notepad is available by default on your system or you can download Microsoft's free Visual Web Developer Express (www.microsoft.com/express/web/) or Web Matrix (www.asp.net/webmatrix/). Mac OS X users can use TextMate, which comes as part of OS X, or download a trial for Coda (www.panic.com/coda/). Linux users can use the built-in VIM.

You also need a modern web browser. Choose any of the following:

- Internet Explorer 8+
- Google Chrome
- Firefox 3.5+
- Apple Safari 4+
- Opera 10+

Create a subfolder called `Lesson25` in the `JS24Hour` folder you created in Lesson 1. Store the files you create in this lesson in the `Lesson25` folder.

Step-by-Step

1. Start by typing the following HTML:

```html
<html>
<head>
    <title>Lesson 25: Example 01</title>
    <style type="text/css">
    .box {
        width: 100px;
        height: 100px;
        background-color: navy;
    }
    </style>
</head>
<body>

<div id="divNavyBox" class="box"></div>

<script type="text/javascript">

</script>
</body>
</html>
```

This is the basis of your web page. It has a style sheet containing a CSS class called box. This class sets the height and width of the element to 100px, and gives it a background color of navy. Inside the <body/> is a <div/> element with an ID of divNavyBox, and it uses the box class.

2. Now add some JavaScript code. Create an object called `animated`, and give it the members in the following code:

```html
<html>
<head>
    <title>Lesson 25: Example 01</title>
    <style type="text/css">
    .box {
        width: 100px;
        height: 100px;
        background-color: navy;
    }
    </style>
</head>
<body>

<div id="divNavyBox" class="box"></div>

<script type="text/javascript">
var animated = {
    timer : null,
    el : document.getElementById("divNavyBox"),
    startGrowAnimation : function() {

    },
    startShrinkAnimation : function() {

    },
    stopAnimation : function() {
        clearInterval(this.timer);
    },
    doAnimation : function(amount) {

    }
};
</script>
</body>
</html>
```

This code adds a few members to the animated object. The `timer` property contains the interval's unique ID; the `el` property contains the `<div/>` element object; and the four methods start, stop, and perform the animations. The `stopAnimation()` method is simple: It calls `clearInterval()` and passes the `timer` property.

3. Let's start with the `doAnimation()` method. Its purpose is to perform the growing and shrinking animations. It accepts one argument, a numeric value, which can be either positive or negative. If positive, the box grows by the amount specified. If negative, the box shrinks by the amount specified. The method's body is in bold:

```html
<html>
<head>
    <title>Lesson 25: Example 01</title>
```

```
      <style type="text/css">
      .box {
          width: 100px;
          height: 100px;
          background-color: navy;
      }
      </style>
</head>
<body>

<div id="divNavyBox" class="box"></div>

<script type="text/javascript">
var animated = {
    timer : null,
    el : document.getElementById("divNavyBox"),
    startGrowAnimation : function() {

    },
    startShrinkAnimation : function() {

    },
    stopAnimation : function() {
        clearInterval(this.timer);
    },
    doAnimation : function(amount) {
        var size = this.el.offsetWidth;

        if ((amount > 0 && size < 200) || (amount < 0 && size > 0)) {
            this.el.style.width = size + amount + "px";
            this.el.style.height = size + amount + "px";
        } else {
            this.stopAnimation();
        }
    }
};
</script>
</body>
</html>
```

Because the <div/> element is in the shape of a square, the doAnimation() method keeps things simple by retrieving only the element's width with the element's offsetWidth property.

Next, an if statement determines whether to grow or shrink the element by determining whether amount is positive or negative. It also determines how big or small the element gets. If amount is positive, the element will grow to a maximum of 200 pixels high and wide. If negative, the element will shrink to a minimum of zero pixels. The element's dimensions are adjusted by the specified amount as long as its size is within the hard-coded limits and the stopAnimation() method executes when either limit is reached.

4. Now add the bold lines in the following code:

```html
<html>
<head>
    <title>Lesson 25: Example 01</title>
    <style type="text/css">
    .box {
        width: 100px;
        height: 100px;
        background-color: navy;
    }
    </style>
</head>
<body>

<div id="divNavyBox" class="box"></div>

<script type="text/javascript">
var animated = {
    timer : null,
    el : document.getElementById("divNavyBox"),
    startGrowAnimation : function() {
        this.stopAnimation();
        this.timer = setInterval(function() {
            animated.doAnimation(5);
        }, 10);
    },
    startShrinkAnimation : function() {

    },
    stopAnimation : function() {
        clearInterval(this.timer);
    },
    doAnimation : function(amount) {
        var size = this.el.offsetWidth;

        if ((amount > 0 && size < 200) || (amount < 0 && size > 0)) {
            this.el.style.width = size + amount + "px";
            this.el.style.height = size + amount + "px";
        } else {
            this.stopAnimation();
        }
    }
};
</script>
</body>
</html>
```

The first line of this code calls `stopAnimation()`. This is absolutely vital because if `startGrowAnimation()` is called while another animation is in progress, the `timer` property will be overwritten with a new timer ID, and the interval timer that was running will stop only when the page is reloaded. By calling `stopAnimation()` first, you can stop the current animation (if there is one) and safely begin the grow animation.

The second statement calls setInterval() and passes an anonymous function to it. Inside the anonymous function is a call to animated.doAnimation(), with a value of 5 being passed. An anonymous function is used here because you need to pass a value to the doAnimation() method in order for it to work.

5. Now add the code for startShrinkAnimation(). It's very similar to that for startGrowAnimation(). The new code is bold in the following:

```html
<html>
<head>
    <title>Lesson 25: Example 01</title>
    <style type="text/css">
    .box {
        width: 100px;
        height: 100px;
        background-color: navy;
    }
    </style>
</head>
<body>

<div id="divNavyBox" class="box"></div>

<script type="text/javascript">
var animated = {
    timer : null,
    el : document.getElementById("divNavyBox"),
    startGrowAnimation : function() {
        this.stopAnimation();
        this.timer = setInterval(function() {
            animated.doAnimation(5);
        }, 10);
    },
    startShrinkAnimation : function() {
        this.stopAnimation();
        this.timer = setInterval(function() {
            animated.doAnimation(-5);
        }, 10);
    },
    stopAnimation : function() {
        clearInterval(this.timer);
    },
    doAnimation : function(amount) {
        var size = this.el.offsetWidth;

        if ((amount > 0 && size < 200) || (amount < 0 && size > 0)) {
            this.el.style.width = size + amount + "px";
            this.el.style.height = size + amount + "px";
        } else {
            this.stopAnimation();
        }
    }
};
```

```
    </script>
</body>
</html>
```

The only difference here is the value passed to doAnimation(). It is -5, so the element will shrink in size by five pixels.

6. Now add the following <a/> elements to call the start and stop methods:

```
<html>
<head>
    <title>Lesson 25: Example 01</title>
    <style type="text/css">
    .box {
        width: 100px;
        height: 100px;
        background-color: navy;
    }
    </style>
</head>
<body>
<a href="#" onclick="animated.startGrowAnimation(); return false;">Grow Box</a>
<a href="#" onclick="animated.startShrinkAnimation(); return false;">Shrink
Box</a>
<a href="#" onclick="animated.stopAnimation(); return false;">Stop
Animation</a>
<div id="divNavyBox" class="box"></div>

<script type="text/javascript">
var animated = {
    timer : null,
    el : document.getElementById("divNavyBox"),
    startGrowAnimation : function() {
        this.stopAnimation();
        this.timer = setInterval(function() {
            animated.doAnimation(5);
        }, 10);
    },
    startShrinkAnimation : function() {
        this.stopAnimation();
        this.timer = setInterval(function() {
            animated.doAnimation(-5);
        }, 10);
    },
    stopAnimation : function() {
        clearInterval(this.timer);
    },
    doAnimation : function(amount) {
        var size = this.el.offsetWidth;

        if ((amount > 0 && size < 200) || (amount < 0 && size > 0)) {
            this.el.style.width = size + amount + "px";
            this.el.style.height = size + amount + "px";
```

```
                } else {
                    this.stopAnimation();
                }
            }
        };
        </script>
        </body>
        </html>
```

7.   Save this file as `lesson25_example01.htm`, and open it in any browser. Click the links to grow and shrink the element, and also click the stop link to stop a running animation.

To get the sample code files, you can download Lesson 25 from the book's website at www.wrox.com.

 Please select Lesson 25 on the DVD to view the video that accompanies this lesson.

26

Forms — A Primer

In early versions of browsers, forms were generally the only means by which a web application could interact with the user. The user could input data into a variety of form controls and send that data to the server, and a server-side application would return a web page that incorporated the data in some way. In many cases a server-side application would have to validate every field in a form, and notify the user of any errors when responding to a form submission. This experience could be frustrating for the user, as sometimes one or more fields would be cleared of any data the user had entered.

Forms are still an important part of any web application that requires input from the user, but today's Web is far more sophisticated than that of yesteryear. With JavaScript, you can validate some form fields before any information is sent to the server — providing a much better experience for the user.

Over the course of the next few lessons, you learn how to script a variety of form controls. But first let's look at some basics of scripting forms with JavaScript.

FORMS AND THE DOM

A form in an HTML page is denoted by the `<form/>` element, and a single web page can have any number of forms. Quite naturally, the `document` object has a `forms` property — a collection of all `<form/>` elements found in the document. Like all array-like objects, `document.forms` has a `length` property, and you can access each form by specifying the index at which a form exists within the document, like this:

```
var firstForm = document.forms[0];
```

This code gets the first form found in the document, and in most cases this is sufficient because the majority of web pages contain only one form. Problems can arise, however, if your page does contain more than one form, and the order in which they're defined in the HTML varies from page to page.

For this reason, you can access any form by using the value set in the `<form/>` element's name attribute. The following code displays the HTML of a form with a specified name of theForm:

```
<form name="theForm"></form>
```

To find this form in the DOM, you can simply use the form's name as a property of the document object, like this:

```
var theForm = document.theForm;
```

This approach is not part of the W3C DOM standard, but it has been incorporated in every JavaScript-supporting browser since Netscape 2.0. It is the clearest way to access a form with JavaScript, and you can be assured that this approach will not go away.

Once you have a `<form/>` element object, you have the ability to submit the form by calling the `submit()` method, or you can clear the form or reset the form control elements to their default values with `reset()`. The `<form/>` element object also has an elements property, which is a collection of all elements contained within the form.

Probably the most frequently used property is the onsubmit event handler. It maps to the `<form/>` element's onsubmit attribute. Handling the submit event allows you to validate form fields and cancel the form's submission to the server if an error is found. So if you ask for a user's e-mail address and he or she provides the answer "Use the Force, Luke," you can identify the invalid data and prohibit the user from submitting the form until his or her data validates.

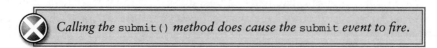

Calling the submit() *method does cause the* submit *event to fire.*

Of course, the use of form validation implies the use of form control elements. Let's look briefly at the various form controls and some common properties their DOM objects expose.

FORM CONTROL ELEMENTS

There are several elements commonly used to allow input from the user. Figures 26-1, 26-2, 26-3, and 26-4 show them grouped by functionality.

The majority of form controls are created via the `<input/>` element, and the type attribute determines what function that `<input/>` element performs. In the coming lessons you'll look at each of these categories and learn how to use JavaScript to access them in the DOM. But first let's look at a few properties and methods common to form controls.

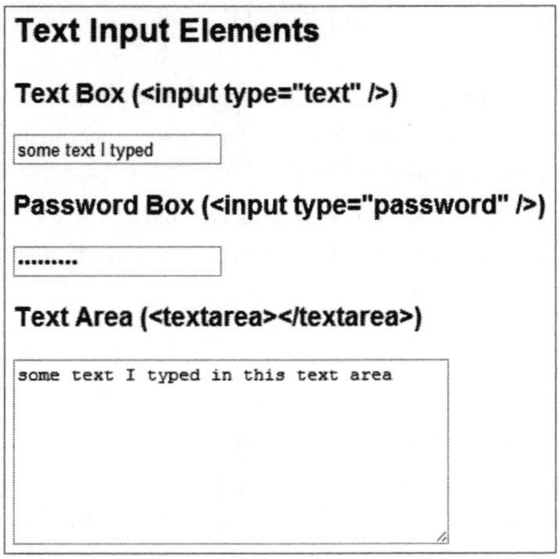

Text Input Elements

Text Box (<input type="text" />)

some text I typed

Password Box (<input type="password" />)

·········

Text Area (<textarea></textarea>)

some text I typed in this text area

FIGURE 26-1

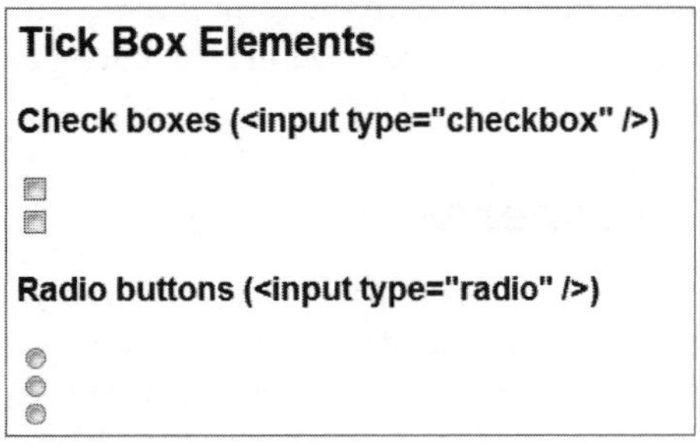

Tick Box Elements

Check boxes (<input type="checkbox" />)

☐
☐

Radio buttons (<input type="radio" />)

◎
◎
◎

FIGURE 26-2

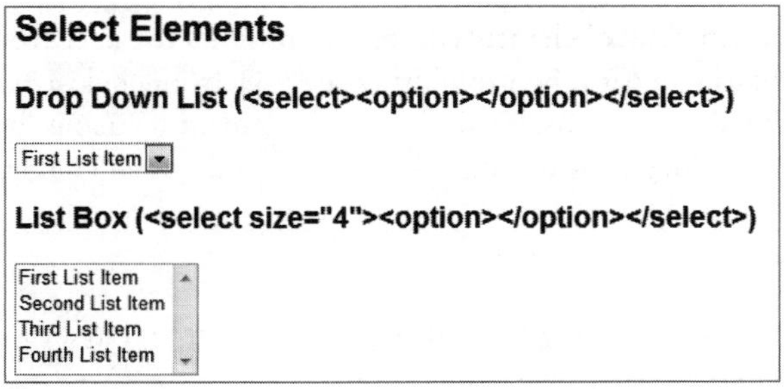

Select Elements

Drop Down List (<select><option></option></select>)

First List Item ▾

List Box (<select size="4"><option></option></select>)

First List Item ▲
Second List Item
Third List Item
Fourth List Item ▾

FIGURE 26-3

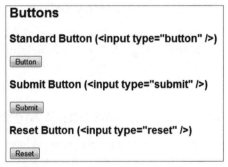

Buttons

Standard Button (<input type="button" />)

Button

Submit Button (<input type="submit" />)

Submit

Reset Button (<input type="reset" />)

Reset

FIGURE 26-4

The name Property

All form control elements have a name attribute, and thus their DOM objects have a name property that maps to that attribute. The value of this property is to provide a unique name for the element so that you can easily access them within the DOM. Also, the name property is part of the information sent to the server when the form is submitted. So nearly every element within a form will have a name property.

The value Property

Chances are that an element has a value attribute if the element in question is used to get data from the user. The corresponding DOM object for that element also has a value property, which gets and sets the value associated with the element. If the form control is a textbox (an <input/> element with type text), the value of that control is the text contained within the textbox. The actual value of an element varies according to the particular form control, so you'll see how the value is determined for each control in the coming lessons.

The form Property

Nearly every element in an HTML page can have an ID attribute. Because of this, those elements that do have an ID attribute can be retrieved via the document.getElementById() method — including form control elements. So it's possible to retrieve a form control element with getElementById() without doing anything with the form it resides in. But what if you need to find the form that particular element is in afterward? You use the form property, which returns the <form/> element object the control resides in.

The type Property

When you do a lot of form processing, you find yourself writing generic functions that you can use on any form to manipulate data or the DOM objects of the controls within the form. In such functions, the type property can be very helpful in determining what part a control plays within the form. The type property maps directly to the HTML element's type attribute.

The disabled Property

There are times when you want to disable a form control element; doing so prohibits the user from using the control. This can be helpful in validating a form by prohibiting the user from clicking the submit button before all required fields are filled in. You disable or enable an element by using the disabled property and assigning it a Boolean value; true disables the element and false enables it.

The focus() and blur() Methods

All form control element objects have the focus() and blur() methods, and they are related to concepts applied not only in web pages but in computer science in general.

In the real world, when you *focus* on an object, you give that object your attention. It may be a coffee mug or a light switch, but whatever it is, it has your attention. Typically, when an item has your focus, your actions are sent to that object. If you're looking at a coffee mug, chances are you are going to reach for it and take a sip. Or if you're looking at a light switch, it's a good indication that you're thinking of switching it on or off.

In JavaScript, focus() works much as it does in the real world. When you give a window in your operating system focus, every keystroke you make goes to that window. When you give a textbox in a web page focus, the keystrokes you make put text inside the textbox. So calling focus() on an element causes the browser to focus on that element.

Blur is a concept that is just the opposite of focus. If something is blurred, it does not have your (or the browser's) attention, and thus any keystroke you make will not be sent to an element that is blurred. So calling blur() on an element doesn't visibly blur that element on the screen, but it removes focus from that element.

These two methods are also linked to two events: focus and blur. An element fires these events when focus is given to and taken away from the element, respectively.

TRY IT

In this lesson, you are briefly introduced to forms and common properties and methods of form controls.

Lesson Requirements

For this lesson, you need a text editor; any plain text editor will do. For Microsoft Windows users, Notepad is available by default on your system or you can download Microsoft's free Visual Web Developer Express (www.microsoft.com/express/web/) or Web Matrix (www.asp.net/webmatrix/). Mac OS X users can use TextMate, which comes as part of OS X, or download a trial for Coda (www.panic.com/coda/). Linux users can use the built-in VIM.

You also need a modern web browser. Choose any of the following:

➤ Internet Explorer 8+

➤ Google Chrome

➤ Firefox 3.5+

➤ Apple Safari 4+

➤ Opera 10+

Create a subfolder called Lesson26 in the JS24Hour folder you created in Lesson 1. Store the files you create in this lesson in the Lesson26 folder.

Step-by-Step

1. Type the following HTML:

```
<html>
<head>
    <title>Lesson 26: Example 01</title>
</head>
<body>
<form name="theForm" action="" onsubmit="trySubmit(event)">
    <input type="submit" value="Submit" />
</form>
<script type="text/javascript" src="eventutility.js"></script>
<script type="text/javascript">
function trySubmit(event) {
    if (confirm("Do you want to stop submission?")) {
        eventUtility.preventDefault(event);
    }
}
</script>
</body>
</html>
```

Save this as `lesson26_example01.htm`. The page consists of one `<form/>` named `theForm`. It has an `onsubmit` event handler set to the `trySubmit()` function. Notice that a variable called `event` is being passed to the function. This ability was not mentioned in Lesson 17, but it's worth mentioning now.

When assigning an event handler using an HTML attribute, you can pass the event object to the handling function by using the word `event`. This gives you access to the event object in the handling function because, by default with HTML attribute event handlers, the event object isn't passed to the function. You must pass it yourself if you want access to that object.

The `trySubmit()` function accepts the event object as an argument. It asks the user if he or she wants to cancel the form submission. If the user clicks OK, the submission is stopped. If the user clicks Cancel, the form submits (although it really doesn't send data to any server).

2. It isn't clear if `trySubmit()` actually works, so add the bold line in the following code:

```
<html>
<head>
    <title>Lesson 26: Example 01</title>
</head>
<body>
<form name="theForm" action="" onsubmit="trySubmit(event)">
    <input type="submit" value="Submit" />
</form>
<script type="text/javascript" src="eventutility.js"></script>
<script type="text/javascript">
alert("Page Loaded");

function trySubmit(event) {
    if (confirm("Do you want to stop submission?")) {
        eventUtility.preventDefault(event);
    }
}
</script>
</body>
</html>
```

The call to `alert()` happens as the page loads into the browser. So when the user clicks the submit button, `alert()` won't execute if the form submission is cancelled. But if the form is allowed to submit, the browser will reload the page and call `alert()` again.

To get the sample code files, you can download Lesson 26 from the book's website at `www.wrox.com`.

 Please select Lesson 26 on the DVD to view the video that accompanies this lesson.

27

Scripting Buttons

Probably the most common form control is the button. Even though you can submit a form by calling its `submit()` method (and thus without using a submit button), most forms have a button because of the relationship between a form and its controls.

Button controls can be created in one of two ways. You can use the `<input/>` element, like this:

```
<input type="submit" name="myButton" value="Button Text" />
```

Or you can use the `<button/>` element, like this:

```
<button type="submit" name="myButton2" value="Button Text"/>
```

Regardless of how you create a button, you can directly access its DOM object in one of two ways. First, you can get to the button through the form. The following code shows how to access the `<input/>` element named `myButton` (from the top of the page), assuming it's in a form named `theForm`:

```
var button = document.theForm.myButton;
```

Form control objects are automatically added as properties to the forms they reside in. So this code first gets the `<form name="theForm" />` element object and then gets the `myButton` property. The second way to get to the button through the form is the ever-easy `document.getElementById()` method, but in the case of the `myButton` button, `getElementById()` will not work because it has no `id` attribute.

After you have access to the DOM object, you can manipulate it however you see fit. For example, the following code sets a `click` event handler (using the event utility) to modify the button every time it's clicked:

```
var count = 0;
var button = document.theForm.myButton;

eventUtility.addEvent(button, "click", function(event) {
```

```
    var eSrc = eventUtility.getTarget(event);

    eSrc.value = "You clicked me " + ++count + " times.";
});
```

This code creates two variables called `count` and `button`. The former is used to count how many times the button is clicked, and the latter gets the `<input/>` element's DOM object. With a reference to that object, the code then sets an event handler to handle the `click` event. When the button is clicked, the button's `value` property is changed to reflect the number of times the button has been clicked. A button's `value` property gets or sets the text that is displayed within the button.

 Remember that ++ is an increment operator, and that when it appears before a variable, the value in the variable is incremented before the variable's value is returned.

There is a flaw in this event handler, however. Assuming that the `myButton` button is part of the `theForm` form, clicking the button causes the form to submit. Its `type` attribute is set to `submit`, so this isn't very surprising. This is easy enough to fix; simply call `eventUtility.preventDefault()` and the form will not submit. The default action of a submit button is to submit the form it resides in. So when you click a submit button, a series of events fire in the following order:

1. `mousedown`
2. `mouseup`
3. `click`
4. `submit`

The `submit` event does not fire until after the `click` event fires, and since `submit` is the default event of a submit button, calling `preventDefault()` will prevent the `submit` event from firing. The same can be said for buttons of type `reset`. The `reset` event fires after `click`, and calling `preventDefault()` in the handler for `click` suppresses the `reset` event.

For the most part these same concepts apply to buttons created with the `<button/>` element. According to the HTML specification, it doesn't really matter how you create a button; the `<button/>` element does allow you to add content to it, however, as shown in the following HTML code:

```
<button name="myButton3" type="submit">
    <p id="buttonContent">Button Text</p>
</button>
```

Here a `<p/>` element with an `id` of `buttonContent` contains the text "Button Text", and it is added as a child to `<button/>`. This content renders inside the `<button/>`, so the content dictates what the user sees as opposed to the `value` property of the `<input/>` element.

What makes `<button/>` elements so different, as far as scripting is concerned, is that the content within the button can also be the target of an event. So in order to replicate the functionality from the `click` event handler for the `myButton` button, a few changes must be made to the event handler function.

Assume the `myButton3` button replaces the `myButton` button in the `theForm` form, and look at the following code:

```
var count = 0;
var button = document.theForm.myButton3;

eventUtility.addEvent(button, "click", function(event) {
    var content = document.getElementById("buttonContent");

    content.innerHTML = "You clicked me " + ++count + " times.";
    eventUtility.preventDefault(event);
});
```

The event handler in this code gets the `<p/>` element by using `getElementById()`, and then sets its `innerHTML` to reflect the number of times the button has been clicked. This is absolutely the easiest approach. Otherwise you would have to acquire the event target, check to see if the target is the `<p/>` element, and, if it's not, search for that element in the DOM tree. So if you plan on using the `<button/>` element, and you want to modify its contents, put an `id` attribute on the elements you want to modify.

Even though you can modify a button in this way, chances are pretty good that the only modification you'll make to a button is disabling it. If you visit discussion boards often you may have noticed something along the lines of a double post. A double post is caused when the user fills out the form, clicks the submit button, and then clicks it again before the browser loads the server's response from the first submission. It's a common problem wherever forms appear, and it can cause serious problems if the user double-posts a form to make a purchase.

You'll look at how to disable a button in the following Try It section.

TRY IT

In this lesson, you learn about the button control, and the differences between creating them with `<input/>` and `<button/>` elements.

Lesson Requirements

For this lesson, you need a text editor; any plain text editor will do. For Microsoft Windows users, Notepad is available by default on your system or you can download Microsoft's free Visual Web Developer Express (www.microsoft.com/express/web/) or Web Matrix (www.asp.net/webmatrix/). Mac OS X users can use TextMate, which comes as part of OS X, or download a trial for Coda (www.panic.com/coda/). Linux users can use the built-in VIM.

You also need a modern web browser. Choose any of the following:

➤ Internet Explorer 8+

➤ Google Chrome

➤ Firefox 3.5+

➤ Apple Safari 4+

➤ Opera 10+

Create a subfolder called Lesson27 in the JS24Hour folder you created in Lesson 1. Store the files you create in this lesson in the Lesson27 folder.

Step-by-Step

1. Type the following HTML:

```
<html>
<head>
    <title>Lesson 27: Example 01</title>
</head>
<body>
<form name="theForm" action="" onsubmit="validateForm(event)">
    <input name="btnSubmit" type="submit" value="Submit" />
</form>
<script type="text/javascript" src="eventutility.js"></script>
<script type="text/javascript">

</script>
</body>
</html>
```

Save this as lesson27_example01.htm. The page consists of one <form/> named theForm. It has an onsubmit event handler set to the validateForm() function. Inside the form is a submit button named btnSubmit.

2. Now add the bold lines in the following code:

```
<html>
<head>
    <title>Lesson 27: Example 01</title>
</head>
<body>
<form name="theForm" action="" onsubmit="validateForm(event)">
    <input name="btnSubmit" type="submit" value="Submit" />
</form>
<script type="text/javascript" src="eventutility.js"></script>
<script type="text/javascript">
function validateForm(event) {
    var button = document.theForm.btnSubmit;

    button.disabled = true;

    var notValidated = confirm("Do you want to simulate an invalid form?");
}
</script>
</body>
</html>
```

This code adds the `validateForm()` function, and it accepts an event object as an argument. The first line of the function gets the submit button and stores it in the button variable. Then you disable the button by assigning `true` to the `disabled` property. The last line of this code simulates a validation error: It calls the `confirm()` method to ask if you want to simulate a validation error. If you click OK, `notValidated` is `true`. If Cancel, `notValidated` is `false`.

3. Nothing happens when you click OK or Cancel in the confirm box at this point, so add the following bold code:

```html
<html>
<head>
    <title>Lesson 27: Example 01</title>
</head>
<body>
<form name="theForm" action="" onsubmit="validateForm(event)">
    <input name="btnSubmit" type="submit" value="Submit" />
</form>
<script type="text/javascript" src="eventutility.js"></script>
<script type="text/javascript">
function validateForm(event) {
    var button = document.theForm.btnSubmit;

    button.disabled = true;

    var notValidated = confirm("Do you want to simulate an invalid form?");

    if (notValidated) {
        alert("Invalid data was found in the form. Please fix and submit
again");
        button.disabled = false;
        eventUtility.preventDefault(event);
    }
}
</script>
</body>
</html>
```

This new code checks the value of `notValidated`. If it's `true` (meaning a simulated validation error took place), an alert box tells the user that something is invalid and to fix the error. After the alert box is dismissed, the button is re-enabled by having its `disabled` property set to `false`, and the call to `eventUtility.preventDefault()` prevents the form from being submitted.

Of course, if the Cancel button is clicked, meaning that `notValidated` is `false`, then the form submits and reloads the page to simulate the validation of all fields.

In some of the future lessons, you build off this example and perform actual validation routines.

To get the sample code files, you can download Lesson 27 from the book's website at www.wrox.com.

Please select Lesson 27 on the DVD to view the video that accompanies this lesson.

28

Scripting Text Elements

If buttons are the most common form control, text-based input elements are a close second. There are several types of text elements, making them the best tool for inputting data to submit to your web application. They are:

➤ The textbox

➤ The password textbox

➤ The hidden textbox

➤ The Multiline textbox

The differences between the textbox types are minimal. Let's start with the simple textbox.

THE TEXTBOX

You create a textbox with the `<input/>` element and set its `type` attribute to the value of `text`, like this:

```
<input type="text" name="textBox" />
```

This HTML creates a textbox named `textBox`. To access it in a form, you get the element either by its `id` attribute (which this example does not have), or through the form it belongs to. Assuming this textbox resides in a form called `theForm`, the following code gets a reference to this textbox:

```
var txtBox = document.theForm.textBox;
```

When you create a textbox, you can set its `value` attribute to contain a text value. The `value` attribute dictates what appears inside the textbox when the browser renders it. This attribute maps directly to the `value` property, so you can get or set the text in a textbox by using the `value` property like this:

```
txtBox.value = "Some new data";
```

The contents of the `value` property are always a string, even if numeric characters are entered. So when you expect a textbox to be used for numeric data, it's always a good idea to convert the textbox's value to a number by using the `parseInt()` or `parseFloat()` methods. Not only does the conversion save you from unwanted string concatenation operations (using the + operator), but it also helps you spot invalid data.

In addition to the common properties and methods discussed in Lesson 26, textbox objects have a method called `select()`; it selects all the text inside the textbox. When used in combination with the `focus()` method, `select()` is useful when you want to direct a user to a particular textbox's value, such as when the user enters invalid data.

Also, textbox objects have more events than just the `focus` and `blur` events discussed in Lesson 26. They have:

➤ `change`: Fires when the textbox loses focus and only if the text inside the textbox changed.

➤ `select`: Fires when a textbox's text is selected (calling `select()` fires this event too).

➤ `keydown`: Fires when a key on the keyboard is pressed down.

➤ `keyup`: Fires when a pressed key on the keyboard is released.

➤ `keypress`: Fires when a key on the keyboard is pressed and released.

THE PASSWORD TEXTBOX

The only purpose of the password textbox is to let users type a password while visually obfuscating each character. This obfuscation is only visual, keeping anyone looking over the user's shoulder from seeing the text the user types. The password textbox object's `value` property contains the actual text without any attempt at obfuscation or encryption of the data. This is actually beneficial, as you can compare the data input in a password textbox with other form data like the data input in a second password textbox, which is common.

To create a password textbox, use an `<input/>` element and set its type as `password`, like this:

```
<input type="password" name="password1" />
```

Password textboxes have the same methods and events as normal textboxes.

THE HIDDEN TEXTBOX

Like the password textbox, the hidden textbox is a specialty control that was derived for one purpose. Hidden textboxes hold the same type of data that other textboxes can hold, the primary difference being that hidden textboxes are hidden from view. Since they are hidden, the only way to get and set data in a hidden textbox is through the `value` attribute and property.

Hidden textboxes are created with the `<input/>` element, like this:

```
<input type="hidden" name="hiddenTextBox />
```

Because you use the `<input/>` element to create this textbox, it has the same properties, methods, and events as the normal and password textboxes. Yes, hidden textboxes even have the keyboard events, but good luck getting them to fire.

THE MULTILINE TEXTBOX

One problem with the normal textbox is that it allows only one line of text. In order to allow the user to input more than one line at a time, you can create a multiline textbox with the `<textarea/>` element:

```
<textarea name="multiLine" cols="30" rows="20">
    Line 1
    Line 2
</textarea>
```

The `cols` and `rows` attributes determines the size of the `<textarea/>` element when rendered by the browser, but CSS can be used to set more exact dimensions. These two attributes are available to you in the DOM, but rarely, if ever, will you want to change them dynamically.

Like the other textboxes, the `<textarea/>` element object has a `value` property, and it gets and sets the text between the opening and closing tags of the element. Also like the other textboxes, `<textarea/>` objects have the `select()` method, as well as the `change`, `keydown`, `keyup`, and `keypress` events.

TRY IT

In this lesson, you learn about the various textbox controls. You also learn basic form validation and how to cope with invalid data with the `value` property and `select()` and `focus()` methods.

Lesson Requirements

For this lesson, you need a text editor; any plain text editor will do. For Microsoft Windows users, Notepad is available by default on your system or you can download Microsoft's free Visual Web Developer Express (www.microsoft.com/express/web/) or Web Matrix (www.asp.net/webmatrix/). Mac OS X users can use TextMate, which comes as part of OS X, or download a trial for Coda (www.panic.com/coda/). Linux users can use the built-in VIM.

You also need a modern web browser. Choose any of the following:

➤   Internet Explorer 8+

➤   Google Chrome

➤   Firefox 3.5+

➤   Apple Safari 4+

➤   Opera 10+

Create a subfolder called Lesson28 in the JS24Hour folder you created in Lesson 1. Store the files you create in this lesson in the Lesson28 folder.

Step-by-Step

1. Type the following HTML:

```
<html>
<head>
    <title>Lesson 28: Example 01</title>
</head>
<body>
<form name="theForm" action="" onsubmit="validateForm(event)">
    <p>
        Name: <input type="text" name="txtName" />
    </p>
    <p>
        Age: <input type="text" name="txtAge" />
    </p>
    <p>
        Email: <input type="text" name="txtEmail" />
    </p>
    <p>
        Password: <input type="password" name="txtPassword1" />
    </p>
    <p>
        Retype Password: <input type="password" name="txtPassword2" />
    </p>

    <input name="btnSubmit" type="submit" value="Submit" />
</form>
<script type="text/javascript" src="eventutility.js"></script>
<script type="text/javascript">

</script>
</body>
</html>
```

Save this as lesson28_example01.htm. The page consists of one <form/> named theForm. It has an onsubmit event handler set to the validateForm() function. Inside the form are several textboxes with which the user can input his or her name, age, e-mail and password, as well as a submit button.

2. The first bit of JavaScript you'll write is a function called isEmpty(). It is bold in the following code; add it to your file.

```
<html>
<head>
    <title>Lesson 28: Example 01</title>
</head>
<body>
<form name="theForm" action="" onsubmit="validateForm(event)">
    <p>
        Name: <input type="text" name="txtName" />
```

```
        </p>
        <p>
            Age: <input type="text" name="txtAge" />
        </p>
        <p>
            Email: <input type="text" name="txtEmail" />
        </p>
        <p>
            Password: <input type="password" name="txtPassword1" />
        </p>
        <p>
            Retype Password: <input type="password" name="txtPassword2" />
        </p>

        <input name="btnSubmit" type="submit" value="Submit" />
    </form>
    <script type="text/javascript" src="eventutility.js"></script>
    <script type="text/javascript">
    function isEmpty(value) {
        return (value === "");
    }
    </script>
    </body>
    </html>
```

Its job is simple: Return a Boolean value based on whether the string is empty.

3. Now start writing the `validateForm()` function. Add the bold code in this sample:

```
    <html>
    <head>
        <title>Lesson 28: Example 01</title>
    </head>
    <body>
    <form name="theForm" action="" onsubmit="validateForm(event)">
        <p>
            Name: <input type="text" name="txtName" />
        </p>
        <p>
            Age: <input type="text" name="txtAge" />
        </p>
        <p>
            Email: <input type="text" name="txtEmail" />
        </p>
        <p>
            Password: <input type="password" name="txtPassword1" />
        </p>
        <p>
            Retype Password: <input type="password" name="txtPassword2" />
        </p>

        <input name="btnSubmit" type="submit" value="Submit" />
    </form>
    <script type="text/javascript" src="eventutility.js"></script>
    <script type="text/javascript">
```

```
function isEmpty(value) {
    return (value === "");
}

function validateForm(event) {
    var theForm = document.theForm;
    var txtName = theForm.txtName;
    var txtAge = theForm.txtAge;
    var txtEmail = theForm.txtEmail;
    var txtPassword1 = theForm.txtPassword1;
    var txtPassword2 = theForm.txtPassword2;
    var button = theForm.btnSubmit;
    var age = parseInt(txtAge.value);

    button.disabled = true;
}
</script>
</body>
</html>
```

This is the beginning of the function. It defines a variety of variables, the majority of which get the DOM object of each control in the form. The value of the txtAge textbox is converted to a number, which is assigned to the final variable, age.

4. Now begin to validate the textboxes in the order in which they appear. Add the bold code:

```
<html>
<head>
    <title>Lesson 28: Example 01</title>
</head>
<body>
<form name="theForm" action="" onsubmit="validateForm(event)">
    <p>
        Name: <input type="text" name="txtName" />
    </p>
    <p>
        Age: <input type="text" name="txtAge" />
    </p>
    <p>
        Email: <input type="text" name="txtEmail" />
    </p>
    <p>
        Password: <input type="password" name="txtPassword1" />
    </p>
    <p>
        Retype Password: <input type="password" name="txtPassword2" />
    </p>

    <input name="btnSubmit" type="submit" value="Submit" />
</form>
<script type="text/javascript" src="eventutility.js"></script>
<script type="text/javascript">
function isEmpty(value) {
    return (value === "");
```

```
    }

    function validateForm(event) {
        var theForm = document.theForm;
        var txtName = theForm.txtName;
        var txtAge = theForm.txtAge;
        var txtEmail = theForm.txtEmail;
        var txtPassword1 = theForm.txtPassword1;
        var txtPassword2 = theForm.txtPassword2;
        var button = theForm.btnSubmit;
        var age = parseInt(txtAge.value);

        button.disabled = true;

        // validate name field
        if (!isEmpty(txtName.value)) {

            // more code here

        } else {
            alert("Please enter your name.");
            txtName.focus();
        }

        button.disabled = false;
        eventUtility.preventDefault(event);
    }
    </script>
    </body>
    </html>
```

This is the basic pattern used to validate all the textboxes. The idea is to ensure that as one textbox passes validation, the validation of the next one begins in the `if` block of the previous textbox's validation check. Once the final validation check is performed and the check passes, the function simply returns and the browser submits the form.

If any textbox fails validation, its `else` block sends a message to the user and gives focus to the textbox. Then the button is re-enabled and the form is prevented from being submitted.

It's a quick and easy way to validate a form.

5. Add the code to validate the age textbox. Use the `isNaN()` method to determine if what the user entered was a number. Also check to make sure the number entered is greater than zero. That code is bold here:

```
    function validateForm(event) {
        var theForm = document.theForm;
        var txtName = theForm.txtName;
        var txtAge = theForm.txtAge;
        var txtEmail = theForm.txtEmail;
        var txtPassword1 = theForm.txtPassword1;
        var txtPassword2 = theForm.txtPassword2;
        var button = theForm.btnSubmit;
        var age = parseInt(txtAge.value);
```

```
        button.disabled = true;

        // validate name field
        if (!isEmpty(txtName.value)) {

            // validate age
            if (!isNaN(age) && age > 0) {

                // more code here

            } else {
                alert("Please enter your age.");
                txtAge.focus();
                txtAge.select();
            }

        } else {
            alert("Please enter your name.");
            txtName.focus();
        }

        button.disabled = false;
        eventUtility.preventDefault(event);
    }
```

For printing, the HTML and `isEmpty()` function were omitted. This code adds the age validation, and it looks similar to the code that validates the name textbox.

6. Now add code to validate the e-mail address. Ensure that the @ symbol is present in the textbox's value, and that it isn't the first character in the string. That code is bold here:

```
function validateForm(event) {
    var theForm = document.theForm;
    var txtName = theForm.txtName;
    var txtAge = theForm.txtAge;
    var txtEmail = theForm.txtEmail;
    var txtPassword1 = theForm.txtPassword1;
    var txtPassword2 = theForm.txtPassword2;
    var button = theForm.btnSubmit;
    var age = parseInt(txtAge.value);

    button.disabled = true;

    // validate name field
    if (!isEmpty(txtName.value)) {

        // validate age
        if (!isNaN(age) && age > 0) {

            // validate email field
            if (txtEmail.value.indexOf("@") > 0) {

                // more code here

            } else {
```

```
                    alert("Please enter a valid email address.");
                    txtEmail.focus();
                    txtEmail.select();
                }

        } else {
            alert("Please enter your age.");
            txtAge.focus();
            txtAge.select();
        }

    } else {
        alert("Please enter your name.");
        txtName.focus();
    }

    button.disabled = false;
    eventUtility.preventDefault(event);
}
```

The same thing as before happens if the validation test fails. An alert box asks the user to enter a valid e-mail address, and focus is given to the textbox.

7. Now add the code to validate the passwords. This is a two-step process: Make sure that one of the password fields isn't empty, and then make sure both fields have the same text. Add the bold code:

```
function validateForm(event) {
    var theForm = document.theForm;
    var txtName = theForm.txtName;
    var txtAge = theForm.txtAge;
    var txtEmail = theForm.txtEmail;
    var txtPassword1 = theForm.txtPassword1;
    var txtPassword2 = theForm.txtPassword2;
    var button = theForm.btnSubmit;
    var age = parseInt(txtAge.value);

    button.disabled = true;

    // validate name field
    if (!isEmpty(txtName.value)) {

        // validate age
        if (!isNaN(age) && age > 0) {

            // validate email field
            if (txtEmail.value.indexOf("@") > 0) {

                // validate password - pass 1
                if (!isEmpty(txtPassword1.value)) {

                    // validate password - pass 2
                    if (txtPassword1.value === txtPassword2.value) {
                        return;
```

```
                        } else {
                            alert("Passwords do not match. Please reenter them.");
                            txtPassword1.focus();
                            txtPassword1.select();
                        }

                    } else {
                        alert("Password cannot be blank.");
                        txtPassword1.focus();
                        txtPassword1.select();
                    }

                } else {
                    alert("Please enter a valid email address.");
                    txtEmail.focus();
                    txtEmail.select();
                }

            } else {
                alert("Please enter your age.");
                txtAge.focus();
                txtAge.select();
            }

        } else {
            alert("Please enter your name.");
            txtName.focus();
        }

        button.disabled = false;
        eventUtility.preventDefault(event);
    }
```

It doesn't matter which password field you check to see if it's empty. This code checks the first password field. If that check passes, the values of both password textboxes are compared. If all validation rules are passed, the function returns and the browser submits the form. If not, an alert box tells the user what he or she needs to do in order to enter valid information, and the browser is prohibited from submitting the form.

To get the sample code files, you can download Lesson 28 from the book's website at www.wrox.com.

 Please select Lesson 28 on the DVD to view the video that accompanies this lesson.

29

Scripting Selection Boxes

The HTML specification provides the `<select/>` element so page authors can add a menu of options to a form. The menu the `<select/>` element generates can look like a drop-down list from which you can select only one item, or like a list box that allows you to select multiple items. These selection boxes have one or more `<option/>` elements inside the opening and closing `<select>` tags. The following HTML shows an example:

```
<select id="dayOfTheWeek" name="dayOfTheWeek" size="5">
    <option value="0">Sunday</option>
    <option value="1">Monday</option>
    <option value="2">Tuesday</option>
    <option value="3">Wednesday</option>
    <option value="4">Thursday</option>
    <option value="5" selected="selected">Friday</option>
    <option value="6">Saturday</option>
</select>
```

The number of options visible in the browser is determined by the `<select/>` element's `size` attribute, and it is this attribute that determines how the browser renders the `<select/>` element. If `size` is greater than 1, the browser renders the element as a list box showing the specified number of options at a time. If `size` is 1 or isn't specified, the browser renders the selection box as a drop-down list.

The `<select/>` element DOM object has a property called `options`, a collection of `<option/>` element objects. Every `<option/>` element inside the `<select/>` element is an item in the `options` collection. So, using the previous `<select/>` element, you can access the `<option/>` element for Monday, like this:

```
var dayOfWeek = document.getElementById("dayOfTheWeek");

var mondayOption = dayOfWeek.options[1];
alert(mondayOption.value); // 1
```

This code first gets the `<select/>` element object from the DOM via the `getElementById()` method (you can also access a `<select/>` element object through its containing form). Then, using the `options` collection, the code gets the `<option/>` element object at the second position and assigns the `<option/>` object to the `mondayOption` variable. The final line of this code uses the `<option/>` object's `value` property, which gets the value contained within the element's `value` attribute — 1 in this case.

You can get the option that is currently selected by combining the `options` collection with the `<select/>` object's `selectedIndex` property, like this:

```
var selectedDay = dayOfWeek.options[dayOfWeek.selectedIndex]; // Friday option

alert(selectedDay.value); // 5
```

Because the `<option/>` element for Friday has the `selected` attribute, it is rendered as the selected option in the menu, and the `<select/>` object's `selectedIndex` property gets the index of that option in the `options` collection.

You can also use the `selectedIndex` property to change the selected option by assigning it the index of the option you want to select. Let's say you want Tuesday to be the selected day. The `<option/>` element for Tuesday is at index position 2. So, to change the selected option to Tuesday, you could use the following code:

```
dayOfWeek.selectedIndex = 2;
```

After this code executes, the browser changes the selected option from Friday to Tuesday.

After you have a reference to an `<option/>` object, you can retrieve two more pieces of information about that option other than its value. You can use the `index` property of the `<option/>` to get its position in the `options` collection, or you can use its `text` property to get or set new text associated with it. Most of the time, however, you simply want its value.

As with most everything in the DOM, you're not stuck with whatever is hardcoded into the HTML. You can add and remove options from `<select/>` elements as you need to.

REMOVING OPTIONS

Options are extremely easy to remove from a selection box. To remove an option you simply assign a value of `null` at the desired index position in the `options` collection, like this:

```
dayOfWeek.options[4] = null;
```

This code removes the Thursday option from the `<select/>` element. Fortunately, removing an `<option/>` object from the `options` collection automatically reorders the remaining options by shifting down the ones at higher index positions. Now the option for Friday is at index 4 and Saturday is at index 5. You don't have to write any code to reposition and reorder the remaining `<option/>` elements; the DOM does it for you.

You can also remove an option with the `<select/>` object's `remove()` method. It accepts a numeric value as an argument specifying the index position you want to remove. So, instead of setting the Thursday `<option/>` to `null`, you could do this:

```
dayOfWeek.remove(4);
```

Now that Thursday is gone from the week, the world is in disarray. We had better put it back...

ADDING OPTIONS

Creating an `<option/>` element object is easy. Simply call the `Option()` constructor and pass it two arguments:

```
var thursOption = new Option("Thursday", 4);
```

This code creates a new `<option/>` object. Its text is `Thursday` and its value is 4. Now that you have created an option, it's time to add it to the `<select/>` element. Unfortunately, adding options to a `<select/>` object isn't as straightforward as removing them.

One way that you can add a new `<option/>` object is by assigning the new object at a particular index in the `options` collection. In doing so, however, you actually overwrite an existing option. Look at the following code:

```
dayOfWeek.options[4] = thursOption;
```

This code assigns the new `<option/>` object to the element at index 4. You may remember that the `<option/>` object at position 4 is now the Friday option. So what this code actually does is overwrite the Friday option with the new Thursday option. Oops. You can, however, add a new option to the end of the options collection without overwriting anything, like this:

```
dayOfWeek.options[dayOfWeek.options.length] = thursOption;
```

This code uses the `length` property to assign the `thursOption` object to the very end of the `options` collection — putting Thursday after Saturday. Oops again. While this may be fine in some cases, it hardly makes sense to have a list of days out of order. You could write code to reorder the options and put them in the correct order, but that requires a lot of extra code (and your author is lazy).

For this reason `<select/>` objects have a method called `add()`, which allows you to add an `<option/>` object at a specified position. This method accepts two arguments: the option to add, and the existing option before which you want to place it. So adding the new option for Thursday can look like this:

```
var fridayOption = dayOfWeek.options[4]; // Friday

dayOfWeek.add(thursOption, fridayOption);
```

This code gets the `<option/>` object for Friday, which is found at index position 4. Then a call to `add()` adds the new `<option/>` for Thursday before the `<option/>` for Friday. All three affected `<option/>` objects (Thursday, Friday, and Saturday) are reorganized and given new index positions. The `<option/>` for Thursday is back at index 4, Friday is at index 5, and Saturday is at index 6.

All is well again…unless you try to run this code in Internet Explorer (IE) 7 (or IE8 non-standards mode). IE7 craps out (yes, that's a technical term) when `add()` is called.

It's not that IE7 (and IE8 in non-standards mode) doesn't have the `add()` method for `<select/>` objects. It does, but it expects the second argument to be the index at which you want to put the new option. So for IE7 the code would look like this:

```
dayOfWeek.add(thursOption, 4);
```

This code inserts the new Thursday option at index position 4, and IE7 then reorganizes the `options` collection, pushing the Friday and Saturday options to positions 5 and 6, respectively.

This is a problem, but it's a problem with an easy solution: *exception handling*. This is actually a topic covered in Lesson 37, and as such it won't be given much coverage here. When a browser craps out (again, it's technical) because of JavaScript code, the JavaScript engine *throws* an *exception*. The term "throw" is used throughout computer science, and in this case it means the engine essentially generates an exception, or error, during the execution of a program.

Exceptions happen. They're a part of programming, so a process called exception handling is used to handle code that may throw an exception. The process goes something like this:

➤   You try to execute code that can cause an exception. If it works, great! If not, an exception is thrown, and…

➤   You catch the exception and execute code that is typically safe to execute — such as code to send a message to the user or achieve the same results as the code that caused the exception.

To put this process into code, you use the `try...catch` statement shown here:

```
try {
    dayOfWeek.add(thursOption, fridayOption);
} catch (exceptionObject) {
    dayOfWeek.add(thursOption, 4);
}
```

This code uses `try...catch` by trying to execute the `add()` method by passing the Friday `<option/>` object. If that code throws an exception, code execution drops to the `catch` block and executes `add()` by specifying the index position 4. Now, when the browser executes this code, the new Thursday `<option/>` is placed in the correct position regardless of the browser used to execute the code.

 Don't worry about the `exceptionObject` *in the previous code. Exception handling is covered in more detail in Lesson 37.*

All right, so let's apply some of this information to the form you've been working with since Lesson 27.

TRY IT

In this lesson, you learn to script selection boxes by getting the selected option, getting data related to that option, and adding and removing options.

Lesson Requirements

For this lesson, you need a text editor; any plain text editor will do. For Microsoft Windows users, Notepad is available by default on your system or you can download Microsoft's free Visual Web Developer Express (www.microsoft.com/express/web/) or Web Matrix (www.asp.net/webmatrix/). Mac OS X users can use TextMate, which comes as part of OS X, or download a trial for Coda (www.panic.com/coda/). Linux users can use the built-in VIM.

You also need a modern web browser. Choose any of the following:

➤ Internet Explorer 8+

➤ Google Chrome

➤ Firefox 3.5+

➤ Apple Safari 4+

➤ Opera 10+

Create a subfolder called Lesson29 in the JS24Hour folder you created in Lesson 1. Store the files you create in this lesson in the Lesson29 folder.

Step-by-Step

1. Type the following HTML:

```
<html>
<head>
    <title>Lesson 29: Example 01</title>
</head>
<body>
<form name="theForm" action="" onsubmit="validateForm(event)">
    <p>
        Name: <input type="text" name="txtName" />
    </p>
    <p>
        Age: <input type="text" name="txtAge" />
    </p>
    <p>
        Email: <input type="text" name="txtEmail" />
    </p>
    <p>
        Password: <input type="password" name="txtPassword1" />
    </p>
    <p>
        Retype Password: <input type="password" name="txtPassword2" />
    </p>
```

```html
    <p>
        Your Favorite Day: <select id="dayOfTheWeek" name="dayOfTheWeek">
                            </select>
    </p>

    <input name="btnSubmit" type="submit" value="Submit" />
</form>
<script type="text/javascript" src="eventutility.js"></script>
<script type="text/javascript">
function isEmpty(value) {
    return (value === "");
}

function validateForm(event) {
    var theForm = document.theForm,
    var txtName = theForm.txtName;
    var txtAge = theForm.txtAge;
    var txtEmail = theForm.txtEmail;
    var txtPassword1 = theForm.txtPassword1;
    var txtPassword2 = theForm.txtPassword2;
    var button = theForm.btnSubmit;
    var age = parseInt(txtAge.value);

    button.disabled = true;

    // validate name field
    if (!isEmpty(txtName.value)) {

        // validate age
        if (!isNaN(age) && age > 0) {

            // validate email field
            if (txtEmail.value.indexOf("@") > 0) {

                // validate password - pass 1
                if (!isEmpty(txtPassword1.value)) {

                    // validate password - pass 2
                    if (txtPassword1.value === txtPassword2.value) {
                        return;
                    } else {
                        alert("Passwords do not match. Please reenter them.");
                        txtPassword1.focus();
                        txtPassword1.select();
                    }

                } else {
                    alert("Password cannot be blank.");
                    txtPassword1.focus();
                    txtPassword1.select();
                }

            } else {
                alert("Please enter a valid email address.");
```

```
                    txtEmail.focus();
                    txtEmail.select();
                }

            } else {
                alert("Please enter your age.");
                txtAge.focus();
                txtAge.select();
            }

        } else {
            alert("Please enter your name.");
            txtName.focus();
        }

        button.disabled = false;
        eventUtility.preventDefault(event);
    }
    </script>
    </body>
    </html>
```

Save this as `lesson29_example01.htm`. It is almost the same as the HTML page at the end of Lesson 28, but it now has a `<select/>` element with an `id` and `name` of `dayOfTheWeek`. It is empty, so you need to write a function to populate the `<select/>` element with options.

2. Add a function called `populateDays()`, and inside the function create an array called `days` containing the seven days of the week. Also add a line at the end of the `<script/>` element to execute `populateDays()`. The new code is bold:

```
    <html>
    <head>
        <title>Lesson 29: Example 01</title>
    </head>
    <body>
    <form name="theForm" action="" onsubmit="validateForm(event)">
        <p>
            Name: <input type="text" name="txtName" />
        </p>
        <p>
            Age: <input type="text" name="txtAge" />
        </p>
        <p>
            Email: <input type="text" name="txtEmail" />
        </p>
        <p>
            Password: <input type="password" name="txtPassword1" />
        </p>
        <p>
            Retype Password: <input type="password" name="txtPassword2" />
        </p>
        <p>
            Your Favorite Day: <select id="dayOfTheWeek" name="dayOfTheWeek">
                            </select>
```

```
    </p>

    <input name="btnSubmit" type="submit" value="Submit" />
</form>
<script type="text/javascript" src="eventutility.js"></script>
<script type="text/javascript">
function populateDays() {
    var days = [ "Sunday", "Monday", "Tuesday", "Wednesday",
        "Thursday", "Friday", "Saturday" ];
}

function isEmpty(value) {
    return (value === "");
}

function validateForm(event) {
    // removed for printing
}

populateDays();
</script>
</body>
</html>
```

3. Now create a few more variables. Get the `<select/>` element by using the `getElementById()` method and assign it to a variable called `dayOfWeek`. Also, create a variable to contain today's day by creating a new `Date` object and calling the `getDay()` method. The new code is bold:

```
<html>
<head>
    <title>Lesson 29: Example 01</title>
</head>
<body>
<form name="theForm" action="" onsubmit="validateForm(event)">
    <p>
        Name: <input type="text" name="txtName" />
    </p>
    <p>
        Age: <input type="text" name="txtAge" />
    </p>
    <p>
        Email: <input type="text" name="txtEmail" />
    </p>
    <p>
        Password: <input type="password" name="txtPassword1" />
    </p>
    <p>
        Retype Password: <input type="password" name="txtPassword2" />
    </p>
    <p>
        Your Favorite Day: <select id="dayOfTheWeek" name="dayOfTheWeek">
                        </select>
```

```
    </p>

    <input name="btnSubmit" type="submit" value="Submit" />
</form>
<script type="text/javascript" src="eventutility.js"></script>
<script type="text/javascript">
function populateDays() {
    var days = [ "Sunday", "Monday", "Tuesday", "Wednesday",
        "Thursday", "Friday", "Saturday" ];
    var dayOfWeek = document.getElementById("dayOfTheWeek");
    var today = (new Date()).getDay();
}

function isEmpty(value) {
    return (value === "");
}

function validateForm(event) {
    // removed for printing
}

populateDays();
</script>
</body>
</html>
```

Notice the code for the `today` variable. The code `new Date()` is encapsulated within a pair of parentheses. This is a trick used by professionals when they don't need a particular object for more than one piece of data. In the case of this script you don't need anything from the `Date` object except the value returned by `getDay()`. So an anonymous `Date` object is created and the `getDay()` method is called on that anonymous object. Remember that `getDay()` returns a numeric value associated with the day of the week. Sunday is 0, Monday is 1, Tuesday is 2, and so on.

4. Loop through the `days` array and add an option for each day. Use the index variable `i` as an option's value:

```
<html>
<head>
    <title>Lesson 29: Example 01</title>
</head>
<body>
<form name="theForm" action="" onsubmit="validateForm(event)">
    <p>
        Name: <input type="text" name="txtName" />
    </p>
    <p>
        Age: <input type="text" name="txtAge" />
    </p>
    <p>
        Email: <input type="text" name="txtEmail" />
    </p>
```

```
    <p>
        Password: <input type="password" name="txtPassword1" />
    </p>
    <p>
        Retype Password: <input type="password" name="txtPassword2" />
    </p>
    <p>
        Your Favorite Day: <select id="dayOfTheWeek" name="dayOfTheWeek">
                            </select>
    </p>

    <input name="btnSubmit" type="submit" value="Submit" />
</form>
<script type="text/javascript" src="eventutility.js"></script>
<script type="text/javascript">
function populateDays() {
    var days = [ "Sunday", "Monday", "Tuesday", "Wednesday",
        "Thursday", "Friday", "Saturday" ];
    var dayOfWeek = document.getElementById("dayOfTheWeek");
    var today = (new Date()).getDay();

    for (var i = 0; i < days.length; i++) {
        var length = dayofWeek.options.length;

        dayOfWeek.add(new Option(days[i], i), length);
    }
}

function isEmpty(value) {
    return (value === "");
}

function validateForm(event) {
    // removed for printing
}

populateDays();
</script>
</body>
</html>
```

The bold code shows the `for` loop iterating over the `days` array. For each element in the array a new `Option` object is created and added to the `<select/>` element. Note that the length of the `options` collection is retrieved and passed as the second parameter to `add()`. This adds the new `<option/>` object at the end of the `options` collection. This code works in all browsers, so you don't have to worry about catching any exceptions.

5. Finally, set the selected option to today's date using the `selectedIndex` property. New code is in bold:

```
<html>
<head>
    <title>Lesson 29: Example 01</title>
</head>
```

```
<body>
<form name="theForm" action="" onsubmit="validateForm(event)">
    <p>
        Name: <input type="text" name="txtName" />
    </p>
    <p>
        Age: <input type="text" name="txtAge" />
    </p>
    <p>
        Email: <input type="text" name="txtEmail" />
    </p>
    <p>
        Password: <input type="password" name="txtPassword1" />
    </p>
    <p>
        Retype Password: <input type="password" name="txtPassword2" />
    </p>
    <p>
        Your Favorite Day: <select id="dayOfTheWeek" name="dayOfTheWeek">
                            </select>
    </p>

    <input name="btnSubmit" type="submit" value="Submit" />
</form>
<script type="text/javascript" src="eventutility.js"></script>
<script type="text/javascript">
function populateDays() {
    var days = [ "Sunday", "Monday", "Tuesday", "Wednesday",
        "Thursday", "Friday", "Saturday" ];
    var dayOfWeek = document.getElementById("dayOfTheWeek");
    var today = (new Date()).getDay();

    for (var i = 0; i < days.length; i++) {
        var length = dayofWeek.options.length;

        dayOfWeek.add(new Option(days[i], i), length);
    }

    dayOfWeek.selectedIndex = today;
}

function isEmpty(value) {
    return (value === "");
}

function validateForm(event) {
    // removed for printing
}

populateDays();
</script>
</body>
</html>
```

This new line of code uses the value contained within the today variable to select the current day from the drop-down list.

Be sure to save the file and run it in any modern browser. You'll find that it works like a charm.

To get the sample code files, you can download Lesson 29 from the book's website at www.wrox.com.

 Please select Lesson 29 on the DVD to view the video that accompanies this lesson.

30

Scripting Checkboxes and Radio Buttons

Checkboxes and radio buttons are used in two different ways. You use radio buttons for a list of multiple options that are mutually exclusive and from which users can select only one. Checkboxes are for multiple options from which users can choose any number. Despite this distinction, the primary purpose of both is to give users a number of options to choose from.

They also have something else in common: Their DOM objects share the same properties, methods, and events. But scripting them can be a little different due to how they are represented in the DOM. This lesson teaches you how to write JavaScript against these controls, starting with the checkbox.

SCRIPTING CHECKBOXES

You generate checkboxes by using the `<input />` element and setting its `type` attribute to `checkbox`, as shown in the following HTML:

```
<input type="checkbox" name="color" value="Red" checked="checked" />
```

This HTML creates a checkbox named `color` with a value of `Red` that is checked by default because of the presence of the `checked` attribute. In the DOM, just as with all other form controls, the `name` and `value` attributes are available to you as properties of the checkbox's DOM object. The `checked` attribute maps to a property of the same name, but the property's value is either `true` or `false` (as opposed to the `checked` attribute's value in the previous HTML code). So you can change the checked state of a checkbox by assigning a Boolean value to the `checked` property, like this:

```
var chkBox = theForm.color;

chkBox.checked = false;
```

This code gets a reference of the checkbox DOM object (assuming it's in a form called `theForm`) and uses the `checked` property to uncheck the box. Scripting a checkbox individually, as in this example, is a common approach to checkbox scripting. Sometimes you need to do something specific when a particular checkbox is checked, and the action performed as a result of the `click` event depends on the checkbox's checked state. For example, you may want to enable or disable parts of a form based on whether or not a particular checkbox is checked. You'll do something similar in code later in this lesson.

You can also group two or more checkboxes together by using the same name for each checkbox, like this:

```
<input type="checkbox" name="color" value="Red" checked="checked" />
<input type="checkbox" name="color" value="Blue" checked="checked" />
<input type="checkbox" name="color" value="Green" checked="checked" />
```

This HTML adds two more checkboxes, and all three `<input/>` elements have the same name: `color`. So this is a checkbox group named `color`. In the DOM, grouping checkboxes creates a `NodeList` of checkboxes, and you access this `NodeList` by using the name of the checkbox group, like this:

```
var colorBoxes = theForm.color;

alert(colorBoxes.length); // 3
```

This code gets a reference to the `color` checkbox group and assigns it to the `colorBoxes` variable. Remember from way back in Lesson 13 that a `NodeList` is an array-like object, and as such has a `length` property. So the alert box shows a value of 3. The `length` property makes it possible to loop through the `NodeList` and determine which checkboxes in the group are checked. Look at the following code:

```
var colors = [];

for (var i = 0; i < colorBoxes.length; i++) {
    var chkBox = colorBoxes[i];

    if (chkBox.checked) {
        colors.push(chkBox.value);
    }
}

alert("You picked: " + colors.join(", "));
```

This code loops through the checkboxes in the `color` group, determines which checkboxes are checked, adds the value of the checked checkboxes to the `colors` array, and then displays the picked colors to the user.

Radio buttons are almost always placed in radio button groups. You can script them as you would script checkbox groups.

SCRIPTING RADIO BUTTONS

Radio buttons are also generated with the `<input/>` element, but their `type` attribute is set to `radio`, like this:

```
<input type="radio" name="color" value="Red" />
<input type="radio" name="color" value="Blue" />
<input type="radio" name="color" value="Green" />
```

This HTML creates the radio button version of the `color` checkbox group from the previous section. In it are three radio buttons, and users can choose only one of these items, since they are grouped together.

Even though it is omitted in this HTML example, radio button controls have a `checked` attribute and property, and you can write code like the checkbox group code from the previous section to determine if a radio button in a particular group has been checked, like this:

```
var colorButtons = theForm.color;

for (var i = 0; i < colorButtons.length; i++) {
    var rdoButton = colorButtons[i];

    if (rdoButton.checked) {
        // do something with verified data
    }
}
```

You use something similar to this code next in the Try It section.

TRY IT

In this lesson, you learn how to script single and multiple checkboxes, as well as radio button groups. You learn that in addition to the standard form control properties, both checkboxes and radio controls have a `checked` property to determine whether or not the control is checked.

Lesson Requirements

For this lesson, you need a text editor; any plain text editor will do. For Microsoft Windows users, Notepad is available by default on your system or you can download Microsoft's free Visual Web Developer Express (www.microsoft.com/express/web/) or Web Matrix (www.asp.net/webmatrix/). Mac OS X users can use TextMate, which comes as part of OS X, or download a trial for Coda (www.panic.com/coda/). Linux users can use the built-in VIM.

You also need a modern web browser. Choose any of the following:

➤ Internet Explorer 8+

➤ Google Chrome

➤ Firefox 3.5+

➤ Apple Safari 4+

➤ Opera 10+

Create a subfolder called `Lesson30` in the `JS24Hour` folder you created in Lesson 1. Store the files you create in this lesson in the `Lesson30` folder.

Step-by-Step

1. Type the following HTML and JavaScript:

```
<html>
<head>
    <title>Lesson 30: Example 01</title>
</head>
<body>
<form name="theForm" action="" onsubmit="validateForm(event)">
    <p>
        Name: <input type="text" name="txtName" />
    </p>
    <p>
        Age: <input type="text" name="txtAge" />
    </p>
    <p>
        Email: <input type="text" name="txtEmail" />
    </p>
    <p>
        Password: <input type="password" name="txtPassword1" />
    </p>
    <p>
        Retype Password: <input type="password" name="txtPassword2" />
    </p>
    <p>
        Your Favorite Day: <select id="dayOfTheWeek" name="dayOfTheWeek">
                           </select>
    </p>
    <p>
        Please choose your favorite color:
    </p>
    <p>
        <input type="radio" name="color" value="Red"  /> Red
    </p>
    <p>
        <input type="radio" name="color" value="Blue" /> Blue
    </p>
    <p>
        <input type="radio" name="color" value="Green" /> Green
    </p>
    <p>
         
    </p>
    <p>
        <input type="checkbox" name="userAgree"
            onclick=" userAgreeClick(event)" />
```

```
            I agree to use this form.
      </p>

      <input name="btnSubmit" type="submit" value="Submit" disabled="disabled" />
</form>
<script type="text/javascript" src="eventutility.js"></script>
<script type="text/javascript">
function populateDays() {
      var days = [ "Sunday", "Monday", "Tuesday", "Wednesday",
          "Thursday", "Friday", "Saturday" ];
      var dayOfWeek = document.getElementById("dayOfTheWeek");
      var today = (new Date()).getDay();

      for (var i = 0; i < days.length; i++) {
          var length = dayofWeek.options.length;

          dayOfWeek.add(new Option(days[i], i), length);
      }

      dayOfWeek.selectedIndex = today;
}

function isEmpty(value) {
      return (value === "");
}

function validateForm(event) {
      var theForm = document.theForm,
          txtName = theForm.txtName,
          txtAge = theForm.txtAge,
          txtEmail = theForm.txtEmail,
          txtPassword1 = theForm.txtPassword1,
          txtPassword2 = theForm.txtPassword2,
          button = theForm.btnSubmit,
          age = parseInt(txtAge.value);

      button.disabled = true;

      // validate name field
      if (!isEmpty(txtName.value)) {

          // validate age
          if (!isNaN(age) && age > 0) {

              // validate email field
              if (txtEmail.value.indexOf("@") > 0) {

                  // validate password - pass 1
                  if (!isEmpty(txtPassword1.value)) {

                      // validate password - pass 2
                      if (txtPassword1.value === txtPassword2.value) {
                          return;
                      } else {
```

```
                                    alert("Passwords do not match. Please reenter them.");
                                    txtPassword1.focus();
                                    txtPassword1.select();
                                }

                        } else {
                            alert("Password cannot be blank.");
                            txtPassword1.focus();
                            txtPassword1.select();
                        }

                } else {
                    alert("Please enter a valid email address.");
                    txtEmail.focus();
                    txtEmail.select();
                }

            } else {
                alert("Please enter your age.");
                txtAge.focus();
                txtAge.select();
            }

        } else {
            alert("Please enter your name.");
            txtName.focus();
        }

        button.disabled = false;
        eventUtility.preventDefault(event);
    }

    populateDays();
</script>
</body>
</html>
```

Save this as `lesson30_example01.htm`. This is a modified version of the form you ended up with at the end of Lesson 29. The bold code shows you what was added to the file. A radio button group, called `color`, was added to the page, and a checkbox named `userAgree` was added as well. It has an `onclick` event handler that calls the function `userAgreeClick()`, which you write in the next step. Also, a `disabled` attribute was added to the submit button, disabling it by default.

2. The checkbox's purpose is similar to that of checkboxes on other forms you may have seen on the Internet, where you must agree to a set of terms before submitting. When the user clicks the checkbox, the submit button should be enabled. Write the `userAgreeClick()` function to enable the button. It is bold in the following code:

```html
<html>
<head>
    <title>Lesson 30: Example 01</title>
</head>
<body>
<form name="theForm" action="" onsubmit="validateForm(event)">
```

```
        <!-- Removed for Printing -->
        <p>
            Please choose your favorite color:
        </p>
        <p>
            <input type="radio" name="color" value="Red"  /> Red
        </p>
        <p>
            <input type="radio" name="color" value="Blue" /> Blue
        </p>
        <p>
            <input type="radio" name="color" value="Green" /> Green
        </p>
        <!-- Removed for Printing -->
    </form>
    <script type="text/javascript" src="eventutility.js"></script>
    <script type="text/javascript">
    function populateDays() {
        // removed for printing
    }

    function userAgreeClick(event) {
        var eSrc = eventUtility.getTarget(event);
        var button = theForm.btnSubmit;

        button.disabled = !eSrc.checked;
    }

    function isEmpty(value) {
        return (value === "");
    }

    function validateForm(event) {
        // removed for printing
    }

    populateDays();
    </script>
    </body>
    </html>
```

The first statement of this function gets the event target (the checkbox) and the form's submit button. Then the button's `disabled` property is set to the opposite of whatever the checkbox's `checked` property is. When `checked` is `true` the button's `disabled` property should be `false`, and vice versa.

3. The `color` radio button group does not have a default option checked so you need to write a function to ensure that users pick one of the three options. Name the function `validateColor()`. It is bold in this code:

```
<html>
<head>
    <title>Lesson 30: Example 01</title>
</head>
<body>
```

```
<form name="theForm" action="" onsubmit="validateForm(event)">
    <!-- Removed for Printing -->
    <p>
        Please choose your favorite color:
    </p>
    <p>
        <input type="radio" name="color" value="Red"  /> Red
    </p>
    <p>
        <input type="radio" name="color" value="Blue" /> Blue
    </p>
    <p>
        <input type="radio" name="color" value="Green" /> Green
    </p>
    <!-- Removed for Printing -->
</form>
<script type="text/javascript" src="eventutility.js"></script>
<script type="text/javascript">
function populateDays() {
    // removed for printing
}

function userAgreeClick(event) {
    // removed for printing
}

function validateColor() {
    var colorButtons = document.theForm.color;

    for (var i = 0; i < colorButtons.length; i++) {
        if (colorButtons[i].checked) {
            return true;
        }
    }

    return false;
}

function isEmpty(value) {
    return (value === "");
}

function validateForm(event) {
    // removed for printing
}

populateDays();
</script>
</body>
</html>
```

The job of this function is simply to return `true` if one of the radio buttons is checked, and `false` otherwise. A `for` loop loops through the radio button group and checks each radio button's `checked` property. If one is checked, the function returns `true`. If the loop iterates over each `color` radio button without finding a checked one, the function returns `false`.

4. Now modify the `validateForm()` function to use the `validateColor()` function. Changes are in bold in the following code:

```
function userAgreeClick(event) {
    // removed for printing
}

function validateColor() {
    var colorButtons = document.theForm.color;

    for (var i = 0; i < colorButtons.length; i++) {
        if (colorButtons[i].checked) {
            return true;
        }
    }

    return false;
}

function isEmpty(value) {
    return (value === "");
}

function validateForm(event) {
    var theForm = document.theForm,
    var txtName = theForm.txtName;
    var txtAge = theForm.txtAge;
    var txtEmail = theForm.txtEmail;
    var txtPassword1 = theForm.txtPassword1;
    var txtPassword2 = theForm.txtPassword2;
    var button = theForm.btnSubmit;
    var age = parseInt(txtAge.value);

    button.disabled = true;

    // validate name field
    if (!isEmpty(txtName.value)) {

        // validate age
        if (!isNaN(age) && age > 0) {

            // validate email field
            if (txtEmail.value.indexOf("@") > 0) {

                // validate password - pass 1
                if (!isEmpty(txtPassword1.value)) {

                    // validate password - pass 2
                    if (txtPassword1.value === txtPassword2.value) {

                        // validate color
                        if (validateColor()) {
                            return;
                        } else {
                            alert("Please choose your favorite color");
```

```
                    }

                } else {
                    alert("Passwords do not match. Please reenter them.");
                    txtPassword1.focus();
                    txtPassword1.select();
                }

            } else {
                alert("Password cannot be blank.");
                txtPassword1.focus();
                txtPassword1.select();
            }

        } else {
            alert("Please enter a valid email address.");
            txtEmail.focus();
            txtEmail.select();
        }

    } else {
        alert("Please enter your age.");
        txtAge.focus();
        txtAge.select();
    }

} else {
    alert("Please enter your name.");
    txtName.focus();
}

button.disabled = false;
eventUtility.preventDefault(event);
}

populateDays();
</script>
</body>
</html>
```

Since `validateColor()` returns a Boolean value, it's used as the condition in the new `if` statement. If it validates, `validateForm()` returns and the form submits. If not, an alert box displays a message to the user asking him or her to pick a color.

Make sure you save the file, and run it in any browser to test the new functionality.

To get the sample code files, you can download Lesson 30 from the book's website at www.wrox.com.

 Please select Lesson 30 on the DVD to view the video that accompanies this lesson.

31

An Introduction to Ajax

Web applications are sometimes considered inferior to conventional applications — that is, applications that run natively on your chosen operating system. That mindset is easy to develop. Imagine a conventional application that has a form that users can use to input data and have it stored in a database. A host of features are common in such conventional applications, such as real-time validation, seamlessly fast response times, and real-time error reporting.

Compare all that to a comparable web application. Users input data into the form and submit it. There is some real-time validation that you can do with JavaScript, but often with such web applications the server is responsible for comprehensive validation. The experience is disjointed when users click the form's submit button: The page has to reload with new data from the server, so not only does the page flicker, but it has to be downloaded again. If an error occurs, users don't know it until the page is completely loaded in the browser.

There are a variety of factors that contribute to the differences between conventional and web applications, but perhaps the largest hurdle web developers face is the HyperText Transfer Protocol (HTTP). The Internet relies upon several components in order to function, and probably the most important component is HTTP, a request-response protocol. When you open a browser and go to any website, your browser sends an HTTP request to the website's server to retrieve an HTML page. The server processes your request and sends an HTTP response back to your browser. If the server is able to fill your request, the response contains the HTML of the page you requested. As the browser finds images, CSS, and JavaScript files referenced in the HTML, it has to make additional HTTP requests for those resources. If, for some reason, the server is not able to fill your request, its response is a simple error code.

It is the request-response nature of HTTP that results in web applications that feel disconnected and disjointed. Every time users click a link or a button in a form, the browser sends a request and waits for a response from the server. While the browser waits, users typically see a blank web page. Users with a broadband connection usually see a flicker of white before the browser loads the requested HTML. Regardless, web applications, by default, still lack the seamless, real-time feel of conventional applications.

Because of this, web developers in the early 2000s began to develop new techniques to make their web applications behave more like conventional applications. These techniques enhanced the applications' performance and usability by enabling them to send and receive data behind the scenes without reloading the entire page.

At the very heart of these techniques was JavaScript and its capability to use hidden frames and a component developed by Microsoft called XMLHttpRequest to make HTTP requests transparent to users. Way back then, the techniques for making transparent HTTP requests were simply referred to as *remote scripting*. Today they're referred to as *Ajax*.

WHAT IS AJAX?

The simplest definition of Ajax is the use of JavaScript to send and receive data using HTTP without reloading the page. The term originates from an article written by Jesse James Garrett in February 2005 entitled "Ajax: A New Approach to Web Applications" (`http://www.adaptivepath.com/ideas/essays/archives/000385.php`). In his article, Garrett stated that the gap between conventional desktop applications and web applications was closing. He pointed to Google's Suggest and Maps as groundbreaking web applications because of their rich experiences and responsiveness.

In his article, Garrett also coined the term Ajax. It originally stood for *Asynchronous JavaScript + XML* because, at the time, XML was the accepted format for client/server communication. XML is still used, although other formats have proven more efficient. However, the term Ajax is now defined as the use of JavaScript to request and receive data from the server without refreshing the page, regardless of what format the data is in. It allows developers to create applications that behave like rich and responsive conventional desktop applications.

A textual representation of Ajax is insufficient, so let's look at some actual uses on the Web. Garrett's examples of Google's Suggest and Maps are still relevant, so let's look at them.

Google Suggest

Google Suggest is an application that stayed in Google Labs for quite some time before being pushed into full-time service on the main search page. It offers suggestions for search terms as users type. With each keystroke, Google Suggest uses Ajax by sending an HTTP request to the server to get search suggestions based on the text contained within the search box. Figure 31-1 shows Suggest in action.

It's fast and responsive, and it gives users a better experience when they're using Google's search — all without reloading the page.

Google Maps

After Google purchased Keyhole and rebranded it as Google Earth, it quickly released a web-based version called Google Maps (`http://maps.google.com`). Google Maps incorporates the use of Ajax, as well as DHTML, to provide an experience rarely found in web applications. Look at Figure 31-2 for the default page of Google Maps.

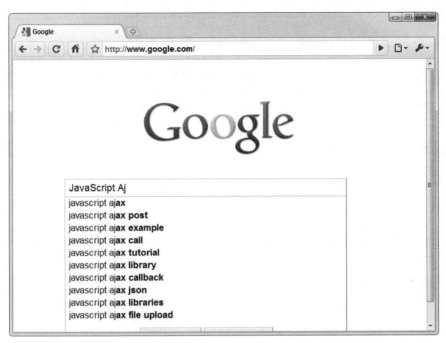

FIGURE 31-1

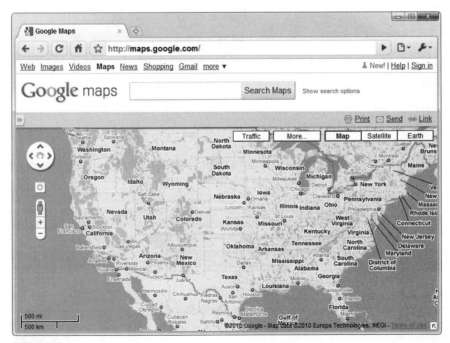

FIGURE 31-2

Entering a location in the textbox and clicking the Search Maps button does not reload the page. Instead, Maps uses Ajax to send and receive data based on the search criteria and dynamically loads the map images in the main area of the page.

The map area is completely interactive. You can drag the map around and zoom in and out using the mouse's scroll wheel. The responsiveness and interactivity rival those of the desktop-based Google Earth. While DHTML techniques are used extensively, Google Maps' success is due to Ajax.

REQUIREMENTS FOR AJAX

So you've seen some remarkable web applications that are remarkable because of Ajax. What do you need to get started with it?

First, you need a web browser that can make transparent HTTP requests and do something with the response. The old techniques of using hidden frames (which is not covered in this book) can be used in IE4+, but the most popular Ajax technique, using the XMLHttpRequest object, can be used only in browsers that support XMLHttp. These browsers are:

- ➤ Internet Explorer 5+
- ➤ Firefox 1+
- ➤ Opera 9+
- ➤ Safari 2+
- ➤ Chrome 1+

Second, you need a webserver because Ajax relies on HTTP communication. The pages in which you want to use Ajax must be served from an actual webserver; otherwise the HTTP requests will fail.

There are several webservers freely available to you, but two stand out and will suit your needs:

- ➤ The Apache HTTP Server (http://httpd.apache.org/)
- ➤ Microsoft's Internet Information Services (IIS)

The Apache HTTP Server is the most popular webserver in the world. The majority of the websites found on the Internet are served by Apache, and you can find a version for just about every operating system. Apache isn't for the faint of heart, however. Configuring the server beyond the default settings requires editing one or more text files. That being said, the default settings are generally fine for developing applications on your computer.

Microsoft's IIS has been freely available to users since Windows 2000, but only users of the Professional/Business or higher versions of XP, Vista, and Windows 7 were able to install it and use it on their machines. IIS is configured through a graphical user interface.

There is a version of IIS that runs on all major Windows operating systems (XP, Vista, and 7) called IIS Express. At the time of this writing, it is only included in Microsoft's WebMatrix beta; no stand-alone version of IIS Express is available to download.

The choice is yours; either server will enable you to learn Ajax in the upcoming lessons.

To get the sample code files, download Lesson 31 from the book's website at www.wrox.com.

 Please check the DVD for Lesson 31: It walks you through the installation of Apache on OS X and Windows and the installation of IIS.

32

Using XMLHttpRequest Objects

In Lesson 31 you learned that there are a variety of ways to incorporate Ajax into a web application. The older technique of using hidden frames can still be found in many modern web applications, but the most popular way to add Ajax functionality to an application is by using the `XMLHttpRequest` (XHR) object. Despite its name, you can retrieve more than XML with XHR. In fact, it's more commonly used to retrieve plain text.

The XHR object originated as a component, called XmlHttp, in Microsoft's MSXML library. The component was first released with Internet Explorer (IE) 5. XmlHttp allowed developers to make HTTP requests, using JavaScript or VBScript, to retrieve XML data. Microsoft updated the MSXML library with every major version of IE, and each new version included an improved XmlHttp component.

As the popularity of Microsoft's XmlHttp grew, the developers behind Mozilla built their own version (calling it XMLHttpRequest) for Firefox. Even though it had a different name, the Mozilla developers copied the majority of the properties and methods of Microsoft's XmlHttp, making cross-browser use easier. Soon after, the developers of Opera and Safari copied Mozilla's XHR object, making transparent HTTP requests through pure JavaScript possible in all modern browsers.

CREATING XHR OBJECTS

There are essentially two types of browsers when it comes to XHR support. The first supports the native XHR object — meaning that XHR is built into the browser. The second does not natively support XHR but can use the XmlHttp component found in the MSXML library.

Let's first look at the browsers that natively support XHR and learn how to make XHR objects.

Browsers with Native Support

All modern browsers have native XHR support. Creating an XHR object in these browsers is incredibly easy. Simply call the constructor using the `new` operator, like this:

```
var xhr = new XMLHttpRequest();
```

It's that simple, and it works in the following browsers:

- ➤ IE7+
- ➤ Firefox 1+
- ➤ Opera 8+
- ➤ Safari 1.2+
- ➤ Chrome 1+

Browsers that Support XmlHttp

The MSXML library is an ActiveX library, so only Internet Explorer supports XmlHttp. So this section focuses on IE5, IE5.5, and IE6. These browsers are quite old, and Microsoft does not support them anymore. Still, despite Microsoft's efforts, IE6 holds an estimated 10% market share at the time of this writing. That's a huge number.

> *Even though IE7+ supports the XHR object and constructor, it actually creates an XmlHttp object from the MSXML library. So while IE7+ does support the XMLHttpRequest identifier, the actual object is not native to the browser.*

Because XmlHttp is an ActiveX component, instantiating an `XmlHttp` object requires the creation of an ActiveX object. Creating ActiveX objects consists of calling the `ActiveXObject` constructor and passing it a string containing the ActiveX component you want to create, like this:

```
var xhr = new ActiveXObject("Microsoft.XMLHttp");
```

This code creates the first version of Microsoft's `XmlHttp`. There are actually several versions, but Microsoft recommends using one of the following:

- ➤ MSXML2.XmlHttp.6.0
- ➤ MSXML2.XmlHttp.3.0

You want to use the latest version possible because it will contain bug fixes and performance gains over previous versions. Unfortunately it's impossible to know if everyone has the latest version installed, but you can write code that determines what version users do have, in order to create appropriate `XmlHttp` objects.

The idea behind this code is to loop through the two recommended version names and attempt to create an XmlHttp object with each — starting with version 6 because it's the latest version. If a user's computer does not have version 6 installed, the browser throws an error when you attempt to create a version 6 XmlHttp object. You can catch that error and continue the loop to attempt the creation of a version 3 object. The following code demonstrates this process:

```
var versions = [ "MSXML2.XmlHttp.6.0",
    "MSXML2.XmlHttp.3.0" ];

for (var i = 0; i < versions.length; i++) {
    try {
        var xhr = new ActiveXObject(versions[i]);
    } catch (error) {
        // do nothing
    }
}
```

The first statement in this code defines an array called versions, and each of its elements is a version string for instantiating an XmlHttp ActiveX object. Next, a for loop iterates over the array, and inside the loop, you see a try...catch block. Remember, the try block "tries" to execute code, and the catch block catches an error if one is thrown from the execution of code in the try block.

This portion of the process is crucial, as the code attempts to create XmlHttp ActiveX objects based on the current version number. The line that can fail is bolded in the previous code. If the code tries to create a version 6 XmlHttp object and fails, the catch block catches the error and does nothing. The loop then iterates and the code tries to create a version 3 object. When an XmlHttp object is successfully created, the xhr variable contains an XmlHttp object. Otherwise it contains the value undefined.

Later in this lesson, you write a function that combines both approaches to creating XHR and XmlHttp objects. But before doing that, let's get started looking at some of these objects' features.

 For the sake of simplicity, both XMLHttpRequest *and* XmlHttp *objects will be referred to as XHR objects unless a distinction between the two needs to be made.*

USING XHR OBJECTS

After creating an XHR object you can begin to make HTTP requests with it. The first step is to initialize the request by calling the open() method. It accepts the following three arguments:

➤ **Request method:** A string indicating what type of request to make. Valid values are GET and POST, and you'll learn about these in Lessons 33 and 34, respectively.

➤ **URL:** A string containing the URL to send the request to

➤ **Asynchronous mode:** A Boolean value determining whether to use asynchronous (true) or synchronous (false) mode

Calling the `open()` method looks something like this:

```
xhr.open("GET", "info.txt", true);
```

This code initializes a GET request to be sent to retrieve a text file called `info.txt` using asynchronous mode. The choice between asynchronous and synchronous mode is an important one because it determines how the XHR affects your application.

Asynchronous mode means that the XHR object sends a request, waits for a response, and processes the response without interrupting the loading of the rest of the page or the execution of other scripts. *Synchronous* mode means the browser stops and waits for the XHR object to send the request, receive a response, and process the response before continuing to load the page or execute other scripts. The mode you use can drastically alter the performance of your application.

Synchronous requests are simpler than asynchronous requests. With synchronous requests you initialize the request, send it, and then process the server's response. The problem is that synchronous requests cause the browser to stop everything until it receives a response. In fact, users can get the feeling that something is wrong with the page, and you don't want that. Asynchronous mode is a better choice even though it requires extra code and complexity.

When you make an asynchronous request the XHR object goes through five different stages called *ready states*, which have numerical values. They are:

➤ 0: The object has been created but not initialized.

➤ 1: The object has been initialized but the request has not been sent.

➤ 2: The request has been sent.

➤ 3: A response has been received from the HTTP server.

➤ 4: The requested data has been fully received.

All XHR objects have a `readyState` property, and it contains one of the aforementioned numerical values. When the `readyState` property's value changes, the XHR's `readystatechange` event fires and calls the `onreadystatechange` event handler. The `onreadystatechange` event handler is usually defined like this:

```
xhr.open("GET", "info.txt", true);

xhr.onreadystatechange = function() {
    // more code here
};
```

Next you need to determine whether the requested data is completely available, because you can't work with data if you don't have it. The ready state you're primarily interested in is the fifth state, which has a value of 4. In order to ensure you have the requested data, check the `readyState` property's value inside the `onreadystatechange` event handler, like this:

```
xhr.open("GET", "info.txt", true);

xhr.onreadystatechange = function() {
    if (xhr.readyState === 4) {
        alert("We got a response");
```

```
    }
};

xhr.send(null);
```

The onreadystatechange event handler fires every time the value of readyState changes; therefore, the function handling the event executes four times. In this code, an if statement checks to see whether readyState is 4, meaning the request is complete. If it is, an alert box displays a message stating that a response was received from the server. The final line of this code sends the request with the send() method. You'll learn more about send() in Lessons 33 and 34.

Even when an XHR's ready state is 4 (fully complete), it is not guaranteed that you have the data you wanted. An error may have occurred.

DETERMINING THE SUCCESS OF A REQUEST

It's entirely possible that the resource you requested doesn't exist, or that the server-side application processing your request had an internal error. There's a whole host of issues that could crop up and cause the server to not provide you with the data you requested. It doesn't matter if you use asynchronous or synchronous mode, errors happen, and you need some way to identify them. Fortunately, determining when these errors happen is rather simple: Look at the response status code.

When sending a response to a client, a server must include a status code that indicates the success or failure of a request. These response codes are standardized parts of the HTTP protocol, they are three digits long, and they fall into five different categories:

➤ 1xx: Informational

➤ 2xx: Success

➤ 3xx: Redirection

➤ 4xx: Client error

➤ 5xx: Server error

You may never actually see the status codes, but they exist behind the scenes and every HTTP-enabled client can understand them. For example, when users go to Google's homepage at http://www.google.com, Google's webserver sends a status code of 200 as part of its response to the browser. This code is the standard response for successful HTTP requests. It literally means "OK." However, if users point their browsers to http://www.google.com/javascript/, Google's web-server responds with a status code of 404. This means that the specified resource could not be found on the server (for example, it doesn't exist).

You can determine whether or not your request was successful by using the XHR object's status property, which contains a three-digit HTTP response code, and comparing it to an HTTP response code, like this:

```
if (xhr.status === 200) {
    alert("Everything is OK.");
}
```

This code uses the `status` property to determine whether the request completed successfully by comparing the `status` property to the status code of `200`. But this check is actually inadequate if you want to determine the success of a request. The `200` status code works in most cases, but the status codes from `200` to `299` are considered successful status codes. Additionally, status code `304` is considered a success because it signifies that the requested resource has not changed since it was last requested. So, in order to adequately determine the success of a request, your code should check if the response status is within the `200`s or is equal to `304`, like this:

```
var status = xhr.status;

if ((status >= 200 && status < 300) || status === 304 ) {
    alert("Everything is OK.");
} else {
    alert("Something went wrong.");
}
```

This code first assigns the XHR's `status` property to a variable called `status`. It then checks if `status` is within the range of `200` through `299` or equal to `304`. This way, all successful status codes result in the message, "Everything is OK." If the request results in any other status code, it is considered an error and the user receives the message "Something went wrong."

Status code checking should be done for both asynchronous and synchronous requests.

SECURITY

There is no doubt that XHR adds a tremendous amount of power to your applications, but this power does not come without limitations. XHR is a JavaScript component, and as such, it is bound to the rules and limitations of the language — notably JavaScript's security.

In order to thwart malicious coders, JavaScript cannot access scripts or documents from a different origin — only scripts or documents from the same origin. The same-origin policy dictates that two pages (or scripts) are from the same origin only if the protocol, port, and host are the same. Consider the following two URLs:

```
http://www.wrox.com
http://www.wrox.com/WileyCDA/
```

These two URLs are of the same origin. They share the same protocol (HTTP), the same host (`www.wrox.com`), and the same port (80 is default). Because these are of the same origin, JavaScript on one page can access the other. Now look at the next two URLs:

```
http://www.wrox.com
https://www.wrox.com/WileyCDA/
```

These two URLs are not of the same origin because their protocols and ports don't match (the default HTTPS port is 443). So JavaScript on one of these pages cannot access the other page.

Why is this important? It's important because Ajax relies on JavaScript. The same-origin policy prohibits any JavaScript component, XHR included, to access any resource from another origin. Developers get around this issue by writing a server-side service to act as a proxy to retrieve the resource from another origin to return to the XHR object.

You've learned about a lot of the components of XHR objects in this lesson, so let's combine them all to give you a clearer picture of how they fit together.

TRY IT

In this lesson, you are introduced to several basic pieces of the XHR object: how to create one, how to determine the object's ready state for asynchronous mode, and how to determine whether a request was successful. You combine all these pieces to create a foundation you use in later lessons.

Lesson Requirements

For this lesson, you need a text editor; any plain text editor will do. For Microsoft Windows users, Notepad is available by default on your system or you can download Microsoft's free Visual Web Developer Express (www.microsoft.com/express/web/) or Web Matrix (www.asp.net/webmatrix/). Mac OS X users can use TextMate, which comes as part of OS X, or download a trial for Coda (www.panic.com/coda/). Linux users can use the built-in VIM.

You also need a modern web browser. Choose any of the following:

➤ Internet Explorer 8+

➤ Google Chrome

➤ Firefox 3.5+

➤ Apple Safari 4+

➤ Opera 10+

Additionally, you need webserver software installed on your computer. Refer to Lesson 31 on the DVD for installation instructions. Create a subfolder called Lesson32 in the root directory of your webserver. Store the files you create in this lesson in the Lesson32 folder.

Step-by-Step

1. Write a function to create an XHR object for all browsers. Call the function createXHR(), and have it return an XHR object. Its code follows:

```
function createXHR() {
    if (typeof XMLHttpRequest !== "undefined") {
        return new XMLHttpRequest();
    } else {
        var versions = [ "MSXML2.XmlHttp.6.0",
```

```
                    "MSXML2.XmlHttp.3.0" ];

            for (var i = 0; i < versions.length; i++) {
                try {
                    var xhr = new ActiveXObject(versions[i]);
                    return xhr;
                } catch (error) {
                    // do nothing
                }
            }
        }

        alert("Your browser does not support XmlHttp");

        return null;
    }
```

This code first uses feature detection to determine whether the browser supports the
XMLHttpRequest identifier, and returns an XHR object if it does. The check for XHR
here is important because IE7+ can use either the XMLHttpRequest constructor or the
ActiveXObject constructor to create an XmlHttp object, and the XHR constructor in IE7+
is guaranteed to create the latest version of XmlHttp available. So the ActiveX code is used
only if the browser doesn't support the XMLHttpRequest identifier.

2. Now call the createXHR() function and assign the resulting XHR object to a variable called
xhr. Then assign a function to the onreadystatechange event handler, as shown in the following code:

```
var xhr = createXHR();

xhr.onreadystatechange = function() {
    if (xhr.readyState === 4) {

    }
};
```

Inside the onreadystatechange event handler is an if statement to determine whether the
ready state is 4 — meaning that the XHR object received the entire response from the server.

3. Now ensure that the request was successful by using the status property. Place the status-
checking code within the if statement checking the ready state. The new code is bold:

```
var xhr = createXHR();

xhr.onreadystatechange = function() {
    if (xhr.readyState === 4) {
        if ((xhr.status >= 200 && xhr.status < 300) || xhr.status === 304 ) {
            // code for success goes here
        } else {
            alert("Something went wrong.");
        }
    }
};
```

By adding this code, you make the onreadystatechange event handler ready to use and process the response from the server. It checks the XHR object's ready state, and then it checks to make sure a proper response was received from the server.

4. Save this file as lesson32_example01.js.

To get the sample code files, download Lesson 32 from the book's website at www.wrox.com.

 Please select Lesson 32 on the DVD to view the video that accompanies this lesson.

33

Making Ajax Requests Using GET

Open a web browser and go to `http://www.google.com`. You've just sent a GET request to Google's webserver. Now point your browser to `http://www.google.com/search?q=JavaScript`. Once again you've sent a GET request to Google. Click any link in the search results. Yep, you just sent a GET request.

The HTTP protocol defines nine HTTP methods (also known as *verbs*) that determine what type of action is taken on the requested resource. The GET verb indicates that the client requesting a resource simply wants to get the data that the resource contains. GET requests are typically thought of as safe requests because they're not meant to cause any change on the server; they are simply used to request a resource's data.

As mentioned in Lesson 32, there are two types of requests you can make with `XMLHttpRequest` (XHR) objects: GET and POST. The majority of requests users make on the Internet are GET requests. Similarly, the majority of requests you'll make with XHR will be GET requests.

MAKING GET REQUESTS

Code samples in Lesson 32 illustrated how you make GET requests, but let's go over everything you need to make these types of requests. First, you create the XHR object and initialize it with the `open()` method, like this:

```
var xhr = createXHR();

xhr.open("GET", "info.txt");
```

The first argument passed to `open()` tells the XHR object to make a GET request to the URL specified as the second argument, and since the third argument is omitted, the request is sent in asynchronous mode.

It's important to fully understand how XHR objects handle the URL you pass to open(). In the case of the preceding code, the XHR object will attempt to find a file called info.txt in the same directory that the code executes in. So, for example, if this code is executed within a web page located at http://www.yourdomain.com/ajax/get_ajax.htm, the XHR object sends a request to the http://www.yourdomain.com/ajax/info.txt URL. The URL passed to open() in the previous code is referred to as a *relative URL* — it is relative to the page currently loaded in the browser. The other type of URL is an *absolute URL*. Absolute URLs contain the protocol, domain, and path of the resource. The URL http://www.yourdomain.com/ajax/info.txt is an absolute URL, and as long as you abide by the same-origin policy discussed in Lesson 32, you can use absolute URLs as well. The following code uses the absolute URL for info.txt in this example:

```
var xhr = createXHR();

xhr.open("GET", "http://www.yourdomain.com/ajax/info.txt");
```

It doesn't really matter if you use relative or absolute URLs. Absolute URLs are clear and less prone to errors; relative URLs are shorter but can cause problems if you do not pay attention to where resources are located in relation to the page.

After you initialize a request you want to handle the readystatechange event, check for ready state 4, and also ensure that the request didn't fail. The following code does all that:

```
xhr.onreadystatechange = function() {
    if (xhr.readyState === 4) {
        var status = xhr.status;
        if ((status >= 200 && status < 300) || status === 304) {
            alert(xhr.responseText);
        } else {
            alert("An error occurred");
        }
    }
};
```

This code looks similar to a snippet in Lesson 32, but there's something different in the bolded line. A new property of the XHR object, called responseText, is passed to the alert() method on a successful request. The responseText property returns the body of the response — the requested resource's data in text format. So whatever text is contained within info.txt is displayed in the alert box.

> There is another property, called responseXML, that returns a DOM object if the returned data is in XML form.

The final step in the process is to send the request, and you do so by calling the send() method. It accepts one argument, which contains the data that makes up the request's body. GET requests do not send data, so you must pass null to the method, like this:

```
xhr.send(null);
```

After calling `send()`, the XHR object then monitors the `readyState` property and fires the `readystatechange` event when its value changes.

ASYNCHRONOUS PROGRAMMING

After the `send()` method executes, the XHR object functions independently of JavaScript code that may be executing after the call to `send()`. This is because the XHR object is operating in asynchronous mode, and programming with asynchronous objects requires a different approach from regular programming. Look at the following code:

```
var xhr = createXHR();

xhr.open("GET", "info.txt");

xhr.onreadystatechange = function() {
    if (xhr.readyState === 4) {
        var status = xhr.status;
        if ((status >= 200 && status < 300) || status === 304) {
            // code removed
        } else {
            alert("An error occurred");
        }
    }
};

xhr.send(null);

alert(xhr.responseText); // wrong!!
```

This code makes a GET request for the `info.txt` file, as in the previous section, but there's one little change. Notice that the line of code calling `alert()` to display the contents of `responseText` was moved out of the `onreadystatechange` event handler and placed after the call to `send()` (the changes are in bold).

Depending on your browser, you'll see either an empty alert box or an error. This is because the browser continues to execute any JavaScript code found after the call to `send()`. When the final line of code executes and attempts to get a value from the `responseText` property, the XHR object has not yet received a complete response from the server. So in some browsers `responseText` is empty and an alert box displays an empty string, while others throw an error.

Perhaps this behavior is better explained with a visual aid. Picture an island in the ocean just off the mainland (Figure 33-1).

The island is connected to the mainland via a one-way bridge, and vehicles travelling on that bridge can travel only from the island to the mainland. An asynchronous XHR object is like this island, and the rest of the page's JavaScript code is like the mainland. All code relying on the XHR object's data is on the island; if code from the

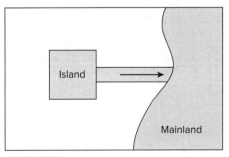

FIGURE 33-1

mainland tried to access code on the island, some kind of error would occur (like a wreck). But the code on the XHR island can access code on the mainland whenever it needs to.

Because this particular request was made using asynchronous mode, all code relying on the request's response must be handled within the `onreadystatechange` event handler (on the island). A common practice is to call a function (on the mainland) when the response is complete and pass the response data as an argument in order to do something with that data. The following code demonstrates this:

```
function processResponse(data) {
    alert(data);
}

var xhr = createXHR();

xhr.open("GET", "info.txt");

xhr.onreadystatechange = function() {
    if (xhr.readyState === 4) {
        var status = xhr.status;
        if ((status >= 200 && status < 300) || status === 304) {
            processResponse(xhr.responseText);
        } else {
            alert("An error occurred");
        }
    }
};

xhr.send(null);
```

This code calls the `processResponse()` function with a successful request, and it makes the code easier to read and maintain.

You can make asynchronous XHR requests even easier to read, maintain, and use by refactoring your XHR code into a function. The only two pieces of information that can vary from request to request are the URL and the function to call when the request is successful (also known as a *callback function*). The following code defines a function called `makeGetRequest()`:

```
function makeGetRequest(url, callback) {
    var xhr = createXHR();

    xhr.open("GET", url);

    xhr.onreadystatechange = function() {
        if (xhr.readyState === 4) {
            var status = xhr.status;
            if ((status >= 200 && status < 300) || status === 304) {
                callback(xhr.responseText);
            } else {
                alert("An error occurred");
            }
        }
    };

    xhr.send(null);
}
```

The request code in makeGetRequest() is almost identical to the code in the previous example. The only changes are that the url variable is in place where info.txt originally was, and that the callback function is invoked in where processResponse() was called. Using makeGetRequest() makes asynchronous requests trivial, as shown in the following code:

```
function processResponse(data) {
    alert(data);
}

makeGetRequest("info.txt", processResponse);
```

In this new code processResponse() stays unchanged, but a call to makeGetRequest() passes info.txt and the processResponse() function as arguments. So now you can make a request using one simple line of code and do something with the request's data when the request completes successfully.

TRY IT

In this lesson, you learn how to make GET requests using XHR objects and work with the data you retrieve with them.

Lesson Requirements

For this lesson, you need a text editor; any plain text editor will do. For Microsoft Windows users, Notepad is available by default on your system or you can download Microsoft's free Visual Web Developer Express (www.microsoft.com/express/web/) or Web Matrix (www.asp.net/webmatrix/). Mac OS X users can use TextMate, which comes as part of OS X, or download a trial for Coda (www.panic.com/coda/). Linux users can use the built-in VIM.

You also need a modern web browser. Choose any of the following:

➤ Internet Explorer 8+

➤ Google Chrome

➤ Firefox 3.5+

➤ Apple Safari 4+

➤ Opera 10+

Additionally, you need webserver software installed on your computer. Refer to Lesson 31 on the DVD for installation instructions. Create a subfolder called Lesson33 in the root directory of your webserver. Store the files you create in this lesson in the Lesson33 folder.

Step-by-Step

1. Create a new text file and add exactly the following text to it:

```
Jeremy,Jason,Jeffrey
```

Note that there are no spaces between the commas and names. Feel free to add more names. Just make sure to separate them with commas and keep the names all in one line. Save this text file as `lesson33_example_data.txt`.

2. Create another new file and type the following JavaScript code. Feel free to copy the `createXHR()` function from `lesson32_example01.js` from Lesson 32:

```javascript
function createXHR() {
    if (typeof XMLHttpRequest !== "undefined") {
        return new XMLHttpRequest();
    } else {
        var versions = [ "MSXML2.XmlHttp.6.0",
            "MSXML2.XmlHttp.3.0" ];

        for (var i = 0; i < versions.length; i++) {
            try {
                var xhr = new ActiveXObject(versions[i]);
                return xhr;
            } catch (error) {
                // do nothing
            }
        }
    }

    alert("Your browser does not support XmlHttp");

    return null;
}

function makeGetRequest(url, callback) {
    var xhr = createXHR();

    xhr.open("GET", url);

    xhr.onreadystatechange = function() {
        if (xhr.readyState === 4) {
            var status = xhr.status;
            if ((status >= 200 && status < 300) || status === 304) {
                callback(xhr.responseText);
            } else {
                alert("An error occurred");
            }
        }
    };

    xhr.send(null);
}
```

These are the functions you've created thus far to aid you in Ajax requests. Save the file as `xhr.js` and place it in the `Lesson33` directory.

3. Copy the `eventUtility.js` file either from the code download or from a previous lesson to the `Lesson33` directory.

4. Type the following HTML:

```html
<html>
<head>
    <title>Lesson 33: Example 01</title>
</head>
<body>

<form name="theForm" action="" onsubmit="validateName(event)">
    <input type="text" name="txtName" value="" />
    <input type="submit" name="btnSubmit" value="Check Name" />
</form>


<script type="text/javascript" src="eventutility.js"></script>
<script type="text/javascript" src="xhr.js"></script>
<script type="text/javascript">

</script>
</body>
</html>
```

This page has a form called `theForm`, and it has a textbox control named `txtName`, and a button named `btnSubmit`. The `eventUtility.js` and `xhr.js` files are also added to the page via two `<script/>` elements, with a third `<script/>` element that will contain inline JavaScript code.

5. The form has an `onsubmit` event handler that calls a function called `validateName()`. This function should verify that the textbox is not empty, and it should make a request to retrieve the `lesson33_example_data.txt` file. Type the following function inside the empty `<script/>` element:

```javascript
function validateName(event) {
    var nameToVerify = document.theForm.txtName.value;
    var button = document.theForm.btnSubmit;

    if (nameToVerify === "") {
        alert("Please enter a name.");
    } else {
        button.disabled = true;
        makeGetRequest("lesson33_example_data.txt", processData);
    }

    eventUtility.preventDefault(event);
}
```

If the textbox is empty, an alert message tells the user to enter a name. Otherwise, a call to `makeGetRequest()` requests the text file and calls a function called `processData()` on a successful request.

The button is also disabled before the request is sent. Latency is an issue when making HTTP requests, and the user can generate many requests by repeatedly clicking the button. By disabling the button when a request is made, you ensure that only one request can be sent at any given time.

The event utility's `preventDefault()` method prevents the form from being submitted.

6. Write the `processData()` function. It should split the data contained in the text file into an array and determine whether the name entered into the textbox has a match in the file. It should also tell the user whether or not a match was found. After everything's been processed, enable the button once again. Type the following function inside the inline `<script/>` element:

```
function processData(data) {
    var names = data.split(",");
    var nameToVerify = document.theForm.txtName.value;
    var button = document.theForm.btnSubmit;
    var nameFound = false;

    for (var i = 0; i < names.length; i++) {
        var name = names[i];

        if (name.toLowerCase() === nameToVerify.toLowerCase()) {
            nameFound = true;
            break;
        }
    }

    if (nameFound) {
        alert("That name is taken.");
    } else {
        alert("That name isn't taken");
    }

    button.disabled = false;
}
```

The names in the text file are separated by commas, so the `String` data type's `split()` method splits the string using a comma as a delimiter. Next a `for` loop iterates over the names array and compares each element in the array to the value contained within the textbox. Both values are converted to their lowercase equivalents to make the search case-insensitive. If a match is found in the array, the `nameFound` variable is set to `true` and the loop ends. Otherwise, the loop continues to iterate over each element until a match is found or the loop exits.

After the loop exits, the function displays a message to the user. The contents of the message depend on `nameFound`'s value. Finally, the button is re-enabled to allow the user to search for another name.

Save the file as `lesson33_example01.htm` and point your browser to `http://localhost/Lesson33/lesson33_example01.htm`. Begin typing names into the textbox and pressing the button to see if the name you typed is found in the text file.

To get the sample code files, download Lesson 33 from the book's website at `www.wrox.com`.

 Please select Lesson 33 on the DVD to view the video that accompanies this lesson.

34

Making Ajax Requests Using POST

If GET requests make up the majority of HTTP requests on the Web, POST requests come in second. POST requests are typically generated by forms. While not every form sends its data using the POST method, many are used to POST information to the server.

POST requests are the exact opposite of GET requests: They are used to submit data to a web application so the application can do something with that data. The request's data is sent in the request's body, unlike with GET requests, in which data can be sent in the URL's query string. Despite these differences, making POST requests with XMLHttpRequest (XHR) objects is strikingly similar to making GET requests. There are, of course, some differences, and you'll learn about them in this lesson.

ASSEMBLING DATA

POST requests are designed to send information from the browser to the server. Because of this the majority of POST requests are made through forms. Forms are the primary means by which users input and send data. The difference with Ajax, however, is in how that data is sent.

Without Ajax, the browser is responsible for gathering the form's data, formatting it, and POSTing it to the server. With Ajax, that responsibility falls to you. So before sending a POST request you must assemble the form's data and format it.

Let's look at an example form:

```
<form name="theForm" method="post" action="ajax_test.php">
    <p>
        Name: <input type="text" name="txtName" value="" />
    </p>
    <p>
        Email: <input type="text" name="txtEmail" value="" />
    </p>
```

```
        <p>
            <input type="submit" name="btnSubmit" value="Submit" />
        </p>
    </form>
```

This form has two textboxes: one for a name and one for an e-mail address. It also has a button to submit the form, and the form POSTs to a file on the server called `ajax_test.php`.

> *PHP is a programming language and server-side framework that allows develop-*
> *ers to write server-side programs. It runs on virtually every operating system.*
> *Explaining PHP is beyond the scope of this book, but I use it in examples. Refer to*
> *Lesson 31 on the DVD for installation instructions for Windows and Mac OS X.*

If a user enters the value `Jeremy` in the name textbox and `jeremy@xyz` in the e-mail textbox, the browser assembles the data into the following format when the user clicks the submit button:

        `txtName=Jeremy&txtEmail=jeremy%40xyz.com&btnSubmit=Submit`

This looks very much like the query portion of a URL. There are three name/value pairs separated by ampersands (`&`). They are:

➤ `txtName=Jeremy`

➤ `txtEmail=jeremy%40xyz.com`

➤ `btnSubmit=Submit`

On the left side of each equals sign (`=`) is the name of a form control from the form, and on the right side is the value of that control. Notice the value of `txtEmail`. Instead of `jeremy@xyz.com`, it's `jeremy%40xyz.com`. The `@` symbol is a special character that has its own meaning in HTTP, and it must be encoded before being transmitted as part of a request's body. Other special characters are:

➤ `,` (comma)

➤ `/`

➤ `?`

➤ `:`

➤ `&`

➤ `=`

➤ `+`

➤ `$`

➤ `#`

When you are POSTing data to a server with XHR, the request's body must be in this format. Having to assemble and format all the information contained within a form may sound daunting, but a function can do it all for you. Look at the beginnings of a function called getRequestBody() in the following code:

```
function getRequestBody(form) {
    var pieces = [];
    var elements = form.elements;

    // more code here

    return pieces.join("&");
}
```

This function accepts one argument, a <form/> element object. So you can pass the function any form and have it generate the body for a request. The first two statements in this function create two variables. The first is an array called pieces, and each element in this array will be a name/value pair. The second variable, elements, is assigned the form's elements collection property. The final line of this function returns the result of calling the pieces array's join() method.

Next, the function loops through the elements collection and constructs a name=value string for each form control. The new code is in bold:

```
function getRequestBody(form) {
    var pieces = [],
        elements = form.elements;

    for (var i = 0; i < elements.length; i++) {
        var element = elements[i];
        var name = encodeURIComponent(element.name);
        var value = encodeURIComponent(element.value);

        pieces.push(name + "=" + value);
    }

    return pieces.join("&");
}
```

Inside the for loop three new variables are initialized. The first variable, element, contains the form control element object as the specified index. The second variable, name, is assigned an encoded version of the element's name property by passing the un-encoded property to the encodeURIComponent() function. The encodeURIComponent() function is a built-in function that encodes special characters into their transmittable equivalents. The third variable, value, is assigned an encoded version of the form control's value property. Finally, the name and value variables are concatenated and added to the pieces array.

Now you can assemble and format a form's contents by simply calling this function and passing it the <form/> element object you want to send, like this:

```
var requestBody = getRequestBody(document.theForm);
```

This code passes the form with the name `theForm` to the `getRequestBody()` function to generate properly formatted data and assign it to the `requestBody` variable.

 The `getRequestBody()` *function, as written in this lesson, does not take into account disabled fields, unchecked radio and check boxes, or* `<select/>` *elements.*

MAKING POST REQUESTS

After you have data in the appropriate format, you can send it with an XHR object. POST requests look a lot like GET requests, so the following code will look familiar to you:

```
var xhr = createXHR();
var data = getRequestBody(document.theForm);

xhr.open("POST", "ajax_test.php");
xhr.setRequestHeader("Content-Type", "application/x-www-form-urlencoded");

xhr.onreadystatechange = function() {
    if (xhr.readyState === 4) {
        var status = xhr.status;
        if ((status >= 200 && status < 300) || status === 304) {
            processResponse(xhr.responseText); // callback function
        } else {
            alert("An error occurred");
        }
    }
};

xhr.send(data);
```

The first major change is the addition of the `data` variable, and it contains a formatted string of name/value pairs to send in the request. The next big change is in the call to the `open()` method: The first argument is now `POST` instead of `GET`. After the call to `open()` is a new line of code that calls the XHR object's `setRequestHeader()` method. This method allows you to set an HTTP header with a supplied value. In the case of POST requests you need to set the `Content-Type` header with the value `application/x-www-form-urlencoded`. Otherwise the request will not work. The last major change is in the call to `send()`. Instead of passing `null` you pass the data generated by `getRequestBody()`.

 Setting the Content-Type header to `application/x-www-form-urlencoded` *is not necessary for all POST requests — it is only required when sending form-formatted data.*

You can simplify POST requests by writing a function like the `makeGetRequest()` function you wrote in Lesson 33. The following code defines a function called `postFromForm()`:

```
function postFromForm(url, form, callback) {
    var xhr = createXHR();
    var data = getRequestBody(form);

    xhr.open("POST", url);
    xhr.setRequestHeader("Content-Type", "application/x-www-form-urlencoded");

    xhr.onreadystatechange = function() {
        if (xhr.readyState === 4) {
            var status = xhr.status;
            if ((status >= 200 && status < 300) || status === 304) {
                callback(xhr.responseText);
            } else {
                alert("An error occurred");
            }
        }
    };

    xhr.send(data);
}
```

This function accepts three arguments: the URL to request, the `<form/>` object that you want to gather data from, and the callback function to execute when the request completes successfully. So using this function means writing something like the following code:

```
function processResponse(responseData) {
    alert(responseData);
}

postFromForm("ajax_text.php", document.theForm, processResponse);
```

Here, a POST request containing the data from a form named `theForm` is sent to `ajax_text.php`, and on a successful request, the `processResponse()` function processes the server's response.

TRY IT

In this lesson, you learn how to make POST requests using XHR objects by formatting the request body's data, supplying the `Content-Type` header, and sending data with the request.

Lesson Requirements

For this lesson, you need a text editor; any plain text editor will do. For Microsoft Windows users, Notepad is available by default on your system or you can download Microsoft's free Visual Web Developer Express (www.microsoft.com/express/web/) or Web Matrix (www.asp.net/webmatrix/). Mac OS X users can use TextMate, which comes as part of OS X, or download a trial for Coda (www.panic.com/coda/). Linux users can use the built-in VIM.

You also need a modern web browser. Choose any of the following:

➤ Internet Explorer 8+

➤ Google Chrome

➤ Firefox 3.5+

➤ Apple Safari 4+

➤ Opera 10+

Additionally, you need webserver software and PHP installed on your computer. Refer to Lesson 31 on the DVD for installation instructions. Create a subfolder called `Lesson34` in the root directory of your webserver. Store the files you create in this lesson in the `Lesson34` folder.

Step-by-Step

1. Copy the `ajax_post.php` file from the code download to the `Lesson34` directory. This is a PHP file that generates random messages based on the information POSTed to it.

2. Write an Ajax utility object. Create a new file called `ajaxUtility.js` and type the following:

```
var ajaxUtility = {
    createXHR : function() {
        if (typeof XMLHttpRequest !== "undefined") {
            return new XMLHttpRequest();
        } else {
            var versions = [ "MSXML2.XmlHttp.6.0",
                "MSXML2.XmlHttp.3.0" ];

            for (var i = 0; i < versions.length; i++) {
                try {
                    var xhr = new ActiveXObject(versions[i]);
                    return xhr;
                } catch (error) {
                    // do nothing
                }
            }
        }

        alert("Your browser does not support XmlHttp");

        return null;
    },

    makeGetRequest : function(url, callback) {
        var xhr = this.createXHR();

        xhr.open("GET", url);

        xhr.onreadystatechange = function() {
            if (xhr.readyState === 4) {
                var status = xhr.status;
```

```
                    if ((status >= 200 && status < 300) || status === 304) {
                        callback(xhr.responseText);
                    } else {
                        alert("An error occurred");
                    }
                }
            }
        };

        xhr.send(null);
    },

    getRequestBody : function(form) {
        var pieces = [];
        var elements = form.elements;

        for (var i = 0; i < elements.length; i++) {
            var element = elements[i];
            var name = encodeURIComponent(element.name);
            var value = encodeURIComponent(element.value);

            pieces.push(name + "=" + value);
        }

        return pieces.join("&");
    },

    postFromForm : function(url, form, callback) {
        var xhr = this.createXHR();
        var data = this.getRequestBody(form);

        xhr.open("POST", url);
        xhr.setRequestHeader("Content-Type", "application/x-www-form-urlencoded");

        xhr.onreadystatechange = function() {
            if (xhr.readyState === 4) {
                var status = xhr.status;
                if ((status >= 200 && status < 300) || status === 304) {
                    callback(xhr.responseText);
                } else {
                    alert("An error occurred");
                }
            }
        };

        xhr.send(data);
    }
};
```

This code creates a new object called `ajaxUtility`. Its `createXHR()` and `makeGetRequest()` methods resemble the functions of the same name from the `xhr.js` file. The other two methods, `getRequestBody()` and `postFromForm()`, are the same as the two functions of the same name from this lesson. Creating a utility like this is advantageous because it keeps all code grouped together in the `ajaxUtility` object.

3. Copy the `eventUtility.js` file from the `Lesson33` directory to the `Lesson34` directory.

4. Type the following HTML:

```html
<html>
<head>
    <title>Lesson 34: Example 01</title>
</head>
<body>
<form name="theForm" method="post" action="ajax_post.php"
onsubmit="addUser(event)">
    <p>
        Name: <input type="text" name="txtName" value="" />
    </p>
    <p>
        Email: <input type="text" name="txtEmail" value="" />
    </p>
    <p>
        <input type="submit" name="btnSubmit" value="Submit" />
    </p>
</form>
<script type="text/javascript" src="eventutility.js"></script>
<script type="text/javascript" src="ajaxUtility.js"></script>
<script type="text/javascript">

</script>
</body>
</html>
```

This page contains the same form from earlier in this lesson, but it POSTs to `ajax_post.php` and has an `onsubmit` event handler. The `eventUtility.js` and `ajaxUtility.js` files are also added to the page via two `<script/>` elements, with a third `<script/>` element that will contain inline JavaScript code.

5. The form's `onsubmit` event handler calls the `addUser()` function. This function should verify that the form is filled out and should POST to the `ajax_post.php` file. Type the following function inside the empty `<script/>` element:

```javascript
function addUser(event) {
    var theForm = document.theForm;
    var name = theForm.txtName.value;
    var email = theForm.txtEmail.value;
    var button = theForm.btnSubmit;

    button.disabled = true;

    if (name === "" || email === "") {
        alert("Please complete the form.");
        button.disabled = false; // so user can resubmit
    } else {
        ajaxUtility.postFromForm(theForm.action, theForm, processData);
    }

    eventUtility.preventDefault(event);
}
```

This function first disables the submit button to prevent the user from submitting more than one request at a time. Then the function determines if the textboxes contain information and asks the user to complete the form if either textbox is empty. If both textboxes contain data you pass the `theForm` object to the `ajaxUtility.postFromForm()` method to send the request.

Instead of the string literal `ajax_post.php`'s being passed to the `postFromForm()` method, the form's `action` property is used instead. This is a nice little technique that allows your XHR object to POST data to whatever URL is specified within the `<form/>` element's `action` attribute. So if you change the value of the `action` attribute you don't have to change the URL in the call to `postFromForm()`.

Finally, the event utility's `preventDefault()` method prevents the form from being submitted.

6. Write the `processData()` function. All it needs to do is alert the response data and re-enable the button. Type the following function inside the inline `<script/>` element:

```
function processData(data) {
    var button = document.theForm.btnSubmit;

    alert(data);

    button.disabled = false;
}
```

Save the file as `lesson34_example01.htm`, and point your browser to `http://localhost/Lesson34/lesson34_example01.htm`. Fill out the form, submit it, and watch the random responses from the server.

 Please select Lesson 34 on the DVD to view the video that accompanies this lesson.

35

JSON

In Lessons 33 and 34, you sent a request to the server and received data that you did something with; in Lesson 33, you retrieved a list of names separated by commas and parsed that data to make a functional application. Lesson 34 had you make a POST request to the server, which responded with text that you displayed in an alert box. The data returned from the server in those two lessons was simple, and you will rarely deal with such a simplistic set of data in a real-world application. So this lesson introduces you to an interchange format suitable for representing complex data. It is today's standard in Ajax communication: JavaScript Object Notation (JSON). First, let's take a look at how JSON came about.

XML RULES THE WORLD...OR DOES IT?

Since its creation, eXtensible Markup Language (XML) has steadily gained ground as the data interchange format of choice. The ability to mark up data and exchange it between different computer systems made XML the de facto standard for data transmission. Don't worry if you're not familiar with XML. The basics of the language are very simple. In fact, it looks a lot like HTML. Following is a simple XML document that describes a person:

```xml
<?xml version="1.0" encoding="utf-8"?>

<person>
    <firstName>John</firstName>
    <lastName>Doe</lastName>
    <address>
        <street>1234 XYZ</street>
        <city>Dallas</city>
        <state>Texas</state>
        <country>USA</country>
    </address>
    <phoneNumbers>
        <phoneNumber type="home">111-123-4567</phoneNumber>
        <phoneNumber type="cell">111-234-5678</phoneNumber>
```

```
    </phoneNumbers>
    <company><![CDATA[John & Joe's Lobster House]]></company>
  </person>
```

XML has a stricter rule set than HTML:

➤ The first line is called the XML declaration, and every XML document must have one.

➤ Every XML document must also have one, and only one, document element, the root element of the document. In this document, `<person/>` is the document element (the `<html/>` element is the document element in HTML documents).

➤ Every beginning tag must have a closing tag, and all elements should be properly nested.

➤ Special characters such as ampersands (`&`) and angle brackets cannot be used in data unless they are inside a CDATA (character data) block.

XML's strict rule set and the ability to create your own formats make it a popular choice for sharing text-based data such as RSS feeds. XML is used everywhere. In fact, you'd be hard pressed to find a web service or a programming interface running on a remote server that doesn't send and receive data in XML.

Naturally, the use of XML as an interchange format trickled into browser/server communication. It seemed perfect for the browser because XML documents could be loaded into a DOM, and developers could traverse the XML document's tree to get the data they needed. As Ajax gained in popularity, XML was the de facto format for exchanging data (remember, the *x* in Ajax stands for XML).

While XML is great for sending and receiving data between networks and computer systems, there are some problems when it comes to using it as a data interchange format with the browser. First, XML documents are inherently verbose because XML is a markup language. Refer back to the sample XML document earlier in this section. Every XML document has an XML declaration at the top of the file, and each element containing data must have a beginning and ending tag. In addition, data containing XML's special/reserved characters has to be represented as character data, as shown in the `<company/>` element in this XML document.

The verbose nature of XML makes this simple document weigh in with a size of 507 bytes. Admittedly, 507 bytes isn't very large, but imagine a document describing over 50 people. The file could get very large fast. File sizes are directly linked to a web application's performance. You want to squeeze as much performance out of your application as possible, and smaller file sizes can help with that.

The second problem with XML is the DOM API. The DOM was developed as a means of programmatically representing structured documents, like HTML and XML. In order for developers to work with an XML document in JavaScript, the document is loaded into its own DOM object (independent from the HTML page's DOM object). JavaScript developers work with DOMs all the time, but the API is cumbersome and unfriendly. For example, the code to directly access the `<country/>` element's value (in the `<address/>` element) looks like this in IE:

```
doc.documentElement.childNodes[2].childNodes[3].nodeValue
```

This code uses `doc` as the top-level DOM object (much as `document` is the top-level DOM object of HTML pages), `documentElement` gets the `<person/>` element, `childNodes[2]` gets the `<address/>` element, `childNodes[3]` accesses the `<country/>` element, and the `nodeValue` property gets the value contained within the element. That's a lot of code to get to one element's value, and it's cryptic, making maintenance difficult.

 The previous code listing is actually incorrect if the XML document is loaded into a standard XML DOM object. Code for accessing the `<country/>` element in standard XML DOM objects are actually more complicated.

So XML is inefficient for data interchange for JavaScript developers. What, then, is the alternative?

JAVASCRIPT OBJECT NOTATION SAVES THE WORLD

Douglas Crockford, a computer scientist, recognized XML's inefficiencies for JavaScript developers and worked to develop an interchange format that would result in smaller files and make working with that data easier. What he developed was a lightweight format dubbed JavaScript Object Notation, or JSON (pronounced *Jason*) for short.

JSON is based on a subset of the JavaScript language, and the idea behind it is that you can adequately describe data by using object and array literals. For example, the XML document in the previous section can be converted into a JavaScript object like this:

```
var person = {
    firstName : "John",
    lastName : "Doe",
    address : {
        street : "1234 XYZ",
        city : "Dallas",
        state : "Texas",
        country : "USA"
    },
    phoneNumbers : [
        {
            type : "home",
            number : "111-123-4567"
        },
        {
            type : "cell",
            number : "111-234-5678"
        }
    ],
    company : "John & Joe's Lobster House"
};
```

This code uses object and array literals to describe the same data as the XML in the previous section. The object is called `person`, and fulfills the same purpose as the `<person/>` root element in the XML file. The `<firstName/>`, `<lastName/>`, and `<address/>` elements are converted to properties of the `person` object. Next, `<phoneNumbers/>` is converted to an array literal, and each item in the array is an object representing a `<phoneNumber/>` element.

Now, this is a JavaScript object, not JSON. The primary difference between JavaScript object/array literals and JSON is that JSON does not have variables, properties, methods, or any other construct of the JavaScript language. JSON is a text format meant to represent data only, so the JSON equivalent of this JavaScript code is the following:

```
{
    "firstName" : "John",
    "lastName" : "Doe",
    "address" : {
        "street" : "1234 XYZ",
        "city" : "Dallas",
        "state" : "Texas",
        "country" : "USA"
    },
    "phoneNumbers" : [
        {
            "type" : "home",
            "number" : "111-123-4567"
        },
        {
            "type" : "cell",
            "number" : "111-234-5678"
        }
    ],
    "company" : "John & Joe's Lobster House"
}
```

This is called a JSON structure. Notice that the property names become string values: JSON is serialized JavaScript objects and arrays. *Serialization* is the process of converting objects into text, and serialization (along with *deserialization* — converting text into objects) is what makes JSON a suitable transmission format for JavaScript developers. JSON is advantageous for JavaScript developers for two reasons:

➤ JSON data is smaller than XML data, and it gets even smaller when you remove all unnecessary whitespace. The JSON data in this example is 462 bytes, and you can shrink that to 256 bytes. Even when compressed into one line, the XML equivalent is still larger at 399 bytes.

➤ Deserializing JSON means you get a JavaScript object that you can use in your program. So after you deserialize the previous JSON and assign the resulting object to a variable called `person`, you can easily find out what country John Doe lives in by using the following code:

```
var country = person.address.country;
```

These two reasons, size and ease of use, make JSON perfect for JavaScript developers. So let's look at how you can serialize to and deserialize from JSON.

CONVERTING TO AND FROM JSON

Since JSON usurped XML as the de facto standard for Ajax data transmission, the latest version of the JavaScript language has had built-in JSON support. A new built-in object, called JSON, exists in the following browsers:

➤ Internet Explorer 8+ (only in IE8 mode)

➤ Firefox 3.5+

➤ Chrome 4+

➤ Safari 5+

JSON support doesn't end with these browsers, however. Before JSON support was built into JavaScript, Crockford wrote a JavaScript script that can be used in any browser. You can find this script at www.json.org/json2.js or in the code download accompanying this book at www.wrox.com. This utility creates a JSON object in browsers that do not support the native JSON object, and its functionality exactly mirrors that of the native JSON object. So until all older browsers are phased out, it's a good idea to include the json2.js file in any page in which you plan on using JSON.

The JSON object has two methods:

➤ parse(): Deserializes JSON to create a JavaScript object or array.

➤ stringify(): Serializes a JavaScript object or array into JSON.

First let's look at the stringify() method. It accepts a JavaScript value as an argument and returns a string containing the JSON text. To get an idea of how stringify() works, let's imagine that you work at a car dealership, and that one of your duties is to write a web application that allows visitors to search for vehicles based on make, model, and year. Part of your code creates a data type called Car. Following is its definition:

```
function Car(make, model, year) {
    this.make = make;
    this.model = model;
    this.year = year;
}
```

The constructor has three parameters: make, model, and year. It uses these values to populate the make, model, and year properties that Car objects will have. Now let's simulate a user's input by creating a Car object with some data and passing it to the JSON.stringify() method, like this:

```
var toyotaCamry = new Car("Toyota", "Camry", 2002);

var carJson = JSON.stringify(toyotaCamry);
```

The first line of this code creates a Car object representing a 2002 Toyota Camry and assigns it to the toyotaCamry variable. In the next line the toyotaCamry object is passed to the JSON.stringify()

method, and the resulting string is returned to the `carJson` variable. This gets you the same result as doing the following:

```
var carJson = '{"make":"Toyota","model":"Camry","year":2002}';
```

Notice that the number `2002` is not a string. By design, the `JSON.stringify()` method does not serialize numeric or Boolean values, in order to preserve their value.

Once you have your data in JSON form, you can do whatever you want with it. More than likely, though, you serialized an object to send it to the server, and you can do so by adding the following method to the `ajaxUtility` object:

```
var ajaxUtility = {
    // other methods snipped for printing

    makePostRequest : function(url, data, callback) {
        var xhr = this.createXHR();

        xhr.open("POST", url);

        xhr.onreadystatechange = function() {
            if (xhr.readyState === 4) {
                var status = xhr.status;
                if ((status >= 200 && status < 300) || status === 304) {
                    callback(xhr.responseText);
                } else {
                    alert("An error occurred");
                }
            }
        };

        xhr.send(data);
    }
};
```

Unlike POSTing data with the `ajaxUtility.postFromForm()` method you wrote in the last lesson, POSTing JSON doesn't require the `application/x-www-form-urlencoded` Content-Type header. So to send the JSON in `carJson` with this new method, all you need to do is this:

```
ajaxUtility.makePostRequest(serverUrl, carJson, processResponse);
```

While there are times when you will want to send data to the server using JSON because of the data's complexity, the simple data in this example would be better sent using the `ajaxUtility` `.postFromForm()` method.

Let's imagine that you sent the car query in a request to a server application that determines if the specified car is in stock. The server processes the request and responds with the following JSON:

```
{
    "searchedCar" : {
        "make" : "Toyota",
        "model" : "Camry",
        "year" : 2002
    },
```

```
        "isFound" : false,
        "results" : [
            {
                "make" : "Toyota",
                "model" : "Camry",
                "year" : 2005
            },
            {
                "make" : "Honda",
                "model" : "Accord",
                "year" : 2002
            }
        ]
    }
```

This JSON structure has three primary pieces of data. First it contains the `searchedCar` object structure that contains the make, model, and year that were searched for. Next it contains a structure called `isFound` containing a Boolean value determining whether or not the searched-for car was found. Last is a structure, called `results`, that contains a list of cars that the user might find suitable.

Of course, the data in this format isn't overly helpful to you, so you want to deserialize it using the `JSON.parse()` method. Now, your request was sent via the `ajaxUtility`, so the following function was executed when the request completed successfully:

```
function processResponse(data) {
    var results = JSON.parse(data);

    // more code here
}
```

In the `processResponse()` function, the first line calls the `JSON.parse()` method, passing it the value of the data parameter, and assigns the resulting object to the results variable. Now you have an actual JavaScript object than you can use in your code, so you can easily provide the user with information regarding his or her query, like this:

```
function processResponse(data) {
    var results = JSON.parse(data);

    if (results.isFound) {
        // do something with the matched data
    } else {
        // do something to let the user know no match was found
        // do something with the suggestions
    }
}
```

By parsing JSON into a JavaScript object you gain immediate access to the data the JSON structure contained in your JavaScript code, and you don't have to traverse a DOM to get it.

The ease of transforming JSON into JavaScript makes JSON the most popular means of transporting data to and from a JavaScript application. Let's expand on this car dealership scenario in the next section.

TRY IT

In this lesson, you learn how to leverage JSON to send, receive, and work with complex data in JavaScript.

Lesson Requirements

For this lesson, you need a text editor; any plain text editor will do. For Microsoft Windows users, Notepad is available by default on your system or you can download Microsoft's free Visual Web Developer Express (www.microsoft.com/express/web/) or Web Matrix (www.asp.net/webmatrix/). Mac OS X users can use TextMate, which comes as part of OS X, or download a trial for Coda (www.panic.com/coda/). Linux users can use the built-in VIM.

You also need a modern web browser. Choose any of the following:

➤ Internet Explorer 8+

➤ Google Chrome

➤ Firefox 3.5+

➤ Apple Safari 4+

➤ Opera 10+

Additionally, you need webserver software and PHP installed on your computer. Refer to Lesson 31 on the DVD for installation instructions. Create a subfolder called Lesson35 in the root directory of your webserver, and copy the eventUtility.js and ajaxUtility.js files into it. Also copy the car_dealership.php and json2.js files from the code download and paste them in the Lesson35 folder. Store the files you create in this lesson in the Lesson35 folder.

The car_dealership.php file responds with one JSON structure. The server's response is as follows:

```
{
    "searchedCar" : {
        "make" : "value",
        "model" : "value",
        "year" : numericValue
    },
    "isFound" : booleanValue,
    "results" : [
        {
            "make" : "value",
            "model" : "value",
            "year" : numericValue
        },
        // more object structures if necessary
    ]
}
```

This JSON structure defines data containing the search query, a Boolean value indicating whether or not a match was found, and an array structure called results containing one or more car-like object structures, each having make, model, and year information.

Step-by-Step

1. Open your text editor, and then type the following:

```html
<html>
<head>
    <title>Lesson 35: Example 01</title>
</head>
<body>
<div id="divResults">
    <div id="divSearchMessage"></div>
    <div id="divSearchResults"></div>
</div>
<form name="theForm" method="post" action="car_dealership.php"
    onsubmit="submitForm(event);">
    <p>
        Make: <input type="text" name="txtMake" value="" />
    </p>
    <p>
        Model: <input type="text" name="txtModel" value="" />
    </p>
    <p>
        Year: <input type="text" name="txtYear" value="" />
    </p>
    <p>
        <input type="submit" name="btnSubmit" value="Submit" />
    </p>
</form>
<script type="text/javascript" src="eventutility.js"></script>
<script type="text/javascript" src="ajaxUtility.js"></script>
<script type="text/javascript" src="json2.js"></script>
<script type="text/javascript">

function submitForm(event) {
    var data = ajaxUtility.getRequestBody(document.theForm);

    ajaxUtility.makeGetRequest("car_dealership.php?" + data,
        processResponse);

    eventUtility.preventDefault(event);
}

function getCarString(carObj) {
    return [carObj.year, carObj.make, carObj.model].join(" ");
}

function processResponse(data) {

}


</script>
</body>
</html>
```

Save it as `lesson35_example01.htm`. At the top of the body is a `<div/>` element with an `id` of `divResults`. Inside this element are two more `<div/>` elements. The one with the `id` of `divSearchMessage` will contain a message to the user telling him or her whether or not the query garnered any results. The `<div/>` element with an `id` of `divSearchResults` will contain the results/suggestions.

Next is a form that that contains `<input/>` elements for the make, model, and year to search for. It has an `onsubmit` event handler that calls the `submitForm()` function. This function uses the `ajaxUtility.getRequestBody()` method to format the data into a URL's query string, and then it makes a `GET` request to the PHP file along with the query string contained within the data.

Another function, called `getCarString()`, is defined. It accepts a car-like object as an argument and formats the object into a "year make model" string, like "2002 Toyota Camry."

The third function is called `processResponse()`, and it's the callback function of the Ajax request made within `submitForm()`.

2. Add the bold lines in the following code to the `processResponse()` function:

```
function processResponse(data) {
    var result = JSON.parse(data);
    var messageDiv = document.getElementById("divSearchMessage");
    var message = "";
    var length = result.results.length;
    var carStr = getCarString(result.searchedCar);

    if (result.isFound) {
        message = "We found " + result.results.length + " matches for " + carStr;
    } else {
        message = "We could not find " + carStr + ". You might like: ";
    }

    messageDiv.innerHTML = message;
}
```

This new code parses the JSON data and assigns the resulting object to the `result` variable, and a reference to the `<div/>` element with an `id` of `divSearchMessage` is retrieved from the document and assigned to the `messageDiv` variable. Another variable, called `message`, is set to an empty string. It will contain a message to tell the user how the search went. Then a variable called `length` is assigned the length of the `result.results` array. Finally, `carStr` is assigned the return value obtained by calling `getCarString()` with the `result.searchedCar` property passed as an argument.

Next some code using the result object's `isFound` property determines if a match was found, and an appropriate message is constructed and displayed in the `<div/>` element for messages.

3. The `processResponse()` function still needs to display a list of suggestions for searches without a match. Add the bold lines in the following code:

```
function processResponse(data) {
    var result = JSON.parse(data);
    var messageDiv = document.getElementById("divSearchMessage");
```

```
var resultsDiv = document.getElementById("divSearchResults");
var message = "";
var results = [];
var length = result.results.length;
var carStr = getCarString(result.searchedCar);

if (result.isFound) {
    message = "We found " + length + " matches for " + carStr;
} else {
    message = "We could not find " + carStr + ". You might like: ";

    for (var i = 0; i < length; i++) {
        results.push(getCarString(result.results[i]));
    }

    resultsDiv.innerHTML = results.join("<br/>");
}

messageDiv.innerHTML = message;
}
```

This new code adds two new variables: resultsDiv and results. The resultsDiv variable points to the <div/> element with an id of divSearchResults, and the results variable is an array.

The next new code is a for loop that loops through the result.results array. Each element in this array is passed to the getCarString() function, and the resulting string value is pushed into the results array.

When the loop exists, the results.join() method is called, concatenating the elements of the results array and separating each element with a <br/> element. The resulting string is assigned to the resultsDiv.innerHTML property to display the list of cars on the page.

4. Save the file again and point your browser to http://localhost/Lesson35/lesson35_example01.htm. Fill out the form, submit it, and watch the random results.

To get the sample code files, download Lesson 35 from the book's website at www.wrox.com.

Please select Lesson 35 on the DVD to view the video that accompanies this lesson.

PART III
Handling Errors, Debugging, and Best Practices

36

Common Coding Mistakes

If there's one thing a novice and a guru have in common, it's that they both make mistakes when writing code. They could introduce a bug that is difficult to find and fix, or something as simple as a typo. As an application's code base grows in size, the chances for the developer to make a mistake increase.

There are some common mistakes that all developers make — even professionals. Mistakes are inevitable, but you can minimize the number of common ones you make by watching out for them as you code.

The majority of mistakes covered in this lesson are syntax mistakes. Most syntax mistakes are reported by the browser, but some, as you'll see, don't cause the browser to throw any errors.

UNDEFINED VARIABLES

JavaScript goes out of its way to be accommodating to developers. It inserts semicolons at the ends of statements if you omit them, and it allows you to assign a value to a variable without first declaring the variable with the `var` keyword. For example, the following code creates a new global variable called `myVariable` and initializes it with a string value:

```
myVariable = "Hello, Global!";
```

While this code executes without any type of error, it is considered bad practice to omit the `var` keyword from variable declarations. Omitting the `var` keyword has an effect on the variable's scope — namely, making the variable global. So always use `var` when declaring a new variable.

Using a variable before it has been given a value results in an error. For example, the following code attempts to use a variable before it has been initialized:

```
alert(someVariable); // error
```

Always make sure to initialize a variable with a value before attempting to use it.

Similarly, be sure to pass arguments to functions that require a value. Consider the following code:

```
function addByTwo(num) {
    return num + 2;
}

var result = addByTwo();

alert(result); // NaN
```

This code defines a function called `addByTwo()`, which accepts a single argument. The function returns the value of the parameter plus two. The final two lines of this code call `addByTwo()`, assigning the result to the `result` variable and alerting `result`. When `addByTwo()` is called in this code, JavaScript assigns the value of `undefined` to the `num` parameter because no value was passed to it. Since `undefined` is not a number, the addition operation fails and results in `NaN`. In general, failing to pass a required value to a function will result in the function's failure.

In addition, you must ensure that function definitions that do have parameters correctly use the parameters' identifiers in the function body. Take a look at the following code:

```
function someFunction(someParameter) {
    alert(someParamter);
}

someFunction("Hello, World!");
```

This code has an error. The `someFunction()` declaration defines a parameter called `someParameter`. However, this parameter isn't used within the function's body. Instead, the `alert()` method attempts to alert the value of `someParamter` (notice the missing e between m and t). A slight typo, such as the omission of one letter, can cause your code to fail. Be mindful of your identifiers, and make sure they match their definitions.

CASE-SENSITIVITY

Slight typos are a nuisance. Just like omitting a single character, not matching an identifier's case can result in your code's failure. For example, see if you can spot all the errors in the following code:

```
var myName = "Jeremy";
If (myname === "Jeremy") {
    alert(myName.toLowercase());
}
```

There are three errors in this code:

➤ The capitol `I` in `If` should be lowercase.

➤ The `myname` identifier is all lowercase when the `n` should be capitalized.

➤ The `toLowercase()` method doesn't exist. Instead, the code should call `toLowerCase()`.

Always be aware of case; knowing the identifier naming conventions can help with that:

➤ All keywords and reserved words are lowercase.

➤ All variables, non-constructor functions, properties, and methods begin with a lowercase letter and use camel-case afterward.

➤ All data type constructor identifiers begin with an uppercase letter and use camel-case afterward.

CLOSING BRACES AND PARENTHESES

Code organization is key to maintainability and readability, and JavaScript has two built-in organizational units with curly braces and parentheses. Unfortunately they are not enough; you need to use whitespace to make code a little easier to read. Following is code that has a few deliberate mistakes. See if you can spot them:

```
function doSomething()
{
var x=1,y=2;
if (x+y)*2<10)
{
if (x+y<5)
{
alert("Alert something");
}
}

doSomething();
```

This code is a mess, and it is a good illustration of why you should strive to format your code. Formatting makes code easier to read, which in turn makes errors easier to identify. So let's format the code as follows:

```
function doSomething() {
    var x = 1,
        y = 2;

    if (x + y) * 2 < 10) {
        if (x + y < 5) {
            alert("Alert something");
        }
    }

doSomething();
```

Now you can easily identify one of the errors: A closing curly brace is missing at the end of the function definition. The second error is a bit trickier to find. Look at the first `if` statement and you'll notice that there is one opening parenthesis and two closing parentheses. An opening parenthesis needs to be added to properly enclose the addition operation. It's very easy to miss an opening or closing parenthesis if you have many parentheses in one statement.

Following is the corrected code with corrections in bold:

```
function doSomething() {
    var x = 1,
        y = 2;

    if ((x + y) * 2 < 10) {
        if (x + y < 5) {
            alert("Alert something");
        }
    }
}

doSomething();
```

OPERATOR MISUSE

It's common to misuse an operator, especially when dealing with assignment (=) and equality (==). Look at the following example:

```
var number = 100;

if (number = 200) {
    alert("Number is 200");
} else {
    alert("Number is " + number);
}
```

At first glance you might think the result of this code will be an alert box displaying the message `"Number is 100"`. That is not the case. This code illustrates the very common mistake of using the assignment operator instead of the equality operator. Instead of comparing `number` with the literal of `200`, the code inside the `if` statement's condition assigns `number` the value of `200`.

What makes misuse like this worse is that JavaScript doesn't throw an error. Assigning a value to a variable inside a condition is perfectly valid, so the only indication you get is abnormal behavior from your application. In a large chunk of code, operator misuse is very easy to overlook. So keep it in mind if your script behaves differently from how you expected.

 Please select Lesson 36 on the DVD to view the video that accompanies this lesson.

37

Handling Errors

The common mistakes covered in Lesson 36 are caused by the developer's breaking some of the syntax rules in JavaScript. As you will undoubtedly find out in your own time, errors in your application can occur even if you follow JavaScript's syntax rules. These are called *runtime errors* because they occur while the program is running. Runtime errors are caused by a variety of factors:

➤ A flaw in your code's logic, such as a failure to validate user input before processing it

➤ Conditions beyond your control, such as a network error on the user's computer

➤ Murphy's Law (anything that can go wrong will go wrong)

 Technically, syntax errors are usually runtime errors as well, because the errors occur while the browser loads and attempts to execute the code.

When writing an application you want to be informed of every error that occurs so that you can fix it. But when you deploy your app, the last thing you want users to see is an error message that means nothing to them. Bugs will occur in our software — it's a given. But we can do our best to prevent them, and handle them when they do occur, to provide the best user experience we can.

PREVENTING ERRORS

There are a number of things you can do if you want error-free web pages. First, ensure that your HTML markup is up to snuff. Close all elements that need closing, and properly nest elements. Many HTML-validator services are available for free on the Internet. A popular one is the W3C's Markup Validation Service at `validator.w3.org`.

Second, thoroughly check your pages in as many browsers as possible. This is easier for developers who use Windows because they have every major browser readily available; developers using OS X or a flavor of Linux have a limited set of browsers to choose from. However, with virtualization technology becoming ubiquitous in our computer systems, it's getting far easier for OS X and Linux users to test in Internet Explorer (IE) by installing Windows on a virtual machine. Alternatively, you can decide which browsers you want to support for your application and verify that your code works in them.

 Keep in mind that IE is the most-used browser at present. As of this writing, 60 percent of all users on the Internet use it. If you're writing a web app for everyone, it needs to work in IE.

Third, validate user input. Users may or may not knowingly input invalid data in your form controls. For example, you may have a textbox that asks for numeric data, and somewhere in your code do some math with it. What would happen if the user typed an alphabetic character in that textbox? The answer is that your code would not work. Either an error would be thrown, or more likely your math operations would return incorrect results — thus breaking your application.

Essentially, thoroughly testing your app, following the best practices for HTML, CSS, and JavaScript, and validating user input will get you on the right track. Let's say you've done all that, and your app works perfectly in your development environment. Unfortunately, things can still go wrong, and issues can crop up that are beyond your control.

Your author wrote a content-management system many years ago that was used by many people to update content on their web pages. While it was in development, Jeremy tested his app and found and fixed bugs. When it was released and in use, some users complained that parts of the application didn't work correctly and that they were receiving errors when adding or editing new content. Come to find out, these users used a particular brand of security software that injected its own JavaScript files into the page, and in doing so caused the application's JavaScript to fail at certain key points.

There was really no way Jeremy could have planned for this, and the only way he could fix the problem was to handle the error using a `try...catch` block to catch the thrown errors and provide an alternative means for the users of that particular security software to add or edit their data.

THE TRY...CATCH STATEMENT

The `try ... catch` statement isn't new to you; you saw them used in Lessons 29 and 32. As a quick refresher, they enable you to write code that can fail gracefully. You *try* to execute code that may fail, and then you *catch* any *exception* that might have been thrown as the result of your code's failing. *Exception* is a programmer's term for an error that occurs as the result of unforeseen circumstances (as opposed to just *error*, which usually refers only to something in the code that has been written incorrectly).

To use `try ... catch` statements, you place the code that could fail inside the `try` block. Then you put code inside the `catch` block, which executes only if an exception is thrown by the `try` code. Look at the following code:

```
try {
    alert("No code to fail here");
} catch(exception) {
    alert("Ooops. " + exception.message);
}
```

In this code, an `alert()` call is placed inside the `try` block. There is no code in `try` that can throw an error, but if one were thrown, code execution would drop to the `catch` block. After the `catch` keyword is a pair of parentheses with an identifier inside. When an exception is thrown, an object of type `Error` is created and passed to the `catch` block. So in this code, `exception` works like a function's parameter (in fact, you can think of `catch` like a function). `Error` objects have a property called `message`, which contains a description of the thrown exception. Let's add a deliberate error to this code:

```
try {
    alert("No code to fail here");
    abert("But now there is");
} catch(exception) {
    alert("Ooops. " + exception.message);
}
```

The bold line in this code adds a call to `abert()`, which doesn't exist. So when JavaScript attempts to execute the bolded statement, the engine throws an exception, which is caught by the `catch` block. In IE9 the `alert()` method displays the message `"Ooops. Function expected"` because `exception` `.message` returns the string `"Function expected"` — no function called `abert()` exists.

THROWING EXCEPTIONS

It may seem strange, but there are times when you want to throw your own exception. For example, this can be useful when users input invalid data. To throw an exception you use the `throw` keyword followed by the object you want to throw. Generally that object is an instance of `Error`. The following code throws an `Error` object:

```
throw new Error("This is my own exception");
```

But the real power behind throwing your own exceptions is the ability to throw any object you want. So if you are validating a form, and the data in a textbox isn't valid, you could do something like this:

```
throw {
    element : txtTextBox,
    message : "Data is invalid"
};
```

This code throws an object defined using object literal notation. It has a property called `element` that contains an HTML element object, and a `message` property containing a description of the error. When throwing your own objects, it's a good idea to include a `message` property because it helps emulate objects of the `Error` data type.

TRY IT

In this lesson, you learn how to handle exceptions that may arise from unforeseen circumstances by encapsulating code inside a `try...catch` block. You also learn how to throw your own exceptions.

Lesson Requirements

For this lesson, you need a text editor; any plain text editor will do. For Microsoft Windows users, Notepad is available by default on your system or you can download Microsoft's Visual Web Developer Express (`www.microsoft.com/express/web/`) or Web Matrix (`www.asp.net/webmatrix/`), both of which are free. Mac OS X users can use TextMate, which comes as part of OS X, or download a trial of Coda (`www.panic.com/coda/`). Linux users can use the built-in VIM.

You also need a modern web browser. Choose any of the following:

- ➤ Internet Explorer 8+
- ➤ Google Chrome
- ➤ Firefox 3.5+
- ➤ Apple Safari 4+
- ➤ Opera 10+

Create a subfolder called `Lesson37` in the `JS24Hour` folder you created in Lesson 1. Store the files you create in this lesson in the `Lesson37` folder. Copy your `eventUtility.js` file into this folder.

Step-by-Step

You will revisit the form-validation routine you wrote in Lesson 28 and use `try ... catch`, along with throwing your own exceptions, to make the code easier to read and maintain. If you like, copy `lesson28_example01.htm` from the `Lesson28` directory and paste it into the `Lesson37` directory, rename it `lesson37_example01.htm`, and make it look like the HTML in Step 1. Or feel free to forego copy/paste and start with Step 1.

1. Open your text editor and type the following:

    ```html
    <html>
    <head>
        <title>Lesson 37: Example 01</title>
    </head>
    <body>
    <form name="theForm" action="" onsubmit="validateForm(event)">
        <p>
            Name: <input type="text" name="txtName" />
        </p>
        <p>
    ```

```
        Age: <input type="text" name="txtAge" />
    </p>
    <p>
        Email: <input type="text" name="txtEmail" />
    </p>
    <p>
        Password: <input type="password" name="txtPassword1" />
    </p>
    <p>
        Retype Password: <input type="password" name="txtPassword2" />
    </p>

    <input name="btnSubmit" type="submit" value="Submit" />
</form>
<script type="text/javascript" src="eventutility.js"></script>
<script type="text/javascript">
function isEmpty(value) {
    return (value === "");
}

function validateForm(event) {
    var theForm = document.theForm;
    var txtName = theForm.txtName;
    var txtAge = theForm.txtAge;
    var txtEmail = theForm.txtEmail;
    var txtPassword1 = theForm.txtPassword1;
    var txtPassword2 = theForm.txtPassword2;
    var button = theForm.btnSubmit;
    var age = parseInt(txtAge.value, 10);

    button.disabled = true;
}
</script>
</body>
</html>
```

Save this file as `lesson37_example01.htm`.

2. Instead of throwing anonymous objects, create a data type called `ValidationException`. It should accept two arguments: an element object and a message. Add the following bold code:

```
<html>
<head>
    <title>Lesson 37: Example 01</title>
</head>
<body>
<form name="theForm" action="" onsubmit="validateForm(event)">
    <p>
        Name: <input type="text" name="txtName" />
    </p>
    <p>
        Age: <input type="text" name="txtAge" />
    </p>
    <p>
        Email: <input type="text" name="txtEmail" />
```

```
        </p>
        <p>
            Password: <input type="password" name="txtPassword1" />
        </p>
        <p>
            Retype Password: <input type="password" name="txtPassword2" />
        </p>

        <input name="btnSubmit" type="submit" value="Submit" />
    </form>
    <script type="text/javascript" src="eventutility.js"></script>
    <script type="text/javascript">
    function ValidationException(element, message) {
        this.element = element;
        this.message = message;
    }

    function isEmpty(value) {
        return (value === "");
    }

    function validateForm(event) {
        var theForm = document.theForm;
        var txtName = theForm.txtName;
        var txtAge = theForm.txtAge;
        var txtEmail = theForm.txtEmail;
        var txtPassword1 = theForm.txtPassword1;
        var txtPassword2 = theForm.txtPassword2;
        var button = theForm.btnSubmit;
        var age = parseInt(txtAge.value, 10);

        button.disabled = true;
    }
    </script>
    </body>
    </html>
```

3. Now start validating each field. Throw a `ValidationException` object if a form field does not validate. Start with the `txtName` textbox. Add the following bolded code to the `validateForm()` function. (Note that the HTML and other JavaScript is removed for printing.)

```
    function validateForm(event) {
        var theForm = document.theForm;
        var txtName = theForm.txtName;
        var txtAge = theForm.txtAge;
        var txtEmail = theForm.txtEmail;
        var txtPassword1 = theForm.txtPassword1;
        var txtPassword2 = theForm.txtPassword2;
        var button = theForm.btnSubmit;
        var age = parseInt(txtAge.value, 10);

        button.disabled = true;

        try {
            if (isEmpty(txtName.value)) {
```

```
            throw new ValidationException(txtName, "Please enter your name.");
        }
    }
}
```

This new code checks to see if the `txtName` textbox is empty and, if so, throws an exception.

4. Now validate the field for the user's age. Ensure that the data is a number and that age is greater than zero. The new code is bold:

```
function validateForm(event) {
    var theForm = document.theForm;
    var txtName = theForm.txtName;
    var txtAge = theForm.txtAge;
    var txtEmail = theForm.txtEmail;
    var txtPassword1 = theForm.txtPassword1;
    var txtPassword2 = theForm.txtPassword2;
    var button = theForm.btnSubmit;
    var age = parseInt(txtAge.value, 10);

    button.disabled = true;

    try {
        if (isEmpty(txtName.value)) {
            throw new ValidationException(txtName, "Please enter your name.");
        }

        if (isNaN(age) || age < 1) {
            throw new ValidationException(txtAge, "Please enter your age.");
        }
    }
}
```

The same basics apply here. If `age` is not a number or is less than 1, throw an exception.

5. Validate the `txtEmail` field. Add the bold code:

```
function validateForm(event) {
    var theForm = document.theForm;
    var txtName = theForm.txtName;
    var txtAge = theForm.txtAge;
    var txtEmail = theForm.txtEmail;
    var txtPassword1 = theForm.txtPassword1;
    var txtPassword2 = theForm.txtPassword2;
    var button = theForm.btnSubmit;
    var age = parseInt(txtAge.value, 10);

    button.disabled = true;

    try {
        if (isEmpty(txtName.value)) {
            throw new ValidationException(txtName,
                "Please enter your name.");
        }

        if (isNaN(age) || !(age > 0)) {
```

```
        throw new ValidationException(txtAge, "Please enter your age.");
    }

    if (!(txtEmail.value.indexOf("@") > 0)) {
        throw new ValidationException(txtEmail,
            "Please enter a valid email address.");
    }


    }
}
```

6. Now validate the password fields. They should match, and they can't be empty. The new code is bold:

```
function validateForm(event) {
    var theForm = document.theForm;
    var txtName = theForm.txtName;
    var txtAge = theForm.txtAge;
    var txtEmail = theForm.txtEmail;
    var txtPassword1 = theForm.txtPassword1;
    var txtPassword2 = theForm.txtPassword2;
    var button = theForm.btnSubmit;
    var age = parseInt(txtAge.value, 10);

    button.disabled = true;

    try {
        if (isEmpty(txtName.value)) {
            throw new ValidationException(txtName, "Please enter your name.");
        }

        if (isNaN(age) || !(age > 0)) {
            throw new ValidationException(txtAge, "Please enter your age.");
        }

        if (!(txtEmail.value.indexOf("@") > 0)) {
            throw new ValidationException(txtEmail,
                "Please enter a valid email address.");
        }

        if (isEmpty(txtPassword1.value)) {
            throw new ValidationException(txtPassword1,
                "Password cannot be blank");
        }

        if (txtPassword1.value !== txtPassword2.value) {
            throw new ValidationException(txtPassword1,
                "Passwords do not match. Please reenter them");
        }
    }
}
```

7. Now add the `catch` block. Use the `alert()` method to alert the exception's message, and use the `element` property to give focus to the element. Also don't forget to prevent the default action of the form's `submit` event, and enable the button. Add the following bold code:

```
function validateForm(event) {
    var theForm = document.theForm;
    var txtName = theForm.txtName;
    var txtAge = theForm.txtAge;
    var txtEmail = theForm.txtEmail;
    var txtPassword1 = theForm.txtPassword1;
    var txtPassword2 = theForm.txtPassword2;
    var button = theForm.btnSubmit;
    var age = parseInt(txtAge.value, 10);

    button.disabled = true;

    try {
        if (isEmpty(txtName.value)) {
            throw new ValidationException(txtName, "Please enter your name.");
        }

        if (isNaN(age) || !(age > 0)) {
            throw new ValidationException(txtAge, "Please enter your age.");
        }

        if (!(txtEmail.value.indexOf("@") > 0)) {
            throw new ValidationException(txtEmail,
                "Please enter a valid email address.");
        }

        if (isEmpty(txtPassword1.value)) {
            throw new ValidationException(txtPassword1,
                "Password cannot be blank");
        }

        if (txtPassword1.value !== txtPassword2.value) {
            throw new ValidationException(txtPassword1,
                "Passwords do not match. Please reenter them");
        }
    } catch(exception) {
        var element = exception.element;

        alert(exception.message);
        element.focus();
        element.select();

        eventUtility.preventDefault(event);
        button.disabled = false;
    }
}
```

In this new code, the `exception.element` property is assigned to the `element` variable. Next, an alert box displays the error message to the user, and then the `focus()` and `select()` methods are called on the `element` object. Then, since an error occurred, the `eventUtility` `.preventDefault()` method prevents the form from being submitted. Finally, the button is enabled to allow the user to resubmit the form.

Open this file in your browser and test it. You'll find that it works very much as it did in Lesson 28, with less code!

To get the sample code files, download Lesson 37 from the book's website at `www.wrox.com`.

 Please select Lesson 37 on the DVD to view the video that accompanies this lesson.

38

Debugging with Firebug

Before JavaScript became the world's most popular programming language, it was actually looked down upon as being a quirky language that wasn't worth any real developer's time. This outlook on JavaScript was primarily caused by two issues:

➤ Developers didn't fully understand the language.

➤ There were no decent development tools available.

The popularity of web applications and Ajax essentially pushed JavaScript into the limelight. As a result, developers finally began to understand the language, and some of them started building development tools for JavaScript.

Today, there are a variety of tools available to developers. Probably the most important are the JavaScript debuggers present in all major browsers. With a debugger, you can pause the code execution of your script, and with a process known as *stepping,* you can execute the lines one at a time to find bugs in your code.

Debugging is universally necessary across all browsers and languages. Although some debugging tools offer features that other tools may not have, all debugging tools are based upon the following concepts:

➤ **Breakpoints:** tell the debugger where it should *break* or halt code execution. You can set a breakpoint on any line in your code; the debugger will pause there.

➤ **Stepping:** lets you execute one statement of code at a time. There are three ways to step through code:

   1. **Step Into:** executes the next line of code. In the case of a function, the debugger executes the function and breaks at the first statement inside the function.

   2. **Step Over:** also executes the next line of code. If the line is a function, the debugger executes the function and breaks at the line after the function call.

3. **Step Out:** returns to the caller when you're inside a function. It executes the function and then breaks at the return point of the function.

➤ **Watches:** let you inspect variables to view their data.

➤ **The call stack:** records the functions and methods that executed up to the breakpoint.

➤ **The console:** lets you execute JavaScript statements within the scope of the breakpoint, as well as displaying unhandled errors that may have occurred.

Although all debuggers offer support for these key concepts, and every modern browser has a JavaScript debugger, the most popular JavaScript debugger is a Firefox add-on called Firebug. Even if you don't use Firefox as your browser, you, like many other developers, may decide to install it just so you can use Firebug.

Unfortunately, Firebug does not come with Firefox by default; you have to install the add-on. You can download the latest version at `www.getfirebug.com` or from Mozilla's add-on site at `addons .mozilla.org/en-US/firefox/addon/1843/`.

Because Firebug is an add-on, you will not find an installer for your operating system. Instead, you have to visit one of the provided URLs with Firefox, click the install button on the web page, and follow the instructions. After the add-on is installed, you need to restart Firefox in order to use the new add-on.

Go ahead and install Firebug and proceed to the next section when you're ready.

GETTING FAMILIAR WITH THE UI

By default, Firebug is not visible when you open a new Firefox window or tab. To access Firebug click the Firebug icon in the status bar at the lower right of the Firefox window. If you do not have the status bar visible you can open Firebug by clicking the Tools menu, moving your mouse over the Firebug option, and then clicking Open Firebug. Or, you can just press the F12 key on your keyboard.

 The F12 key will generally open a browser's developer tools.

By default Firebug opens as a panel at the bottom of the window (Figure 38-1), but you can pop it out into its own window by clicking the middle panel control button at the top right corner.

At the top of the panel is a list of tabs that give you information about the web page. The far left tab is the Console tab, shown in Figure 38-2. The top portion is an information area that lists errors and results of the JavaScript code you execute in the lower portion.

Tab Controls

Firebug
Panel
Controls

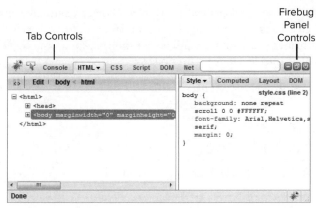

FIGURE 38-1

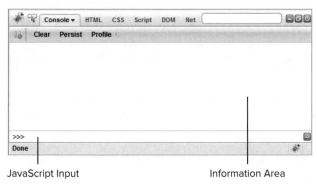

JavaScript Input

Information Area

FIGURE 38-2

By default the console allows only single-line JavaScript statements to be input and executed, but you can click the up arrow to allow multi-statement JavaScript code. When you do so, the Console tab divides into a left panel (the informational panel) and a right panel (the JavaScript input panel).

The next tab is the HTML tab, and it provides information regarding the HTML structure as it's rendered in the browser (Figure 38-3).

Document Tree

Information Area

Info Tabs

FIGURE 38-3

On the left side is a tree that lets you drill down to any element in the page. You can actually edit the HTML on-the-fly to see how a change affects its rendering. It's a powerful tool for any web developer. On the right is a panel that provides you with CSS and layout information of the element you have selected in the left panel, as well as the element's DOM object.

The next tab is the CSS tab (Figure 38-4). It displays the source code of all the CSS style sheets referenced in the page.

CSS File Selection Menu   CSS Source Code

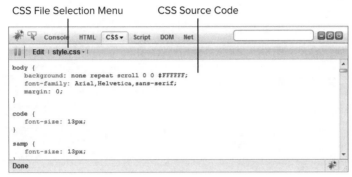

FIGURE 38-4

By clicking the menu you can select any style sheet and edit it to see how a change makes the page look in the browser. While it isn't overly useful for JavaScript developers, it is handy for those responsible for a page's look-and-feel.

The Script tab is next, shown in Figure 38-5, and this is where you'll spend the majority of your time in this lesson.

The left panel displays the source code of all the JavaScript referenced in the page. You can view the other JavaScript files by clicking the menu and choosing the JavaScript file you want to view. The area to the very left of the source code panel, where the line numbers are shown, is called the *gutter*. You'll use the gutter to set and remove breakpoints.

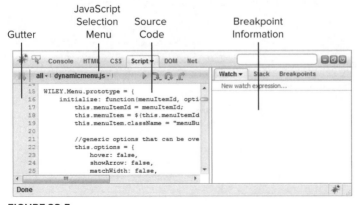

FIGURE 38-5

The right-hand panel of the Script tab is an information area that allows you to specify watches, view the call stack, and view the statements that have breakpoints.

The next tab is the DOM tab (Figure 38-6). It displays everything loaded by the DOM, as well as JavaScript variables, functions, and objects in the currently loaded page.

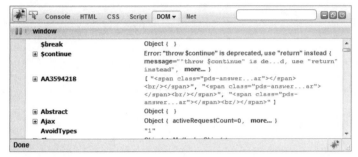

FIGURE 38-6

Finally is the Net tab, which is disabled by default, but which gives you instructions on how to enable it if you want. This tab shows you all the requests made on this page, as shown in Figure 38-7.

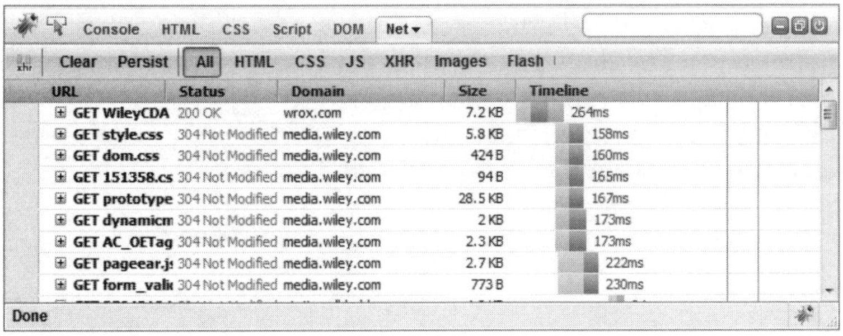

FIGURE 38-7

It gives you just about all the information you need regarding each request: headers, response code, what domain the request was sent to, and the amount of time it took to download the resource. It's a very useful tool when you're trying to optimize the network portion of a web application.

So that's a quick rundown of the UI. Let's focus on the tools central to JavaScript development, starting with the Script tab.

Setting Breakpoints

When the debugger reaches a breakpoint, it pauses code execution and waits for an action from you. This is useful because it allows you to inspect your code while it executes. To create a breakpoint, simply left-click in the gutter on the line where you want to break. Breakpoints are denoted by a red circle in the gutter on the line where you clicked (Figure 38-8).

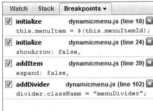

FIGURE 38-8

You can also hard-code a breakpoint in your JavaScript code by using the debugger keyword, like this:

```
function someFunction() {
    var someVariable = "Doing some work";
    debugger;
    someVariable = "Doing more work";
}
```

When code execution reaches the debugger statement in this code, Firebug will break and wait for an action from you.

To view all the breakpoints that you've set, you can click the Breakpoints tab in the right panel (Figure 38-9). Each entry in the list lets you enable or disable a breakpoint by checking or unchecking the checkbox, and also features the name of the function containing the statement the breakpoint is on (if applicable), the file name and line number of the source file, the source text of the breakpoint, and a delete button to remove the breakpoint.

FIGURE 38-9

Stepping through Code

You control code stepping with four buttons in the upper right of the source code panel (Figure 38-10).

➤ The first button is the Continue button (its shortcut key is F8). When code execution is stopped at a breakpoint, the Continue action will restart it until either the next breakpoint or the code's end is reached.

➤ The second button is Step Into (its shortcut key is F11). It executes the current line of code and pauses at the next statement. If the current line is a function, it steps to the first line of the function.

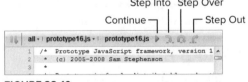

FIGURE 38-10

➤ Next is Step Over (F10), and it executes the current line of code and pauses at the next statement.

➤ Last is the Step Over button (Shift+F11). When evoked inside a function, Step Out executes the remaining code of the function and returns to the caller.

TRY IT

In this lesson, you are introduced to Firebug, the most popular JavaScript debugger. You learn how to set breakpoints, step through code, and use the console to get information and change values as you need to.

Lesson Requirements

For this lesson, you will need a text editor; any plain text editor will do. For Microsoft Windows users, Notepad is available by default on your system, or you can download Microsoft's Visual Web Developer Express (www.microsoft.com/express/web/) or Web Matrix (www.asp.net/webmatrix/), both of which are free. Mac OS X users can use TextMate, which comes as part of OS X, or download a trial of Coda (www.panic.com/coda/). Linux users can use the built-in VIM.

You also need Firefox and the Firebug add-on installed. If you do not have Firefox installed on your computer, visit www.getfirefox.com to download and install it. After it is installed, install the Firebug add-on as described previously in this lesson.

Create a subfolder called Lesson38 in the JS24Hour folder, and then open your text editor and type the following HTML. The bold line has a deliberate typo.

```
<html>
<head>
    <title>Lesson 38: Example 01</title>
</head>
<body>

<script type="text/javascript">
function writeTimesTable(timesTable) {
   var writeString = "";

   for (var counter = 1; counter < 12; counter++) {
       writeString = counter + " * " + timesTable + " = ";
       writeString = writeString + (timesTable * counter);
       writeString = writeString + "<br />";

       documents.write(writeString);
   }
}

writeTimesTable(2);
</script>

</body>
</html>
```

Save this file as lesson38_example01.htm, and make sure it is in the Lesson38 folder.

Step-by-Step

1. Open `lesson38_example01.htm` in Firefox. Firebug should automatically open. If not, that's fine.

If your status bar is enabled, look at the lower right of the browser window and you'll see that an error occurred in this page (Figure 38-11).

FIGURE 38-11

2. If your status bar is enabled, click the "1 Error" message in the status bar.

3. If your status bar is disabled, and if it isn't open already, open Firebug by pressing the F12 key, and click the Console tab.

4. You'll now see the error. Notice that you are given the error message, the source code that caused the error, and the number of the file and line where the error occurred.

5. Go back to your text editor and fix the error by removing the s from `documents`. Save the file again, and refresh the page in your browser.

6. Now set a breakpoint on line 13. The code on that line is:

```
writeString = writeString + (timesTable * counter);
```

To set a breakpoint, click the Script tab and left-click the gutter at line 13. You should now see a red circle next to the line number.

7. Reload the page. Notice that it looks as if nothing has happened. That's because Firebug has paused JavaScript execution. Look at the source code in the Scripts tab. You'll see an arrow inside the red circle, and the line will be highlighted (Figure 38-12). The debugger has not yet executed this line of code — it is waiting for an action from you. You'll give it an action shortly.

8. Look over at the pane on the right. The Watch tab should be active. If not, click it.

The breakpoint caused the debugger to pause at line 13, which is inside the `writeTimesTable()` function. The items being displayed in the Watch tab are variables that have scope inside `writeTimesTable()`. You can see that `this` is the `window` object, the `counter` variable is 1, `timesTable` is 2, and `writeString` is `"1 * 2 = "`. You can click where it says "New watch expression" to add a new watch. There aren't any that you want to add at this time.

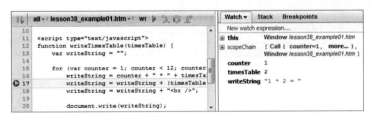
FIGURE 38-12

9. Now Step Into the next line by pressing the F11 key (or clicking the Step Into button). The debugger executes the currently highlighted line and then pauses at the next line.

10. Look back at the Watch tab and at the value of `writeString`. It is now as follows:

```
"1 * 2 = 2"
```

The values of watched items are updated in real time.

11. Step Into the code two more times. Notice that Firefox updates the page as you step through code. Unfortunately, not all JavaScript debuggers do this (IE's debugger doesn't).

12. Now Step Out of the code (Shift+F11). The loop iterates and code execution pauses again at line 13. You cannot Step Out of a function if a breakpoint is set on a statement within a loop. While the remainder of the loop's iteration executes, the debugger stops at the breakpoint again in the next iteration.

To Step Out of a function while inside a loop, you must disable or remove the breakpoint that is inside the loop.

13. Click the Breakpoints tab in the right panel and you'll see the information about the breakpoint on line 13. Uncheck the checkbox and Step Out again. The loop finished executing without breaking again and you Stepped Out of the function. Now code execution is paused at line 20, the call to `writeTimesTable()`.

14. Step Into the code again, and it looks as if nothing happens. When you Step Out of the function, it finishes executing and returns you to the point at which the function was called. Since there is no other code to execute, Step Into doesn't really do anything.

15. Enable the breakpoint again and refresh the page. The code pauses again at line 13.

16. Let's mess this up. Click the Console tab and type the following code in the input box at the bottom of the Console tab:

```
writeString = "I messed this up!";
```

17. Now press the enter key on your keyboard. It will seem as if nothing happens.

18. This time remove the breakpoint by clicking the red circle in the gutter and press F8 to Continue (or click the button). The page in Firefox should look like Figure 38-13.

This happened because you changed the value of `writeString` while paused at line 13.

FIGURE 38-13

To get the sample code files, download Lesson 38 from the book's website at www.wrox.com.

 Please select Lesson 38 on the DVD to view the video that accompanies this lesson.

39

Coding Guidelines

Whether you're working on a project by yourself or with a group of other developers, it's very important that you follow a set of guidelines as you write code. Following guidelines promotes code quality, making it easier for you and others to find bugs, read, and maintain. The heart of most sets of guidelines is code conventions inherent to the programming language. For example, when you were introduced to variables and identifiers in Lesson 2, you were taught how identifiers should follow the code conventions already in use by the language itself.

Aside from naming identifiers, JavaScript developers follow a varying set of guidelines, usually based on conventions, to make their code easier to read and maintain. Let's look at some of them.

USE WHITESPACE

Whitespace, while not actually code, is one of the most important pieces of a programming language. It allows you to visually organize your code into readable and maintainable chunks of text. Without whitespace code would be a jumbled mess of text. Look at the following code for an example:

```
function doSomethingUseless(num){if(num===1){num=num+1;
doSomethingUseless(1);}
else{num=num*2;for(var i=0;i<num;i++){
num--;}
return num;
}
}
```

This code is difficult to read. By scanning it you can see that it's a function with some decisions and loops, but the lack of whitespace makes it difficult to discern what the code actually does. So let's add some whitespace to make it more readable:

```
function doSomethingUseless(num) {
    if (num === 1) {
```

```
            num = num + 1;
            doSomethingUseless(num);
        } else {
            num = num * 2;
            for (var i = 0; i < num; i++) {
                num--;
            }
            return num;
        }
    }
```

To visually organize your code, follow these guidelines:

➤ Put each statement on its own line.

➤ Organize code blocks by doing the following:

   ➤ Put the opening curly brace ({)at the end of the line that begins the code block.

   ➤ Put the closing curly brace (}) at the beginning of a new line. It should be indented to align with the statement that contains the opening curly brace.

   ➤ Indent each line of code so that you can see what lines of code are contained within a particular code block.

➤ Add a single space between values and operators. The code 2+2 is easier to read as 2 + 2.

VARIABLE DECLARATIONS

Something else that makes code easier to read and maintain is declaring all variables at the beginning of a function (using the var keyword, of course). Consider the following code as an example:

```
function nothingSpecial(value) {
    var multiplier = 2;
    var result = value;

    for (var i = 0; i < value; i++) {
        result = result * 2 + num;
    }

    return result;
}
```

Placing variables declarations at the top of a function also has the side effect of pointing out possible errors. For example, this code uses a variable called num inside the for loop. It's obviously important to the nothingSpecial() function because it's used in the calculation of result.

So is num supposed to be global, or is it supposed to be a local variable? Can you count on its having a value before trying to use it in a calculation? By declaring variables at the top of a function you can catch little things like the num variable since you know what variables to expect in the function. Also remember that JavaScript has no block-level scope. Placing variable declarations at the beginning of a function makes that fact explicit.

Variables serving as loop counters are an exception. Typically, they're declared with the loop they count.

AVOID THE GLOBAL SCOPE

The previous section posed a valid question regarding a variable that was not declared within a function. Is it global? One of JavaScript's faults is its dependency on the global scope. JavaScript assumes undeclared variables are global, and that can lead to undesired results in your application. So it's best to avoid the global scope.

Avoiding the global scope is also advantageous because it helps you avoid naming conflicts (that is, having more than one variable or function with the same name). As you develop more and more applications you may find yourself using code written by someone else, such as the code in the popular jQuery library. The more code written by a third party you add to a project, the greater the chance of a naming conflict. While avoiding the global scope entirely is next to impossible, you can minimize naming conflicts by keeping as much of your code out of the global scope as possible. You'll learn exactly how to do this in Lesson 42.

USE LITERALS

The performance of your web application is linked to how fast it downloads to the user's browser. Obviously, larger files take more time to download. With broadband connections becoming more and more the norm, it may seem that file size doesn't matter. After all, a 50KB file takes .05 seconds to download on a 1MB/s line, but it can add up. So cutting out unnecessary characters not only makes typing easier, but also trims down the size of your code.

Perhaps the best way to type less is to use literal notation when creating objects and arrays instead of calling their constructors. Remember, object literals use curly braces ({}) and array literals use square brackets ([]). For example, the following code creates an object with three properties, one of which is an array, using the `Object` and `Array` constructors:

```
var person = new Object();
person.firstName = "John";
person.lastName = "Doe";
person.friends = new Array();
person.friends[0] ="Jim";
person.friends[1] = "Jane";
person.friends[2] = "Bartholomew";
```

That's a lot of typing to create one `person` object: 203 bytes worth of characters. Contrast that with the following code:

```
var person = {
    firstName : "John",
    lastName : "Doe",
```

```
        friends : [
            "Jim",
            "Jane",
            "Bartholomew"
        ]
    };
```

This code uses literal notation to create the same `person` object. Even though it has two more lines than the previous code, it's less typing and weighs in at 146 bytes. That's a significant decrease in size, and the size difference would only grow as more properties or array elements were added.

Many professionals use a tool called JSLint (`http://www.jslint.com/`), written by Douglas Crockford, to analyze code and check its quality. The guidelines mentioned in this lesson are just a few of the items JSLint looks at, and future lessons touch on other items scrutinized by JSLint.

40

Separating JavaScript and HTML

Web applications are naturally separated into different layers. The HTML layer is responsible for getting data to the user, the CSS layer is responsible for the visual representation of that data, and JavaScript adds behavior to the page. Despite this separation, developers have a tendency to tie HTML, CSS, and JavaScript together by using inline style sheets or scripts, as well as by using the style and event handler attributes (such as onclick).

Proof of this is found in this book. In many examples you'll find the use of inline scripts or event handler attributes. It makes explanations and demonstrations easier while at the same time making maintenance a headache. The more tightly you integrate multiple layers, the more work you face when making changes down the road.

Using inline scripts and event handler attributes is technically correct. After all, the examples in this book use them, but their use made the examples harder to maintain and, in the case of errors, fix. Consider the following code as an example:

```
<form name="theForm" onsubmit="submitFom(event);" />

<script type="text/javascript">
function submitForm(event) {
    alert("Submitting!");
}
</script>
```

There is an error in this code. But where? Is it in the `<form/>` element's onsubmit attribute or in the JavaScript code? You have a 50 percent chance of picking the correct spot to start debugging, and if you pick wrong you've wasted time. The actual error is in the onsubmit event handler: It calls submitFom(), not submitForm(). Now, this is a very simple example, so imagine having to debug several HTML attributes and inline scripts on multiple pages. That's a daunting task.

This example also brings up another way in which an error might occur: The form could be submitted before the submitForm() function is available to the browser. In other words, the submitForm() function isn't loaded by the browser when the user submits the form. It's one of those errors that you personally may not experience when developing your application, but that users on varying connections, especially slow ones, could experience.

Decoupling your JavaScript and HTML is one of the tenants of *progressive enhancement*, a Web development philosophy that champions accessibility. The idea behind progressive enhancement is to create a bare-bones document that works in all browsers (no CSS or JavaScript whatsoever). Then the developer adds enhancements to the page via external style sheets or JavaScript. Progressive enhancement enables users with the latest browsers to experience the full-feature page; whereas, users with JavaScript-disabled browsers can still use the page's basic functionality without having to download the unnecessary JavaScript files.

The previous form submittal example is a perfect illustration of how progressive enhancement can improve a user's experience. Examine the following HTML:

```
<form name="theForm" onsubmit="submitForm(event);" />

<script type="text/javascript">
function submitForm(event) {
    alert("Submitting!");
}
</script>
```

Browsers with JavaScript disabled still have to download the inline JavaScript because it's part of the HTML document. Compare that code with the following HTML:

```
<form name="theForm" />

<script type="text/javascript" src="formStuff.js"></script>
```

The JavaScript code within `formStuff.js` contains all the code necessary to provide enhanced features and usability for users of modern web browsers. For users of browsers with JavaScript enabled, the external file is downloaded. Users of browsers with JavaScript disabled don't need the file; the browser ignores the external file and doesn't download it. So by following the progressive enhancement philosophy (and thus separating your JavaScript and HTML), you provide features for users that want them while improving performance for users that don't.

Decoupling HTML and JavaScript means that JavaScript files are served separately from HTML documents. This gives you the ability to compress JavaScript files with gzip to make them smaller, serve them as cacheable so they only have to be downloaded once, and *minify* them, or remove unnecessary characters, using various tools like Yahoo!'s UI Compressor (`http://developer.yahoo` `.com/yui/compressor/`) or Douglas Crockford's JSMIN (`http://crockford.com/javascript/jsmin`).

So how can you separate your JavaScript and HTML? The first step is to remove all inline JavaScript and put it in external files. Second, remove all event handler attributes from your HTML elements, and finally, wire up events in your JavaScript.

TRY IT

In this lesson, you learn how to separate your JavaScript from HTML to avoid errors and make your application easier to maintain and debug.

Lesson Requirements

For this lesson, you need a text editor; any plain text editor will do. For Microsoft Windows users, Notepad is available by default on your system or you can download Microsoft's Visual Web Developer Express (`www.microsoft.com/express/web/`) or Web Matrix (`www.asp.net/webmatrix/`), both of which are free. Mac OS X users can use TextMate, which comes as part of OS X, or download a trial of Coda (`www.panic.com/coda/`). Linux users can use the built-in VIM.

You also need a modern web browser. Choose any of the following:

➤ Internet Explorer 8+

➤ Google Chrome

➤ Firefox 3.5+

➤ Apple Safari 4+

➤ Opera 10+

Additionally, you need a webserver installed with PHP support. Refer to Lesson 31 on the DVD for installation instructions.

This lesson modifies Lesson 35's JSON example, so you need a directory called `Lesson40` in your webserver's root directory, containing the `eventUtility.js`, `ajaxUtility.js`, `car_dealership.php`, and the `json2.js` files used in Lesson 35. You can also copy `lesson35_example01.htm` and paste it into the `lesson40` folder. Just remember to rename it to `lesson40_example01.htm`.

Step-by-Step

1. If you didn't copy `lesson35_example01.htm`, open your text editor and type the following:

```
<html>
<head>
    <title>Lesson 40: Example 01</title>
</head>
<body>
<div id="divResults">
    <div id="divSearchMessage"></div>
    <div id="divSearchResults"></div>
</div>
<form name="theForm" method="post" action="car_dealership.php"
    onsubmit="submitForm(event);">
    <p>
        Make: <input type="text" name="txtMake" value="" />
    </p>
    <p>
        Model: <input type="text" name="txtModel" value="" />
    </p>
    <p>
        Year: <input type="text" name="txtYear" value="" />
    </p>
    <p>
        <input type="submit" name="btnSubmit" value="Submit" />
```

```
      </p>
   </form>
   <script type="text/javascript" src="eventutility.js"></script>
   <script type="text/javascript" src="ajaxUtility.js"></script>
   <script type="text/javascript" src="json2.js"></script>
   <script type="text/javascript">
   function submitForm(event) {
       var data = ajaxUtility.getRequestBody(document.theForm);

       ajaxUtility.makeGetRequest("car_dealership.php?" + data, processResponse);

       eventUtility.preventDefault(event);
   }

   function getCarString(carObj) {
       return [carObj.year, carObj.make, carObj.model].join(" ");
   }

   function processResponse(data) {
       var result = JSON.parse(data),
       var messageDiv = document.getElementById("divSearchMessage");
       var resultsDiv = document.getElementById("divSearchResults");
       var message = "";
       var results = [];
       var length = result.results.length;
       var carStr = getCarString(result.searchedCar);

       if (result.isFound) {
           message = "We found " + length + " matches for " + carStr;
       } else {
           message = "We could not find " + carStr + ". You might like: ";

           for (var i = 0; i < length; i++) {
               results.push(getCarString(result.results[i]));
           }

           resultsDiv.innerHTML = results.join("<br/>");
       }

       messageDiv.innerHTML = message;
   }
   </script>
   </body>
   </html>
```

Save it as `lesson40_example01.htm`.

2.   Copy the inline JavaScript code and paste it into a new text file. Save this new file as `lesson40_example01.js`. Be sure to save it in the `lesson40` directory.

3.   Now remove the inline code from your HTML file and reference the new `lesson40_example01.js` file as shown in the following HTML:

```
<html>
<head>
```

```
        <title>Lesson 40: Example 01</title>
    </head>
    <body>
    <div id="divResults">
        <div id="divSearchMessage"></div>
        <div id="divSearchResults"></div>
    </div>
    <form name="theForm" method="post" action="car_dealership.php"
        onsubmit="submitForm(event);">
        <p>
            Make: <input type="text" name="txtMake" value="" />
        </p>
        <p>
            Model: <input type="text" name="txtModel" value="" />
        </p>
        <p>
            Year: <input type="text" name="txtYear" value="" />
        </p>
        <p>
            <input type="submit" name="btnSubmit" value="Submit" />
        </p>
    </form>
    <script type="text/javascript" src="eventutility.js"></script>
    <script type="text/javascript" src="ajaxUtility.js"></script>
    <script type="text/javascript" src="json2.js"></script>
    <script type="text/javascript" src="lesson40_example01.js"></script>
    </body>
    </html>
```

Doesn't that look cleaner?

4. Remove the `onsubmit` attribute from the `<form/>` element. The new code should look like the following:

```
    <html>
    <head>
        <title>Lesson 40: Example 01</title>
    </head>
    <body>
    <div id="divResults">
        <div id="divSearchMessage"></div>
        <div id="divSearchResults"></div>
    </div>
    <form name="theForm" method="post" action="car_dealership.php">
        <p>
            Make: <input type="text" name="txtMake" value="" />
        </p>
        <p>
            Model: <input type="text" name="txtModel" value="" />
        </p>
        <p>
            Year: <input type="text" name="txtYear" value="" />
        </p>
        <p>
            <input type="submit" name="btnSubmit" value="Submit" />
```

```
        </p>
    </form>
    <script type="text/javascript" src="eventutility.js"></script>
    <script type="text/javascript" src="ajaxUtility.js"></script>
    <script type="text/javascript" src="json2.js"></script>
    <script type="text/javascript" src="lesson40_example01.js"></script>
    </body>
</html>
```

JavaScript code is now completely absent from your HTML. It is good.

5.   All you need to do now is handle the `<form/>`'s submit event. In `lesson40_example01.js`, add the following line at the end of the file:

```
eventUtility.addEvent(document.forms[0], "submit", submitForm);
```

This code uses the `eventUtility` object to add a `submit` event handler to the form.

Now your JavaScript is completely separate from your HTML. Any change you make to the JavaScript code is done without your touching any of the HTML. Also, any JavaScript error that might occur can originate only from the JavaScript contained in the external files. There's no more guessing involved in determining if the error originated from HTML or JavaScript.

 Even by completely separating HTML and JavaScript, the form in this can still be submitted before the `submitForm()`, *or the code that assigns it to handle the* `submit` *event is loaded by the browser. Premature form submission cannot be prevented.*

You'll continue this best practices study in Lesson 41 when you learn how to decouple JavaScript and CSS.

To get the sample code files, download Lesson 32 from the book's website at www.wrox.com.

 Please select Lesson 40 on the DVD to view the video that accompanies this lesson.

41

Separating JavaScript and CSS

The HTML layer is arguably the most important because of its responsibility for getting data to the user, and the interaction between the HTML and JavaScript layers is important to the user's overall experience. JavaScript can interact with another layer, the CSS layer, which is responsible for how the page is displayed in the browser. Just as the HTML and JavaScript layers can be tightly integrated, the CSS and JavaScript layers can be coupled.

In Lesson 15, you learned how to change an element's style by using an element object's `style` property, like this:

```
var someEl = document.getElementById("someElement");

someEl.style.color = "red";
someEl.style.backgroundColor = "gray";
someEl.style.border = "1px solid black";
```

This code retrieves an element with an `id` of `someElement` and then changes various CSS properties to change how the element renders in the browser. The code works fine, but it suffers from problems like those of coupled HTML and JavaScript in that it makes maintenance more difficult. Not only do you have to revisit this code whenever you want to change the `color`, `backgroundColor`, and `border` properties, but making additional style changes requires an additional line of code for every property you want to change. Code such as this essentially makes JavaScript share the presentation role that is supposed to be the role of CSS.

Another issue is performance. To use the `style` object you access a DOM object — a poorly performing operation. As you add more lines of code to change an element's style, you not only make your application slower, but you potentially cause the browser to re-render the page multiple times.

Admittedly, it's impossible to completely separate CSS and JavaScript (unless you don't use JavaScript to change an element's style), but you can minimize the integration of CSS and

JavaScript by using the `className` property to add CSS classes to and remove them from an element's `className` property, as you did in Lesson 15, like this:

```
someEl.className = "cssClassName";
```

By doing so, you make only one call to the DOM instead of multiple, and any modification to the CSS is made where it needs to be made — in the CSS file. If you want to add another CSS class to the element represented by `someEl`, you can write the following code:

```
someEl.className = someEl.className + " anotherCssClass";
```

This code adds a CSS class called `anotherCssClass`, and when you want to remove it you can do this:

```
someEl.className = someEl.className.replace(" anotherCssClass", "");
```

There are, however, exceptions to this rule of separation. There are times when changing an element's CSS class cannot provide the functionality you want. Remember the drag-and-drop script from Lesson 24? You had to move an element by changing the `top` and `left` CSS properties while also manipulating the element's `z-index`. This type of fine control is impossible to achieve with CSS classes. So when you need that level of control, setting individual CSS properties with JavaScript is acceptable.

42

Avoiding Global Scope

In Lesson 39, I mentioned that it's good practice to avoid the global scope. This is crucial when you incorporate someone else's code in your page, as it helps you avoid *naming conflicts* between the variable and function names given in yours and the other party's code. What exactly is a naming conflict? A naming conflict occurs when you use an identifier that is used in another script on the same level of scope.

Let's look at an example. The following code is a truncated version of the `eventUtility` object used throughout this book:

```
// your code
var eventUtility = {
    addEvent : (function() {
        if (typeof addEventListener !== "undefined") {
            return function(obj, evt, fn) {
                obj.addEventListener(evt, fn, false);
            };
        } else {
            return function(obj, evt, fn) {
                obj.attachEvent("on" + evt, fn);
            };
        }
    }())
};
```

This code creates the `eventUtility` object with the `addEvent()` method. This code is defined in the global scope, and your event-driven code heavily relies on this particular object and method. But you wanted to add some extra functionality to your page, and you incorporated code written by someone else. It too uses a global object called `eventUtility`, but it's different from yours. Its code is as follows:

```
// third party code
var eventUtility = {
    addEventHandler : function(obj, evt, fn) {
```

```
        obj.addEventListener(evt, fn, false);
    }
};
```

The browser loads this code after loading yours. Since they both share the same identifier and they exist on the same level of scope (global), this second `eventUtility` object overwrites your `eventUtility` object. That's a huge problem because the rest of your code in the page makes extensive use of the `eventUtility.addEvent()` method, and it no longer exists because `eventUtility` was overwritten by someone else's code. So your page breaks, and you could spend a lot of time trying to figure out why. Obviously, you want to avoid naming conflicts. Let's see how you can do just that.

USING FUNCTIONS

In Lesson 6 you learned about scope and that functions have their own levels of scope; the variables, objects, and functions defined inside another function cannot be accessed from outside that function. In Lesson 20, while writing a cross-browser event utility, you learned about self-executing functions — anonymous functions that were executed immediately after they were defined. These two ideas, functional scope and self-executing functions, can be combined in order to hide your code from the global scope.

Let's look at an example. The following is some code using a self-executing function to isolate code from the global scope:

```
var someVariable = "Hello, Global!"; ///

(function() {

var someVariable = "Hello, Privacy!";

alert(someVariable); // Hello, Privacy!

}());

alert(someVariable); // Hello, Global!
```

The first line of this code creates a global variable called `someVariable`. It can be accessed anywhere in the page, and as a result it can potentially be overwritten by some other data.

Next a self-executing function is defined, and its body consists of a local variable called `someVariable` (the same name as the global variable) and a call to `alert()` to display the value of `someVariable`. Remember, Lesson 6 discussed how a variable or function in a local scope can *override* (not the same as *overwrite*) a global variable or function with the same name. The global variable or function is still intact with its value, but in the local scope the variable or function defined locally is used in place of the global variable or function. So when this self-executing function executes, the value of the local `someVariable` variable is displayed in an alert window.

After the function finishes, the final line of this code executes and alerts the text `"Hello, Global!"` because the global `someVariable` variable was not altered.

Let's look at another example. This one uses the `eventUtility` example from earlier in the lesson:

```
(function() {

var eventUtility = {
    addEvent : (function() {
        if (typeof addEventListener !== "undefined") {
            return function(obj, evt, fn) {
                obj.addEventListener(evt, fn, false);
            };
        } else {
            return function(obj, evt, fn) {
                obj.attachEvent("on" + evt, fn);
            };
        }
    }())
};

function documentLoad(event) {
    alert("Document loaded!");
}

// use local version of eventUtility and documentLoad()
eventUtility.addEvent(document, "load", documentLoad);

}());

function documentLoad(event) {
    alert("Event handled with third party");
}

// use third party eventUtility and global documentLoad()
eventUtility.addEventHandler(document, "load", documentLoad);
```

This code first executes a self-executing function. Inside this function your `eventUtility` object is defined and used to assign an event handler to handle the `document` object's `load` event. When the event fires, an alert window displays the text `"Document loaded!"`

After the function executes, another event handler is assigned to handle the `document`'s `load` event using the third-party `eventUtility` object. When a page loads with this JavaScript you'll see two alert boxes: The first tells you the document was loaded, and the second says, `"Event handled with third party"` in browsers supporting `addEventListener()`.

So by putting your code into a self-executing function, you can effectively protect it from the rest of the JavaScript code loaded in the page. But there is a problem here. The `eventUtility` object is something you want to use throughout your application — possibly in different JavaScript files. If it's hidden inside a function, how can other pieces of code use it? Shouldn't it be globally accessible so that you can use it wherever you need to? Yes, it should, and you can make it so by emulating namespaces.

EMULATING NAMESPACES

Many programming languages have built-in constructs called *namespaces* to help avoid naming collisions. A namespace is a container that provides context for the objects it contains while protecting the names of those objects from colliding with the names of other objects outside the namespace. Namespaces aren't a foolproof means of preventing naming collisions, but they do a good enough job.

Unfortunately, JavaScript does not support a formal namespace feature, but you can emulate namespaces by using object literals.

 This book refers to emulated namespaces as pseudo-namespaces, *since they are not technically namespaces but serve the same purpose.*

A namespace should be something meaningful, and yet somewhat unique to you, such as your name or your site's domain name. Your author's website is `www.wdonline.com`, so you could create a pseudo-namespace for him by typing the following:

```
var wdonline = {};
```

Then you can start to tack on the code you need to globally access, as in the following code:

```
wdonline.eventUtility = {
    addEvent : (function() {
        if (typeof addEventListener !== "undefined") {
            return function(obj, evt, fn) {
                obj.addEventListener(evt, fn, false);
            };
        } else {
            return function(obj, evt, fn) {
                obj.attachEvent("on" + evt, fn);
            };
        }
    }())
};
```

In the case of this code, the `wdonline` object is global, but the likelihood of `wdonline` being overwritten by a third party's code is slim. The `eventUtility` object is now a property of `wdonline`, giving it protection from being overwritten. If the chances of `wdonline`'s being overwritten are slim, they're even smaller for `wdonline.eventUtility`.

The reality is that you cannot get away from the global scope if you want certain pieces of your code to be accessible anywhere in the page, but you can do your best to avoid naming collisions by using self-executing functions and pseudo-namespaces.

TRY IT

In this lesson, you learn how to minimize the impact your code has on the global scope in order to reduce the likelihood of naming collisions.

Lesson Requirements

To practice the techniques outlined in this lesson, you will refactor the eventUtility and ajaxUtility objects to include the use of self-executing anonymous functions and pseudo-namespaces. To do this, you will change the example in Lesson 35, the car dealership search using JSON.

You need a text editor. For Microsoft Windows users, Notepad is available by default on your system or you can download Microsoft's Visual Web Developer Express (www.microsoft.com/express/web/) or Web Matrix (www.asp.net/webmatrix/), both of which are free. Mac OS X users can use TextMate, which comes as part of OS X, or download a trial version of Coda (www.panic.com/coda/). Linux users can use the built-in VIM.

You also need a modern web browser. Choose any of the following:

➤ Internet Explorer 8+

➤ Google Chrome

➤ Firefox 3.5+

➤ Apple Safari 4+

➤ Opera 10+

You also need a webserver installed with PHP support. Refer to Lesson 31 on the DVD for installation instructions.

Create a subfolder called Lesson42 in your webserver's root directory. Copy the contents of the Lesson35 directory into Lesson42, and rename the lesson35_example01.htm file to lesson42_example01.htm.

Step-by-Step

1. Open lesson42_example01.htm in your text editor, and change the <title/> element to contain the text Lesson 42: Example 01.

2. Create a new file called lesson42_example01.js, and move all the in-line JavaScript to that new file. Also remove the onsubmit event handler from the <form/> element. The altered HTML should look like this:

```
<html>
<head>
    <title>Lesson 42: Example 01</title>
</head>
<body>
```

```
<div id="divResults">
    <div id="divSearchMessage"></div>
    <div id="divSearchResults"></div>
</div>
<form name="theForm" method="post" action="car_dealership.php">
    <p>
        Make: <input type="text" name="txtMake" value="" />
    </p>
    <p>
        Model: <input type="text" name="txtModel" value="" />
    </p>
    <p>
        Year: <input type="text" name="txtYear" value="" />
    </p>
    <p>
        <input type="submit" name="btnSubmit" value="Submit" />
    </p>
</form>
<script type="text/javascript" src="eventutility.js"></script>
<script type="text/javascript" src="ajaxUtility.js"></script>
<script type="text/javascript" src="json2.js"></script>
<script type="text/javascript" src="lesson42_example01.js"></script>
</body>
</html>
```

3. Open the `eventUtility.js` file in your text editor. You will create a pseudo-namespace called `js24Hour` and add the `eventUtility` object to the pseudo-namespace. Add the following code at the beginning of the file:

```
if (typeof js24Hour === "undefined") {
    var js24Hour = {};
}
```

This code adds flexibility to your pseudo-namespace. Remember that the `eventUtility` and `ajaxUtility` objects exist in two separate files. If you create a `js24Hour` object in both files you will overwrite one of them. By using this code you check to see if `js24Hour` does not exist, and create it if necessary. This way both your `eventUtility` and `ajaxUtility` objects exist within the same `js24Hour` pseudo-namespace.

4. Make changes to the file as shown in bold in the following code:

```
if (!js24Hour) {
    var js24Hour = {};
}

js24Hour.eventUtility = {
    addEvent : (function() {
        if (typeof addEventListener !== "undefined") {
            return function(obj, evt, fn) {
                obj.addEventListener(evt, fn, false);
            };
        } else {
            return function(obj, evt, fn) {
                obj.attachEvent("on" + evt, fn);
```

```
                };
            }
        }()),
        removeEvent : (function() {
            if (typeof removeEventListener !== "undefined") {
                return function(obj, evt, fn) {
                    obj.removeEventListener(evt, fn, false);
                };
            } else {
                return function(obj, evt, fn) {
                    obj.detachEvent("on" + evt, fn);
                };
            }
        }()),
        getTarget : (function() {
            if (typeof addEventListener !== "undefined") {
                return function(event) {
                    return event.target;
                }
            } else {
                return function(event) {
                    return event.srcElement;
                }
            }
        }()),
        preventDefault : (function() {
            if (typeof addEventListener !== "undefined") {
                return function(event) {
                    event.preventDefault();
                }
            } else {
                return function(event) {
                    event.returnValue = false;
                }
            }
        }())
    };
```

This code adds the eventUtility object to the js24Hour pseudo-namespace. There are no other changes. Save the file.

5. Now open ajaxUtility.js and make the changes as marked in bold in the following code:

```
if (typeof js24Hour === "undefined") {
    var js24Hour = {};
}

js24Hour.ajaxUtility = {
    createXHR : function() {
        if (typeof XMLHttpRequest !== "undefined") {
            return new XMLHttpRequest();
        } else {
            var versions = [ "MSXML2.XmlHttp.6.0",
                "MSXML2.XmlHttp.3.0" ];

            for (var i = 0; i < versions.length; i++) {
```

```
                try {
                    var xhr = new ActiveXObject(versions[i]);
                    return xhr;
                } catch (error) {
                    // do nothing
                }
            }
        }

        alert("Your browser does not support XmlHttp");

        return null;
    },

    makeGetRequest : function(url, callback) {
        var xhr = this.createXHR();

        xhr.open("GET", url);

        xhr.onreadystatechange = function() {
            if (xhr.readyState === 4) {
                var status = xhr.status;
                if ((status >= 200 && status < 300) || status === 304) {
                    callback(xhr.responseText);
                } else {
                    alert("An error occurred");
                }
            }
        };

        xhr.send(null);
    },

    getRequestBody : function(form) {
        var pieces = [];
        var elements = form.elements;

        for (var i = 0; i < elements.length; i++) {
            var element = elements[i];
            var name = encodeURIComponent(element.name);
            var value = encodeURIComponent(element.value);

            pieces.push(name + "=" + value);
        }

        return pieces.join("&");
    },

    makePostRequest : function(url, data, callback) {
        var xhr = this.createXHR();

        xhr.open("POST", url);

        xhr.onreadystatechange = function() {
```

```
            if (xhr.readyState === 4) {
                var status = xhr.status;
                if ((status >= 200 && status < 300) || status === 304) {
                    callback(xhr.responseText);
                } else {
                    alert("An error occurred");
                }
            }
        };

        xhr.send(data);
    },

    postFromForm : function(url, form, callback) {
        var xhr = this.createXHR();

        xhr.open("POST", url);
        xhr.setRequestHeader("Content-Type", "application/x-www-form-urlencoded");

        xhr.onreadystatechange = function() {
            if (xhr.readyState === 4) {
                var status = xhr.status;
                if ((status >= 200 && status < 300) || status === 304) {
                    callback(xhr.responseText);
                } else {
                    alert("An error occurred");
                }
            }
        };

        xhr.send(this.getRequestBody(form));
    }
};
```

Once again the first lines ensure that you do not overwrite any existing js24Hour object. Save the file.

6. Now you need to open lesson42_example01.js and make changes to this file. First, surround the code in this file with a self-executing anonymous function. Then, because you removed the onsubmit event handler from the <form/> element's HTML, you need to wire up the submitForm() function to handle the form's submit event. Finally, you need to modify the submitForm() function to use the js24Hour.ajaxUtility and js24Hour.eventUtility objects. The changes to this file are bold in the following code:

```
(function() {

var ajaxUtility = js24Hour.ajaxUtility;
var eventUtility = js24Hour.eventUtility;

function submitForm(event) {
    var data = ajaxUtility.getRequestBody(document.theForm);

    ajaxUtility.makeGetRequest("car_dealership.php?" + data, processResponse);

    eventUtility.preventDefault(event);
```

```
    }

    function getCarString(carObj) {
        return [carObj.year, carObj.make, carObj.model].join(" ");
    }

    function processResponse(data) {
        var result = JSON.parse(data);
        var messageDiv = document.getElementById("divSearchMessage");
        var resultsDiv = document.getElementById("divSearchResults");
        var message = "";
        var results = [];
        var length = result.results.length;
        var carStr = getCarString(result.searchedCar);

        if (result.isFound) {
            message = "We found " + length + " matches for " + carStr;
        } else {
            message = "We could not find " + carStr + ". You might like: ";

            for (var i = 0; i < length; i++) {
                results.push(getCarString(result.results[i]));
            }

            resultsDiv.innerHTML = results.join("<br/>");
        }

        messageDiv.innerHTML = message;
    }

    eventUtility.addEvent(document.forms[0], "submit", submitForm);

}());
```

Using a self-executing anonymous function in this file protects this code from any accidental damage from other JavaScript that may be loaded in the page. The first two statements in the self-executing function cache the js24Hour.ajaxUtility and js24Hour.eventUtility objects in the ajaxUtility and eventUtility variables, respectively. Caching these objects enables you to use them inside the self-executing function exactly as you have in previous lessons.

This code also decouples your JavaScript code from your HTML by using your event utility to assign a function to handle the form's submit event.

7. Save lesson42_example01.js and point your browser to http://localhost/Lesson42/ lesson42_example01.htm. Fill out the form and submit it, and you'll see that it works just as it did in Lesson 35.

You can also download the sample code for all lessons from the book's website at www.wrox.com.

 Please select Lesson 42 on the DVD to view the video that accompanies this lesson.

43

Optimizing Your Code

The applications you use every day have more than likely been in development for many years. The code behind them has been refined to make them more efficient and responsive to the user than they were at first. When first written, code is rarely the best it could be — usually far from it.

There's an old adage that most professional developers follow: "Make it run, and then make it run well." When you first write an application, don't worry about optimizing your code. Another adage is "Premature optimization is the root of all evil." Worry about making your application work, and after it works, *then* start optimizing your code.

There are three major aspects of JavaScript optimization. They are:

➤ Refactoring code

➤ Optimizing DOM code

➤ Using event delegation

Let's start by looking at how to refactor your code.

REFACTORING CODE

It's been recounted many times, but it's worth repeating: The faster your code downloads, the faster your application feels to the user. You don't have control over your users' connection speed, but you do have control over how big your code files are. The size of your code files depends on a variety of factors, but two things that often add to code size are code duplication and unnecessary statements.

Refactoring Duplicate Code

You can cut the size of your code by *refactoring* duplicated code. When you refactor your code, you improve it without changing its external behavior. The most common means of refactoring code is identifying duplicated code and modifying it to be reused and easily maintained.

Recall the lesson on functions (Lesson 3). At the beginning of the lesson you were given an example of code duplication. It is listed here for your convenience:

```
var valueOne = 100;
valueOne = valueOne + 150;
valueOne = valueOne / 2;
valueOne = "The value is: " + valueOne; // results in "The value is: 125"

var valueTwo = 50;
valueTwo = valueTwo + 150;
valueTwo = valueTwo / 2;
valueTwo = "The value is: " + valueTwo; // results in "The value is: 100"

var valueThree = 2;
valueThree = valueThree + 150;
valueThree = valueThree / 2;
valueThree = "The value is: " + valueThree; // results in "The value is: 76"
```

This code performs the same exact operations on three different variables. Later in that lesson, that code was refactored to use the following function:

```
function augmentValue(originalValue) {
    var augmentedValue = originalValue;
    augmentedValue = augmentedValue + 150;
    augmentedValue = augmentedValue / 2;
    augmentedValue = "The value is: " + augmentedValue;

    return augmentedValue;
}

var valueOne = augmentValue(100); // results in "The value is: 125"
var valueTwo = augmentValue(50);  // results in "The value is: 100"
var valueThree = augmentValue(2); // results in "The value is: 76"
```

This refactor session saved two lines of code. Now, that may not seem like much right now, but let's look at the benefits. First, the code is reusable. If you need to augment more values in the same way, you can simply call the function as shown in the following example:

```
var valueFour = augmentValue(10); // results in "The value is: 80"
var valueFive = augmentValue(40); // results in "The value is: 90"
var valueSix = augmentValue(0); // results in "The value is: 75"
```

Now you begin to see real code savings from reusing the augmentValue() function. Before refactoring, each set of operations on one variable took four lines of code, including the variable declaration. If you were to perform the same set of operations on six variables, you'd do so in 24 lines of code. By refactoring the code you shrink the number of lines to 13 (seven for the function and six for each variable) — that's a nice savings.

Second, the code is more maintainable. Let's imagine that you wanted to add one to each value after dividing the number by two. Before refactoring you would have had to modify each set of operations like the bolded lines in the following code:

```
var valueOne = 100;
valueOne = valueOne + 150;
valueOne = (valueOne / 2) + 1;
valueOne = "The value is: " + valueOne; // results in "The value is: 125"

var valueTwo = 50;
valueTwo = valueTwo + 150;
valueTwo = (valueTwo / 2) + 1;
valueTwo = "The value is: " + valueTwo; // results in "The value is: 100"

// etc, etc, etc
```

Making changes like this makes your code more prone to error (what if you missed a variable?), and consumes too much time. You can achieve the same modification by editing one line of code, shown in bold in the following example:

```
function augmentValue(originalValue) {
    var augmentedValue = originalValue;
    augmentedValue = augmentedValue + 150;
    augmentedValue = (augmentedValue / 2) + 1;
    augmentedValue = "The value is: " + augmentedValue;

    return augmentedValue;
}
```

So by identifying duplicated code and refactoring it, you not only gain a performance increase by reducing the amount of code, you also save time and avoid potential errors.

Reducing Statements

The `augmentValue()` function in the previous section certainly eliminated duplicated code, but the function's body can be made to be more efficient and consume less space. The first change you can make is to remove the `augmentedValue` variable. The value passed to this function is supposed to be a number. Numbers are primitive values in JavaScript, so the value passed to this function is copied and contained within the `originalValue` variable. Because of this there's no need to copy the value in `originalValue` to `augmentedValue`. So the first refactor would result in the following:

```
function augmentValue(originalValue) {
    originalValue = originalValue + 150;
    originalValue = (originalValue / 2) + 1;
    originalValue = "The value is: " + originalValue;

    return originalValue;
}
```

You can refactor this function some more by combining statements. The JavaScript engine can execute one statement containing multiple operations faster than it can execute multiple statements performing one operation each. While you could combine all the statements in this function into one, a better approach (as far as maintainability is concerned) would be to combine statements that perform similar operations. For example, there are two statements that perform arithmetic operations. You can combine them into one statement, as shown in this code:

```
function augmentValue(value) {
    originalValue = ((value + 150) / 2) + 1;
    return "The value is: " + originalValue;
}
```

First, the `originalValue` parameter was changed to just `value`. This was done for two reasons:

➤ Before the removal of the `augmentedValue` variable, the `originalValue` identifier made sense. Now, since `augmentedValue` is no longer used, `originalValue` is not meaningful.

➤ Because `originalValue` is no longer meaningful, it makes sense to use the word `value` alone. It's short and saves space, while providing a meaningful name for the parameter.

Next, the first two statements are combined. This isn't always a good idea. If there are many mathematical operations to perform, they would be easier to read and maintain if they were in multiple statements. But here, combining them is fine.

Last, the concatenation and `return` statements are combined. Because there are no other operations that need to be performed after `value` is concatenated with a string, it makes sense to simply return the result of the concatenation operation.

Now the `augmentValue()` function is much smaller than it was before. That, combined with the refactoring of duplicated code into the `augmentValue()` function, makes this code efficient and ready for download.

Combining statements also applies to variables. Lesson 2 introduced the idea of initializing multiple variables within one statement as demonstrated in the following code:

```
var variableOne = "data",
    variableTwo = 10,
    variableThree = [];
```

Each variable initialization is separated by a comma. This code executes faster than the following code:

```
var variableOne = "data";
var variableTwo = 10;
var variableThree = [];
```

This book, for the sake of clarity, opted to declare and initialize multiple variables in separate statements like this code. Many professionals declare variables in this manner, but bear in mind that the single statement approach is more efficient.

OPTIMIZING DOM CODE

Refactoring code is only one piece of the optimization puzzle; you also need to look at your code that interacts with the DOM. As a JavaScript developer you'll spend a lot of your time working with the DOM — the slowest part of an application you'll deal with (other than connection-based parts like Ajax).

The DOM's slowness is primarily caused by two factors: re-rendering of the page caused by changes in the DOM, and the sheer amount of data the DOM manages. You can optimize your code that interacts with the DOM by limiting the number of updates you make to the DOM.

Using Document Fragments

In Lesson 14 you learned how to dynamically create HTML elements and text nodes with the `document.createElement()` and `document.createTextNode()` methods, and how to add them to the page with the `appendChild()` and `insertBefore()` methods. As a quick refresher, look at the following code:

```
for (var i = 0; i < 20; i++) {
    var el = document.createElement("p");
    el.appendChild(document.createTextNode("Paragraph " + i));
    document.body.appendChild(el);
}
```

This code creates 20 `<p/>` elements, adds a text node to them, and adds them to the page. Figure 43-1 shows you what it looks like in the browser.

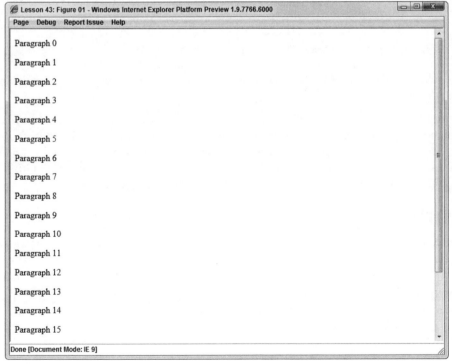

FIGURE 43-1

There is technically nothing wrong with this code, but it is horribly inefficient because the DOM is updated 20 separate times, once for each <p/> element that is added to the page. With each update the browser has to redraw the page. This kind of page update can be noticeable by the user and inhibit performance. To solve this problem you want to reduce the number of updates made to the DOM, and you can do so by creating a *document fragment*.

Document fragments are lightweight document objects that can contain element objects that you can manipulate as if they were inside the HTML document. To create a document fragment you use the `createDocumentFragment()` method of the `document` object, like this:

```
var fragment = document.createDocumentFragment();
```

After you have created a fragment you can start adding element objects to it. In the case of this example you can append each <p/> element to a document fragment and then add the fragment to the HTML document. The following code illustrates this:

```
var fragment = document.createDocumentFragment();

for (var i = 0; i < 20; i++) {
    var el = document.createElement("p");
    el.appendChild(document.createTextNode("Paragraph " + i));
    fragment.appendChild(el);
}

document.body.appendChild(fragment);
```

Here, each <p/> element is appended to the document fragment. After the loop exits, the fragment is appended to the `document`'s `body` node.

Using a document fragment in this way is advantageous because it reduces the amount of DOM updates to one. Even though you append each <p/> element to the fragment, the fragment exists outside of the DOM. So you don't cause an update to occur until you append the fragment to `document.body`. The document fragment object doesn't generate HTML itself, but its children do. So the resulting HTML in this code is exactly the same as it was without a document fragment.

Using innerHTML

Also in Lesson 14 you learned about the `innerHTML` property that you can use to add HTML to an element. Instead of creating node objects you simply construct a string containing HTML markup and assign it to an element's `innerHTML` property. It's simple, quick, and efficient — unless of course you make multiple updates to the DOM. Let's recreate the example from the previous section by using `innerHTML` to add <p/> elements to the page with the following code:

```
for (var i = 0; i < 20; i++) {
    var el = "<p>Paragraph " + i + "</p>";
    document.body.innerHTML = document.body.innerHTML + el;
}
```

As in the previous section, this code creates 20 <p/> elements and adds them to the document's body. As you might have realized, this code is inefficient because you make 20 updates to the body — causing the browser to render the page with every update. You could fix this by creating a variable and adding each HTML string to it, like this:

```
var html = "";

for (var i = 0; i < 20; i++) {
    html = html + "<p>Paragraph " + i + "</p>";
}

document.body.innerHTML = html;
```

But this code is inefficient too, because strings are immutable in JavaScript. The string value in `html` has to be copied, destroyed, and recreated with every loop iteration. A better solution is to create an array and push each HTML string to it, as shown in the following code:

```
var html = [];

for (var i = 0; i < 20; i++) {
    html.push("<p>Paragraph " + i + "</p>");
}

document.body.innerHTML = html.join();
```

In this code a string value is added as an element in the `html` array. After the loop exits, the `html` array's `join()` method is called to convert the array to a string value, which is then assigned to the body's `innerHTML` property. By building a HTML string, or in this case an array, you can limit the number of updates to the page.

USE EVENT DELEGATION

Events are a crucial part of a JavaScript application, and the more event handlers you use on a page the slower it responds to the user. Lesson 21 introduced you to event delegation — a technique by which you set a single event handler on a parent element to take advantage of event bubbling.

To reuse the example from Lesson 21, let's assume you want to handle the click event for two `<div/>` elements in a page. Here is the HTML:

```
<body>
    <div id="divElement"
        style="width: 100px; height: 100px; background-color: red; "></div>
<br/><br/>
    <div id="divElement2"
        style="width: 100px; height: 100px; background-color: red; "></div>
</body>
```

You want the color of these `<div/>` elements to change when they're clicked. You could add an `onclick` event handler to each element, but you also want to limit the amount of event handlers used in the page. To solve this problem, use event delegation by handling the `document` object's `click` event, like this:

```
var eventUtility = js24Hour.eventUtility;

eventUtility.addEvent(document, "click", function(event) {
```

```
        var eSrc = eventUtility.getTarget(event);

    if (eSrc.tagName.toUpperCase() === "DIV") {
        var bgColor = eSrc.style.backgroundColor,
            color = "red";

        if (bgColor === color) {
            color = "green";
        }

        eSrc.style.backgroundColor = color;
    }
});
```

When the user clicks anywhere in the document, the event handler executes, and the code determines whether the element that received the mouse click is a <div/> element. If it is, its background color is changed.

Using event delegation is an efficient way to handle events in your page. Simply assign a single event handler for a particular event (click in this example), and use it to handle the same event for all elements in the page.

TRY IT

In this lesson, you learn how to optimize your code after you have written it by refactoring, limiting DOM updates, and using event delegation.

Lesson Requirements

You need a text editor. For Microsoft Windows users, Notepad is available by default on your system or you can download Microsoft's Visual Web Developer Express (www.microsoft.com/express/web/) or Web Matrix (www.asp.net/webmatrix/), both of which are free. Mac OS X users can use TextMate, which comes as part of OS X, or download a trial of Coda (www.panic.com/coda/). Linux users can use the built-in VIM.

You also need a modern web browser. Choose any of the following:

➤ Internet Explorer 8+

➤ Google Chrome

➤ Firefox 3.5+

➤ Apple Safari 4+

➤ Opera 10+

You also need a webserver installed with PHP support. Refer to Lesson 31 on the DVD for installation instructions.

Create a subfolder called `Lesson43` in your webserver's root directory. Copy all the files from the `Lesson42` directory and paste them into the `Lesson43` folder. Rename the `lesson42_example01.htm` file to `lesson43_example01.htm`. As an exercise in code optimization you'll refactor the `ajaxUtility` object.

Step-by-Step

1. Open the `ajaxUtility.js` file in your text editor and look at it; specifically, look at the `makeGetRequest()`, `makePostRequest()`, and `postFromForm()` methods. They are listed here for your convenience:

```
makeGetRequest : function(url, callback) {
    var xhr = this.createXHR();

    xhr.open("GET", url);

    xhr.onreadystatechange = function() {
        if (xhr.readyState === 4) {
            var status = xhr.status;
            if ((status >= 200 && status < 300) || status === 304) {
                callback(xhr.responseText);
            } else {
                alert("An error occurred");
            }
        }
    };

    xhr.send(null);
}

makePostRequest : function(url, data, callback) {
    var xhr = this.createXHR();

    xhr.open("POST", url);

    xhr.onreadystatechange = function() {
        if (xhr.readyState === 4) {
            var status = xhr.status;
            if ((status >= 200 && status < 300) || status === 304) {
                callback(xhr.responseText);
            } else {
                alert("An error occurred");
            }
        }
    };

    xhr.send(data);
}

postFromForm : function(url, form, callback) {
    var xhr = this.createXHR();

    xhr.open("POST", url);
```

```
            xhr.setRequestHeader("Content-Type", "application/x-www-form-urlencoded");

            xhr.onreadystatechange = function() {
                if (xhr.readyState === 4) {
                    var status = xhr.status;
                    if ((status >= 200 && status < 300) || status === 304) {
                        callback(xhr.responseText);
                    } else {
                        alert("An error occurred");
                    }
                }
            };

            xhr.send(this.getRequestBody(form));
        }
```

There's a lot of code duplication here. All these methods create an XHR object, open the connection, assign the onreadystatechange event handler (which calls the callback function), and send the request. These operations can be refactored into their own method, so let's do it.

2. Create a new method called openAndSend(). It will be responsible for creating the XHR object, opening a GET or POST request, setting the onreadystatechange event handler, and sending data (if applicable). So it should accept four arguments: the request type, the URL to send the request to, the data to send in the request, and the callback function. Its code follows:

```
        openAndSend : function(type, url, data, callback) {
            var xhr = this.createXHR();

            xhr.open(type, url);

            xhr.onreadystatechange = function() {
                if (xhr.readyState === 4) {
                    var status = xhr.status;
                    if ((status >= 200 && status < 300) || status === 304) {
                        callback(xhr.responseText);
                    } else {
                        alert("An error occurred");
                    }
                }
            };

            xhr.send(data);
        }
```

Compare this code to the makeGetRequest() and makePostRequest() methods. They look very similar, don't they? In fact, the only differences are in the values passed to the XHR object's open() and send() methods.

3. So let's refactor makeGetRequest() and makePostRequest() to call openAndSend(). Following is the new code:

```
        makeGetRequest : function(url, callback) {
            this.openAndSend("GET", url, null, callback);
```

```
        },

        makePostRequest : function(url, data, callback) {
            this.openAndSend("POST", url, data, callback);
        },
```

In `makeGetRequest()`, `openAndSend()` is called by passing four things: the string `"GET"` for the request type, the `url` parameter, `null` for the data, and the value passed to the `callback` parameter. The `makePostRequest()` was altered to pass `"POST"`, as well as the `url`, `data`, and `callback` parameters.

Notice how these two methods did not change from an API perspective; you still call `makeGetRequest()` and `makePostRequest()` as you did before. But underneath the hood these methods do something different by calling the new `openAndSend()` method to do all the work. When you're refactoring code that's already in use, it's important to do your best to keep the external portions the same. That way you can drop in the newly revised `ajaxUtility.js` file without having to rewrite any code relying on the `ajaxUtility` object. For example, when you're finished refactoring this code you can use it in any example in this book that uses the `ajaxUtility` object, without having to make any additional changes.

4. Now let's look at the `postFromForm()` method. It's the same as the `makeGetRequest()` and `makePostRequest()` methods except for one small detail: It sets a Content-Type header using the XHR object's `setRequestHeader()` method. At first glance it looks as if we can't refactor this method the way you did the other two. Fortunately, however, you can.

The only thing `postFromForm()` does is set that header, so you can add another parameter to `openAndSend()` to determine whether or not the Content-Type header is set — essentially refactoring again. Following is the revised `openAndSend()` with the changes in bold:

```
    openAndSend : function(type, url, data, callback, contentType) {
        var xhr = this.createXHR();

        xhr.open(type, url);

        if (contentType) {
            xhr.setRequestHeader("Content-Type", contentType);
        }

        xhr.onreadystatechange = function() {
            if (xhr.readyState === 4) {
                var status = xhr.status;
                if ((status >= 200 && status < 300) || status === 304) {
                    callback(xhr.responseText);
                } else {
                    alert("An error occurred");
                }
            }
        };

        xhr.send(data);
    }
```

In this revision, the `contentType` parameter is a string value (a content type). If data is passed to it, the value passed to the `contentType` argument is used to set the Content-Type header using the XHR object's `setRequestHeader()`. If omitted, the header code is skipped and the method continues executing as normal.

5. Now change `postFromForm()` to call `openAndSend()`, like this:

```
postFromForm : function(url, form, callback) {
    this.openAndSend("POST", url, this.getRequestBody(form), callback,
        "application/x-www-form-urlencoded");
}
```

Even though you changed the parameter list of `openAndSend()`, you do not have to change the `makeGetRequest()` and `makePostRequest()` methods. Parameters in JavaScript are always optional. You technically don't have to pass anything to a function in order to execute it, but the function may not do what it's supposed to do if you do not provide it with the data it needs.

When an argument is not passed, the parameter contains a value of `undefined`. So when `makeGetRequest()` and `makePostRequest()` call `openAndSend()` without passing a value as the `contentType` parameter, `contentType` becomes `undefined`, a false value.

So once again your refactor session changed the way something worked without causing you to rewrite the code that depended on it.

6. The `ajaxUtility.js` file should now look like this:

```
js24Hour.ajaxUtility = {
    createXHR : function() {
        if (typeof XMLHttpRequest !== "undefined") {
            return new XMLHttpRequest();
        } else {
            var versions = [ "MSXML2.XmlHttp.6.0",
                "MSXML2.XmlHttp.3.0" ];

            for (var i = 0; i < versions.length; i++) {
                try {
                    var xhr = new ActiveXObject(versions[i]);
                    return xhr;
                } catch (error) {
                    // do nothing
                }
            }
        }

        alert("Your browser does not support XmlHttp");

        return null;
    },

    getRequestBody : function(form) {
        var pieces = [],
```

```
            elements = form.elements;

        for (var i = 0; i < elements.length; i++) {
            var element = elements[i],
                name = encodeURIComponent(element.name),
                value = encodeURIComponent(element.value);

            pieces.push(name + "=" + value);
        }

        return pieces.join("&");
    },

    makeGetRequest : function(url, callback) {
        this.openAndSend("GET", url, null, callback);
    },

    makePostRequest : function(url, data, callback) {
        this.openAndSend("POST", url, data, callback);
    },

    postFromForm : function(url, form, callback) {
        this.openAndSend("POST", url, this.getRequestBody(form), callback,
            "application/x-www-form-urlencoded");
    },

    openAndSend : function(type, url, data, callback, contentType) {
        var xhr = this.createXHR();

        xhr.open(type, url);

        if (isForm) {
            xhr.setRequestHeader("Content-Type", contentType);
        }

        xhr.onreadystatechange = function() {
            if (xhr.readyState === 4) {
                var status = xhr.status;
                if ((status >= 200 && status < 300) || status === 304) {
                    callback(xhr.responseText);
                } else {
                    alert("An error occurred");
                }
            }
        };

        xhr.send(data);
    }
};
```

7. Save ajaxUtility.js. Let's test it to make sure everything works as it should. Point your browser to http://localhost/Lesson43/lesson43_example01.htm. Fill out the form, submit it, and you'll see that it works exactly as it should.

Please select Lesson 43 on the DVD to view the video that accompanies this lesson. You can also download the sample code for all lessons from the book's website at www.wrox.com.

What's on the DVD?

This appendix provides you with information on the contents of the DVD that accompanies this book. For the most up to date information, please refer to the ReadMe file located at the root of the DVD. Here is what you will find in this appendix:

➤ System requirements

➤ Using the DVD

➤ What's on the DVD

➤ Troubleshooting

SYSTEM REQUIREMENTS

Most reasonably up-to-date computers with a DVD drive should be able to play the screencasts that are included on the DVD. You might also find an Internet connection helpful for downloading updates to this book.

You need a text editor to finish nearly every lesson. Most operating systems have one installed by default, but you might want to download and install another text editor that offers more features (especially if you're using Windows). I use Microsoft's Visual Web Developer Express 2010 in the screencasts (www.microsoft.com/express/).

You also need a web browser. Almost all major consumer operating systems have one installed by default, but you can download other browsers (or update yours) if you want. The following list details the latest versions of the most used browsers and where you can download their latest versions:

➤ Microsoft Internet Explorer 8 (www.microsoft.com/ie/ — for Windows only)

➤ Google Chrome 7 (www.google.com/chrome/)

➤ Mozilla Firefox 3.6 (www.getfirefox.com)

➤ Apple Safari 5 (www.apple.com/safari/)

➤ Opera 10.62 (www.opera.com)

USING THE DVD ON A PC

To access the content from the DVD, follow these steps.

1. Insert the DVD into your computer's DVD-ROM drive. The license agreement appears.

 *The interface won't launch if you have autorun disabled. In that case, click Start ➪ Run (For Windows Vista, Start ➪ All Programs ➪ Accessories ➪ Run). In the dialog box that appears, type **D:\Start.exe**. (Replace D with the proper letter if your DVD drive uses a different letter. If you don't know the letter, see how your CD drive is listed under My Computer.) Click OK.*

2. Read through the license agreement, and then click the Accept button if you want to use the DVD.

3. The DVD interface appears. Simply select the lesson video you want to view.

USING THE DVD ON A MAC

To install the items from the DVD to your hard drive, follow these steps:

1. Insert the DVD into your computer's DVD-ROM drive.

2. The DVD icon will appear on your desktop; double-click to open.

3. Double-click the Start button.

4. Read the license agreement and click the Accept button to use the DVD.

5. The DVD interface will appear. Here you can install the programs and run the demos.

WHAT'S ON THE DVD

Nothing beats watching how something is done, and that's why a DVD accompanies this book. Most lessons in the book have a corresponding screencast that illustrates examples in the lesson and provides content beyond what is covered in print.

I recommend using the following steps when reading a lesson:

1. Read the lesson's text.

2. Read the step-by-step instructions of the lesson's Try It section.

3. Watch me complete the exercise in the screencast.

You can also download all of the solutions to the Try Its at the book's website. If you get stuck and don't know what to do next, visit the p2p forums (`p2p.wrox.com`), locate the forum for the book, and leave a post. You can also contact me through my website at `www.wdonline.com/contact/`.

TROUBLESHOOTING

If you have difficulty installing or using any of the materials on the companion DVD, try the following solutions:

➤ **Turn off any anti-virus software that you may have running:** Installers sometimes mimic virus activity and can make your computer incorrectly believe that it is being infected by a virus. (Be sure to turn the anti-virus software back on later.)

➤ **Close all running programs:** The more programs you're running, the less memory is available to other programs. Installers also typically update files and programs; if you keep other programs running, installation may not work properly.

➤ **Reference the ReadMe:** Please refer to the ReadMe file located at the root of the CD-ROM for the latest product information at the time of publication.

➤ **Reboot if necessary:** If all else fails, rebooting your machine can often clear any conflicts in the system.

CUSTOMER CARE

If you have trouble with the CD-ROM, please call the Wiley Product Technical Support phone number at (800) 762-2974. Outside the United States, call 1(317) 572-3994. You can also contact Wiley Product Technical Support at `http://support.wiley.com`. John Wiley & Sons will provide technical support only for installation and other general quality control items. For technical support on the applications themselves, consult the program's vendor or author.

To place additional orders or to request information about other Wiley products, please call (877) 762-2974.

INDEX

WILEY PUBLISHING, INC.
END-USER LICENSE AGREEMENT

READ THIS. You should carefully read these terms and conditions before opening the software packet(s) included with this book "Book". This is a license agreement "Agreement" between you and Wiley Publishing, Inc. "WPI". By opening the accompanying software packet(s), you acknowledge that you have read and accept the following terms and conditions. If you do not agree and do not want to be bound by such terms and conditions, promptly return the Book and the unopened software packet(s) to the place you obtained them for a full refund.

1. License Grant. WPI grants to you (either an individual or entity) a nonexclusive license to use one copy of the enclosed software program(s) (collectively, the "Software") solely for your own personal or business purposes on a single computer (whether a standard computer or a workstation component of a multi-user network). The Software is in use on a computer when it is loaded into temporary memory (RAM) or installed into permanent memory (hard disk, CD-ROM, or other storage device). WPI reserves all rights not expressly granted herein.

2. Ownership. WPI is the owner of all right, title, and interest, including copyright, in and to the compilation of the Software recorded on the physical packet included with this Book "Software Media". Copyright to the individual programs recorded on the Software Media is owned by the author or other authorized copyright owner of each program. Ownership of the Software and all proprietary rights relating thereto remain with WPI and its licensers.

3. Restrictions on Use and Transfer.

(a) You may only (i) make one copy of the Software for backup or archival purposes, or (ii) transfer the Software to a single hard disk, provided that you keep the original for backup or archival purposes. You may not (i) rent or lease the Software, (ii) copy or reproduce the Software through a LAN or other network system or through any computer subscriber system or bulletin-board system, or (iii) modify, adapt, or create derivative works based on the Software.

(b) You may not reverse engineer, decompile, or disassemble the Software. You may transfer the Software and user documentation on a permanent basis, provided that the transferee agrees to accept the terms and conditions of this Agreement and you retain no copies. If the Software is an update or has been updated, any transfer must include the most recent update and all prior versions.

4. Restrictions on Use of Individual Programs. You must follow the individual requirements and restrictions detailed for each individual program in the "About the CD" appendix of this Book or on the Software Media. These limitations are also contained in the individual license agreements recorded on the Software Media. These limitations may include a requirement that after using the program for a specified period of time, the user must pay a registration fee or discontinue use. By opening the Software packet(s), you agree to abide by the licenses and restrictions for these individual programs that are detailed in the "About the CD" appendix and/or on the Software Media. None of the material on this Software Media or listed in this Book may ever be redistributed, in original or modified form, for commercial purposes.

5. Limited Warranty.

(a) WPI warrants that the Software and Software Media are free from defects in materials and workmanship under normal use for a period of sixty (60) days from the date of purchase of this Book. If WPI receives notification within the warranty period of defects in materials or workmanship, WPI will replace the defective Software Media.

(b) WPI AND THE AUTHOR(S) OF THE BOOK DISCLAIM ALL OTHER WARRANTIES, EXPRESS OR IMPLIED, INCLUDING WITHOUT LIMITATION IMPLIED WARRANTIES OF MERCHANTABILITY AND FITNESS FOR A PARTICULAR PURPOSE, WITH RESPECT TO THE SOFTWARE, THE PROGRAMS, THE SOURCE CODE CONTAINED THEREIN, AND/OR THE TECHNIQUES DESCRIBED IN THIS BOOK. WPI DOES NOT WARRANT THAT THE FUNCTIONS CONTAINED IN THE SOFTWARE WILL MEET YOUR REQUIREMENTS OR THAT THE OPERATION OF THE SOFTWARE WILL BE ERROR FREE.

(c) This limited warranty gives you specific legal rights, and you may have other rights that vary from jurisdiction to jurisdiction.

6. Remedies.

(a) WPI's entire liability and your exclusive remedy for defects in materials and workmanship shall be limited to replacement of the Software Media, which may be returned to WPI with a copy of your receipt at the following address: Software Media Fulfillment Department, Attn.: *JavaScript 24-Hour Trainer*, Wiley Publishing, Inc., 10475 Crosspoint Blvd., Indianapolis, IN 46256, or call 1-800-762-2974. Please allow four to six weeks for delivery. This Limited Warranty is void if failure of the Software Media has resulted from accident, abuse, or misapplication. Any replacement Software Media will be warranted for the remainder of the original warranty period or thirty (30) days, whichever is longer.

(b) In no event shall WPI or the author be liable for any damages whatsoever (including without limitation damages for loss of business profits, business interruption, loss of business information, or any other pecuniary loss) arising from the use of or inability to use the Book or the Software, even if WPI has been advised of the possibility of such damages.

(c) Because some jurisdictions do not allow the exclusion or limitation of liability for consequential or incidental damages, the above limitation or exclusion may not apply to you.

7. U.S. Government Restricted Rights. Use, duplication, or disclosure of the Software for or on behalf of the United States of America, its agencies and/or instrumentalities "U.S. Government" is subject to restrictions as stated in paragraph (c)(1)(ii) of the Rights in Technical Data and Computer Software clause of DFARS 252.227-7013, or subparagraphs (c) (1) and (2) of the Commercial Computer Software - Restricted Rights clause at FAR 52.227-19, and in similar clauses in the NASA FAR supplement, as applicable.

8. General. This Agreement constitutes the entire understanding of the parties and revokes and supersedes all prior agreements, oral or written, between them and may not be modified or amended except in a writing signed by both parties hereto that specifically refers to this Agreement. This Agreement shall take precedence over any other documents that may be in conflict herewith. If any one or more provisions contained in this Agreement are held by any court or tribunal to be invalid, illegal, or otherwise unenforceable, each and every other provision shall remain in full force and effect.